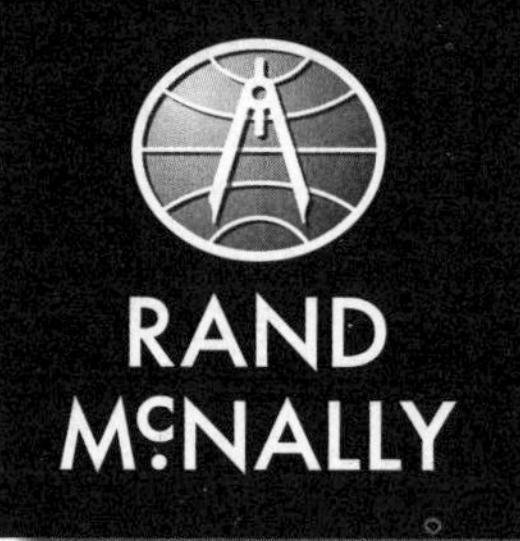

2019 Road Atlas

Contents

Travel Information

National Parks 2-6

Our editors' picks of America's 59 national parks—big and small, east and west—showcase this country's astonishing beauty, highlight essential visitor information, and offer insightful travel tips.

Mileage Chart 7

Driving distances between 77 North American cities.

Mileage and Driving Times Map inside back cover

Distances and driving times between over a hundred North American cities.

Maps

Map legend **inside front cover**
United States overview map **8-9**
U.S. states **10-109**
Canada overview map **110-111**
Canadian provinces **112-127**
Mexico overview map and Puerto Rico **160**
U.S. and Canadian cities **128-159**

Photo Credits: p. 2 ©Mak_photo / Getty; p. 3 ©Brian W. Downs / Getty; p. 4 ©Deborah Garber / Getty; p. 5 ©Filippo Bacci / Getty; p. 6 ©Ilflan / Getty.

Published and printed in U.S.A.

For licensing information and copyright permissions, contact us at permissions@randmcnally.com

If you have a comment, suggestion, or even a compliment, please visit us at randmcnally.com/contact or write to:
Rand McNally Consumer Affairs
P.O. Box 7600
Chicago, Illinois 60680-9915

1 2 3 VE 19 18

State & Province Maps

United States

Alabama .... 10 - 11
Alaska .... 12 - 13
Arizona .... 14 - 15
Arkansas .... 16 - 17
California .... 18 - 21
Colorado .... 22 - 23
Connecticut .... 24 - 27
Delaware .... 28 - 29
Florida .... 30 - 31
Georgia .... 32 - 33
Hawaii 13
Idaho .... 34 - 35
Illinois .... 36 - 37
Indiana .... 38 - 39
Iowa .... 40 - 41
Kansas .... 42 - 43
Kentucky .... 44 - 47
Louisiana .... 48 - 49
Maine .... 50 - 51
Maryland .... 28 - 29
Massachusetts .... 24 - 27
Michigan .... 52 - 53
Minnesota .... 54 - 55
Mississippi .... 56 - 57
Missouri .... 58 - 59
Montana .... 60 - 61
Nebraska .... 62 - 63
Nevada .... 18 - 21
New Hampshire .... 64 - 65
New Jersey .... 66 - 67
New Mexico .... 68 - 69
New York .... 70 - 73
North Carolina .... 74 - 77
North Dakota .... 78 - 79
Ohio .... 80 - 83
Oklahoma .... 84 - 85
Oregon .... 86 - 87
Pennsylvania .... 88 - 91
Rhode Island .... 24 - 27
South Carolina .... 74 - 77
South Dakota .... 92 - 93
Tennessee .... 45 - 47
Texas .... 94 - 97
Utah .... 98 - 99
Vermont .... 64 - 65
Virginia .... 100 - 103
Washington .... 104 - 105
West Virginia .... 100 - 103
Wisconsin .... 106 - 107
Wyoming .... 108 - 109

Canada

Alberta .... 112 - 115
British Columbia .... 112 - 115
Manitoba .... 116 - 119
New Brunswick .... 126 - 127
Newfoundland and Labrador .... 126 - 127
Nova Scotia .... 126 - 127
Ontario .... 120 - 123
Prince Edward Island .... 126 - 127
Québec .... 124 - 125
Saskatchewan .... 116 - 119

City Maps

Albuquerque 129
Atlanta 128
Austin 130
Baltimore 129
Birmingham 129
Boston .... 130 - 131
Buffalo 132
Charlotte 130
Chicago .... 132 - 133
Cincinnati 134
Cleveland 137
Columbus 135
Dallas .... 134 & 136
Denver 135
Detroit .... 138 - 139
Fort Lauderdale .... 142 - 143
Fort Worth .... 134 & 136
Greensboro .... 138 - 139
Hartford 137
Houston 140
Indianapolis 139
Jacksonville 137
Kansas City .... 142 - 143
Las Vegas 143
Los Angeles .... 144 - 145
Louisville 139
Memphis 146
Mexico City 160
Miami .... 142 - 143
Milwaukee .... 146 - 147
Minneapolis 141
Nashville 144
New Orleans 146
New York .... 148 - 149
Newark .... 148 - 149
Norfolk .... 146 - 147
Orlando 153
Ottawa 111
Philadelphia .... 150 - 151
Phoenix 147
Pittsburgh .... 152 - 153
Portland 151
Raleigh 154
St. Louis .... 150 - 151
St. Paul 141
St. Petersburg .... 154 - 155
Sacramento .... 154 - 155
Salt Lake City 157
San Antonio 155
San Diego 154
San Francisco .... 156 - 157
Seattle .... 152 - 153
Tampa .... 154 - 155
Toronto 158
Vancouver 158
Washington D.C. .... 158 - 159
Winston-Salem .... 138 - 139

America's 59 national parks not only inspire wonder and awe but also restore our souls. Here are 5 of our favorite parks—big and small, east and west—that showcase this country's astonishing beauty.

ACADIA NATIONAL PARK, ME

Bass Harbor Head Lighthouse

New England's only national park represents the region well. As you wind your way to Mount Desert Island, home to most of Acadia, the magic of Maine begins to enchant you. The park's breathtaking coast features granite boulders, tidal pools, moss-covered rocks, and sandy beaches. Its interior—peppered with lakes, ponds, and overlooks—is also spectacular. So, too, are its separate, less-congested areas: the craggy Schoodic Peninsula and Isle au Haut, a remote islet that's partially under park stewardship.

GETTING ORIENTED

Bangor, Maine is 45 miles inland and northwest of the park; Portland is 160 miles to its southwest along the coast. The park's **Hulls Cove Visitor Center** (25 Visitor Center Rd.)—with access to the Park Loop Road and Carriage Road network—is just north of the town of **Bar Harbor** (www.barharbormaine.gov), a hub for dining and lodging.

Northeast Harbor (www mountdesertchamber.org) and **Southwest Harbor** (www.southwestharbor.org), each just 1 mile from a park entrance, also make good bases. Seasonal **Island Explorer** (207/667-5796, www.exploreacadia.com) shuttle buses will scoot you around the island for free. In-park lodging options include the 600 sites (mostly for small tents) at the **Blackwoods**, **Seawall**, and **Schoodic Woods campgrounds**, booked through Recreation.gov. **Park Contact Info:** *207/288-3338, www.nps.gov/acad.*

Atlas map **p. 51, G-5**

PARK HIGHLIGHTS

Natural Attractions. Peek at tidal pools teeming with life, gaze at striated granite boulders, flex your toes in the sand, or (if you're really brave) dip those same toes in the frigid Atlantic. Or hop a ferry, book a cruise, or rent a motorboat or sailboat. Acadia's impossibly green woods are also picture-worthy, as are the "reveals" when you happen upon a secluded pond or lake.

Trails, Drives & Viewpoints. The 27-mile **Park Loop Road** gives you a great orientation to much of the park's Mount Desert Island portion. Be sure to hike, bike, or drive to the summit of **Cadillac Mountain**. Intrepid folks do this very early to watch one of the nation's first sunrises (the first from early October through early March).

Park trails include everything from short, level hikes to the shoreline like the 1.4-mile round-trip **Wonderland Trail**, to lakeside trails such as the moderate 3.2-mile **Jordan Pond Path** loop, to extreme trails like the aptly named **Perpendicular Trail** (2.2 miles, with stairs and iron rungs). The **Friends of Acadia Village Connector Trails** (www.friendsofacadia.org) enable you to walk from Mount Desert Island's various towns directly into the park.

To escape peak-season Mount Desert Island crowds, head to **Isle au Haut** (www.isleauhaut.org), home to 73 full-time residents and a general store. **Isle au Haut Boat Services** (207/367-5193, www.isleauhautferryservice.com) ferries depart from picturesque **Stonington** (www.deerisle.com), roughly 58 miles southwest of Bar Harbor, for Isle au Haut's Town Landing (year-round) or Duck Harbor Boat Landing (summer only), which is in the park.

Alternatively, head to Acadia's **Schoodic Peninsula**—about 39 miles from the Hulls Cove Visitor Center via Route 3 and US 1 north—for still more (and more peaceful) Maine woods and rocky shore. The 6-mile, one-way **Schoodic Loop Road** runs to **Schoodic Point**, a coastal outcrop with stunning views of crashing waves.

Museums & Sites. Between mid-May and mid-October, stop at **Jordan Pond House** (7.6 miles from Hulls Cove Visitor Center, 207/276-3316, acadiajordanpondhouse.com) for afternoon tea—a time-honored tradition since the late 1800s (reservations advised). Outside the park, the **Mount Desert Oceanarium** (off ME-3 just past Mount Desert Island Bridge, 207/288-5005, www.theoceanarium.com) has a great lobster touch tank that kids love.

Programs & Activities. Night talks and other **ranger-led events** happen at both Blackwoods and Seawall campgrounds. There are also guided sunrise strolls, cruises to Baker Island to spot seabirds and lighthouses, and plenty of family activities.**Acadian Boat Tours** (207/801-2300, www.acadianboattours.com) offers daily sightseeing/nature cruises. To sail, kayak, or canoe on area ponds and lakes, contact **Acadia Boat Rental** (207/370-7663, www.acadiaboatrental.com) or **National Park Canoe & Kayak Rentals** (207/244-5854, www.nationalparkcanoerental.com).

CONGAREE NATIONAL PARK, SC

Congaree might not be the largest national park, but it is one of the most essential—preserving 11,000 acres of old-growth bottomland hardwood forest. Before the late 19th century, 35 to 50 *million* acres of floodplain forests covered the land from Florida to Texas and Maryland to Missouri. Some trees died naturally; others were used for building materials or fuel. But many were felled owing to development. In the 1960s, grassroots environmental efforts helped to save the modest slice of wilderness that is today Congaree.

Hiking the elevated boardwalk through the park

GETTING ORIENTED

Congaree is in central South Carolina, close to several urban hubs, including Columbia, 20 miles northwest of the Harry Hampton Visitor Center (100 National Park Rd., Hopkins); Charleston, 106 miles southeast; and, in North Carolina, Charlotte, 112 miles north.

Aside from tent camping at Longleaf and Bluff campgrounds (Recreation.gov), and primitive backcountry camping, the park has no lodging. Columbia (www.columbiacvb.com) has abundant restaurant and hotel choices. Though they have fewer options, several smaller nearby communities make good hubs, including Eastover (www.townofeastoversc.com), 13 miles northeast of the visitors center; Hopkins, 7 miles northwest; and Santee (www.santeetourism.com), 40 miles southeast. **Park Contact Info:** ***803/776-4396, www.nps.gov/cong.***

PARK HIGHLIGHTS

Natural Attractions. Even if you usually can't see the forest for the trees, dig a little deeper here. A visit to Congaree puts you inside a marvel of biodiversity and natural engineering, surrounded by a spectacular world that sustains and recycles itself. It's a time machine that shows how the South once looked.

With the wilderness largely off limits to cars and motorized watercraft, Congaree is even more calming than most forests. It has one of the world's highest temperate deciduous forest canopies and North America's largest concentrations of champion trees—the largest known examples of a tree species within a geographic area. Here, these include the cherrybark oak, sweetgum, American elm, swamp chestnut oak, common persimmon, and more than a dozen other towering giants.

Bobcats, deer, feral pigs, opossums, raccoons, coyotes, and armadillos are just some of this park's wildlife. In the creeks, wetlands, and oxbow lakes (created when a curve of a river becomes cut off from the main flow) are turtles, snakes, alligators, frogs, otters, and catfish. The Carolina Bird Club notes about 200 year-round and migrating species including the wild turkey, yellow-crowned night heron, barred owl, and rose-breasted grosbeak, as well as several species of warblers and woodpeckers.

Trails & Viewpoints. Congaree has no public roads. Between hiking and paddling, you can spend about half a day here, longer if you work your way into the backcountry. Park brochures highlight the 20 miles of hiking trails, including an easy tour through the wetlands via a 2.4-mile elevated boardwalk. If you plan to delve deeper into the wilderness, ask the rangers for guidance, including a checklist of necessary gear.

Canoeing or kayaking through a primeval old-growth forest on a 15-mile marked trail along Cedar Creek is an unforgettable experience. One of the park's most popular trails for canoeists and kayakers is the 50-mile Congaree River Blue Trail, designated a National Recreation Trail by the U.S. Department of the Interior. Beginning in Columbia, it flows downriver and around the park's western perimeter.

On the eastern side of the park, the Wateree River Blue Trail is another option. Note that Congaree has no concessionaires, so it's BYOC (Bring Your Own Canoe). Outfitters in Columbia such as River Runner Outdoor Center (803/771-0353, shopriverrunner.com) can help you out with canoe and kayak rentals, and some companies also offer guided trips.

Museum. An orientation film at the Harry Hampton Visitor Center explains Congaree's story, and interpretive exhibits feature artifacts and information on Native American history, forestry, logging, and the settlements that spelled opportunity for pioneers (and tragedy for the trees).

Programs & Activities. Bird-watching is popular: Even before Congaree became a national park, the National Audubon Society designated it an Important Bird Area. Rangers and volunteers host Nature Discovery Tours to the park boardwalk and big trees each Saturday morning; they also occasionally schedule guided canoe tours and evening programs celebrating owls (the Owl Prowl) and the fireflies which, incredibly, synchronize their glow. Check ahead for details.

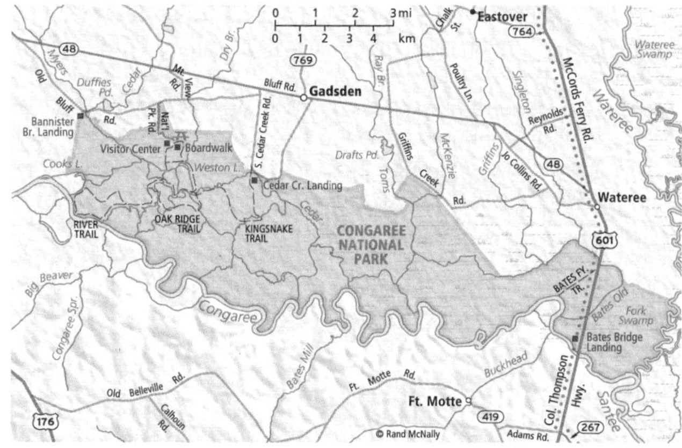

Atlas map **p. 75, F-5**

GRAND TETON NATIONAL PARK, WY

Canoeing the Snake River at Oxbow Bend

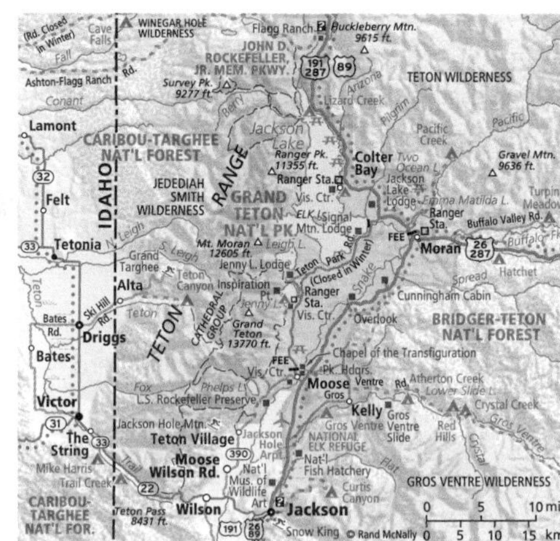

Atlas map **p. 108, B-1**

There are spectacular mountain views; then there are those in the Tetons—truly mesmerizing. You can enjoy northwestern Wyoming's stunning Rocky Mountain scenery from afar, along valley roads (a drive through the park only takes about two hours), trails, or the Snake River. But this landscape really merits an up-close look. Myriad routes take you from merely seeing the majestic peaks to truly experiencing them, as they rise 7,000 feet from the valley floor.

GETTING ORIENTED

Grand Teton is 290 miles northwest of Salt Lake City, the closest major urban gateway. The posh resort town of **Jackson** (www.jacksonholechamber.com) is just to the park's south; **Yellowstone National Park** (307/344-7381, www.nps.gov/yell) is to its north. US 26/89/191 and Teton Park Road traverse the park. The main **Craig Thomas Discovery and Visitor Center** is in the town of Moose; others are at **Jenny Lake** and **Colter Bay** on Jackson Lake.

Six park campgrounds have a total of 1,000 sites for tents and/or RVs (with and without hookups). **Grand Teton Lodging Company** (307/543-3100, www.gtlc.com) operates several classic in-park lodges, and there are plenty of amenities in Jackson and the towns of Wilson and Kelly. **Park Contact Info:** ***307/739-3300, www.nps.gov/grte.***

PARK HIGHLIGHTS

Natural Attractions. The **Teton Range** is the park's undeniable superstar. Jutting skyward 7,000 feet from the floor of a valley with few foothills, the range consists of aptly named Grand Teton (13,770 feet), Middle Teton, Mt. Owen, and Teewinot—part of the Cathedral Group—as well as Mt. Moran to the north.

Between the peaks, glaciers cut a series of dramatic canyons into the mountains, feeding a series of jewel-like lakes below. The trout-rich **Snake River** winds across the valley, which itself offers varied habitats for the park's resident wildlife, including bears, bald eagles, bison, and elk.

Trails, Drives & Viewpoints. If you're going to hike just one trail, try the moderate, 7.6-mile **Jenny Lake Loop Trail**; you can cut it in half by taking the shuttle (fee) across the lake. From the West Dock, it's worth the uphill hike to Hidden Falls and Inspiration Point, which adds another 2.4 miles but rewards the extra effort with sweeping views.

Diehards can continue on the **Cascade Canyon Trail**, the prime route for mountaineers looking to summit Grand Teton and its sister Cathedral Group peaks. On the park's south side, the Laurance S. Rockefeller Preserve offers a network of fairly level trails, such as the 6.3-mile **Phelps Lake Loop Trail**, which culminates with mountain and canyon views from its namesake lake.

Scenic drives and viewpoints abound. The lesser-traveled **Moose-Wilson Road** enters the park 8 miles north of Teton Village and has many hiking and moose-spotting opportunities. For superlative views on the park's north side, drive the 5-mile **Signal Mountain Summit Road** (May–Oct.) and stop at the Jackson Point Overlook.

Museum/Site. On the park's south side, off Teton Park Road, the famed **Chapel of the Transfiguration**, with an altar window framing the Cathedral Group, is in **Menor's Ferry Historic District**, an important Snake River crossing before a new bridge put it out of business in 1927.

Programs & Activities. Free ranger programs include daily, **guided hikes and talks** from spring through fall and guided **snowshoe walks** Monday through Saturday in winter. Rivers and lakes provide **boating opportunities** (307/543-2811, www.gtlc.com), including rafting trips on the Snake River and narrated cruises on Jackson Lake. **Jenny Lake Boating** (307/734-9227, www.jennylakeboating.com) offers shuttles to the Hidden Falls trailhead and lake cruises.

Based in Jackson, Teton Science Schools' **Wildlife Expeditions** (307/733-1313, www.tetonscience.org) runs safari tours of Grand Teton and Yellowstone. Just south of the park off US 26/89/191, the **National Elk Refuge** (307/733-9212, www.fws.gov) is set aside as a wintering ground for the local herd. Sleigh rides tour the refuge in winter.

Outside yet nearby the park, **Jackson Hole Mountain Resort** (3395 Cody Ln., Teton Village, 307/733-2292, www.jacksonhole.com) is a major ski destination with 133 runs on 2,500 acres and the nation's longest (4,139 feet) continuous vertical drop. In summer, the resort offers mountain biking, hiking, and golf.

BRYCE CANYON NATIONAL PARK, UT

Hoodoos rise, hawks soar. The setting sun turns the landscape crimson. The stars emerge, and all is still and quiet. Welcome to Bryce Canyon. Despite its name, this southwestern Utah park doesn't consist of a canyon but rather natural amphitheaters with tall, reddish rock spires called hoodoos—some of the planet's most awe-inspiring formations. Be sure to take in views from both above and amid the hoodoos.

GETTING ORIENTED

The **Bryce Canyon Visitor Center** is 1 mile south of the park's sole entrance—itself 272 miles north of Salt Lake City and 270 miles southwest of Las Vegas. Bryce's **Sunset** and **North campgrounds** (Recreation.gov) are near the visitors center. Permits are required for (and water is scarce at) the 12 **backcountry campsites**, but you get to camp among the hoodoos. The seasonal, circa-1925 **Bryce Canyon Lodge** (435/834-8700, www.brycecanyonforever.com) is the only in-park lodging. In summer, **park shuttles** let you enjoy the scenery without adding to the traffic.

Natural Bridge

Bryce Canyon Resort (13500 E. UT 12, Bryce, 435/834-5351, www.brycecanyonresort.com) is one of several hotels just outside the park. The towns of **Escalante** (www.escalanteut.com), 49 miles east, and **Panguitch** (www.panguitch.com), 28 miles northwest, make good bases.

Park Contact Info: ***435/834-5322, www.nps.gov/brca.***

PARK HIGHLIGHTS

Natural Attractions. The park is arranged in a "line" of **natural amphitheaters** along the edge of the Paunsaugunt Plateau. The fantastic-looking **hoodoos** in the world's largest collection have variable thicknesses (like totem poles) and were formed by rain, erosion, and "frost wedging"—a process that occurs when water freezes overnight and then expands in the morning, causing rock to split.

Walking *among* the hoodoos is as cool as gazing at them from above, with more chances to spot **wildlife**. Plenty of mammals, reptiles, and insects inhabit the park. So do about 175 species of birds—including California condors, ospreys, peregrine falcons, and ravens—either year-round or seasonally.

The other real show is the night sky: Bryce is more than 20 miles from the nearest town and hundreds of miles from the nearest large city. Pull up a chair at Bryce Canyon Lodge, or peer from your tent to see more than 7,500 stars on a moonless night. You'll understand why Bryce is one of America's Dark Sky–certified parks.

Trails, Drives & Viewpoints. Sunrise Point, Sunset Point, Inspiration Point, Bryce Point, Natural Bridge, and Rainbow Point are all must-see **viewpoints** along the sole park road (UT 63), which runs for 19 miles between the visitors center and the terminus at Rainbow Point. If you're into photography or simply want to stop at every viewpoint, it will take half a day to make your way to Rainbow Point and back. Sunset Point is, indeed, the best stop for sunsets, but every stop has postcard-worthy vistas.

Following the strenuous, backcountry 23-mile **Under-the-Rim Trail** (a full-day hike or more) and the moderate 8.6-mile **Riggs Spring Loop Trail** (half a day, minimum) is an excellent way to experience the park and avoid the crowds at the top of the plateau. What's more, the park shuttle is handy if you want to hike only part of the Under-the-Rim Trail—just be prepared, and mind the elevation.

Programs & Activities. Attending a **geology talk** or the park's annual two-day **Geology Festival** in July is a must to fully comprehend how the hoodoos came into

Bryce Canyon Amphitheater at sunrise

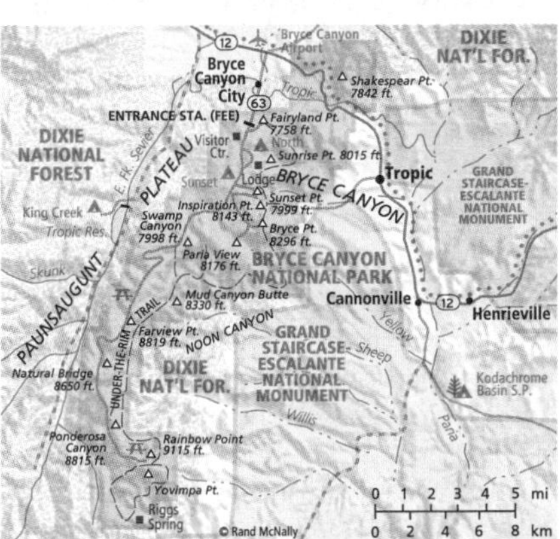

Atlas map **p. 99, H-3**

existence. The festival features bus tours with a geologist, special exhibits and guest speakers, and family-oriented activities. At night, **full-moon hikes** and **stargazing programs** are fun for the whole family. You can also join a 1-mile evening **Rim Walk**, and let a park ranger point out wonders that your eye might have missed. In addition, during June's four-day **Astronomy Festival**, local and national astronomy experts join park rangers to present special programs and viewings.

In spring, summer, and fall, a two- or three-hour horseback-riding excursion with **Canyon Trail Rides** (435/679-8665, www.canyonrides.com) is a classic way to explore Bryce's geology and terrain. (The company also offers rides in Zion and Grand Canyon national parks.) In winter, try a 1- to 2-mile, ranger-guided **snowshoe hike**—the park will provide the snowshoes. When the snow is deep enough, rangers also lead full-moon snowshoe hikes.

YOSEMITE NATIONAL PARK, CA

Yosemite's granite peaks, plunging waterfalls, giant-sequoia groves, and high-alpine meadows are truly iconic. Although more than 5 million people visit each year, never fear. With nearly 1,200 square miles to explore, it's easy to get away from the crowds of Yosemite Valley . . . once you've seen the valley, of course.

Yosemite Valley and Half Dome from Olmstead Point

GETTING ORIENTED

Yosemite is 200 miles east of San Francisco amid eastern California's Sierra Nevadas. Yosemite Valley and Village, home to the main **Yosemite Valley Visitor Center and Theater**, are closest to the western **Big Oak Flat** and **Arch Rock** entrances. The **Hetch Hetchy Entrance** is in the northwest, the **South Entrance** is close to Mariposa Giant Sequoia Grove, and the seasonal **Tioga Pass Entrance** is near Tuolumne Meadows to the east.

The park is open year-round, but conservation projects and the weather can result in closures; check ahead. Reservations for Yosemite's classic hotels (some of them seasonal) and most of its 13 campgrounds (9 of which allow RVs) are a must. Book through **Aramark** (888/413-8869 or 602/278-8888, www.travelyosemite.com), the park's primary concessionaire, or look into options in nearby towns such as El Portal, Fish Camp, or Lee Vining. **Park Contact Info:** ***209/372-0200, www.nps.gov/yose.***

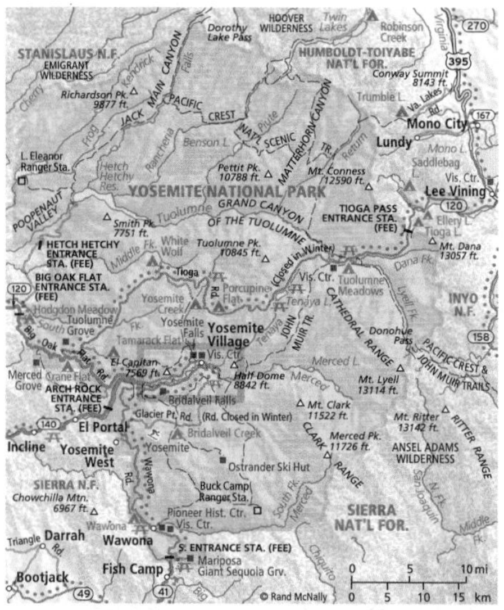

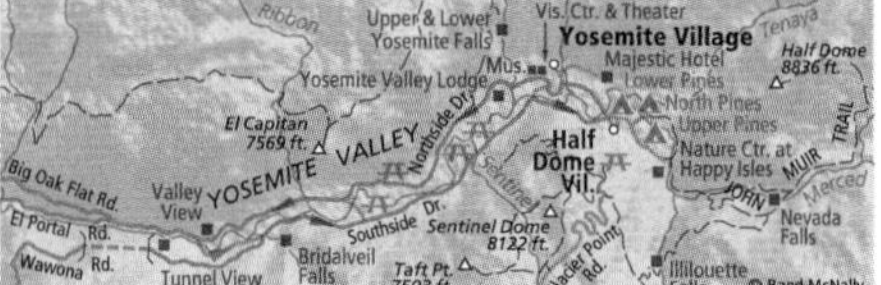

Atlas map **p. 18, F-5**

PARK HIGHLIGHTS

Natural Attractions. "Granite rocks" might sound boring—until you gaze upon **El Capitan**, a colossal cliff rising 3,000 feet from the Yosemite Valley floor, or massive **Half Dome**, the iconic, sliced-in-half, rounded rock. Also awe-inspiring are the 1,000-foot **Horsetail Fall**, on the east side of El Capitan, and the three-tiered **Yosemite Falls**, plunging 2,400 feet into Yosemite Valley. Snaking through it all is the glittering **Merced River**.

There are also the wildflower-covered slopes of **Tuolumne Meadows**, 8,600 feet above the Valley in the park's northeastern quadrant, and the hundreds of majestic *Sequoiadendron giganteum* (giant sequoias) of **Mariposa Grove**, in the park's southern reaches.

Trails, Drives & Viewpoints. There's no way to prepare for the sheer beauty of the **Tunnel View**: namely, the awesome sight of the entire Yosemite Valley as you emerge from the tunnel on **Wawona Road** en route from the South Entrance to the Valley.

On a drive along the **Valley Road**, stop for the easy, 0.5-mile, round-trip hike to 620-foot **Bridalveil Fall**, which flows year-round, or the easy, 1-mile loop to **Lower Yosemite Falls**. Escape (some) of the crowds along the **Mist Trail**, a strenuous, 2.4-mile, round-trip trek to from the top of powerful, 318-foot **Vernal Fall**.

Don't miss the views from, 7,200-foot **Glacier Point**. It's about 30 miles from Yosemite Valley, with 17 or so miles of the drive along winding **Glacier Point Road** (open seasonally).

Museums & Sites. The Valley's **Yosemite Museum**, in a National Park Service Rustic–style structure (circa 1925), offers a fascinating look into the history of both the park and the Native Americans who lived in the area for thousands of years before the trappers and traders arrived. Be sure to stop by **The Ansel Adams Gallery** (650/692-3285, www.anseladams.com), also in the Valley. Prints by the great American landscape photographer are on view and on sale.

In the south, near Mariposa Grove, you cross a covered bridge to reach the **Pioneer Yosemite History Center**, a collection of historic structures built in different eras throughout the park and moved here in the 1950s and '60s.

Programs & Activities. Yosemite has many programs on tap. A free, hour-long **Naturalist Stroll** is a good way to learn about the park; it's also a good warm-up for an art or photography class, a guided hike, or a **Yosemite Valley Floor Tram Tour**. There's also the fun 2.5-hour **Bike to Hike Tour** or the **Ask a Climber** program.

Rafting the Merced River is a pastoral way to wind through Yosemite Valley; rentals are available when the water is high, typically June and July. **Canoeing** and **kayaking** are also permitted at other park waterways. The **Yosemite Mountaineering School & Guide Service** (209/372-8344) provides guided rock climbs and classes—from free-form to fixed-rope to everything in between. In winter, **cross-country skiing** through the Valley will put you *inside* an Ansel Adams photograph. Sublime.

Mileage Chart

This handy chart offers more than 2,400 mileages covering 77 North American cities. Want more mileages? Visit **randmcnally.com/MC** and type in any two cities or addresses.

	Albuquerque, NM	Atlanta, GA	Billings, MT	Boston, MA	Charlotte, NC	Chicago, IL	Cincinnati, OH	Dallas, TX	Denver, CO	Detroit, MI	Houston, TX	Indianapolis, IN	Kansas City, MO	Los Angeles, CA	Memphis, TN	Miami, FL	Milwaukee, WI	Minneapolis, MN	New Orleans, LA	New York, NY	Omaha, NE	Orlando, FL	Philadelphia, PA	Phoenix, AZ	Pittsburgh, PA	Portland, OR	St. Louis, MO	Salt Lake City, UT	San Francisco, CA	Seattle, WA	Washington, DC	Wichita, KS
Albuquerque, NM		1386	998	2219	1626	1333	1387	647	446	1570	884	1279	784	786	1008	1952	1354	1225	1165	2001	863	1730	1924	425	1641	1363	1037	599	1086	1438	1885	591
Amarillo, TX	288	1102	965	1935	1342	1049	1103	363	424	1286	589	995	570	1072	720	1668	1132	1009	881	1716	647	1446	1640	746	1357	1669	752	883	1370	1743	1600	418
Atlanta, GA	1386		1831	1095	244	715	461	780	1404	722	794	533	800	2174	379	661	809	1127	468	882	992	440	780	1844	684	2603	555	1878	2472	2649	637	955
Atlantic City, NJ	1985	831	2072	338	590	818	632	1518	1792	644	1598	703	1187	2774	1063	1248	910	1232	1273	126	1272	1038	60	2447	365	2922	948	2201	2934	2889	188	1379
Austin, TX	705	920	1495	1959	1164	1121	1128	196	950	1358	163	1067	702	1381	643	1341	1204	1136	503	1737	839	1124	1658	1010	1411	2068	825	1304	1760	2143	1524	542
Baltimore, MD	1887	683	1953	400	442	699	513	1368	1673	524	1448	584	1068	2670	914	1082	792	1112	1124	192	1153	889	97	2349	246	2804	829	2081	2816	2771	39	1260
Billings, MT	998	1831		2236	1990	1246	1546	1425	551	1535	1652	1435	1026	1240	1477	2497	1173	838	1868	2041	845	2275	2011	1210	1713	891	1278	552	1173	818	1951	1064
Birmingham, AL	1241	146	1780	1177	390	660	466	636	1329	724	668	478	749	2030	233	746	754	1072	343	960	939	534	880	1700	748	2551	502	1826	2327	2598	745	810
Boise, ID	938	2177	621	2660	2336	1693	1943	1702	830	1960	1930	1835	1372	842	1825	2844	1732	1461	2216	2465	1225	2622	2435	914	2137	431	1622	340	639	503	2375	1338
Boston, MA	2219	1095	2236		841	983	870	1764	1970	724	1844	937	1421	2983	1312	1482	1074	1396	1520	216	1436	1288	306	2681	570	3086	1182	2365	3098	3054	439	1613
Branson, MO	864	652	1241	1433	868	545	601	435	806	784	602	493	209	1651	274	1284	630	643	597	1201	402	1062	1138	1326	851	2013	249	1288	1950	2060	1081	292
Calgary, AB	1542	2357	541	2615	2400	1627	1925	1967	1096	1916	2209	1814	1567	1557	2028	3018	1555	1221	2419	2439	1387	2797	2391	1524	2093	787	1820	869	1500	678	2334	1606
Charleston, SC	1703	319	2133	970	209	908	620	1099	1706	826	1105	726	1103	2491	696	583	1002	1324	742	768	1294	380	668	2165	654	2904	857	2180	2789	2951	532	1272
Charlotte, NC	1626	244	1990	841		769	477	1023	1566	616	1038	583	961	2414	619	728	867	1180	712	641	1151	526	539	2088	446	2761	714	2037	2712	2808	398	1092
Chicago, IL	1333	715	1246	983	769		289	926	1002	282	1085	181	526	2015	531	1381	90	408	923	787	470	1153	757	1795	459	2118	295	1398	2130	2063	697	724
Cincinnati, OH	1387	461	1546	870	477	289		934	1187	259	1055	109	584	2172	482	1127	381	703	804	637	722	905	571	1849	288	2369	348	1647	2380	2363	512	779
Cleveland, OH	1598	714	1597	638	514	344	248	1194	1330	169	1315	315	799	2342	729	1240	434	756	1057	460	797	1043	428	2060	134	2446	560	1725	2458	2414	370	992
Columbus, OH	1457	567	1606	763	426	354	107	1039	1261	212	1174	189	657	2244	587	1164	445	766	910	533	792	954	468	1920	174	2439	421	1718	2451	2425	411	851
Corpus Christi, TX	855	1001	1622	2051	1244	1338	1262	410	1077	1542	207	1228	919	1494	782	1394	1421	1353	554	1844	1056	1172	1754	1122	1561	2218	1042	1454	1873	2292	1619	758
Dallas, TX	647	780	1425	1764	1023	926	934		880	1163	239	873	489	1437	453	1307	1010	928	519	1548	656	1086	1467	1066	1221	2128	630	1403	1734	2193	1332	361
Denver, CO	446	1404	551	1970	1566	1002	1187	880		1270	1035	1083	603	1015	1097	2069	1042	913	1398	1775	534	1851	1732	908	1447	1256	854	533	1268	1320	1671	519
Des Moines, IA	983	902	946	1299	1057	335	580	683	670	599	938	474	194	1682	617	1567	375	244	1008	1105	135	1339	1074	1445	777	1786	350	1065	1798	1764	1015	391
Detroit, MI	1570	722	1535	724	616	282	259	1163	1270		1319	277	764	2281	742	1354	374	696	1066	613	736	1144	583	2032	285	2385	533	1664	2397	2353	522	964
Duluth, MN	1375	1187	860	1370	1239	466	760	1092	1063	754	1331	651	586	2076	963	1852	394	152	1354	1264	530	1632	1230	1838	932	1749	679	1458	2033	1677	1171	785
Edmonton, AB	1724	2391	722	2549	2443	1670	1968	2149	1278	1958	2391	1857	1626	1755	2147	3058	1598	1264	2538	2482	1445	2836	2434	1721	2136	966	1878	1069	1695	793	2377	1787
El Paso, TX	266	1418	1257	2373	1662	1455	1569	635	707	1702	744	1398	929	796	1089	1934	1497	1377	1095	2202	1004	1712	2102	424	1774	1630	1157	866	1175	1705	1967	730
Fargo, ND	1318	1361	607	1629	1414	641	937	1079	873	930	1321	825	600	1848	1054	2025	569	234	1445	1438	420	1807	1405	1780	1107	1497	841	1160	1781	1424	1348	685
Gatlinburg, TN	1439	196	1803	922	202	578	290	884	1376	552	964	396	773	2226	431	865	672	994	640	707	964	640	625	1901	493	2574	527	1850	2525	2621	490	905
Guadalajara, JA	1194	1739	2194	2789	1982	1954	1962	1028	1639	2191	948	1901	1535	1501	1482	2131	2037	1969	1292	2592	1672	1910	2492	1212	2261	2545	1658	1792	1963	2631	2356	1377
Gulfport, MS	1221	399	1912	1482	643	896	767	562	1386	1025	403	780	883	1949	365	792	988	1196	78	1266	1073	572	1180	1577	1052	2633	647	1909	2307	2730	1036	867
Houston, TX	884	794	1652	1844	1038	1085	1055	239	1035	1319		1021	732	1550	575	1186	1163	1171	348	1632	898	965	1547	1178	1354	2356	784	1634	1929	2431	1411	595
Indianapolis, IN	1279	533	1435	937	583	181	109	873	1083	277	1021		482	2068	464	1198	272	591	818	707	613	968	643	1742	359	2260	243	1541	2273	2253	582	674
Jacksonville, FL	1636	346	2183	1146	379	1068	796	992	1756	1002	871	874	1152	2421	677	349	1163	1474	547	939	1344	141	844	2050	825	2954	907	2230	2723	3001	706	1272
Kansas City, MO	784	800	1026	1421	961	526	584	489	603	764	732	482		1616	451	1466	565	436	844	1196	184	1246	1127	1246	840	1797	248	1073	1808	1844	1066	198
Key West, FL	2099	809	2646	1659	886	1534	1275	1455	2222	1515	1334	1348	1617	2884	1159	160	1632	1944	1010	1446	1807	387	1357	2514	1332	3417	1370	2693	3186	3464	1213	1735
Las Vegas, NV	572	1959	973	2714	2199	1746	1932	1220	747	2013	1457	1828	1349	270	1581	2525	1786	1656	1739	2518	1278	2303	2480	285	2190	1023	1600	419	569	1128	2428	1164
Lexington, KY	1371	369	1610	917	400	370	83	876	1186	344	996	184	581	2158	423	1030	464	782	745	701	771	817	638	1833	370	2381	334	1657	2392	2428	533	773
Little Rock, AR	877	515	1407	1447	754	650	617	319	965	885	439	583	381	1666	136	1147	724	815	425	1230	574	925	1150	1340	905	2211	345	1488	1963	2275	1015	446
Los Angeles, CA	786	2174	1240	2983	2414	2015	2172	1437	1015	2281	1550	2068	1616		1794	2735	2055	1925	1894	2787	1546	2515	2713	370	2428	963	1821	688	380	1134	2670	1377
Memphis, TN	1008	379	1477	1312	619	531	482	453	1097	742	575	464	451	1794		1012	622	831	394	1094	641	778	1014	1471	768	2245	283	1524	2095	2299	879	577
Mexico City, DF	1404	1718	2301	2768	1962	2017	1979	1090	1756	2254	924	1963	1598	1839	1500	2111	2100	2032	1272	2571	1735	1889	2471	1469	2279	2768	1721	2003	2218	2842	2336	1440
Miami, FL	1952	661	2497	1482	728	1381	1127	1307	2069	1354	1186	1198	1466	2735	1012		1475	1791	861	1288	1658	235	1180	2362	1173	3260	1221	2544	3038	3315	1044	1587
Milwaukee, WI	1354	809	1173	1074	867	90	381	1010	1042	374	1163	272	565	2055	622	1475		337	1015	879	509	1258	849	1817	551	2062	379	1437	2170	1990	788	763
Minneapolis, MN	1225	1127	838	1396	1180	408	703	928	913	696	1171	591	436	1925	831	1791	337		1223	1204	372	1573	1171	1687	874	1727	563	1308	2040	1655	1110	634
Mobile, AL	1234	328	1874	1427	571	917	721	589	1414	978	468	733	850	2014	382	719	1011	1224	144	1202	1038	497	1101	1643	1000	2661	645	1936	2320	2727	965	894
Montréal, QC	2129	1218	2099	310	980	847	824	1722	1832	560	1884	847	1330	2845	1314	1647	938	1262	1640	382	1302	1437	454	2591	603	2948	1092	2228	2960	2916	587	1529
Nashville, TN	1219	248	1586	1099	408	469	273	664	1158	534	786	287	555	2006	209	913	564	881	532	884	747	692	802	1682	560	2357	307	1633	2306	2404	667	688
New Orleans, LA	1165	468	1868	1520	712	923	804	519	1398	1066	348	818	844	1894	394	861	1015	1223		1304	1032	641	1222	1523	1090	2642	675	1920	2252	2716	1087	880
New York, NY	2001	882	2041	216	641	787	637	1548	1775	613	1632	707	1196	2787	1094	1288	879	1204	1304		1245	1089	95	2463	369	2891	954	2170	2902	2858	228	1391
Norfolk, VA	1910	558	2132	569	328	878	605	1350	1758	704	1362	720	1155	2707	898	950	969	1295	1026	370	1335	755	271	2373	425	2962	911	2238	2973	2949	193	1349
Oklahoma City, OK	542	844	1203	1678	1084	792	846	206	631	1029	437	739	348	1326	466	1476	876	788	722	1460	452	1254	1384	1005	1101	1922	496	1200	1627	1948	1344	160
Omaha, NE	863	992	845	1436	1151	470	722	656	534	736	898	613	184	1546	641	1658	509	372	1032	1245		1436	1212	1325	914	1650	439	930	1662	1663	1151	298
Orlando, FL	1730	440	2275	1288	526	1153	905	1086	1851	1144	965	968	1246	2515	778	235	1258	1573	641	1089	1436		986	2145	975	3048	999	2323	2816	3093	849	1365
Ottawa, ON	2039	1158	1768	428	920	760	732	1632	1748	471	1804	757	1240	2763	1230	1618	859	1032	1582	440	1213	1408	447	2501	546	2660	1002	2142	2877	2586	566	1439
Philadelphia, PA	1924	780	2011	306	539	757	571	1467	1732	583	1547	643	1127	2713	1014	1180	849	1171	1222	95	1212	986		2387	305	2861	888	2140	2873	2828	137	1319
Phoenix, AZ	425	1844	1210	2681	2088	1795	1849	1066	908	2032	1178	1742	1246	373	1471	2362	1817	1687	1523	2463	1325	2145	2387		2104	1332	1499	653	749	1414	2348	1053
Pittsburgh, PA	1641	684	1713	570	446	459	288	1221	1447	285	1354	359	840	2428	768	1173	551	874	1090	369	914	975	305	2104		2563	604	1842	2574	2530	243	1035
Portland, ME	2315	1192	2333	107	938	1079	967	1861	2067	825	1940	1034	1518	3082	1408	1585	1176	1492	1616	304	1533	1385	402	2778	666	3186	1279	2461	3196	3151	535	1710
Portland, OR	1363	2603	891	3086	2761	2118	2369	2128	1256	2385	2356	2260	1797	963	2245	3260	2062	1727	2642	2891	1650	3048	2861	1332	2563		2050	765	635	174	2800	1764
Rapid City, SD	843	1508	323	1900	1670	912	1208	1061	397	1200	1291	1100	704	1312	1160	2173	840	575	1551	1708	525	1956	1675	1305	1378	1215	959	649	1384	1142	1618	699
Reno, NV	1019	2396	958	2881	2555	1913	2163	1668	1051	2180	1904	2056	1591	470	2029	3063	1953	1818	2186	2685	1445	2841	2656	733	2357	578	1844	518	218	720	2595	1558
Richmond, VA	1832	532	2051	547	293	797	512	1278	1671	622	1329	627	1069	2620	824	944	888	1210	1002	334	1259	742	245	2294	344	2869	822	2145	2880	2868	108	1261
St. Louis, MO	1037	555	1278	1182	714	295	348	630	854	533	784	243	248	1821	284	1221	379	563	675	954	439	999	888	1499	604	2050		1326	2061	2096	827	442
Salt Lake City, UT	599	1878	552	2365	2037	1398	1647	1403	533	1664	1634	1541	1073	688	1524	2544	1437	1308	1920	2170	930	2323	2140	653	1842	765	1326		735	839	2079	1042
San Antonio, TX	712	986	1480	2039	1230	1202	1210	276	935	1439	195	1149	766	1357	727	1379	1285	1205	541	1822	920	1160	1742	985	1495	2076	906	1311	1736	2150	1607	625
San Diego, CA	810	2138	1302	3046	2381	2080	2196	1359	1077	2346	1472	2089	1597	120	1819	2656	2118	1986	1816	2809	1613	2436	2738	355	2452	1083	1845	750	501	1256	2693	1401
San Francisco, CA	1086	2472	1173	3098	2712	2130	2380	1734	1268	2397	1929	2273	1808	382	2095	3038	2170	2040	2252	2902	1662	2816	2873	749	2574	635	2061	735		807	2812	1775
Santa Fe, NM	58	1379	943	2212	1618	1313	1379	640	391	1562	877	1272	766	846	998	1944	1336	1207	1158	1994	891	1723	1917	520	1634	1388	1029	625	1144	1463	1879	572
Sault Ste. Marie, ON	1777	1040	1273	923	947	483	577	1370	1428	348	1527	540	951	2465	972	1685	400	545	1355	921	850	1475	911	2240	614	2166	740	1848	2581	2090	854	1150
Seattle, WA	1438	2649	818	3054	2808	2063	2363	2193	1320	2353	2431	2253	1844	1134	2299	3315	1990	1655	2716	2858	1663	3093	2828	1414	2530	174	2096	839	807		2768	1828
Spokane, WA	1320	2369	541	2774	2528	1785	2084	1964	1091	2075	2192	1973	1564	1216	2018	3035	1712	1377	2409	2580	1383	2814	2550	1381	2252	352	1817	720	874	279	2490	1600
Tampa, FL	1746	451	2293	1342	578	1166	916	1102	1860	1178	980	984	1252	2525	779	280	1260	1578	651	1138	1445	85	1040	2153	1023	3064	1008	2340	2832	3111	904	1381
Toronto, ON	1800	963	1771	548	756	519	493	1393	1504	231	1551	518	1001	2517	983	1483	609	933	1306	489	974	1284	497	2262	316	2620	763	1899	2632	2588	486	1188
Tulsa, OK	645	782	1234	1576	1022	687	738	258	692	927	487	635	263	1433	402	1414	773	704	671	1350	380	1192	1282	1107	994	1938	392	1215	1731	2012	1234	175
Vancouver, BC	1575	2785	953	3188	2944	2198	2499	2338	1465	2487	2565	2389	1980	1275	2437	3451	2125	1790	2851	2993	1799	3229	2963	1550	2665	313	2232	973	947	141	2903	1973
Washington, DC	1885	637	1951	439	398	697	512	1332	1671	522	1411	582	1066	2670	879	1044	788	1110	1087	228	1151	849	137	2348	244	2800	827	2079	2812	2768		1258
Wichita, KS	591	955	1064	1613	1092	724	779	361	519	964	595	674	198	1377	577	1587	763	634	880	1391	298	1365	1319	1053	1035	1764	442	1042	1775	1828	1258	

Mileages in this chart are based upon the routes usually followed by motorists. Highway systems include interstate, U.S., and state highways.

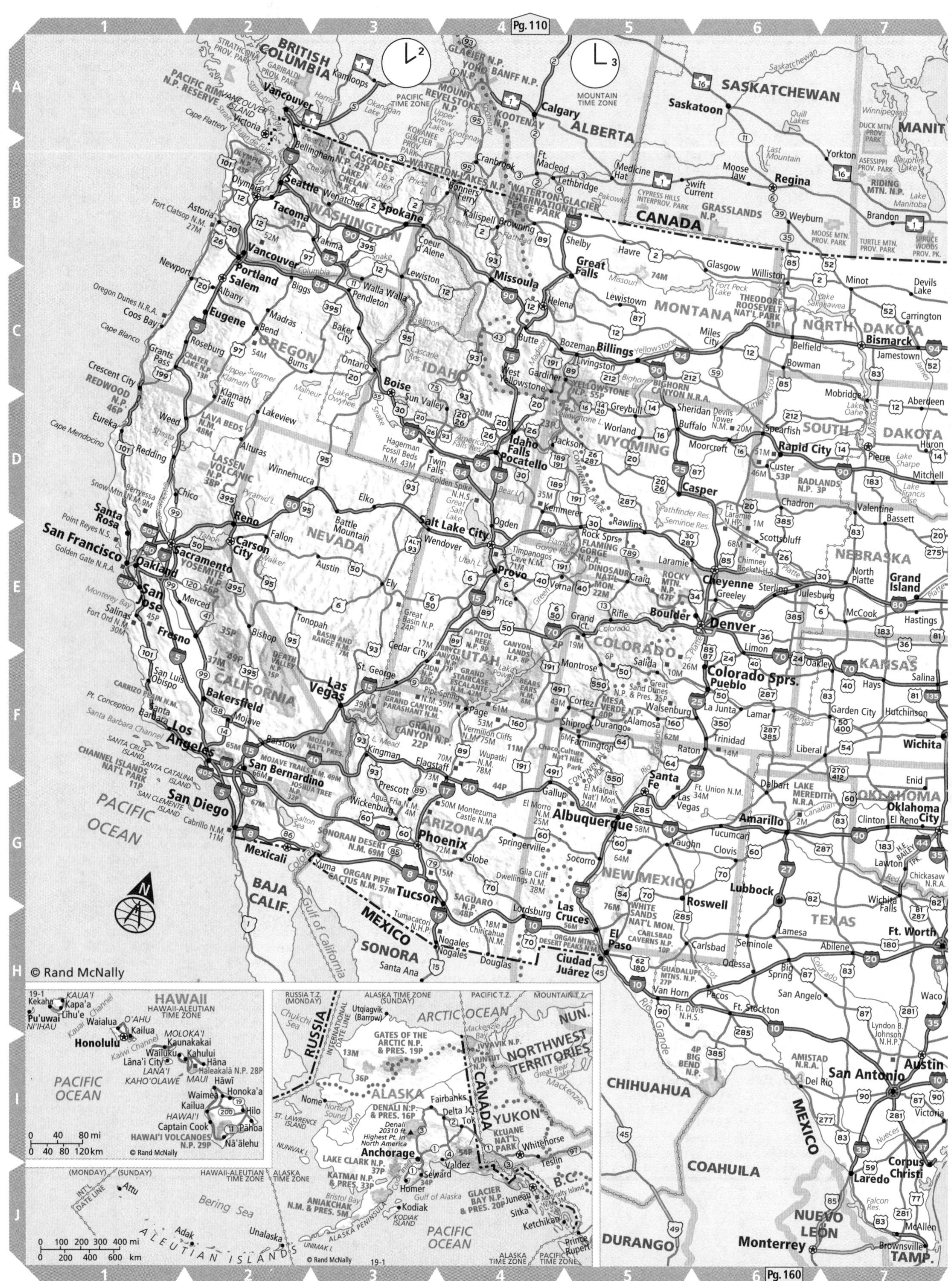

Pg. 110
BRITISH COLUMBIA
ALBERTA
SASKATCHEWAN
CANADA
WASHINGTON
OREGON
IDAHO
MONTANA
NORTH DAKOTA
SOUTH DAKOTA
WYOMING
NEBRASKA
NEVADA
UTAH
COLORADO
KANSAS
CALIFORNIA
ARIZONA
NEW MEXICO
OKLAHOMA
TEXAS
MEXICO
BAJA CALIF.
SONORA
CHIHUAHUA
COAHUILA
DURANGO
NUEVO LEÓN
TAMP.
PACIFIC OCEAN
PACIFIC TIME ZONE
MOUNTAIN TIME ZONE
Vancouver
Victoria
Calgary
Saskatoon
Regina
Seattle
Tacoma
Spokane
Portland
Salem
Eugene
Boise
Missoula
Helena
Great Falls
Billings
Bismarck
Pierre
Rapid City
Casper
Cheyenne
Salt Lake City
Reno
Carson City
Sacramento
San Francisco
Oakland
San Jose
Fresno
Las Vegas
Los Angeles
San Bernardino
San Diego
Phoenix
Tucson
Albuquerque
Santa Fe
Denver
Boulder
Colorado Sprs.
Pueblo
El Paso
Ciudad Juárez
Lubbock
Amarillo
Oklahoma City
Wichita
Ft. Worth
Austin
San Antonio
Laredo
Corpus Christi
Monterrey
Mexicali
© Rand McNally
HAWAII
HAWAII-ALEUTIAN TIME ZONE
Honolulu
Hilo
PACIFIC OCEAN
ALASKA
RUSSIA
CANADA
YUKON
NORTHWEST TERRITORIES
ARCTIC OCEAN
Anchorage
Fairbanks
Juneau
Bering Sea
ALEUTIAN ISLANDS
Pg. 160

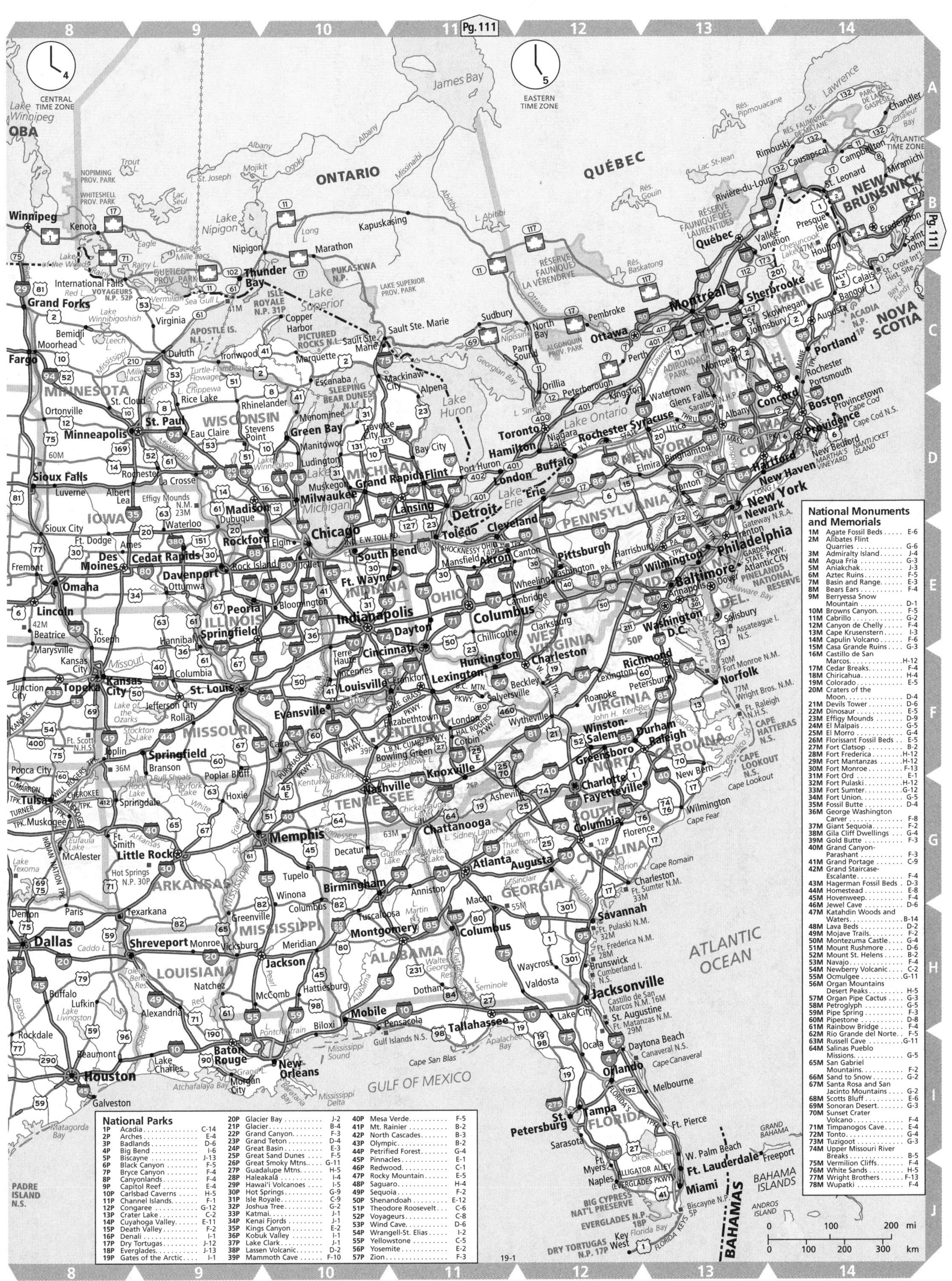

National Parks

1P	Acadia	C-14
2P	Arches	E-4
3P	Badlands	D-6
4P	Big Bend	I-6
5P	Biscayne	J-13
6P	Black Canyon	F-5
7P	Bryce Canyon	F-4
8P	Canyonlands	F-4
9P	Capitol Reef	E-4
10P	Carlsbad Caverns	H-5
11P	Channel Islands	F-1
12P	Congaree	G-12
13P	Crater Lake	C-2
14P	Cuyahoga Valley	E-11
15P	Death Valley	F-2
16P	Denali	I-1
17P	Dry Tortugas	J-12
18P	Everglades	J-13
19P	Gates of the Arctic	I-1
20P	Glacier Bay	J-2
21P	Glacier	B-4
22P	Grand Canyon	F-3
23P	Grand Teton	D-4
24P	Great Basin	E-3
25P	Great Sand Dunes	F-5
26P	Great Smoky Mtns.	G-11
27P	Guadalupe Mtns.	H-5
28P	Haleakalā	I-4
29P	Hawai'i Volcanoes	I-5
30P	Hot Springs	G-9
31P	Isle Royale	C-9
32P	Joshua Tree	G-2
33P	Katmai	J-1
34P	Kenai Fjords	J-1
35P	Kings Canyon	E-2
36P	Kobuk Valley	I-1
37P	Lake Clark	J-1
38P	Lassen Volcanic	D-2
39P	Mammoth Cave	F-10
40P	Mesa Verde	F-5
41P	Mt. Rainier	B-2
42P	North Cascades	B-3
43P	Olympic	B-2
44P	Petrified Forest	G-4
45P	Pinnacles	E-1
46P	Redwood	C-1
47P	Rocky Mountain	E-5
48P	Saguaro	H-4
49P	Sequoia	F-2
50P	Shenandoah	E-12
51P	Theodore Roosevelt	C-6
52P	Voyageurs	C-8
53P	Wind Cave	D-6
54P	Wrangell-St. Elias	I-2
55P	Yellowstone	C-5
56P	Yosemite	E-2
57P	Zion	F-3

National Monuments and Memorials

1M	Agate Fossil Beds	E-6
2M	Alibates Flint Quarries	G-6
3M	Admiralty Island	J-4
4M	Agua Fria	G-3
5M	Aniakchak	J-3
6M	Aztec Ruins	F-5
7M	Basin and Range	E-3
8M	Bears Ears	F-4
9M	Berryessa Snow Mountain	D-1
10M	Browns Canyon	F-5
11M	Cabrillo	G-2
12M	Canyon de Chelly	F-4
13M	Cape Krusenstern	I-3
14M	Capulin Volcano	F-6
15M	Casa Grande Ruins	G-3
16M	Castillo de San Marcos	H-12
17M	Cedar Breaks	F-4
18M	Chiricahua	H-4
19M	Colorado	E-5
20M	Craters of the Moon	D-4
21M	Devils Tower	D-6
22M	Dinosaur	E-5
23M	Effigy Mounds	D-9
24M	El Malpais	G-5
25M	El Morro	G-4
26M	Florissant Fossil Beds	E-5
27M	Fort Clatsop	B-2
28M	Fort Frederica	H-12
29M	Fort Mantanzas	H-12
30M	Fort Monroe	F-13
31M	Fort Ord	E-1
32M	Fort Pulaski	H-12
33M	Fort Sumter	G-12
34M	Fort Union	G-5
35M	Fossil Butte	D-4
36M	George Washington Carver	F-8
37M	Giant Sequoia	F-2
38M	Gila Cliff Dwellings	G-4
39M	Gold Butte	F-3
40M	Grand Canyon-Parashant	F-3
41M	Grand Portage	C-9
42M	Grand Staircase-Escalante	F-4
43M	Hagerman Fossil Beds	D-3
44M	Homestead	E-8
45M	Hovenweep	F-4
46M	Jewel Cave	D-6
47M	Katahdin Woods and Waters	B-14
48M	Lava Beds	D-2
49M	Mojave Trails	F-2
50M	Montezuma Castle	G-4
51M	Mount Rushmore	D-6
52M	Mount St. Helens	B-2
53M	Navajo	F-4
54M	Newberry Volcanic	C-2
55M	Ocmulgee	G-11
56M	Organ Mountains Desert Peaks	H-5
57M	Organ Pipe Cactus	G-3
58M	Petroglyph	G-5
59M	Pipe Spring	F-3
60M	Pipestone	D-8
61M	Rainbow Bridge	F-4
62M	Río Grande del Norte	F-5
63M	Russell Cave	G-11
64M	Salinas Pueblo Missions	G-5
65M	San Gabriel Mountains	F-2
66M	Sand to Snow	G-2
67M	Santa Rosa and San Jacinto Mountains	G-2
68M	Scotts Bluff	E-6
69M	Sonoran Desert	G-3
70M	Sunset Crater Volcano	F-4
71M	Timpanogos Cave	E-4
72M	Tonto	G-4
73M	Tuzigoot	G-3
74M	Upper Missouri River Breaks	B-5
75M	Vermilion Cliffs	F-4
76M	White Sands	H-5
77M	Wright Brothers	F-13
78M	Wupatki	F-4

Alabama state facts

Nickname: The Heart of Dixie
Capital: Montgomery, F-4
Population: 4,779,736 (rank: 23rd)
Largest city: Birmingham, 212,237, D-3
Land area: 50,645 sq. mi. (rank: 28th)
Highest point: Cheaha Mountain, 2,407 ft., D-5

Pg. 45
Pg. 56
Pg. 32

Alabama

Cities and Towns

Abbeville . . . H-6
Alabaster . . . D-3
Albertville . . . B-4
Alexander City . . . E-5
Aliceville . . . E-1
Andalusia . . . H-4
Anniston . . . C-5
Arab . . . B-4
Ashland . . . D-5
Ashville . . . C-4
Athens . . . A-3
Atmore . . . I-2
Attalla . . . C-4
Auburn . . . F-5
Bay Minette . . . I-2
Bessemer . . . D-3
Birmingham . . . D-3
Boaz . . . B-4
Brent . . . E-3
Brewton . . . H-3
Bridgeport . . . A-5
Butler . . . G-1
Calera . . . E-3
Camden . . . G-3
Carrollton . . . D-1
Centre . . . C-5
Centreville . . . E-3
Chatom . . . H-1
Childersburg . . . D-4
Citronelle . . . H-1
Clanton . . . E-4
Clayton . . . G-6
Columbiana . . . D-4
Cullman . . . B-3
Dadeville . . . E-5
Daleville . . . H-5
Daphne . . . I-1
Decatur . . . B-3
Demopolis . . . F-2
Dothan . . . H-6
Double Springs . . . C-2
East Brewton . . . H-3
Elba . . . H-5
Enterprise . . . H-5
Eufaula . . . G-6
Eutaw . . . E-2
Evergreen . . . H-3
Fairhope . . . J-1
Fayette . . . C-2
Florence . . . A-2
Foley . . . J-2
Fort Payne . . . B-5
Fultondale . . . D-3
Gadsden . . . C-5
Geneva . . . I-5
Greensboro . . . E-2
Greenville . . . G-4
Grove Hill . . . G-2
Guin . . . C-2
Gulf Shores . . . J-2
Guntersville . . . B-4
Haleyville . . . B-2
Hamilton . . . C-1
Hanceville . . . C-3
Hartford . . . H-5
Hartselle . . . B-3
Hayneville . . . F-4
Hazel Green . . . A-4
Headland . . . H-6
Heflin . . . C-5

NOTE: Maps are not always in alphabetical order.
See Page 1 for map location in this atlas.

Henagar B-5
Homewood D-3
Hoover D-3
Huntsville A-4
Irondale D-3
Jackson H-2
Jacksonville C-5
Jasper C-3
LaFayette E-6
Lanett E-6
Leeds D-4
Lincoln D-4
Linden F-2
Lineville D-5
Livingston F-1
Luverne G-4
Madison A-3
Marion E-2
Midfield D-3
Mobile I-1
Monroeville H-2
Montevallo E-3
Montgomery F-4
Moulton B-3
Muscle Shoals A-2
Northport D-2
Oneonta C-4
Opelika E-6
Opp H-4
Orange Beach J-2
Oxford D-5
Ozark H-5
Pelham D-3
Pell City D-4
Phenix City F-6
Piedmont C-5
Pinson C-4
Prattville F-4
Prichard I-1
Rainbow City C-5
Rainsville B-5
Red Bay B-1
Roanoke D-6
Robertsdale J-2
Rockford E-4
Russellville B-2
Saraland I-1
Scottsboro B-5
Selma F-3
Sheffield A-2
Spanish Fort I-1
Springville C-4
Sumiton C-3
Sylacauga D-4
Talladega D-4
Tallassee F-5
Theodore J-1
Thomasville G-2
Troy G-5
Trussville D-4
Tuscaloosa D-2
Tuscumbia A-2
Tuskegee F-5
Union Springs F-5
Valley E-6
Vernon C-1
Warrior C-3
Wedowee D-5
Wetumpka F-4
Winfield C-2
York F-1

Travel planning & on-the-road resources

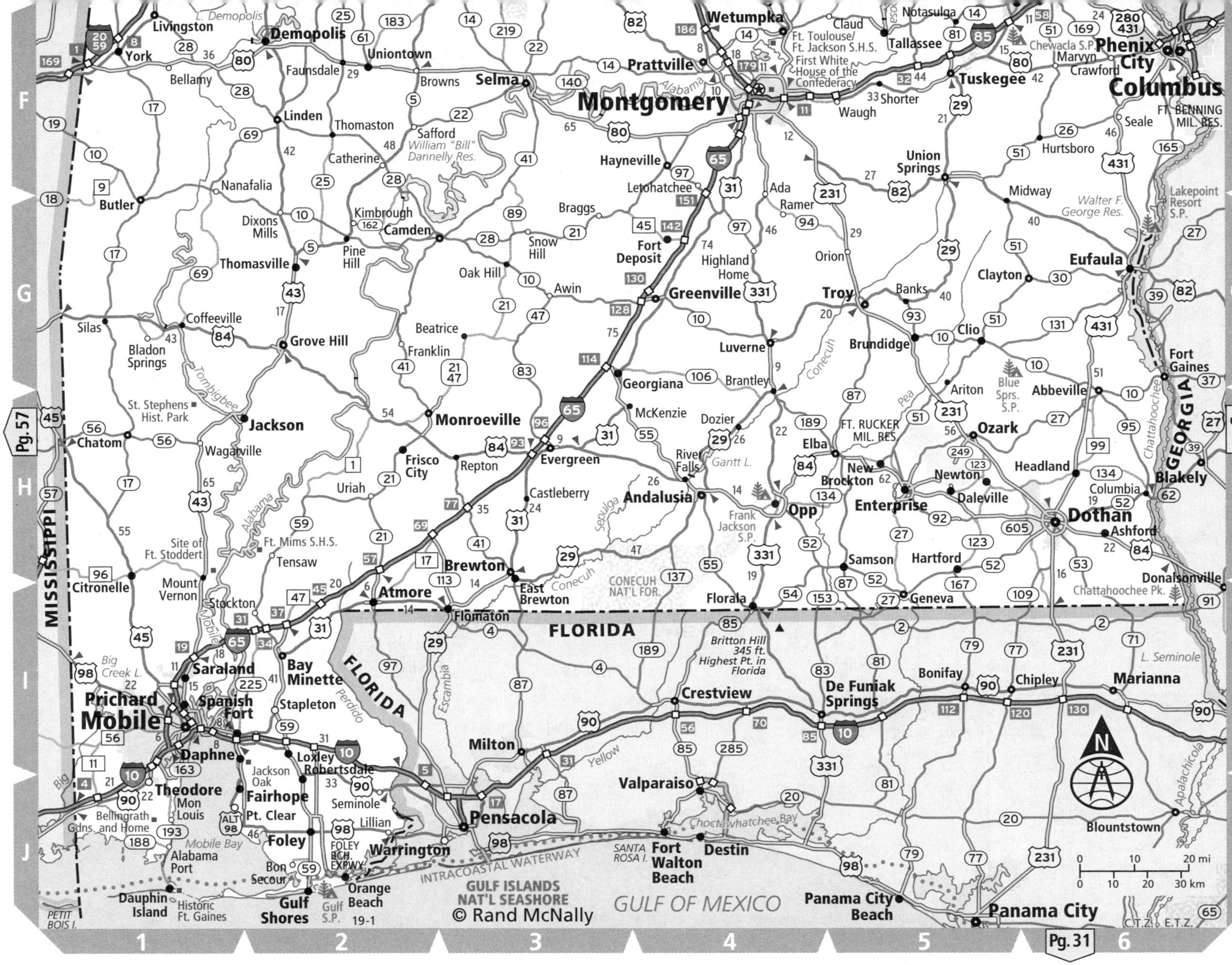

Tourism Information	Alabama Tourism Department (800) 252-2262, (334) 242-4169 www.alabama.travel, tourism.alabama.gov	**Road Conditions & Construction**	(888) 588-2848 www.dot.state.al.us alitsweb2.dot.state.al.us/RoadConditions

Alaska state facts

Nickname: The Last Frontier
Capital: Juneau, E-6
Population: 710,231 (rank: 47th)
Largest city: Anchorage, 291,826, D-4
Land area: 570,641 sq. mi. (rank: 1st)
Highest point: Denali, 20,310 ft., D-3

Travel planning & on-the-road resources

Tourism Information	Alaska Tourism www.travelalaska.com	**Road Conditions & Construction**	511, (907) 465-8952 511.alaska.gov www.dot.state.ak.us

Alaska

Cities and Towns

Place	Grid
Alakanuk	C-2
Allakaket	C-3
Anchorage	D-3
Aniak	D-2
Bethel	D-2
Big Delta	C-4
Cantwell	C-4
Chignik	E-2
Circle	C-4
Circle Hot Springs	C-4
Cold Bay	E-1
Cordova	D-4
Delta Junction	C-4
Dillingham	E-2
Eagle	C-5
Eek	D-2
Fairbanks	C-4
Fort Yukon	C-4
Glenallen	D-4
Haines	D-5
Homer	D-3
Hoonah	E-6
Hooper Bay	D-1
Iditarod	D-2
Juneau	E-6
Kaltag	C-2
Karluk	E-3
Kenai	D-3
Ketchikan	E-6
Kodiak	E-3
Kotlik	C-2
Kotzebue	B-2
Kwethluk	D-2
Kwigillingok	D-2
Livengood	C-4
McGrath	D-3
Nenana	C-4
Ninilchik	D-3
Noatak	B-2
Nome	C-2
Palmer	D-4
Perryville	E-2
Petersburg	E-6
Port Graham	E-3
Point Hope	B-2
Prudhoe Bay	B-4
Ruby	C-3
Sand Point	F-2
Savoonga	C-1
Scammon Bay	D-1
Seward	D-4
Shungnak	B-3
Sitka	E-6
Skagway	D-5
Soldotna	D-3
Tanana	C-3
Taylor	C-2
Tok	D-4
Umiat	B-3
Unalaska	F-1
Utqiagvik (Barrow)	A-3
Valdez	D-4
Wainwright	A-3
Wasilla	D-4
Willow	D-3
Wrangell	E-6
Yakutat	D-5

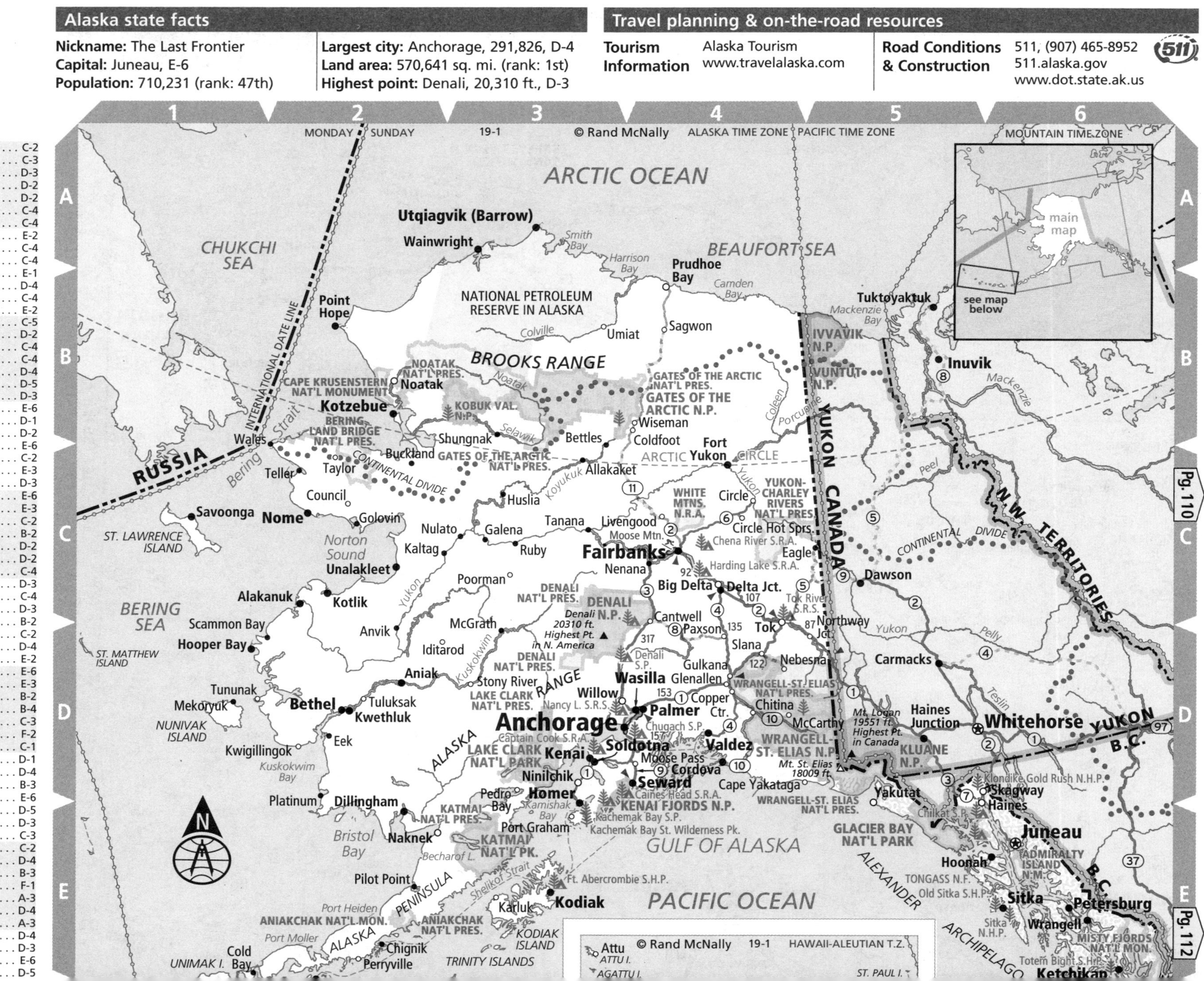

NOTE: Maps are not always in alphabetical order.
See Page 1 for map location in this atlas.

Hawaii

Cities and Towns

'Aiea J-2
'Ewa Beach J-2
'Ewa Villages J-2
Hala'ula I-5
Hale'iwa H-2
Hāna H-5
Hau'ula H-3
Hilo I-6
Hōlualoa J-5
Hōnaunau J-5
Honoka'a I-6
Honolulu J-3
Honomū I-6
Ho'olehua H-4
Kahalu'u I-3
Kahana I-3
Kahuku H-2
Kahului G-5
Kailua I-3
Kailua Kona I-5
Kainaliu J-5
Kalāheo G-1
Kalaupapa H-4
Kāne'ohe I-3
Kapa'a G-2
Kaunakakai H-4
Kea'au I-6
Kekaha G-1
Kīhei G-5
Kīlauea G-2
Kīpahulu G-6
Kōloa G-1
Kukuihaele I-6
Kurtistown J-6
Lahaina G-5
Lā'ie H-2
Lāna'i City H-4
Līhu'e G-2
Mā'alaea G-5
Mā'ili I-1
Makakilo City J-2
Mākaha I-1
Makawao G-6
Maunaloa H-4
Nā'ālehu J-6
Nānākuli J-1
Ō'ōkala I-6
Pāhala J-6
Pāhoa J-6
Pāpa'ikou I-6
Pa'uwela G-6
Pearl City I-2
Pukalani G-5
Volcano J-6
Wahiawā I-2
Waialua H-1
Wai'anae I-1
Wailuku G-5
Waimānalo J-4
Waimānalo Beach J-4
Waimea H-2
Waipahu I-2
Whitmore Village I-2

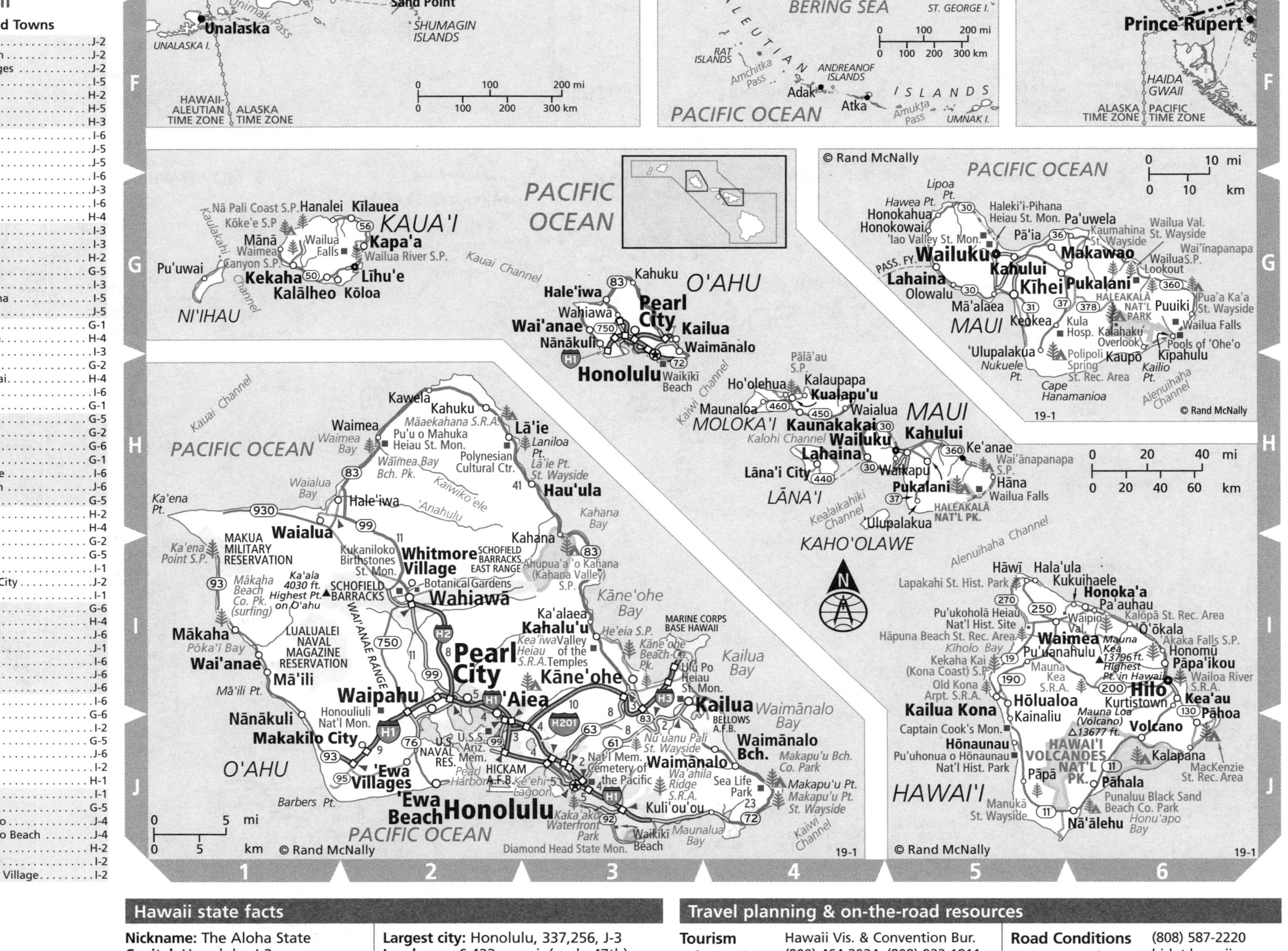

Hawaii state facts

Nickname: The Aloha State
Capital: Honolulu, J-3
Population: 1,360,301 (rank: 40th)
Largest city: Honolulu, 337,256, J-3
Land area: 6,423 sq. mi. (rank: 47th)
Highest point: Mauna Kea, 13,796 ft., I-6

Travel planning & on-the-road resources

Tourism Information Hawaii Vis. & Convention Bur. (800) 464-2924, (808) 923-1811 www.gohawaii.com

Road Conditions & Construction (808) 587-2220 hidot.hawaii.gov

Arizona state facts

Nickname: The Grand Canyon State
Capital: Phoenix; F-4

Population: 6,392,017 (rank: 16th)
Largest city: Phoenix, 1,445,632, F-4

Land area: 113,594 sq. mi. (rank: 6th)
Highest point: Humphreys Peak, 12,633 ft., C-4

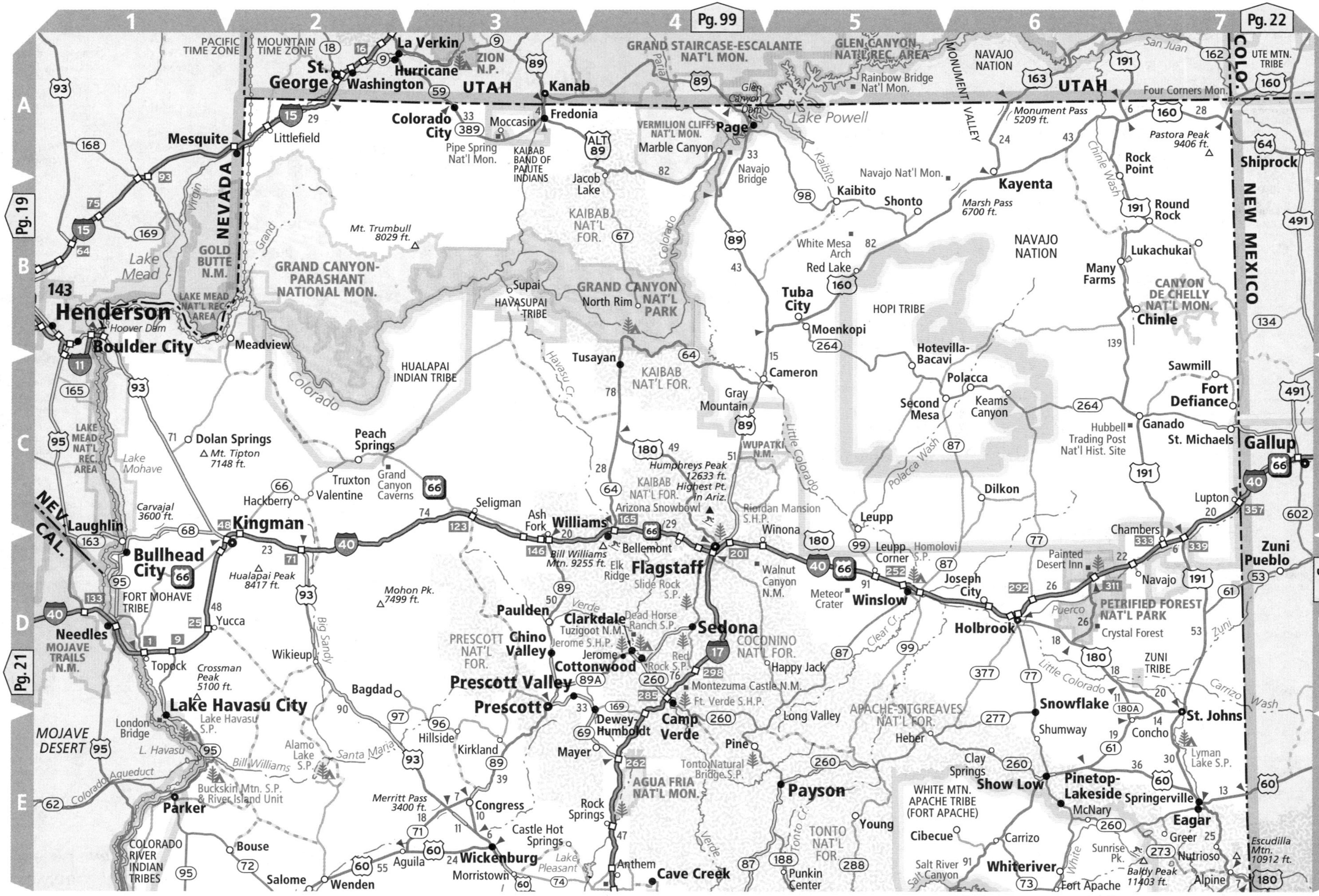

NOTE: Maps are not always in alphabetical order.
See Page 1 for map location in this atlas.

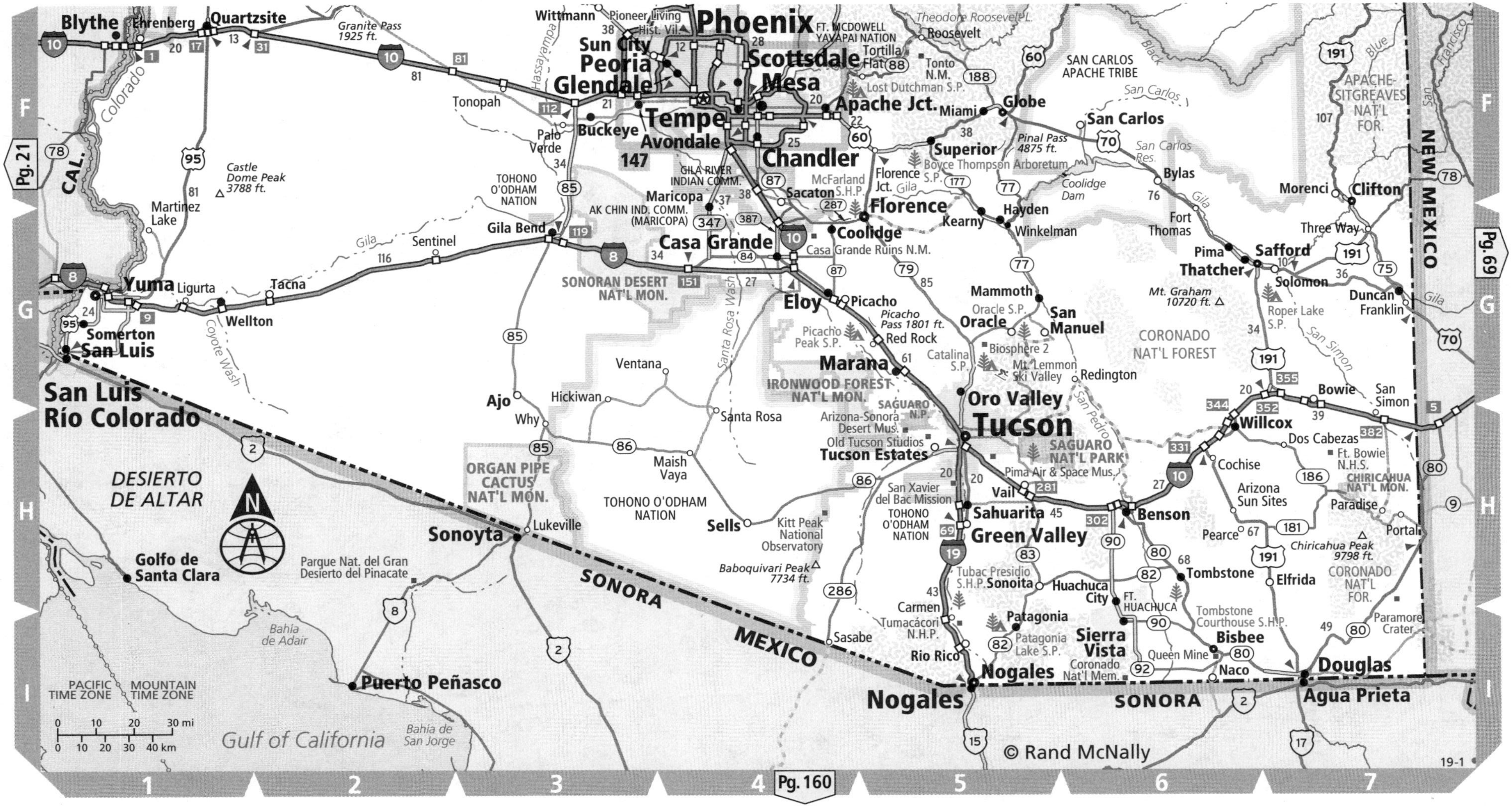

Pg. 69

Pg. 21

Pg. 160

© Rand McNally

Arizona

Cities and Towns

Anthem E-4
Apache Junction F-4
Avondale F-3
Bagdad D-2
Bellemont D-4
Benson H-6
Bisbee I-6
Buckeye F-3
Bullhead City D-1
Camp Verde D-4
Casa Grande G-4
Cave Creek E-4
Chandler F-4
Chinle B-7
Chino Valley D-3
Clarkdale D-4
Clifton F-7
Colorado City A-3
Congress E-3
Coolidge G-4
Cottonwood D-4
Dolan Springs C-1
Douglas I-7
Eagar E-7
Eloy G-4
Flagstaff D-4
Florence G-5
Fort Defiance C-7
Ganado C-7
Gila Bend G-3
Glendale F-4
Globe F-5
Green Valley H-5
Holbrook D-6
Huachuca City H-6
Kaibito B-5
Kayenta A-6
Kearny G-5
Kingman D-2
Lake Havasu City E-1
Lukachukai B-7
Mammoth G-5
Many Farms B-6
Marana G-5
Mayer E-4
Mesa F-4
Miami F-5
Morenci F-7
Nogales I-5
Oracle G-5
Oro Valley G-5
Page A-4
Parker E-1
Paulden D-3
Payson E-5
Peoria F-4
Phoenix F-4
Pima G-6
Pine E-4
Pinetop-Lakeside E-6
Prescott D-3
Prescott Valley D-3
Quartzsite F-1
Sacaton F-4
Safford G-6
Sahuarita H-5
St. Johns D-7
Salome E-2
San Carlos F-6
San Luis G-1
San Manuel G-5
Scottsdale F-4
Sedona D-4
Sells H-4
Show Low E-6
Sierra Vista I-6
Snowflake D-6
Somerton G-1
Springerville E-7
Sun City F-3
Superior F-5
Tempe F-4
Thatcher G-6
Tombstone H-6
Tuba City B-5
Tucson H-5
Tucson Estates H-5
Vail H-5
Wellton G-1
Whiteriver E-6
Wickenburg E-3
Willcox H-6
Williams D-4
Winslow D-5
Yuma G-1

Travel planning & on-the-road resources

Tourism Information
Arizona Office of Tourism
(866) 275-5816, (602) 364-3700
www.visitarizona.com

Road Conditions & Construction
511
(888) 411-7623
www.az511.com, www.azdot.gov

Arkansas

Cities and Towns

Arkadelphia E-3
Arkansas City F-6
Ash Flat A-6
Ashdown F-2
Augusta C-6
Batesville B-6
Bella Vista A-1
Benton D-4
Bentonville A-2
Berryville A-3
Blytheville B-8
Booneville C-2
Cabot D-5
Camden F-4
Charleston C-2
Clarendon D-6
Clarksville C-3
Clinton B-4
Conway C-4
Corning A-7
Crossett G-5
Danville C-3
Dardanelle C-3
De Queen E-1
De Valls Bluff D-6
De Witt E-6
Des Arc D-6
Dumas F-6
El Dorado G-4
Eureka Springs A-2
Fayetteville A-2
Fordyce F-4
Forrest City D-7
Fort Smith C-1
Greenwood C-1
Hamburg G-5
Hampton F-4
Harrisburg B-7
Harrison A-3
Heber Springs C-5
Helena-W. Helena D-7
Hope F-2
Hot Springs E-3
Hot Springs Village D-3
Huntsville A-2
Jacksonville D-5
Jasper B-3
Jonesboro B-7
Lake City B-7
Lake Village G-6
Lewisville G-2
Little Rock D-4
Lonoke D-5
Magnolia G-3
Malvern E-4
Marianna D-7
Marion C-8
Marshall B-4
McGehee F-6
Melbourne B-5
Mena D-1
Monticello F-5
Morrilton C-4
Mount Ida D-2
Mountain Home A-4
Mountain View B-5
Murfreesboro E-2
Nashville F-2
Newport B-6
North Little Rock D-5
Osceola B-8
Ozark C-2
Paragould B-7
Paris C-2
Perryville D-4
Piggott A-8
Pine Bluff E-5
Pocahontas A-7
Prescott F-3
Rison F-5
Rogers A-2
Russellville C-3
Salem A-5
Searcy C-5
Sheridan E-4
Siloam Springs A-1
Springdale A-2
Star City F-5
Stuttgart E-6
Texarkana G-2
Trumann B-7
Van Buren C-1
Waldron D-2
Walnut Ridge A-7
Warren F-5
West Memphis C-8
Wynne C-7
Yellville A-4

Land area: 52,035 sq. mi. (rank: 27th)
Highest point: Magazine Mtn., 2753 ft., C-2

Population: 2,915,918 (rank: 32nd)
Largest city: Little Rock, 193,524, D-4

Nickname: The Natural State
Capital: Little Rock, D-4

Arkansas state facts

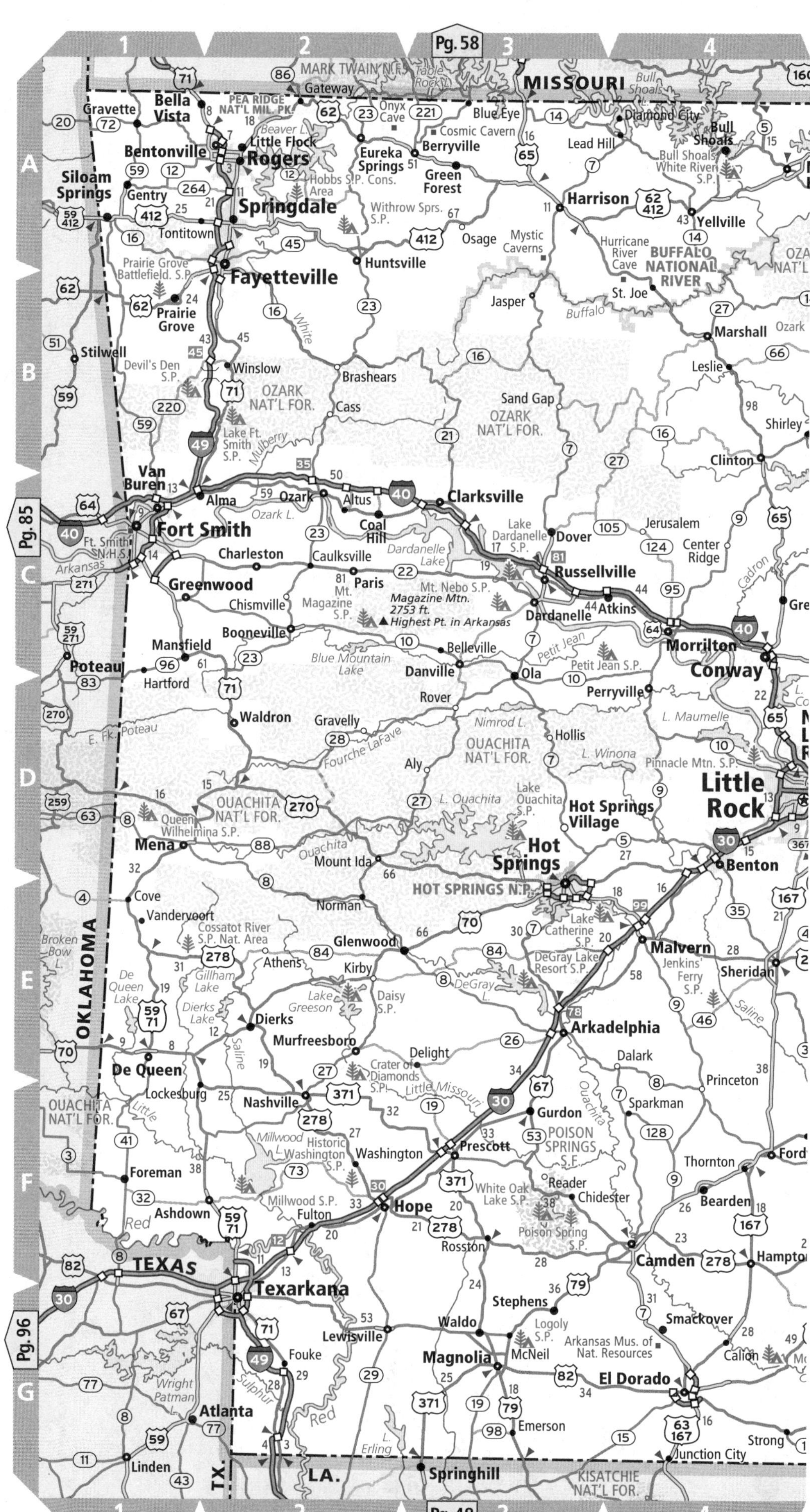

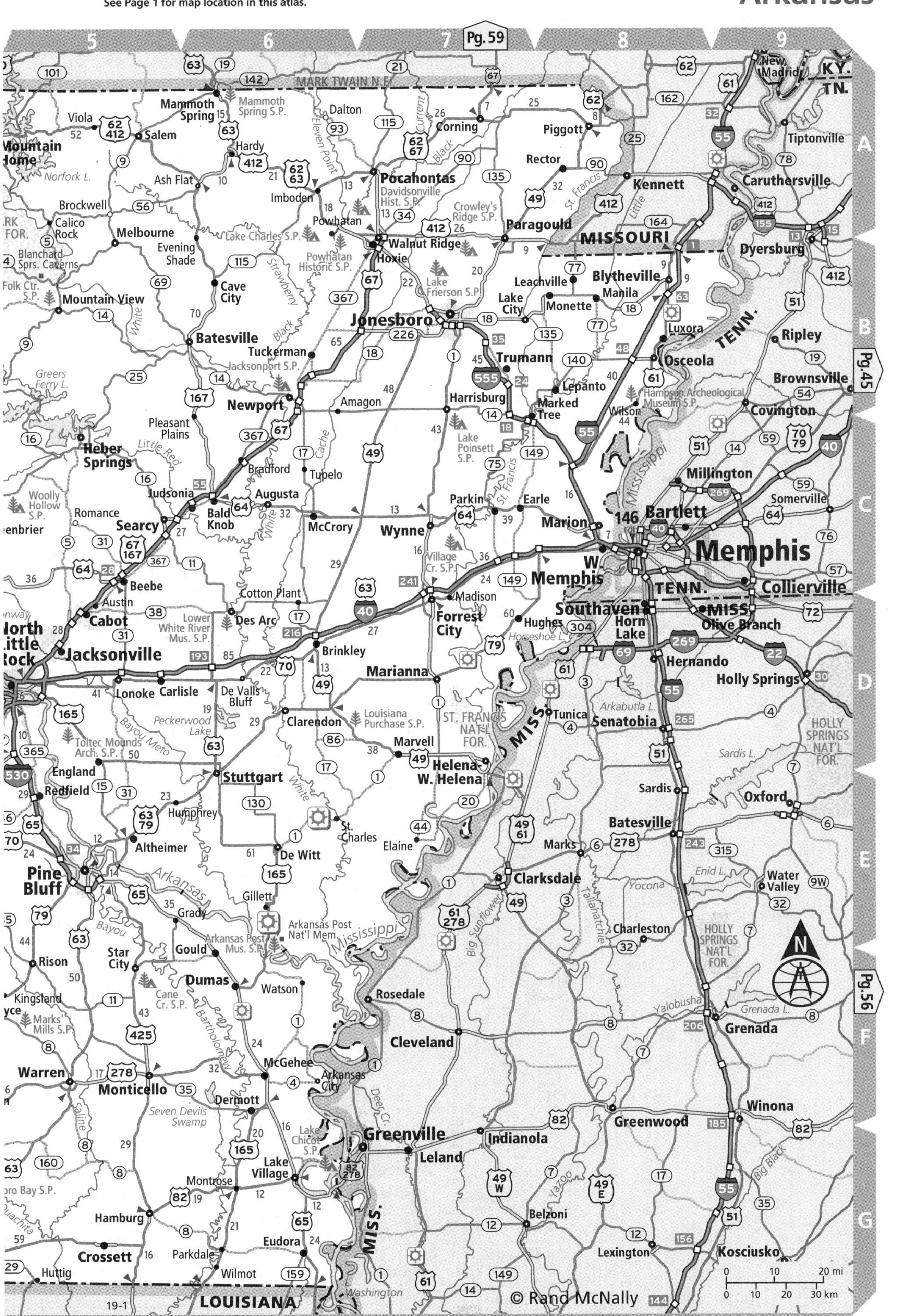

Road Conditions & Construction
(800) 245-1672, (501) 569-2374, (501) 569-2000
www.arkansashighways.com
www.idrivearkansas.com

Tourism Information
Arkansas Dept. of Parks & Tourism
(800) 628-8725, (501) 682-7777
www.arkansas.com

Travel planning & on-the-road resources

California state facts

Nickname: The Golden State
Capital: Sacramento, E-3
Population: 37,253,956 (rank: 1st)
Largest city: Los Angeles, 3,792,621, J-6
Land area: 155,799 sq. mi. (rank: 3rd)
Highest point: Mt. Whitney, 14,494 ft., G-6

Pg. 86

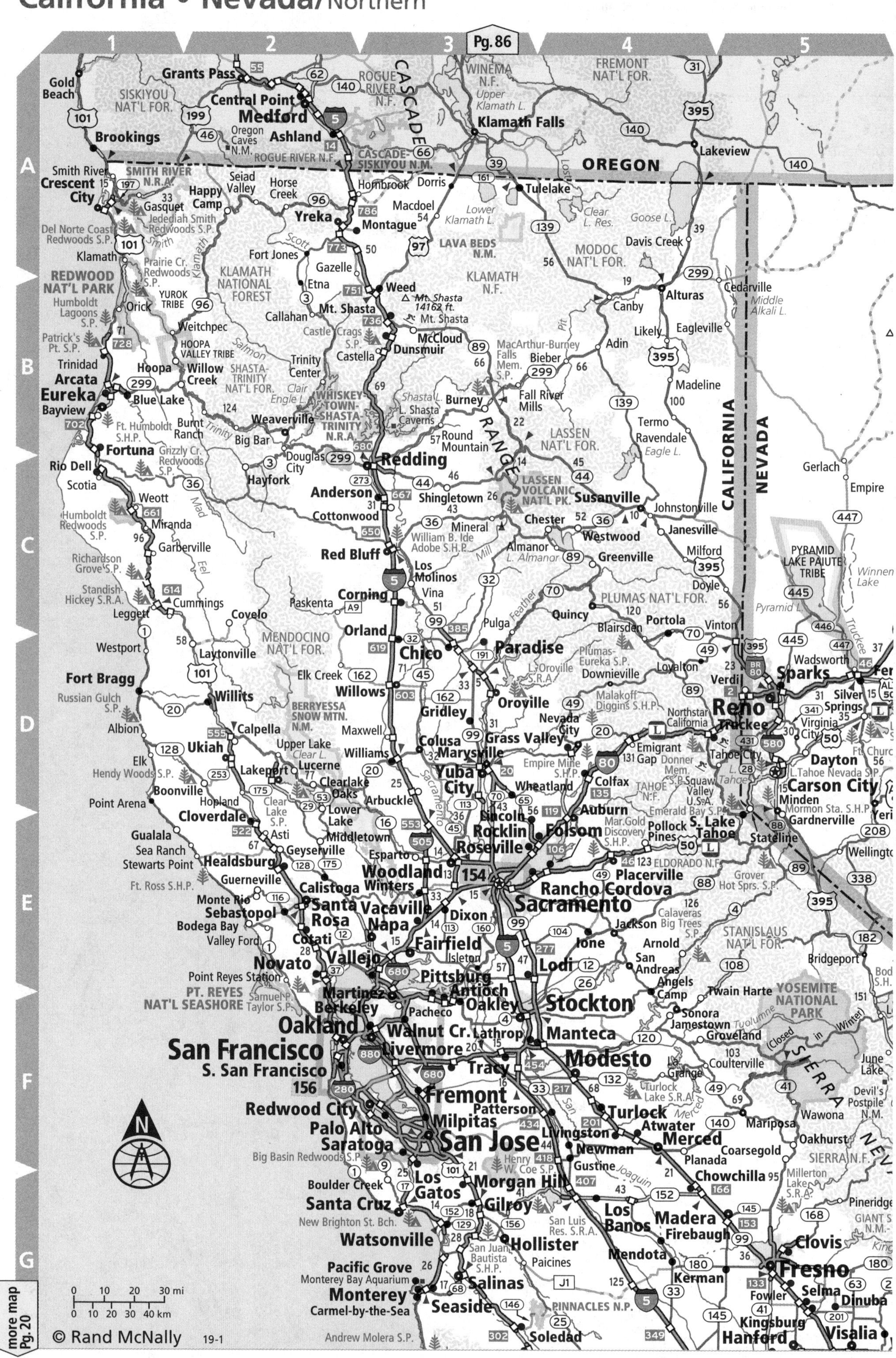

more map Pg. 20

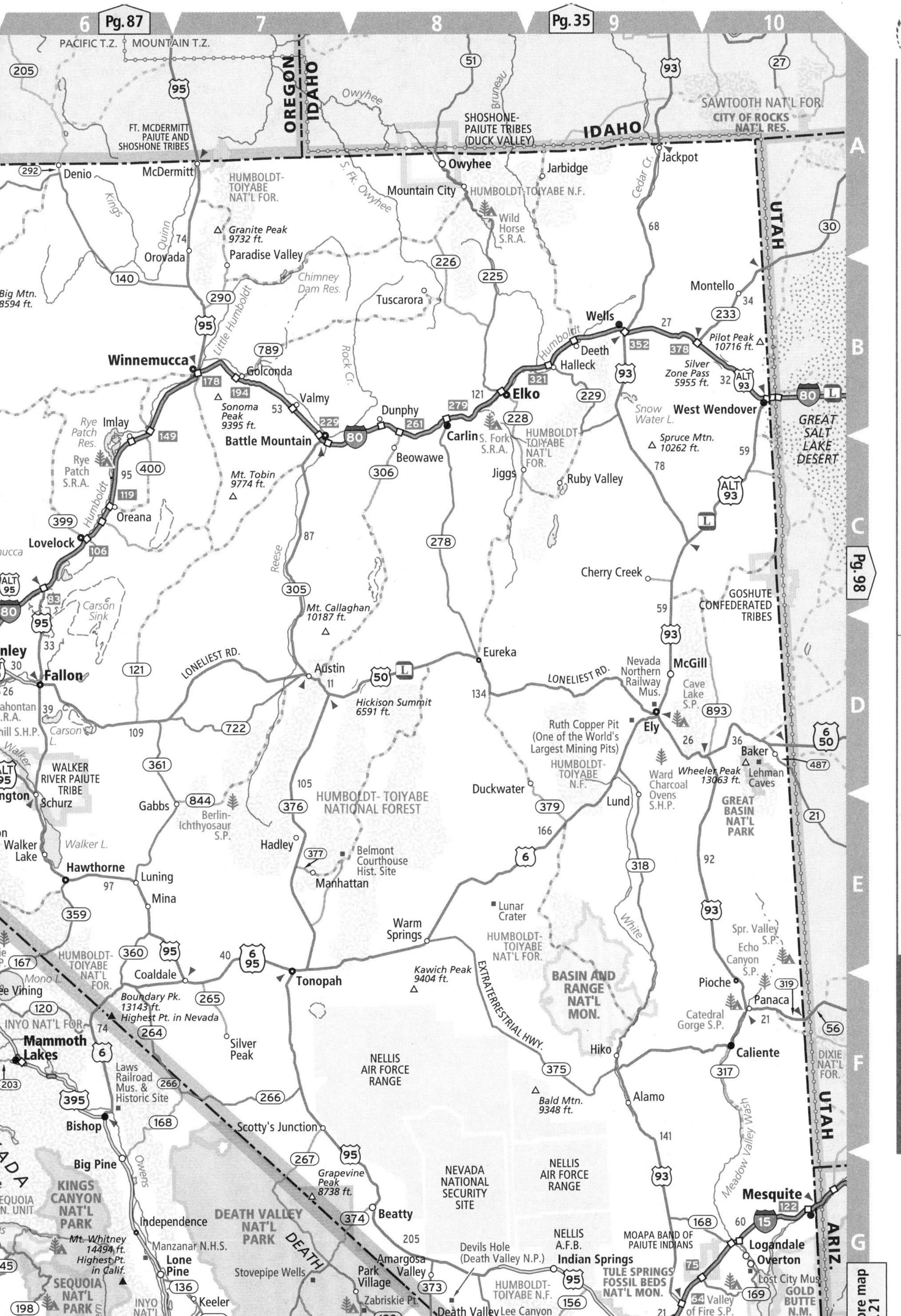

Road Conditions & Construction

(800) 427-7623
www.dot.ca.gov

Los Angeles metro area: 511, www.go511.com
Sacramento area: 511, www.sacregion511.org
San Diego area: 511, (619) 669-1900, www.511.sd.com
San Francisco Bay area: 511, www.511.org

Tourism Information

California Tourism
(877) 225-4367, (916) 444-4429
www.visitcalifornia.com

Travel planning & on-the-road resources

more map Pg. 18

Nevada state facts

Nickname: The Silver State
Capital: Carson City, D-5

Population: 2,700,551 (rank: 35th)
Largest city: Las Vegas, 583,756, H-9

Land area: 109,781 sq. mi. (rank: 7th)
Highest point: Boundary Pk., 13,143 ft., F-6

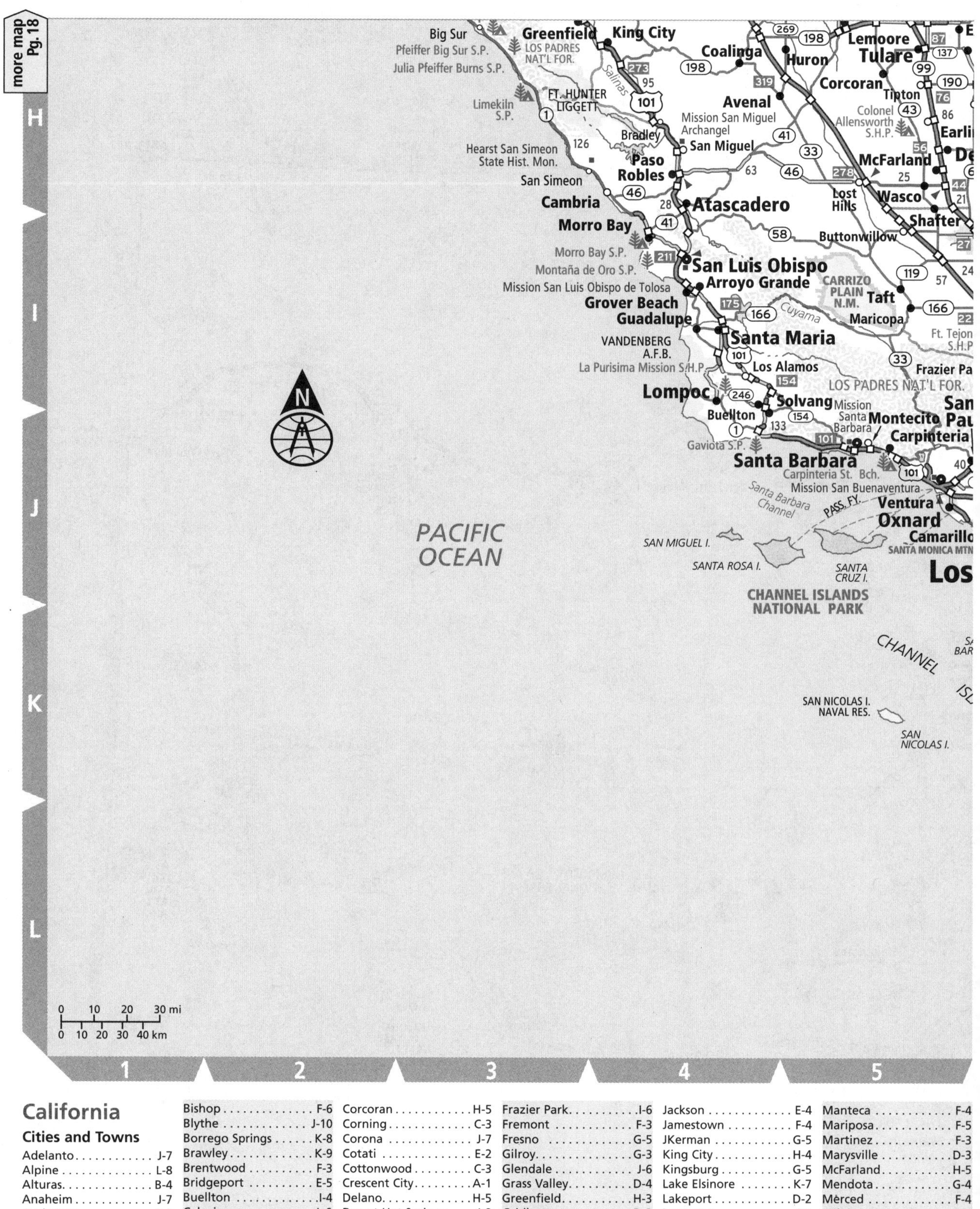

California

Cities and Towns

Adelanto J-7
Alpine L-8
Alturas B-4
Anaheim J-7
Anderson C-3
Angels Camp E-4
Antioch F-3
Apple Valley J-7
Arcata B-1
Arroyo Grande I-4
Arvin I-6
Atascadero H-4
Atwater F-4
Auburn E-4
Avalon K-6
Avenal H-4
Bakersfield I-6
Barstow I-7
Bayview B-1
Beaumont J-8
Berkeley F-3
Bishop F-6
Blythe J-10
Borrego Springs K-8
Brawley K-9
Brentwood F-3
Bridgeport E-5
Buellton I-4
Calexico L-9
California City I-7
Calipatria K-9
Calistoga E-2
Camarillo J-6
Cambria H-4
Carlsbad K-7
Carmel-by-the-Sea G-3
Carpinteria J-5
Chico D-3
Chowchilla G-4
Chula Vista L-7
Clearlake Oaks D-2
Cloverdale E-2
Clovis G-5
Coalinga H-4
Colusa D-3
Corcoran H-5
Corning C-3
Corona J-7
Cotati E-2
Cottonwood C-3
Crescent City A-1
Delano H-5
Desert Hot Springs J-8
Dinuba G-5
Dixon E-3
Downieville D-4
Earlimart H-5
El Cajon L-8
El Centro K-9
Encinitas K-7
Escondido K-7
Eureka B-1
Exeter H-5
Fairfield E-3
Firebaugh G-4
Folsom E-4
Fort Bragg D-1
Fortuna B-1
Fowler G-5
Frazier Park I-6
Fremont F-3
Fresno G-5
Gilroy G-3
Glendale J-6
Grass Valley D-4
Greenfield H-3
Gridley D-3
Grover Beach I-4
Guadalupe I-4
Guerneville E-2
Gustine F-4
Hanford G-5
Healdsburg E-2
Hemet J-8
Hesperia J-7
Hollister G-3
Holtville K-9
Huron H-5
Imperial K-9
Independence G-6
Indio J-8
Ione E-4
Irvine K-7
Jackson E-4
Jamestown F-4
JKerman G-5
King City H-4
Kingsburg G-5
Lake Elsinore K-7
Lakeport D-2
Lancaster I-6
Lathrop F-3
Lemoore H-5
Lincoln E-3
Lindsay H-5
Livermore F-3
Livingston F-4
Lodi E-3
Loma Linda J-7
Lompoc I-4
Long Beach J-6
Los Angeles J-6
Los Banos G-4
Los Gatos F-3
Lucerne D-2
Madera G-5
Mammoth Lakes F-6
Manteca F-4
Mariposa F-5
Martinez F-3
Marysville D-3
McFarland H-5
Mendota G-4
Merced F-4
Milpitas F-3
Modesto F-4
Montecito J-5
Monterey G-3
Moorpark J-6
Morgan Hill G-3
Morro Bay I-4
Mount Shasta B-3
Napa E-3
National City L-7
Needles I-10
Nevada City D-4
Newman F-4
Newport Beach K-7
Novato E-2
Oakhurst F-5
Oakland F-3

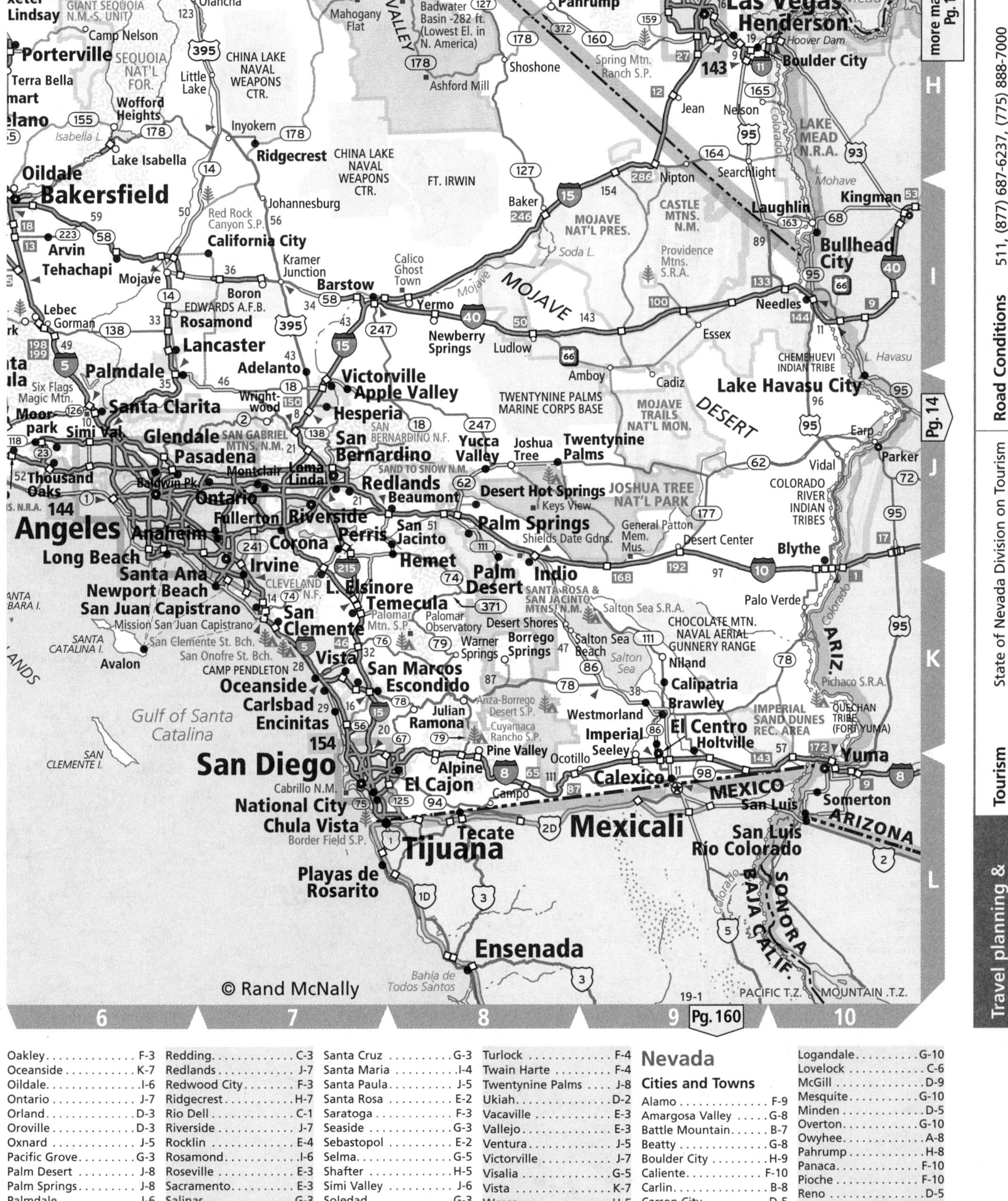

Road Conditions & Construction
511, (877) 687-6237, (775) 888-7000
www.nevadadot.com
www.nvroads.com

Tourism Information
State of Nevada Division on Tourism
(800) 638-2328, (775) 687-4322
www.travelnevada.com

Travel planning & on-the-road resources

- Oakley . . . F-3
- Oceanside . . . K-7
- Oildale . . . I-6
- Ontario . . . J-7
- Orland . . . D-3
- Oroville . . . D-3
- Oxnard . . . J-5
- Pacific Grove . . . G-3
- Palm Desert . . . J-8
- Palm Springs . . . J-8
- Palmdale . . . J-6
- Palo Alto . . . F-3
- Paradise . . . D-3
- Pasadena . . . J-6
- Paso Robles . . . H-4
- Patterson . . . F-4
- Perris . . . J-7
- Pittsburg . . . F-3
- Placerville . . . E-4
- Porterville . . . H-6
- Quincy . . . C-4
- Ramona . . . K-8
- Rancho Cordova . . . E-3
- Red Bluff . . . C-3
- Redding . . . C-3
- Redlands . . . J-7
- Redwood City . . . F-3
- Ridgecrest . . . H-7
- Rio Dell . . . C-1
- Riverside . . . J-7
- Rocklin . . . E-4
- Rosamond . . . I-6
- Roseville . . . E-3
- Sacramento . . . E-3
- Salinas . . . G-3
- San Andreas . . . E-4
- San Bernardino . . . J-7
- San Clemente . . . K-7
- San Diego . . . L-7
- San Francisco . . . F-2
- San Jacinto . . . J-8
- San Jose . . . F-3
- San Juan Capistrano . . . K-7
- San Luis Obispo . . . I-4
- San Marcos . . . K-7
- Santa Ana . . . J-7
- Santa Barbara . . . J-5
- Santa Clarita . . . J-6
- Santa Cruz . . . G-3
- Santa Maria . . . I-4
- Santa Paula . . . J-5
- Santa Rosa . . . E-2
- Saratoga . . . F-3
- Seaside . . . G-3
- Sebastopol . . . E-2
- Selma . . . G-5
- Shafter . . . H-5
- Simi Valley . . . J-6
- Soledad . . . G-3
- Solvang . . . I-4
- Sonora . . . F-4
- South Lake Tahoe . . . E-5
- South San Francisco . . . F-2
- Stockton . . . F-3
- Susanville . . . C-4
- Taft . . . I-5
- Tehachapi . . . I-6
- Temecula . . . K-7
- Thousand Oaks . . . J-6
- Tracy . . . F-3
- Truckee . . . D-4
- Tulare . . . H-5
- Turlock . . . F-4
- Twain Harte . . . F-4
- Twentynine Palms . . . J-8
- Ukiah . . . D-2
- Vacaville . . . E-3
- Vallejo . . . E-3
- Ventura . . . J-5
- Victorville . . . J-7
- Visalia . . . G-5
- Vista . . . K-7
- Wasco . . . H-5
- Watsonville . . . G-3
- Weaverville . . . B-2
- Williams . . . D-3
- Willits . . . D-2
- Willows . . . D-3
- Winters . . . E-3
- Woodlake . . . G-5
- Woodland . . . E-3
- Yreka . . . A-2
- Yuba City . . . D-3
- Yucca Valley . . . J-8

Nevada

Cities and Towns

- Alamo . . . F-9
- Amargosa Valley . . . G-8
- Battle Mountain . . . B-7
- Beatty . . . G-8
- Boulder City . . . H-9
- Caliente . . . F-10
- Carlin . . . B-8
- Carson City . . . D-5
- Dayton . . . D-5
- Elko . . . B-8
- Ely . . . D-9
- Eureka . . . D-8
- Fallon . . . D-6
- Fernley . . . D-5
- Gardnerville . . . E-5
- Hawthorne . . . E-6
- Henderson . . . H-9
- Indian Springs . . . G-9
- Jackpot . . . A-9
- Las Vegas . . . H-9
- Laughlin . . . I-10
- Logandale . . . G-10
- Lovelock . . . C-6
- McGill . . . D-9
- Mesquite . . . G-10
- Minden . . . D-5
- Overton . . . G-10
- Owyhee . . . A-8
- Pahrump . . . H-8
- Panaca . . . F-10
- Pioche . . . F-10
- Reno . . . D-5
- Schurz . . . D-6
- Searchlight . . . H-9
- Silver Springs . . . D-5
- Sparks . . . D-5
- Stateline . . . D-5
- Tonopah . . . E-7
- Verdi . . . D-5
- Virginia City . . . D-5
- Wadsworth . . . D-5
- Walker Lake . . . E-6
- Wells . . . B-9
- West Wendover . . . B-10
- Winnemucca . . . B-7
- Yerington . . . D-5

Colorado state facts

Nickname: The Centennial State
Capital: Denver, C-6

Population: 5,029,196 (rank: 22nd)
Largest city: Denver, 600,158, C-6

Land area: 103,642 sq. mi. (rank: 8th)
Highest point: Mt. Elbert, 14,433 ft., D-4

Colorado

Cities and Towns

Akron B-8
Alamosa F-5
Arvada C-6
Aspen D-3
Aurora C-6
Basalt D-3
Bennett C-6
Boulder C-5
Breckenridge C-4
Brighton C-6
Brush B-7
Buena Vista D-4
Burlington D-9
Cañon City E-5
Carbondale D-3
Castle Rock D-6
Center F-4
Central City C-5
Cheyenne Wells D-9
Clifton D-2
Colorado City F-6
Colorado Springs D-6
Conejos G-4
Cortez G-1
Craig B-3
Creede F-3
Cripple Creek E-5
Del Norte F-4
Delta D-2
Denver C-6
Dove Creek F-1
Durango G-2
Eads E-8
Eagle C-4
Eaton B-6
Englewood C-6
Estes Park B-5
Evans B-6
Fairplay D-4
Florence E-6
Fort Collins B-6
Fort Lupton C-6
Fort Morgan B-7
Fountain E-6
Frederick B-6
Fruita D-1
Fruitvale D-2
Georgetown C-5
Glenwood Springs C-3
Golden C-5
Grand Junction D-1
Greeley B-6
Gunnison E-3
Gypsum C-3
Holyoke B-9
Hot Sulphur Springs C-4
Hugo D-7
Julesburg A-9
Kiowa D-6
Lake City F-3
Lakewood C-6
Lamar E-8
Las Animas F-8
Leadville D-4
Limon D-7
Lincoln Park E-5
Littleton C-6
Longmont B-6
Loveland B-6
Manitou Springs D-6
Meeker C-2
Monte Vista F-4
Montrose E-2
Ordway E-7
Ouray F-2
Pagosa Springs G-3
Palisade D-2
Parker C-6
Penrose E-6
Platteville B-6
Pueblo E-6
Rangely B-1
Rifle C-2
Rocky Ford F-7
Saguache F-4
Salida E-4
San Luis G-5
Silverton F-2
Springfield G-9
Steamboat Springs B-4
Sterling B-8
Telluride F-2
Thornton C-6
Trinidad G-6
Vail C-4
Walden B-4
Walsenburg F-6
Wellington B-6
Westcliffe E-5
Windsor B-6
Woodland Park D-6
Wray B-9
Yuma B-8

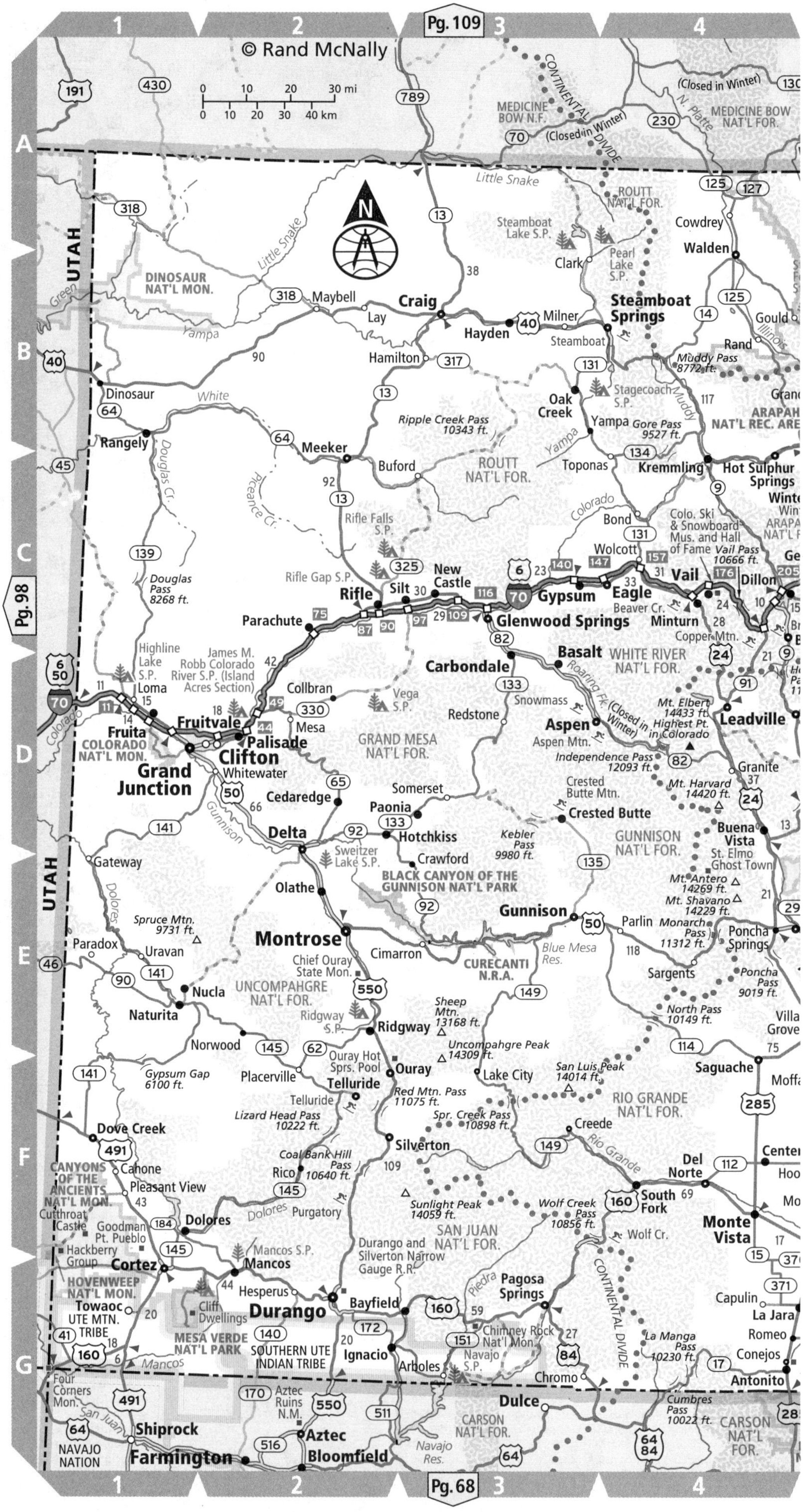

NOTE: Maps are not always in alphabetical order.
See Page 1 for map location in this atlas.

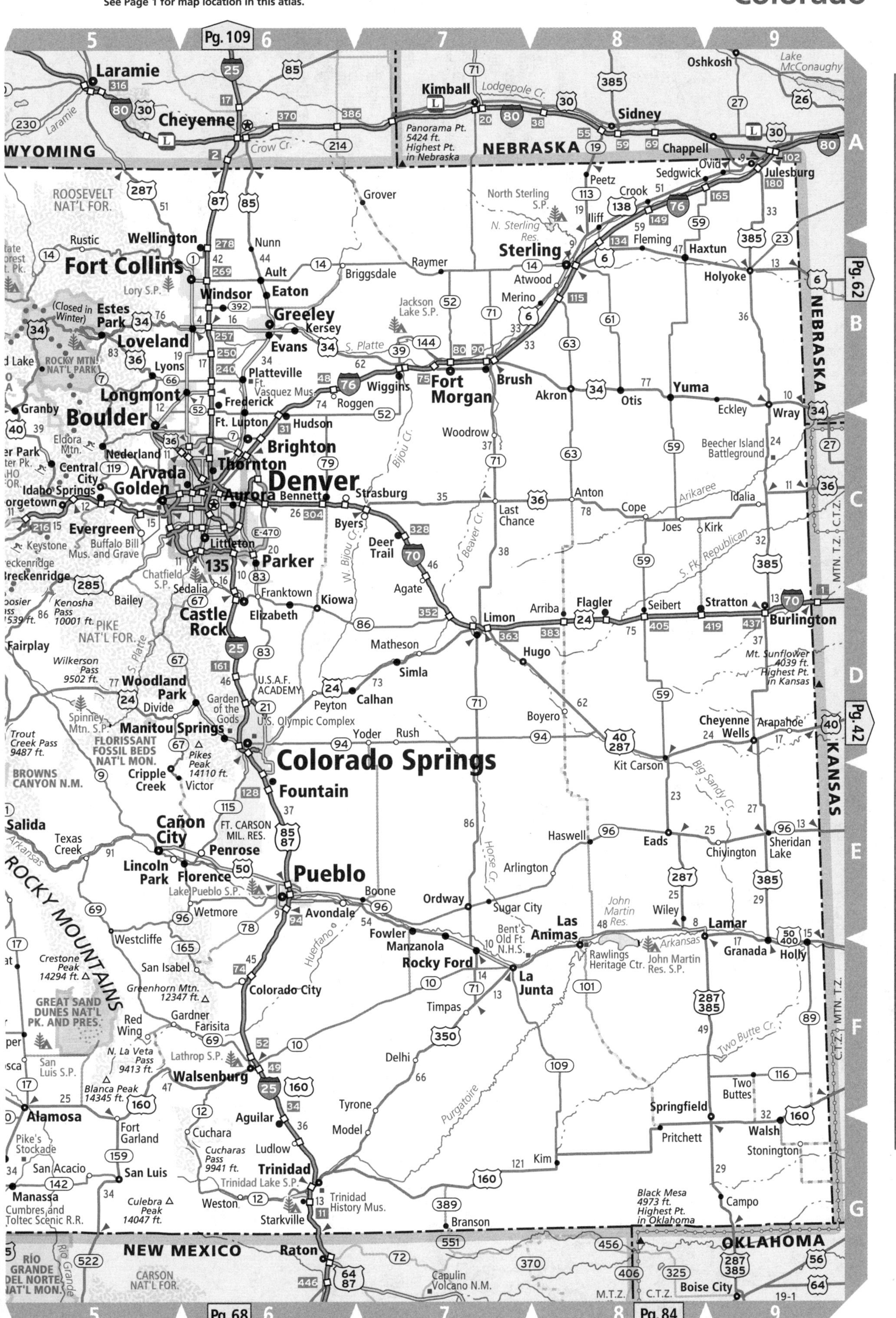

Road Conditions & Construction
511
(303) 639-1111, (877) 315-7623
www.cotrip.org, www.codot.gov

Tourism Information
Colorado Tourism Office
(800) 265-6723
www.colorado.com

Travel planning & on-the-road resources

Connecticut state facts

Nickname: The Constitution State
Capital: Hartford, F-4
Population: 3,574,097 (rank: 29th)
Largest city: Bridgeport, 144,229, I-2
Land area: 4,842 sq. mi. (rank: 48th)
Highest point: Mt. Frissell, 2,380 ft., E-1

Travel planning & on-the-road resources

Tourism Information
Connecticut Office of Tourism
(888) 288-4748, (860) 256-2800
www.ctvisit.com

Road Conditions & Construction
(860) 594-2000,
(860) 594-2650
www.ct.gov/dot

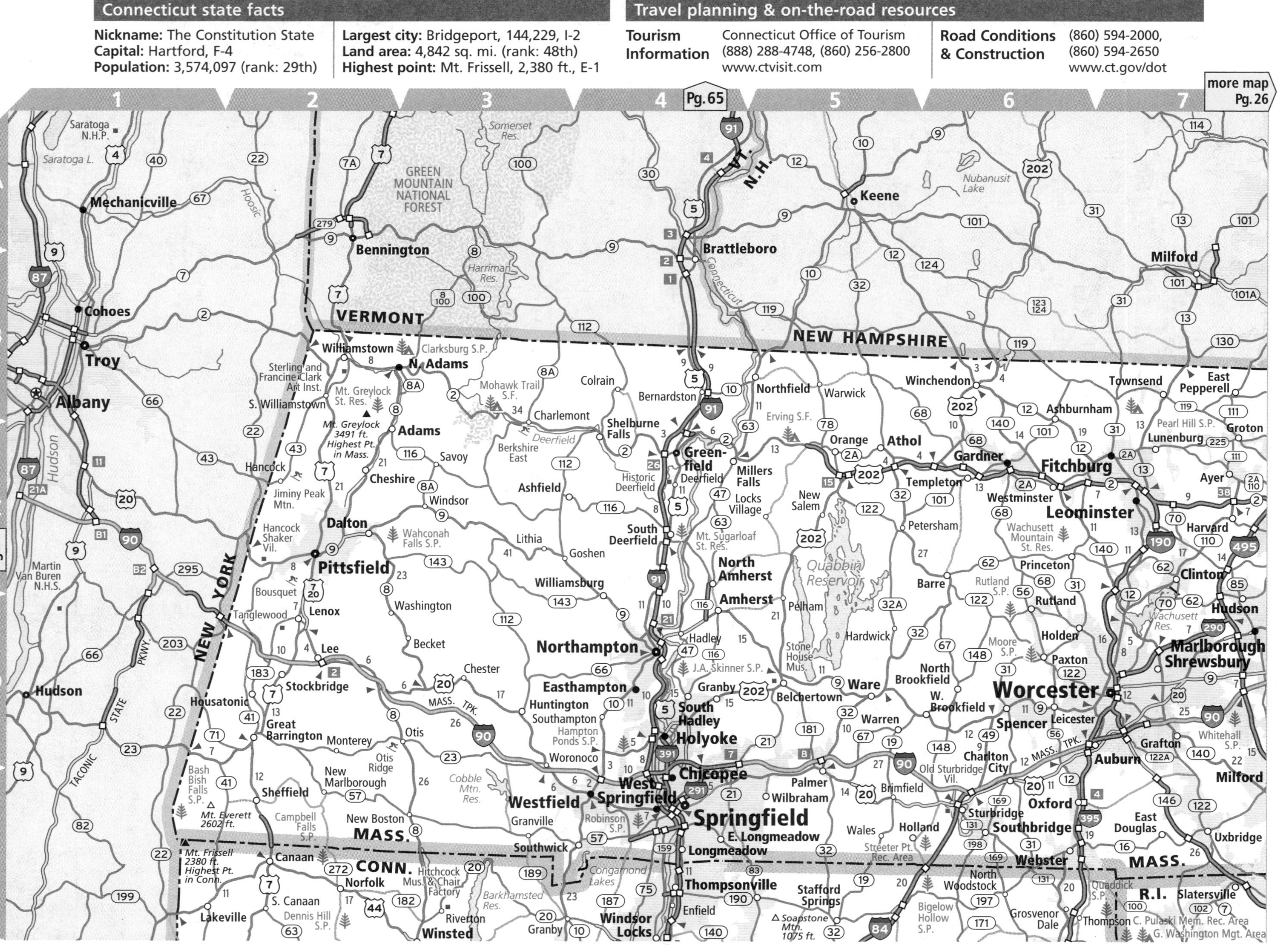

more map Pg. 26
Pg. 65
Pg. 73

Rhode Island state facts

Nickname: The Ocean State
Capital: Providence, F-8
Population: 1,052,567 (rank: 43rd)
Largest city: Providence, 178,042, F-8
Land area: 1,034 sq. mi. (rank: 50th)
Highest point: Jerimoth Hill, 812 ft., F-7

Travel planning & on-the-road resources

Tourism Information	Rhode Island Tourism Division (800) 556-2484 www.visitrhodeisland.com
Road Conditions & Construction	511, (888) 401-4511, (401) 222-2450 www.dot.ri.gov/travel

Massachusetts state facts

Nickname: The Bay State
Capital: Boston, D-9
Population: 6,547,629 (rank: 14th)
Largest city: Boston, 617,594, D-9
Land area: 7,800 sq. mi. (rank: 45th)
Highest point: Mt. Greylock, 3,491 ft., B-2

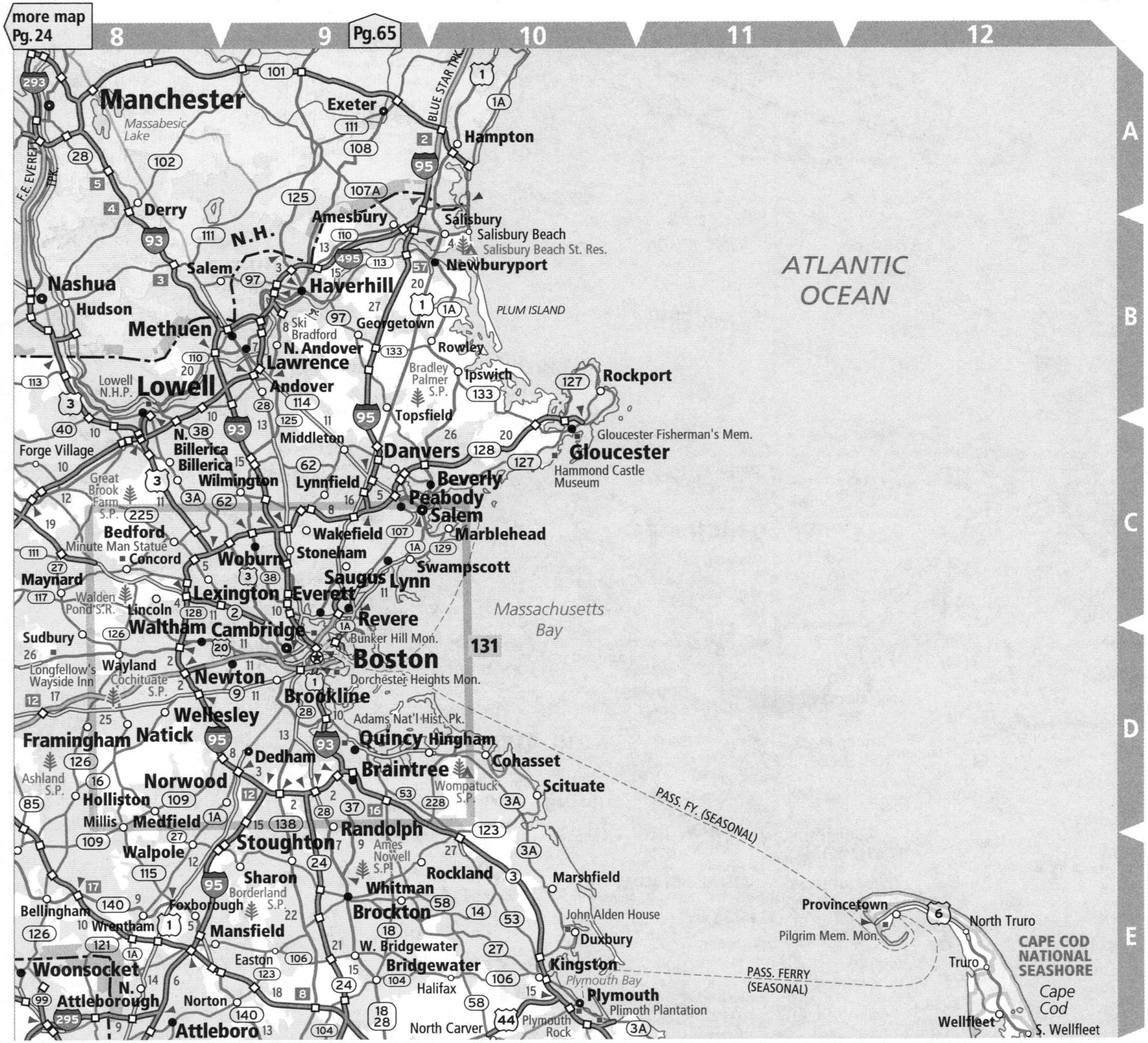

more map Pg. 24
Pg.65

Connecticut

Cities and Towns

Ansonia H-3
Avon F-3
Baltic G-6
Beacon Falls H-3
Bethel H-1
Bloomfield F-4
Branford H-3
Bridgeport I-2
Bristol G-3
Brooklyn F-6
Canaan E-2
Cheshire G-3
Colchester G-5
Columbia F-5
Cromwell G-4
Danbury H-1
Danielson F-6
Darien I-1
Deep River H-5
Derby H-2
East Hampton G-4
East Hartford F-4
East Haven H-3
Ellington F-4
Fairfield I-2
Farmington F-3
Georgetown H-1
Greenwich I-1
Groton H-6
Guilford H-4
Hamden H-3
Hartford F-4
Kensington G-4
Lakeville E-1
Litchfield F-2
Manchester F-4
Meriden G-3
Middlebury G-2
Middletown G-4
Milford H-3
Moosup F-6
Mystic H-6
Naugatuck G-3
New Britain G-3
New Canaan I-1
New Fairfield G-1
New Haven H-3
New London H-6
New Milford G-1
Newington F-4
Newtown H-2
Norfolk E-2
Northford H-3
Norwalk I-1
Norwich G-6
Old Mystic H-6
Pawcatuck H-6
Plainfield G-6
Plainville G-3
Plymouth G-3
Portland G-4
Putnam F-6
Ridgefield H-1
Seymour H-3
Shelton H-2
Simsbury F-3
South Windham G-5
South Windsor F-4
Southbury G-2
Stafford Springs E-5

Gloucester C-10
Great Barrington D-2
Greenfield C-4
Harwich F-12
Harwich Port G-12
Haverhill B-9
Hingham D-9
Holden D-6
Holliston D-8
Holyoke D-4
Hudson D-7
Hyannis G-11
Ipswich B-10
Kingston E-10
Lawrence B-9
Lee D-2
Leicester D-6
Leominster C-7
Lexington C-8
Lincoln C-8
Longmeadow E-4
Lowell B-8
Lunenburg C-7
Lynn C-9
Lynnfield C-9
Mansfield E-8
Marblehead C-10
Marlborough D-7
Marshfield E-10
Maynard C-8
Medfield D-8
Methuen B-9
Middleborough F-9
Middleton C-9
Milford E-8
Millis D-8
Nantucket H-12
Natick D-8
New Bedford G-9
Newburyport B-10
Newton D-9
North Adams B-3
North Amherst C-4
North Andover B-9
North Attleboro E-8
North Billerica C-8
North Brookfield D-6
Northampton D-4
Norton E-9
Norwood D-9
Oak Bluffs G-11
Orange C-5
Orleans F-12
Oxford E-6
Palmer E-5
Peabody C-9
Pittsfield C-2
Plymouth E-10
Pocasset F-10
Provincetown E-12
Quincy D-9
Randolph D-9
Revere C-9
Rockland E-9
Rockport B-10
Rutland D-6
Salem C-9
Salisbury B-10
Sandwich F-11
Saugus C-9
Scituate D-10
Sharon E-9
Shelburne Falls C-4
Shrewsbury D-7

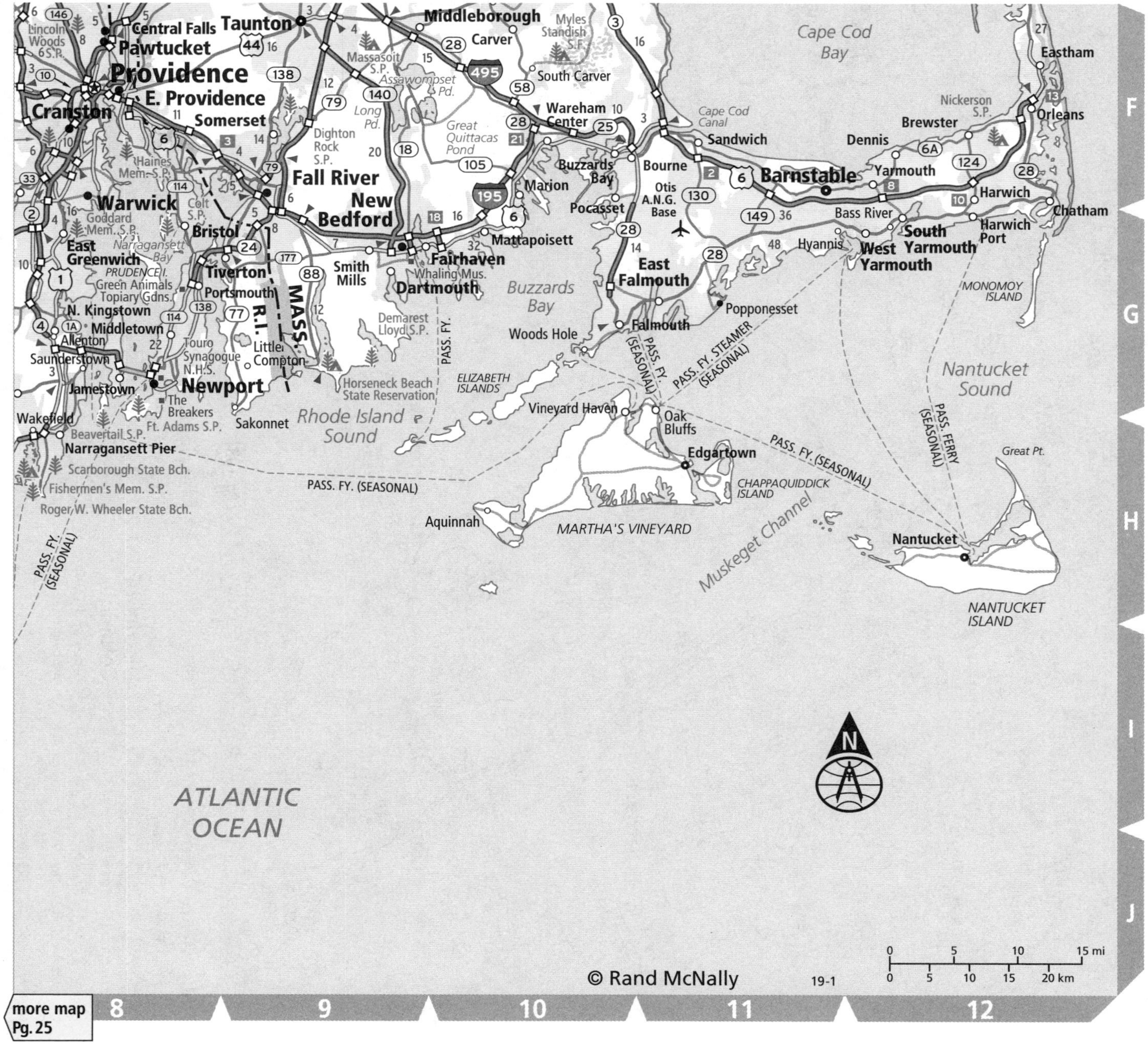

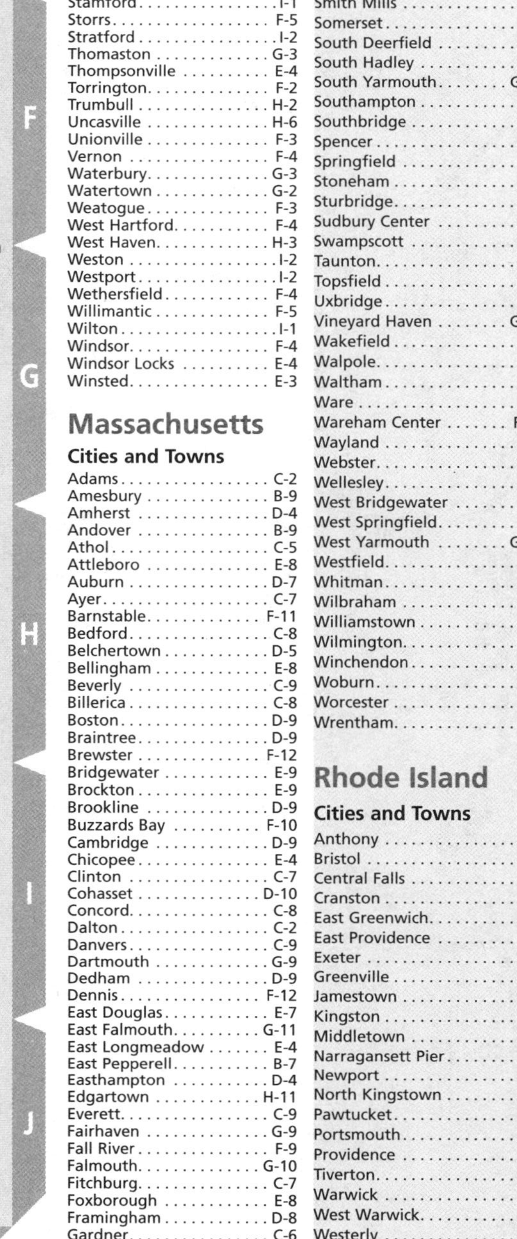

more map Pg. 25

- Stamford I-1
- Storrs F-5
- Stratford I-2
- Thomaston G-3
- Thompsonville E-4
- Torrington F-2
- Trumbull H-2
- Uncasville H-6
- Unionville F-3
- Vernon F-4
- Waterbury G-3
- Watertown G-2
- Weatogue F-3
- West Hartford F-4
- West Haven H-3
- Weston I-2
- Westport I-2
- Wethersfield F-4
- Willimantic F-5
- Wilton I-1
- Windsor F-4
- Windsor Locks E-4
- Winsted E-3

Massachusetts

Cities and Towns

- Adams C-2
- Amesbury B-9
- Amherst D-4
- Andover B-9
- Athol C-5
- Attleboro E-8
- Auburn D-7
- Ayer C-7
- Barnstable F-11
- Bedford C-8
- Belchertown D-5
- Bellingham E-8
- Beverly C-9
- Billerica C-8
- Boston D-9
- Braintree D-9
- Brewster F-12
- Bridgewater E-9
- Brockton E-9
- Brookline D-9
- Buzzards Bay F-10
- Cambridge D-9
- Chicopee E-4
- Clinton C-7
- Cohasset D-10
- Concord C-8
- Dalton C-2
- Danvers C-9
- Dartmouth G-9
- Dedham D-9
- Dennis F-12
- East Douglas E-7
- East Falmouth G-11
- East Longmeadow E-4
- East Pepperell B-7
- Easthampton D-4
- Edgartown H-11
- Everett C-9
- Fairhaven G-9
- Fall River F-9
- Falmouth G-10
- Fitchburg C-7
- Foxborough E-8
- Framingham D-8
- Gardner C-6
- Georgetown B-9
- Smith Mills G-9
- Somerset F-9
- South Deerfield C-4
- South Hadley D-4
- South Yarmouth G-12
- Southampton D-4
- Southbridge E-6
- Spencer D-6
- Springfield E-4
- Stoneham C-9
- Sturbridge E-6
- Sudbury Center D-8
- Swampscott C-9
- Taunton F-9
- Topsfield B-9
- Uxbridge E-7
- Vineyard Haven G-10
- Wakefield C-9
- Walpole E-8
- Waltham D-8
- Ware D-5
- Wareham Center F-10
- Wayland D-8
- Webster E-6
- Wellesley D-8
- West Bridgewater E-9
- West Springfield E-4
- West Yarmouth G-12
- Westfield E-4
- Whitman E-9
- Wilbraham E-5
- Williamstown B-2
- Wilmington C-9
- Winchendon B-6
- Woburn C-9
- Worcester D-7
- Wrentham E-8

Rhode Island

Cities and Towns

- Anthony F-7
- Bristol G-8
- Central Falls F-8
- Cranston F-8
- East Greenwich G-8
- East Providence F-8
- Exeter G-7
- Greenville F-7
- Jamestown G-8
- Kingston G-8
- Middletown G-8
- Narragansett Pier H-8
- Newport G-8
- North Kingstown G-8
- Pawtucket F-8
- Portsmouth G-8
- Providence F-8
- Tiverton G-9
- Warwick F-8
- West Warwick F-8
- Westerly H-7
- Woonsocket E-8

Tourism Information Mass. Office of Travel & Tourism (800) 227-6277, (617) 973-8500 www.massvacation.com

Road Conditions & Construction 511, Metro Boston: (617) 986-5511, Central: (508) 499-5511, Western: (413) 754-5511 www.mass511.com

Travel planning & on-the-road resources

Delaware state facts

Nickname: The First State
Capital: Dover, C-9
Population: 897,934 (rank: 45th)
Largest city: Wilmington, 70,851, A-9
Land area: 1,949 sq. mi. (rank: 49th)
Highest point: Ebright Azimuth, 448 ft., A-9

Travel planning & on-the-road resources

Tourism Information
Delaware Tourism Office
(866) 284-7483
www.visitdelaware.com

Road Conditions & Construction
(800) 652-5600
(302) 760-2080
www.deldot.gov

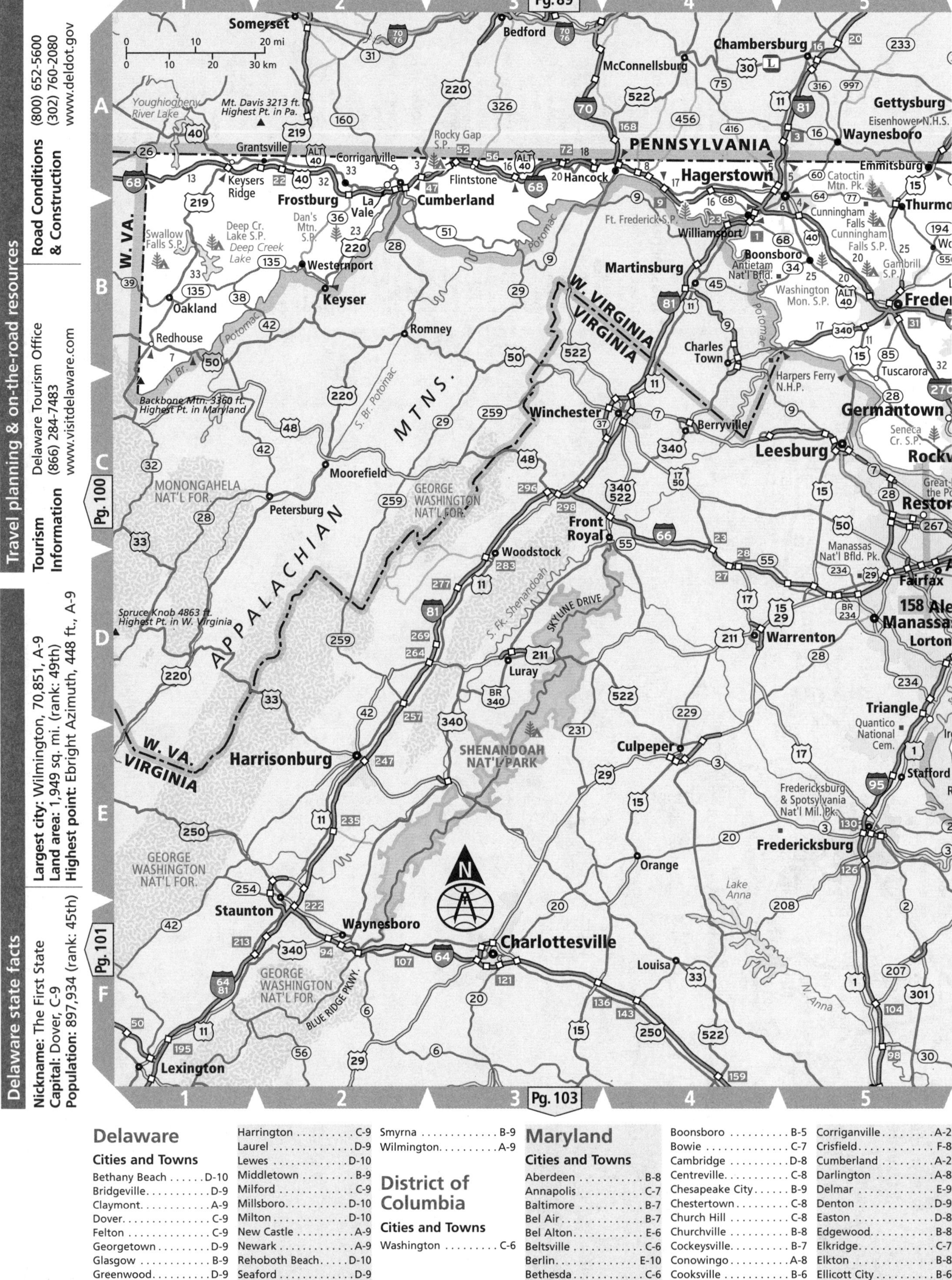

Delaware

Cities and Towns

Bethany Beach D-10
Bridgeville. D-9
Claymont. A-9
Dover. C-9
Felton C-9
Georgetown D-9
Glasgow B-9
Greenwood. D-9
Harrington C-9
Laurel D-9
Lewes D-10
Middletown B-9
Milford C-9
Millsboro. D-10
Milton D-10
New Castle A-9
Newark A-9
Rehoboth Beach. D-10
Seaford D-9
Smyrna B-9
Wilmington. A-9

District of Columbia

Cities and Towns

Washington C-6

Maryland

Cities and Towns

Aberdeen B-8
Annapolis C-7
Baltimore B-7
Bel Air. B-7
Bel Alton. E-6
Beltsville C-6
Berlin. E-10
Bethesda C-6
Boonsboro B-5
Bowie C-7
Cambridge D-8
Centreville. C-8
Chesapeake City. B-9
Chestertown C-8
Church Hill C-8
Churchville B-8
Cockeysville. B-7
Conowingo. A-8
Cooksville B-6
Corriganville A-2
Crisfield. F-8
Cumberland A-2
Darlington A-8
Delmar E-9
Denton D-9
Easton. D-8
Edgewood. B-8
Elkridge. C-7
Elkton B-8
Ellicott City B-6

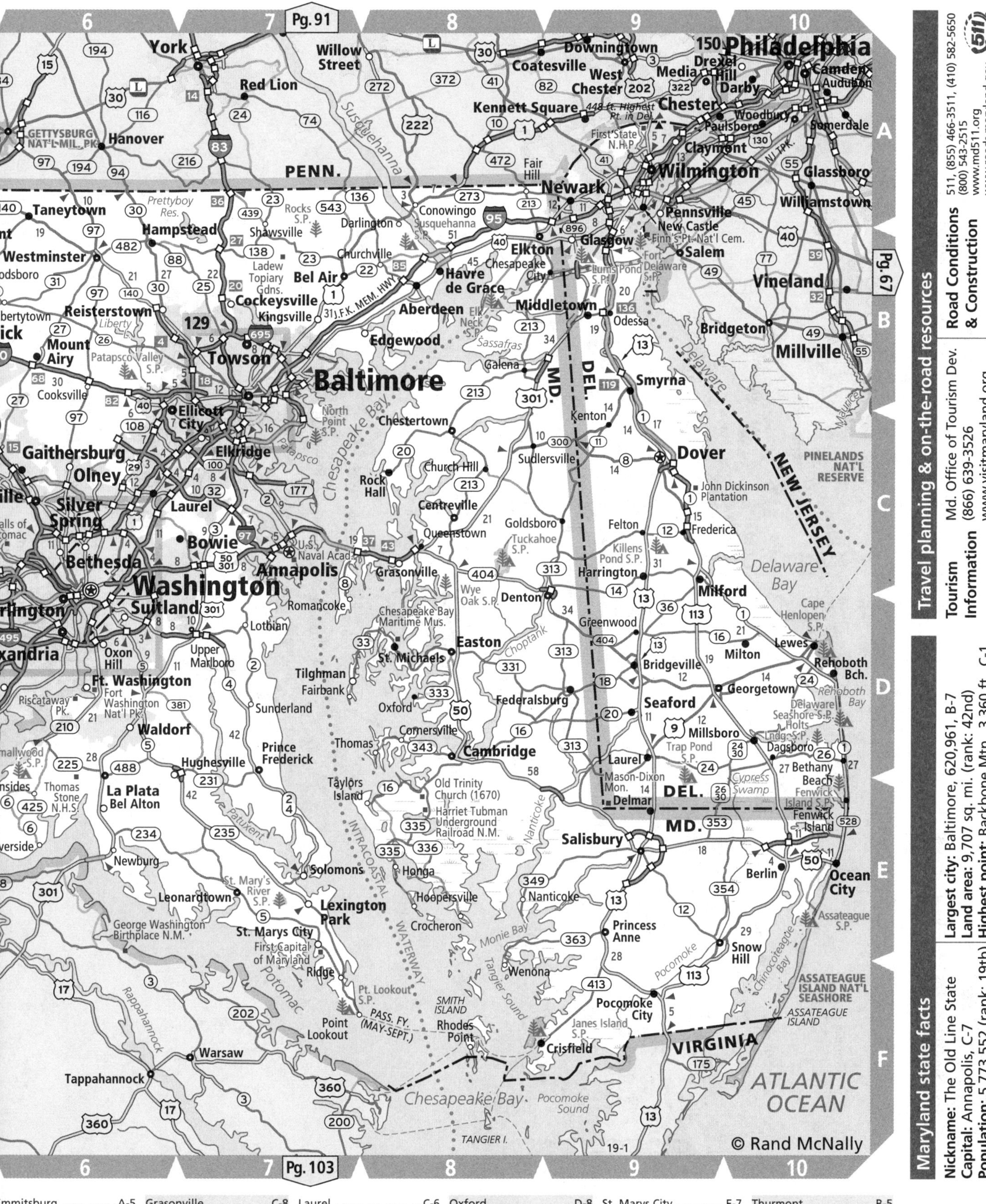

Travel planning & on-the-road resources

Tourism Information: Md. Office of Tourism Dev. (866) 639-3526 www.visitmaryland.org

Road Conditions & Construction: 511, (855) 466-3511, (410) 582-5650 (800) 543-2515 www.md511.org www.roads.maryland.gov

Maryland state facts

Nickname: The Old Line State
Capital: Annapolis, C-7
Population: 5,773,552 (rank: 19th)
Largest city: Baltimore, 620,961, B-7
Land area: 9,707 sq. mi. (rank: 42nd)
Highest point: Backbone Mtn., 3,360 ft., C-1

Emmitsburg . . . A-5
Federalsburg . . . D-9
Flintstone . . . A-3
Fort Washington . . . D-6
Frederick . . . B-5
Frostburg . . . A-2
Gaithersburg . . . C-6
Galena . . . B-8
Germantown . . . C-5
Goldsboro . . . C-9
Grantsville . . . A-2
Grasonville . . . C-8
Hagerstown . . . A-5
Hampstead . . . B-6
Hancock . . . A-4
Havre de Grace . . . B-8
Hoopersville . . . E-8
Hughesville . . . D-6
Ironsides . . . E-6
Kingsville . . . B-7
La Plata . . . D-6
La Vale . . . A-2
Laurel . . . C-6
Leonardtown . . . E-7
Lexington Park . . . E-7
Libertytown . . . B-6
Lothian . . . D-7
Mount Airy . . . B-6
Nanticoke . . . E-8
Newburg . . . E-6
Oakland . . . B-1
Ocean City . . . E-10
Olney . . . C-6
Oxford . . . D-8
Pocomoke City . . . F-9
Prince Frederick . . . D-7
Princess Anne . . . E-9
Queenstown . . . C-8
Reisterstown . . . B-6
Rhodes Point . . . F-8
Ridge . . . F-7
Rock Hall . . . C-8
Rockville . . . C-6
Romancoke . . . D-7
St. Marys City . . . E-7
St. Michaels . . . D-8
Salisbury . . . E-9
Silver Spring . . . C-6
Snow Hill . . . E-9
Solomons . . . E-7
Sudlersville . . . C-8
Suitland . . . D-6
Sunderland . . . D-7
Taneytown . . . A-6
Taylors Island . . . E-8
Thurmont . . . B-5
Tilghman . . . D-7
Towson . . . B-7
Tuscarora . . . C-5
Upper Marlboro . . . D-7
Waldorf . . . D-6
Wenona . . . F-8
Westernport . . . B-2
Westminster . . . B-6
Williamsport . . . B-4
Woodsboro . . . B-5

Florida state facts

Nickname: The Sunshine State
Capital: Tallahassee, B-1

Population: 18,801,310 (rank: 4th)
Largest city: Jacksonville, 821,784, B-4

Land area: 53,625 sq. mi. (rank: 26th)
Highest point: Britton Hill, 345 ft., I-2

Pg. 33

For continuation see inset below

Florida

Cities and Towns

City	Grid
Altamonte Springs	D-4
Apalachicola	I-3
Arcadia	F-4
Atlantic Beach	B-4
Bartow	E-4
Belle Glade	G-5
Blountstown	H-3
Boca Raton	G-6
Bonifay	H-3
Bradenton	F-3
Brandon	E-3
Brooksville	D-3
Bunnell	C-4
Bushnell	D-4
Cape Canaveral	E-5
Cape Coral	G-4
Chipley	H-3
Clearwater	E-3
Clermont	D-4
Cocoa Beach	E-5
Coral Gables	H-6
Crawfordville	B-1
Crestview	H-2
Cross City	C-2
Dade City	E-3
Dania Beach	H-6
Daytona Beach	D-5
De Funiak Springs	H-2
DeBary	D-4
Deerfield Beach	G-6
DeLand	D-4
Delray Beach	G-6
Dunedin	E-3
Edgewater	D-5
Englewood	F-3
Eustis	D-4
Fernandina Beach	B-4
Fort Lauderdale	H-6
Fort Myers	G-4
Fort Pierce	F-6
Fort Walton Beach	H-2
Gainesville	C-3
Green Cove Springs	C-4
Haines City	E-4
Hallandale Beach	H-6
Hialeah	H-6
Holly Hill	C-5
Hollywood	H-6
Homestead	H-6
Homosassa	D-3
Homosassa Springs	D-3
Hudson	E-3
Immokalee	G-4
Inverness	D-3
Jacksonville	B-4
Jacksonville Beach	B-4
Jasper	B-3
Jensen Beach	F-6
Jupiter	F-6
Kendall	H-6
Key Largo	I-6
Key West	J-4
Kissimmee	E-4
La Belle	G-4
Lady Lake	D-4
Lake Buena Vista	E-4
Lake Butler	B-3
Lake City	B-3
Lake Wales	E-4
Lake Worth	G-6

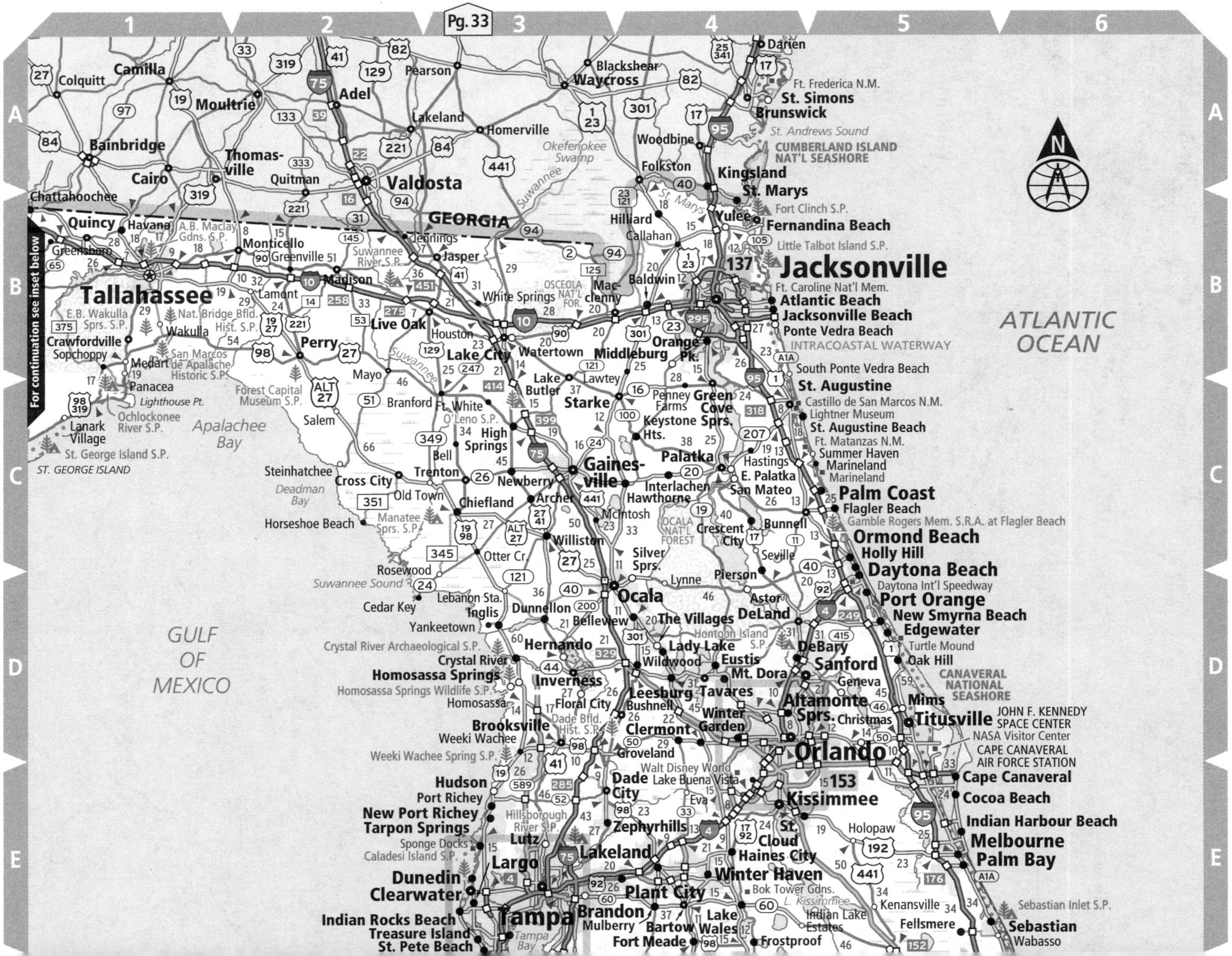

NOTE: Maps are not always in alphabetical order.
See Page 1 for map location in this atlas.

Lakeland E-4
Largo E-3
Leesburg D-4
Lehigh Acres G-4
Live Oak B-3
Lutz E-3
Macclenny B-3
Madeira Beach E-3
Madison B-2
Marathon I-5
Marco H-4
Marianna H-3
Melbourne E-5
Miami H-6
Miami Beach H-6
Middleburg B-4
Milton H-1
Monticello B-2
Moore Haven G-5
Naples H-4
New Port Richey E-3
New Smyrna Beach D-5
North Palm Beach G-6
Ocala D-3
Okeechobee F-5
Orange Park B-4
Orlando D-4
Ormond Beach C-5
Palatka C-4
Palm Bay E-5
Palm Beach G-6
Palm Coast C-5
Palmetto F-3
Panama City I-3
Pensacola H-1
Perry B-2
Plant City E-4
Pompano Beach G-6
Port Charlotte F-4
Port Orange D-5
Port St. Joe I-3
Port St. Lucie F-6
Punta Gorda G-4
Quincy B-1
St. Augustine C-4
St. Cloud E-4
St. Pete Beach E-3
St. Petersburg E-3
Sanford D-4
Sarasota F-3
Sebastian E-5
Sebring F-4
Starke C-4
Stuart F-6
Sunrise G-6
Tallahassee B-1
Tampa E-3
Tarpon Springs E-3
Tavares D-4
Titusville D-5
Trenton C-3
Venice F-3
Vero Beach F-6
Warrington H-1
Wauchula F-4
West Palm Beach G-6
Weston H-6
Winter Garden D-4
Winter Haven E-4
Yeehaw Junction E-5
Zephyrhills E-3

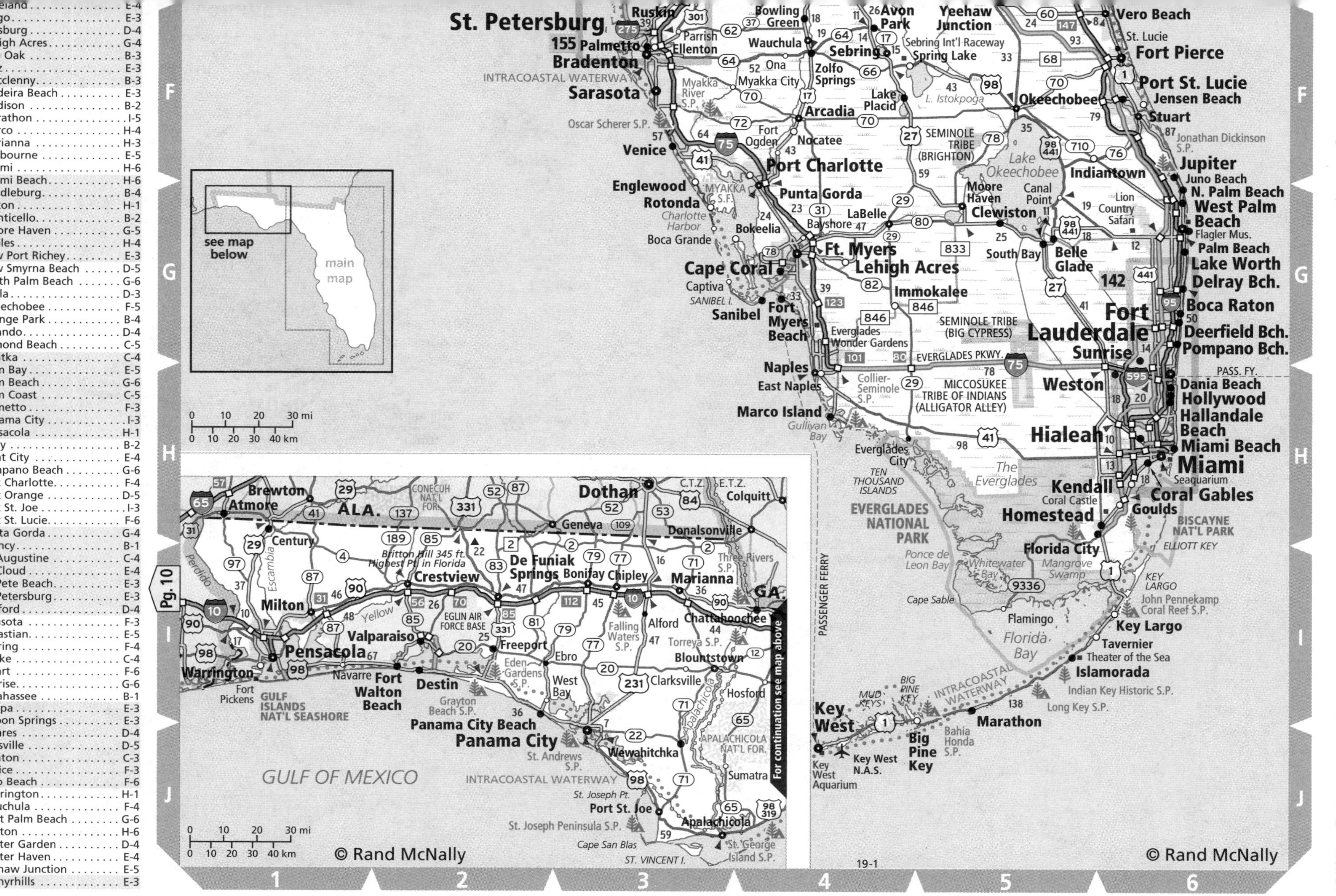

Travel planning & on-the-road resources

Tourism Information	Visit Florida (888) 735-2872, (850) 488-5607 www.visitflorida.com
Road Conditions & Construction	511 www.fl511.com www.fdot.gov

Georgia state facts

Nickname: The Peach State

Capital: Atlanta, C-2

Population: 9,687,653 (rank: 9th)

Largest city: Atlanta, 420,003, C-2

Land area: 57,513 sq. mi. (rank: 21st)

Highest point: Brasstown Bald, 4,784 ft., A-3

Pg. 47

Pg. 74

Pg. 75

Pg. 10

NOTE: Maps are not always in alphabetical order.
See Page 1 for map location in this atlas.

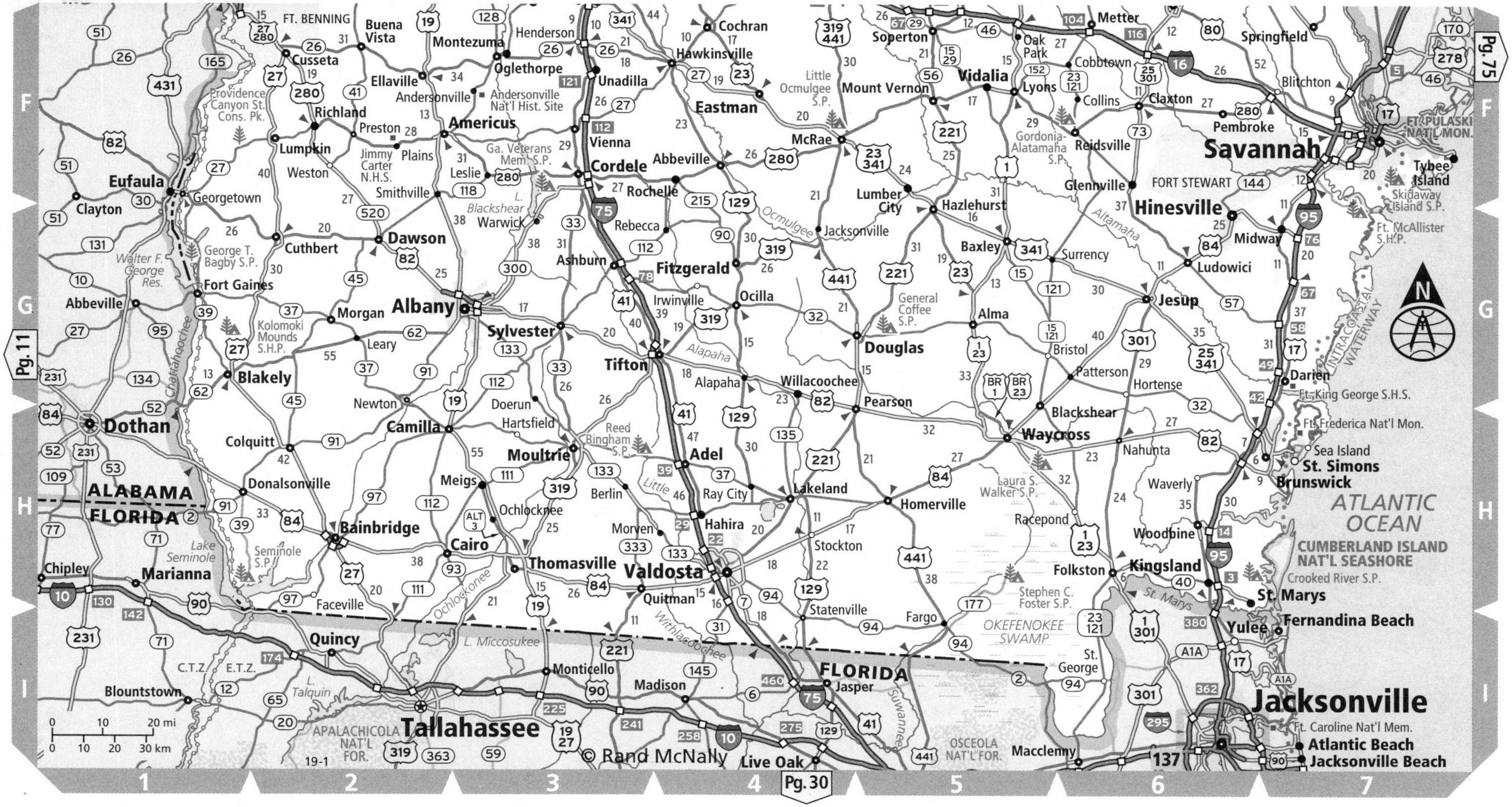

Pg. 75
Pg. 11
Pg. 30

© Rand McNally

Georgia

Cities and Towns

Adel H-4
Albany G-3
Alpharetta C-2
Americus F-2
Ashburn G-3
Athens C-4
Atlanta C-2
Augusta D-6
Austell C-2
Bainbridge H-2
Barnesville D-3
Blakely G-1
Bremen C-1
Brunswick H-7
Buford C-3
Cairo H-2
Calhoun B-1
Camilla H-2
Canton B-2
Carrollton D-1
Cartersville C-2
Cedartown C-1
Cochran F-4
College Park C-2
Columbus E-1
Commerce B-4
Conyers C-3
Cordele F-3
Covington D-3
Cumming B-3
Dallas C-2
Dalton A-1
Dawson G-2
Decatur C-2
Douglas G-4
Douglasville C-2
Dublin E-4
Duluth C-3
East Point C-2
Eastman F-4
Eatonton D-4
Elberton C-4
Fairburn D-2
Fayetteville D-2
Fitzgerald G-4
Fort Oglethorpe A-1
Fort Valley E-3
Gainesville B-3
Glennville F-6
Griffin D-2
Hawkinsville F-4
Hinesville G-6
Jesup G-6
Kingsland H-6
La Grange D-1
LaFayette B-1
Lawrenceville C-3
Lilburn C-3
Lithia Springs C-2
Macon E-3
Marietta C-2
McDonough D-3
Milledgeville D-4
Monroe C-3
Morrow D-2
Moultrie H-3
Newnan D-2
Norcross C-3
Perry E-3
Quitman H-3
Rome B-1
Roswell C-2
St. Marys H-6
Sandersville E-5
Savannah F-7
Smyrna C-2
St. Simons H-7
Statesboro E-6
Stockbridge D-2
Stone Mountain C-3
Summerville B-1
Swainsboro E-5
Sylvester G-3
Thomaston E-2
Thomasville H-3
Thomson D-5
Tifton G-4
Toccoa B-4
Valdosta H-4
Vidalia F-5
Warner Robins E-3
Washington C-5
Waycross H-5
Waynesboro D-6
Winder C-3

Travel planning & on-the-road resources

Tourism Information
Explore Georgia
(800) 847-4842
www.exploregeorgia.org

Road Conditions & Construction
511
(877) 694-2511, (404) 635-8000
www.511ga.org

Idaho state facts

Nickname: The Gem State
Capital: Boise, H-2

Population: 1,567,582 (rank: 39th)
Largest city: Boise, 205,671, H-2

Land area: 82,643 sq. mi. (rank: 11th)
Highest point: Borah Peak, 12,662 ft., G-4

Idaho

Cities and Towns

Aberdeen I-5
Albion I-4
American Falls I-5
Arco H-4
Ashton G-6
Athol B-1
Bancroft I-6
Bellevue H-3
Blackfoot H-5
Bliss I-3
Bloomington I-6
Boise H-2
Bonners Ferry A-2
Bovill D-2
Buhl I-3
Burley I-4
Caldwell H-1
Cambridge G-1
Carey H-4
Cascade G-2
Castleford I-3
Cataldo C-2
Challis G-3
Chester G-6
Clark Fork B-2
Coeur d'Alene C-1
Cottonwood E-2
Council F-1
Craigmont D-1
Culdesac D-1
Dayton J-5
Deary D-1
Declo I-4
Downey I-5
Driggs H-6
Dubois G-5
Eden I-3
Elk City E-2
Emmett G-1
Fairfield H-3
Fernwood C-2
Filer I-3
Firth H-5
Franklin J-6
Fruitland G-1
Georgetown I-6
Glenns Ferry I-2
Gooding I-3
Grace I-6
Grand View I-2
Grangeville E-2
Hagerman I-3
Hailey H-3
Hammett I-2
Hansen I-3
Harrison C-1
Hollister I-3
Homedale H-1
Horseshoe Bend G-2
Idaho City G-2
Idaho Falls H-5
Inkom I-5
Jerome I-3
Kamiah D-2
Kellogg C-2
Kendrick D-1
Ketchum H-3
Kimberly I-3
Kooskia E-2
Kootenai B-2

Lava Hot Springs I-5
Letha G-1
Lewiston D-1
Mackay G-4
Malad City J-5
Marsing H-1
McCall F-2
McCammon I-5
Melba H-1
Meridian H-1
Montpelier I-6
Moreland H-5
Moscow D-1
Mountain Home H-2
Moyie Springs A-2
Mud Lake G-5
Mullan C-2
Murphy H-1
Nampa H-1
Naples A-2
New Meadows F-2
New Plymouth G-1
Newdale G-6
Nezperce D-2
Oakley I-4
Orofino D-2
Osburn C-2
Paris I-6
Paul I-4
Payette G-1
Pierce D-2
Pinehurst C-2
Pleasantview J-5
Plummer C-1
Pocatello I-5
Post Falls C-1
Potlatch D-1
Preston J-6
Priest River B-1
Rathdrum B-1
Rexburg G-6
Richfield H-3
Rigby H-5
Riggins E-2
Ririe H-6
Roberts H-5
Rockland I-5
Rupert I-4
St. Anthony G-6
St. Maries C-1
Salmon F-4
Sandpoint B-1
Shelley H-5
Shoshone I-3
Silverton C-2
Soda Springs I-6
Spirit Lake B-1
Star H-1
Sugar City G-6
Sun Valley H-3
Swan Valley H-6
Sweet G-2
Tetonia G-6
Troy D-1
Twin Falls I-3
Victor H-6
Wallace C-2
Weippe D-2
Weiser G-1
Wendell I-3
Weston J-5

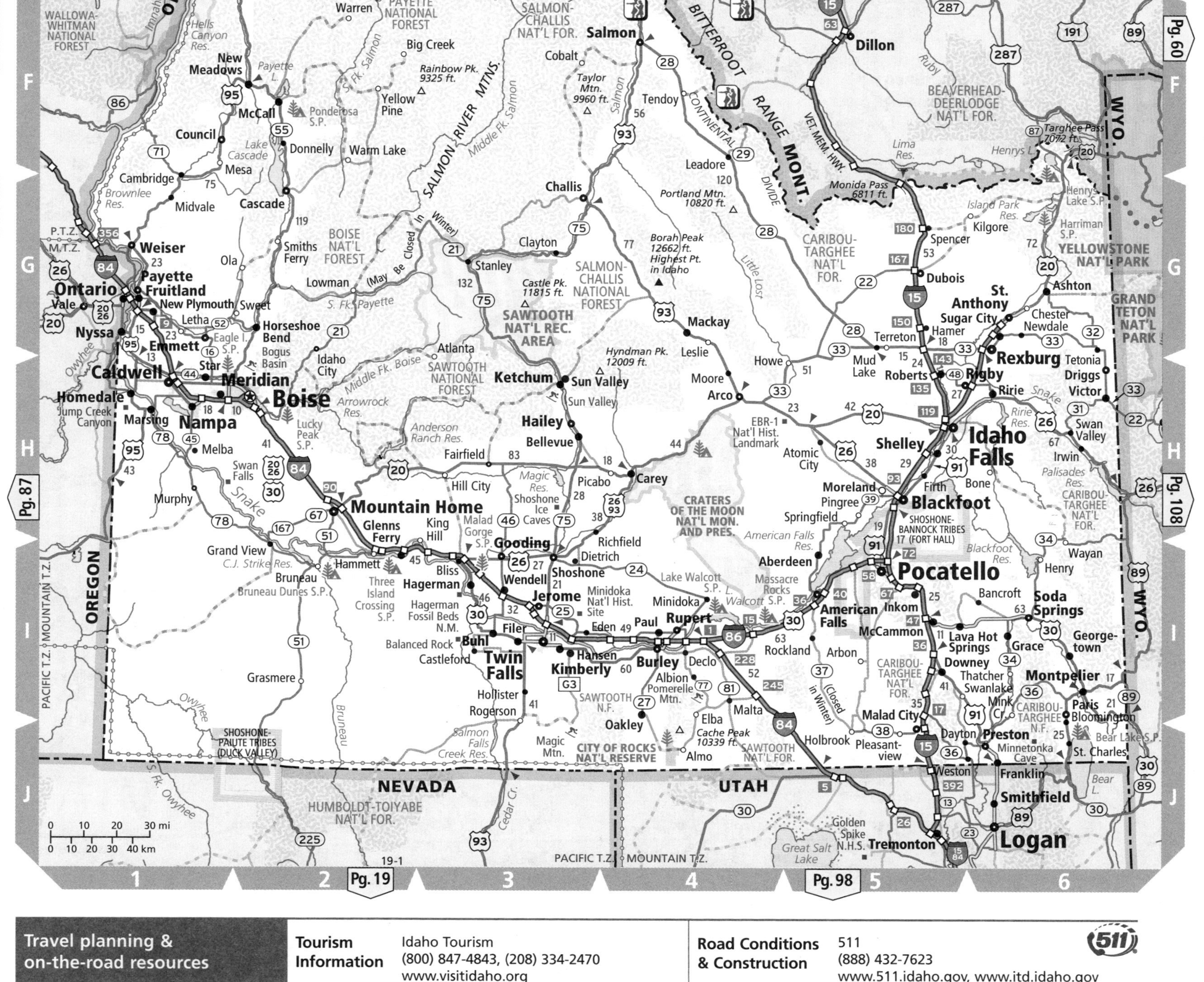

Travel planning & on-the-road resources

Tourism Information	Idaho Tourism (800) 847-4843, (208) 334-2470 www.visitidaho.org	**Road Conditions & Construction**	511 (888) 432-7623 www.511.idaho.gov, www.itd.idaho.gov

511

Illinois state facts

Nickname: Land of Lincoln
Capital: Springfield, E-3
Population: 12,830,632 (rank: 5th)
Largest city: Chicago, 2,695,598, B-6
Land area: 55,519 sq. mi. (rank: 24th)
Highest point: Charles Mound, 1,235 ft., A-2

Illinois

Cities and Towns

Albion H-5
Aledo C-2
Alton G-2
Arlington Heights B-5
Aurora B-5
Belleville H-3
Belvidere A-4
Benton I-4
Bloomington D-4
Cairo J-4
Cambridge C-3
Canton D-3
Carbondale I-4
Carlinville F-3
Carlyle G-4
Carmi H-5
Carrollton F-2
Carthage D-1
Centralia H-4
Champaign E-5
Charleston F-5
Chester I-3
Chicago B-6
Chicago Heights C-6
Clinton E-4
Collinsville G-3
Crete C-6
Crystal Lake A-5
Danville E-6
Decatur E-4
DeKalb B-4
Des Plaines B-5
Dixon B-3
East Moline C-2
East St. Louis G-3
Edwardsville G-3
Effingham G-5
Elgin B-5
Eureka D-4
Evanston B-6
Fairfield H-5
Forsyth E-4
Freeport A-3
Galena A-2
Galesburg C-2
Granite City G-3
Greenville G-3
Harrisburg I-5
Havana E-3
Herrin I-4
Highland Park A-6
Hillsboro G-3
Jacksonville F-2
Jerseyville G-2
Joliet B-5
Jonesboro I-4
Kankakee C-5
Kewanee C-3
La Salle C-4
Lacon C-3
Lake Forest A-5
Lawrenceville G-6
Lewistown D-3
Libertyville A-5
Lincoln E-4
Lisle B-5
Louisville G-5
Macomb D-2
Manteno C-6
Marion I-4

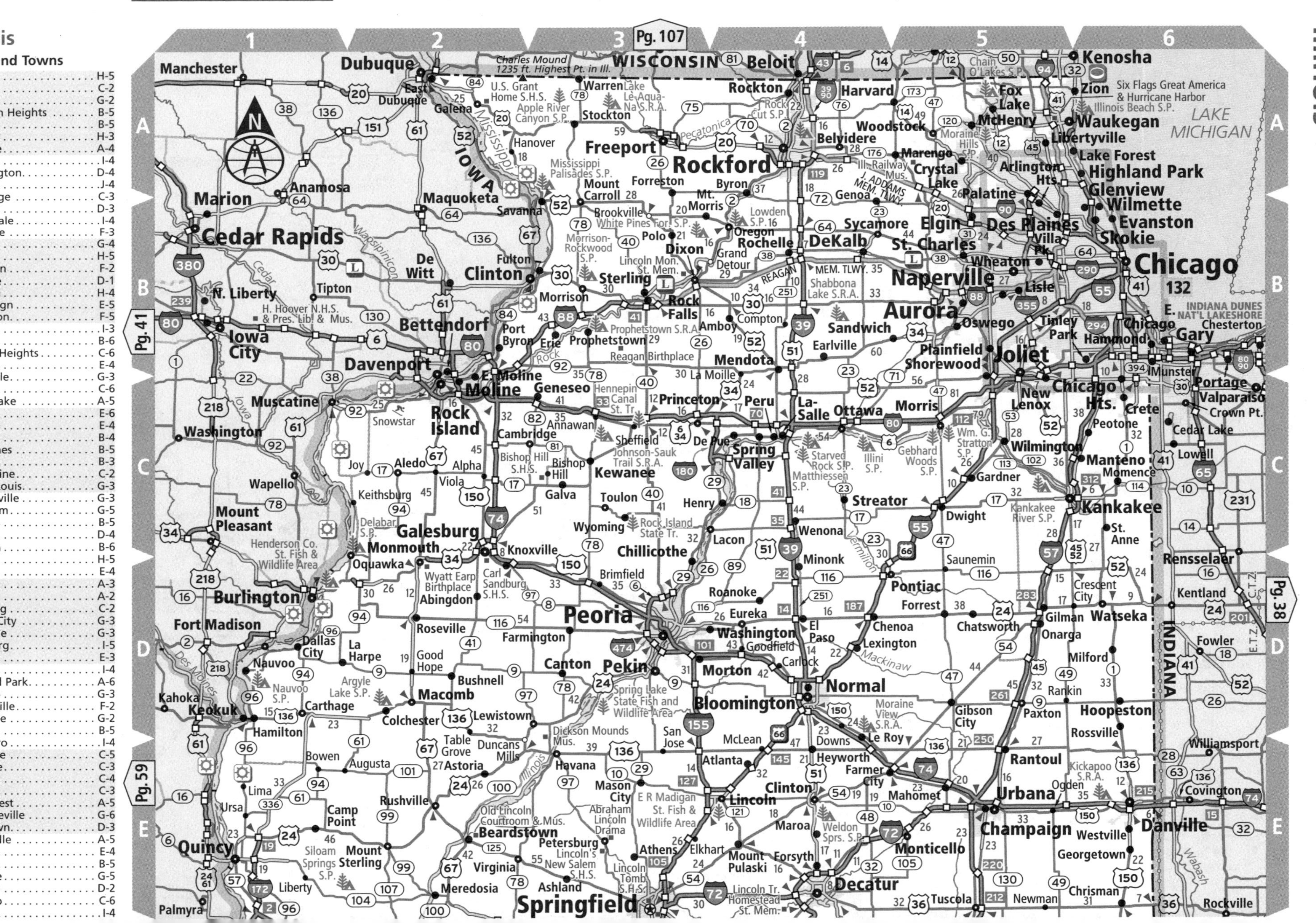

Marshall F-6
Mattoon F-5
McHenry A-5
McLeansboro H-5
Metropolis J-4
Moline C-2
Monmouth D-2
Monticello E-5
Morris C-5
Morrison B-3
Morton D-3
Mount Carmel H-6
Mount Carroll B-3
Mount Sterling E-2
Mount Vernon H-4
Murphysboro I-4
Naperville B-5
Nashville H-4
New Lenox C-5
Newton G-5
Normal D-4
O'Fallon G-3
Olney G-5
Oquawka C-2
Oregon B-4
Oswego B-5
Ottawa C-4
Paris F-6
Paxton D-5
Pekin D-3
Peoria D-3
Peru C-4
Petersburg E-3
Pinckneyville H-4
Pittsfield F-2
Plainfield B-5
Pontiac D-4
Princeton C-3
Quincy E-1
Rantoul E-5
Robinson G-6
Rock Falls B-3
Rock Island C-2
Rockford A-4
Rushville E-2
St. Charles B-5
Salem G-4
Shawneetown I-5
Shelbyville F-4
Shorewood C-5
Skokie B-6
Springfield E-3
Sterling B-3
Streator C-4
Sycamore B-4
Taylorville F-4
Toulon C-3
Tuscola E-5
Urbana E-5
Vandalia G-4
Virginia E-2
Washington D-3
Waterloo H-2
Watseka D-6
Waukegan A-5
Wheaton B-5
Wilmette B-6
Winchester F-2
Winnetka B-6
Woodstock A-5
Zion A-6

Travel planning & on-the-road resources

Tourism Information
Illinois Office of Tourism
(800) 226-6632
www.enjoyillinois.com

Road Conditions & Construction
(800) 452-4368
www.gettingaroundillinois.com
www.dot.il.gov

Indiana state facts

Nickname: The Hoosier State
Capital: Indianapolis, F-4

Population: 6,483,802 (rank: 15th)
Largest city: Indianapolis, 820,445, F-4

Land area: 35,826 sq. mi. (rank: 38th)
Highest point: Hoosier Hill, 1,257 ft., E-6

Indiana

Cities and Towns

Albion . . . B-5
Alexandria . . . D-5
Anderson . . . E-5
Angola . . . A-6
Attica . . . D-2
Auburn . . . B-6
Batesville . . . G-6
Bedford . . . H-3
Berne . . . D-6
Bicknell . . . H-2
Bloomfield . . . G-3
Bloomington . . . G-3
Bluffton . . . C-6
Boonville . . . I-2
Brazil . . . F-2
Bremen . . . B-4
Brookville . . . F-6
Brownsburg . . . E-4
Brownstown . . . H-4
Carmel . . . E-4
Cedar Lake . . . B-2
Charlestown . . . I-5
Chesterton . . . A-2
Clarksville . . . I-5
Clinton . . . F-2
Columbia City . . . B-5
Columbus . . . G-4
Connersville . . . F-6
Corydon . . . I-4
Covington . . . E-2
Crawfordsville . . . E-3
Crown Point . . . B-2
Danville . . . F-3
Decatur . . . C-6
Delphi . . . D-3
DeMotte . . . B-2
East Chicago . . . A-2
Edinburgh . . . G-4
Elkhart . . . A-4
Elwood . . . D-4
English . . . I-3
Evansville . . . J-1
Fort Wayne . . . C-6
Fortville . . . E-4
Fowler . . . D-2
Frankfort . . . D-3
Franklin . . . F-4
French Lick . . . H-3
Garrett . . . B-6
Gary . . . B-2
Gas City . . . D-5
Goshen . . . B-4
Greencastle . . . F-3
Greenfield . . . F-5
Greensburg . . . G-5
Greenwood . . . F-4
Hammond . . . A-2
Hartford City . . . D-5
Hebron . . . B-2
Huntingburg . . . I-3
Huntington . . . C-5
Indianapolis . . . F-4
Jasper . . . I-3
Jeffersonville . . . I-5
Kendallville . . . B-5
Kentland . . . C-2
Knox . . . B-3
Kokomo . . . D-4
Lafayette . . . D-3
Lagrange . . . A-5

Pg. 53
Pg. 80
Pg. 36

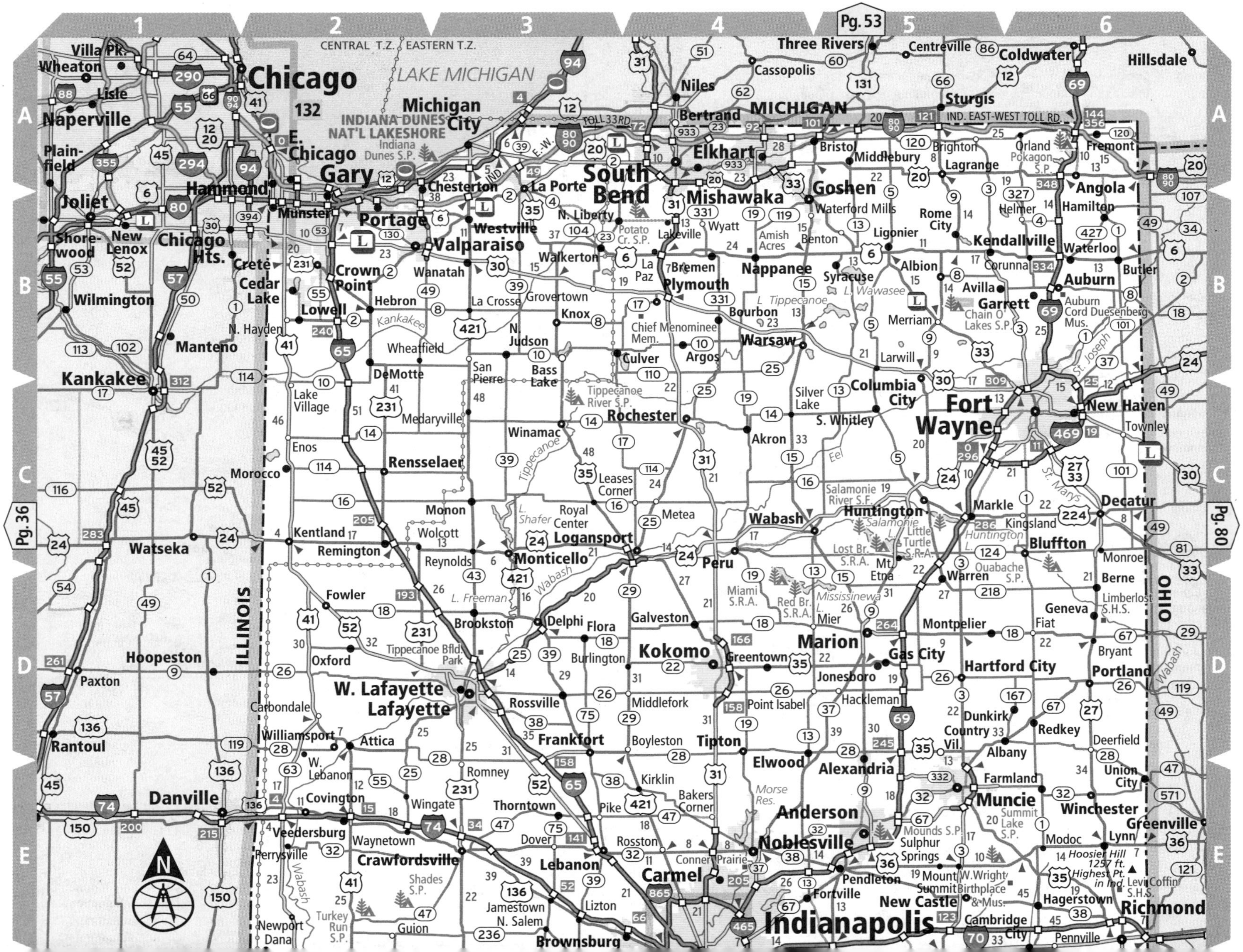

NOTE: Maps are not always in alphabetical order.
See Page 1 for map location in this atlas.

La Porte A-3
Lawrenceburg G-6
Lebanon E-3
Liberty F-6
Ligonier B-5
Linton G-2
Logansport C-4
Lowell B-2
Madison H-5
Marion D-5
Martinsville F-3
Michigan City A-3
Mishawaka A-4
Mitchell H-3
Monticello C-3
Mooresville F-4
Mount Vernon J-1
Muncie E-5
Nappanee B-4
Nashville G-4
New Albany I-5
New Castle E-5
New Haven C-6
Newport E-2
Noblesville E-4
North Terre Haute F-2
North Vernon G-5
Paoli H-3
Pendleton E-5
Peru C-4
Petersburg H-2
Plainfield F-4
Plymouth B-4
Portage B-2
Portland D-6
Princeton I-1
Rensselaer C-2
Richmond E-6
Rising Sun G-6
Rochester C-4
Rockport J-2
Rockville F-2
Rushville F-5
Salem H-4
Schererville B-2
Scottsburg H-5
Sellersburg I-5
Seymour G-4
Shelbyville F-5
Shoals H-3
South Bend A-4
Spencer G-3
Sullivan G-2
Syracuse B-5
Tell City J-3
Terre Haute F-2
Tipton D-4
Union City E-6
Valparaiso B-2
Vernon G-5
Versailles G-6
Vevay H-6
Vincennes H-2
Wabash C-5
Warsaw B-4
Washington H-2
West Lafayette D-3
Westville B-3
Williamsport D-2
Winamac C-3
Winchester E-6

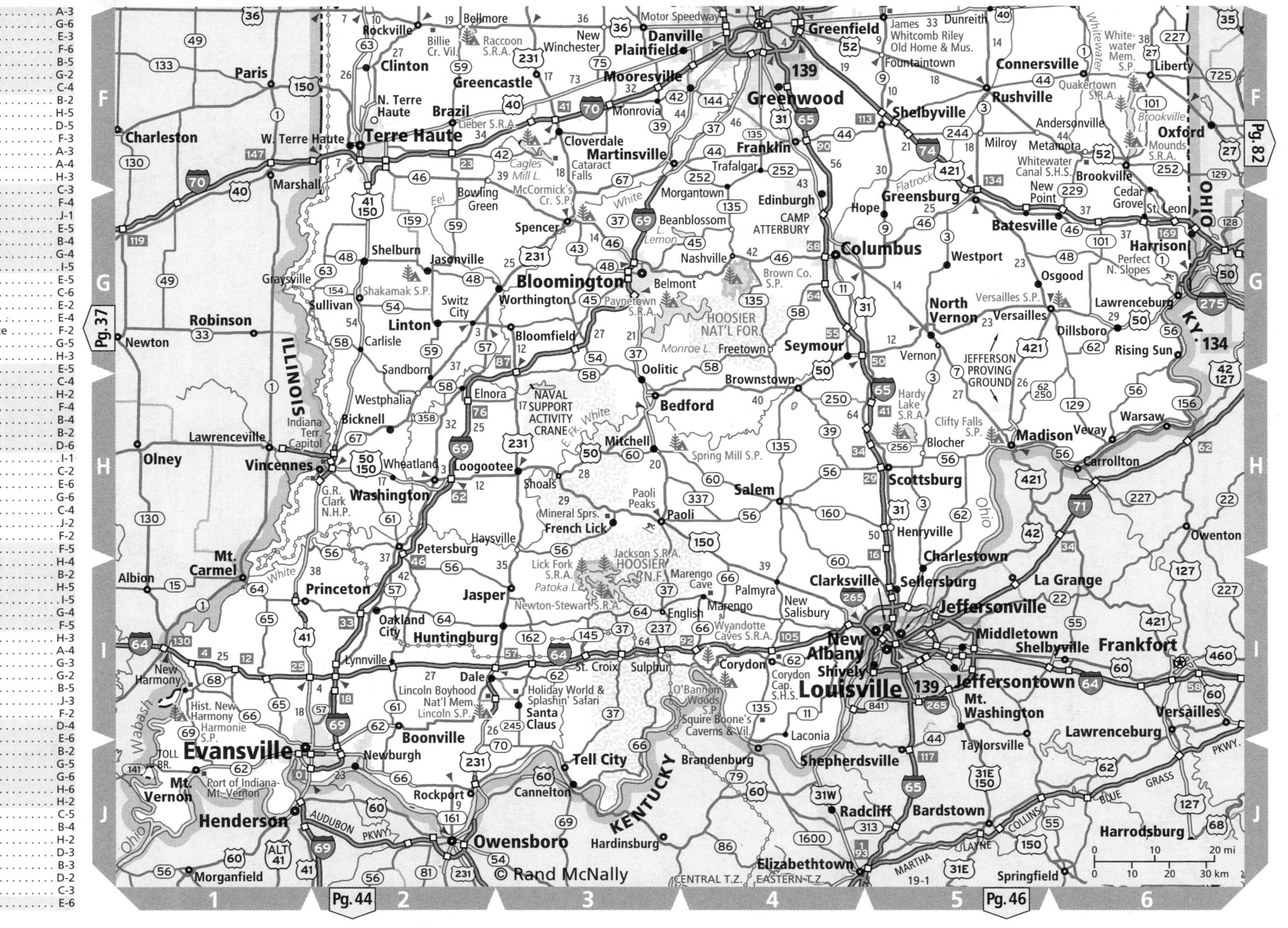

Travel planning & on-the-road resources

Tourism Information Indiana Office of Tourism Development
(800) 677-9800
www.visitindiana.com

Road Conditions & Construction (800) 261-7623, (866) 849-1368
www.in.gov/dot
www.in.gov/indot/2420.htm

Iowa state facts

Nickname: The Hawkeye State
Capital: Des Moines, D-5
Population: 3,046,355 (rank: 30th)
Largest city: Des Moines, 203,433, D-5
Land area: 55,857 sq. mi. (rank: 23rd)
Highest point: Hawkeye Point, 1,670 ft., A-2

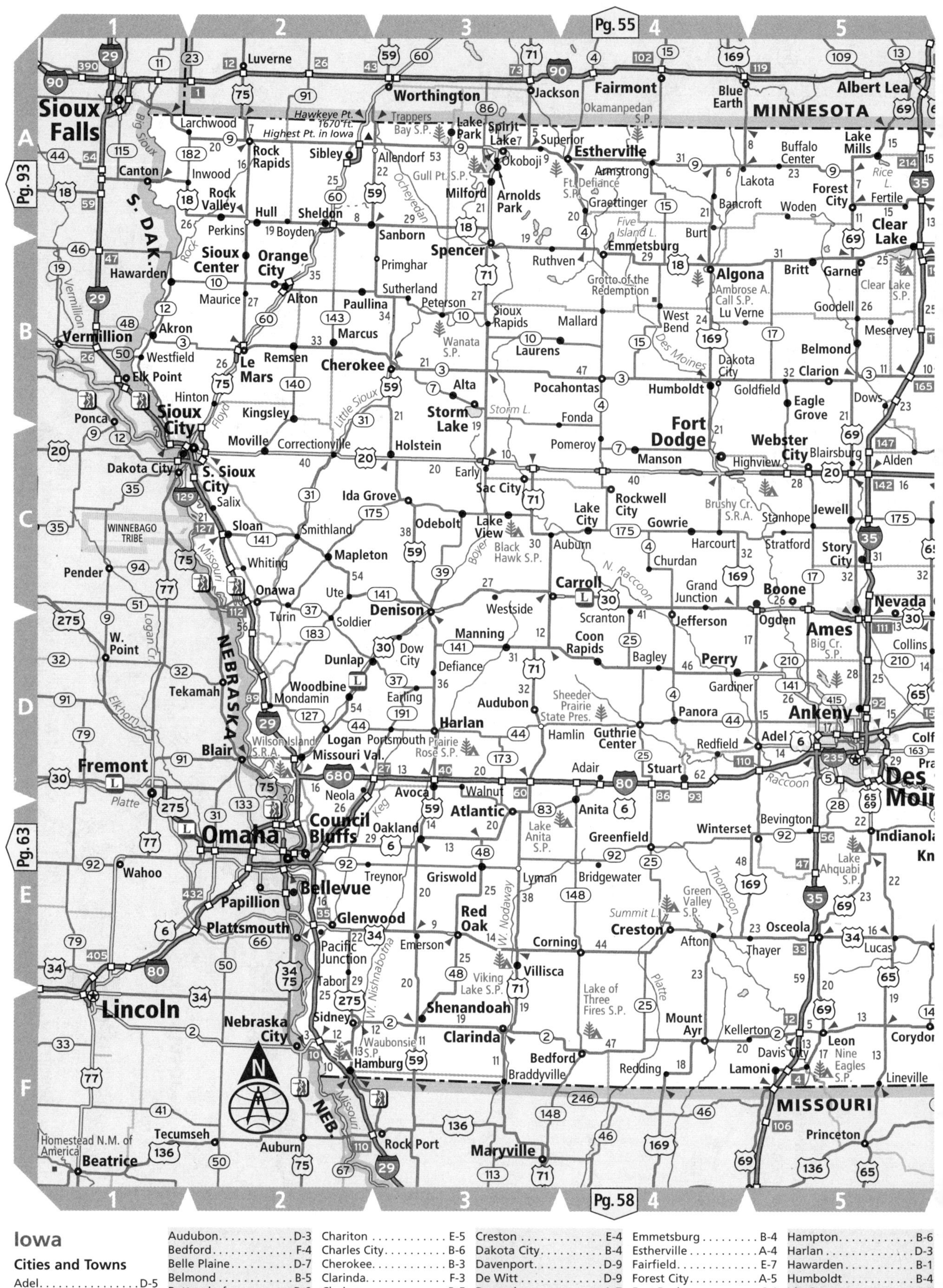

Iowa

Cities and Towns

Adel D-5
Albia E-6
Algona B-4
Allison B-6
Ames C-5
Anamosa C-8
Ankeny D-5
Atlantic E-3
Audubon D-3
Bedford F-4
Belle Plaine D-7
Belmond B-5
Bettendorf D-9
Bloomfield F-7
Boone C-5
Burlington F-8
Carroll C-3
Cedar Falls C-7
Cedar Rapids D-8
Centerville F-6
Chariton E-5
Charles City B-6
Cherokee B-3
Clarinda F-3
Clarion B-5
Clear Lake B-5
Clinton D-10
Coralville D-8
Corning E-4
Corydon F-5
Council Bluffs E-2
Cresco A-7
Creston E-4
Dakota City B-4
Davenport D-9
De Witt D-9
Decorah A-7
Denison C-3
Des Moines D-5
Dubuque C-9
Dyersville C-8
Eagle Grove B-5
Eldora C-6
Elkader B-8
Emmetsburg B-4
Estherville A-4
Fairfield E-7
Forest City A-5
Fort Dodge C-4
Fort Madison F-8
Garner B-5
Glenwood E-2
Greenfield E-4
Grinnell D-6
Grundy Center C-6
Guthrie Center D-4
Hampton B-6
Harlan D-3
Hawarden B-1
Humboldt B-4
Ida Grove C-3
Independence C-7
Indianola E-5
Iowa City D-8
Iowa Falls C-6
Jefferson D-4
Keokuk F-8
Keosauqua F-7

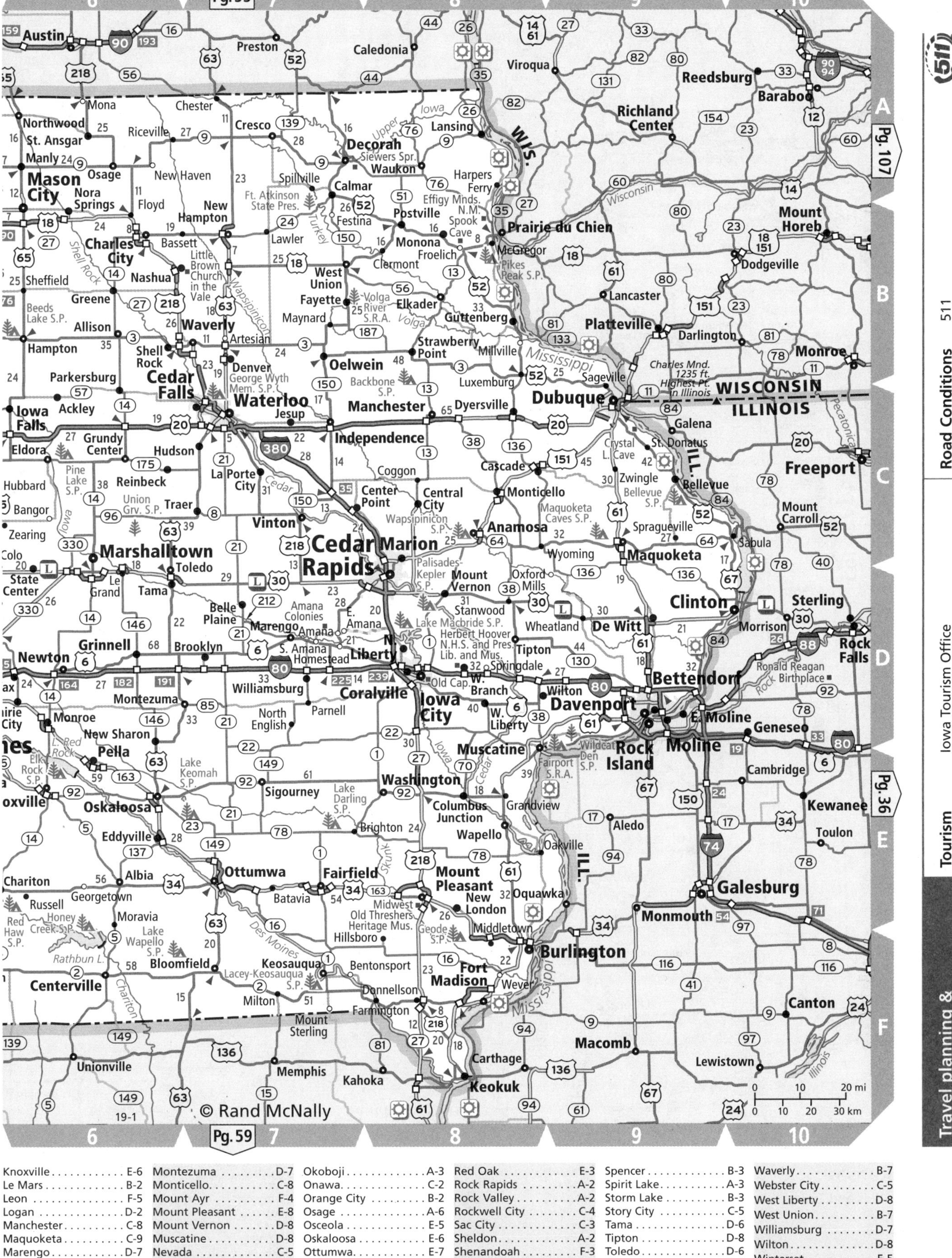

Road Conditions & Construction
511
(800) 288-1047
www.511ia.org, www.iowadot.gov

Tourism Information
Iowa Tourism Office
(888) 472-6035, (800) 345-4692
www.traveliowa.com

Travel planning & on-the-road resources

Knoxville . . . E-6
Le Mars . . . B-2
Leon . . . F-5
Logan . . . D-2
Manchester . . . C-8
Maquoketa . . . C-9
Marengo . . . D-7
Marion . . . C-8
Marshalltown . . . C-6
Mason City . . . B-6
Milford . . . A-3
Missouri Valley . . . D-2
Montezuma . . . D-7
Monticello . . . C-8
Mount Ayr . . . F-4
Mount Pleasant . . . E-8
Mount Vernon . . . D-8
Muscatine . . . D-8
Nevada . . . C-5
New Hampton . . . B-7
Newton . . . D-6
North Liberty . . . D-8
Northwood . . . A-6
Oelwein . . . B-7
Okoboji . . . A-3
Onawa . . . C-2
Orange City . . . B-2
Osage . . . A-6
Osceola . . . E-5
Oskaloosa . . . E-6
Ottumwa . . . E-7
Pacific Junction . . . E-2
Pella . . . E-6
Perry . . . D-4
Pocahontas . . . B-4
Primghar . . . B-3
Red Oak . . . E-3
Rock Rapids . . . A-2
Rock Valley . . . A-2
Rockwell City . . . C-4
Sac City . . . C-3
Sheldon . . . A-2
Shenandoah . . . F-3
Sibley . . . A-2
Sidney . . . F-2
Sigourney . . . E-7
Sioux Center . . . B-2
Sioux City . . . C-2
Spencer . . . B-3
Spirit Lake . . . A-3
Storm Lake . . . B-3
Story City . . . C-5
Tama . . . D-6
Tipton . . . D-8
Toledo . . . D-6
Vinton . . . C-7
Wapello . . . E-8
Washington . . . E-8
Waterloo . . . C-7
Waukon . . . A-8
Waverly . . . B-7
Webster City . . . C-5
West Liberty . . . D-8
West Union . . . B-7
Williamsburg . . . D-7
Wilton . . . D-8
Winterset . . . E-5

Kansas state facts

Nickname: The Sunflower State
Capital: Topeka, C-9

Population: 2,853,118 (rank: 33rd)
Largest city: Wichita, 382,368, E-7

Land area: 81,759 sq. mi. (rank: 13th)
Highest point: Mount Sunflower, 4,039 ft., C-1

Pg. 62

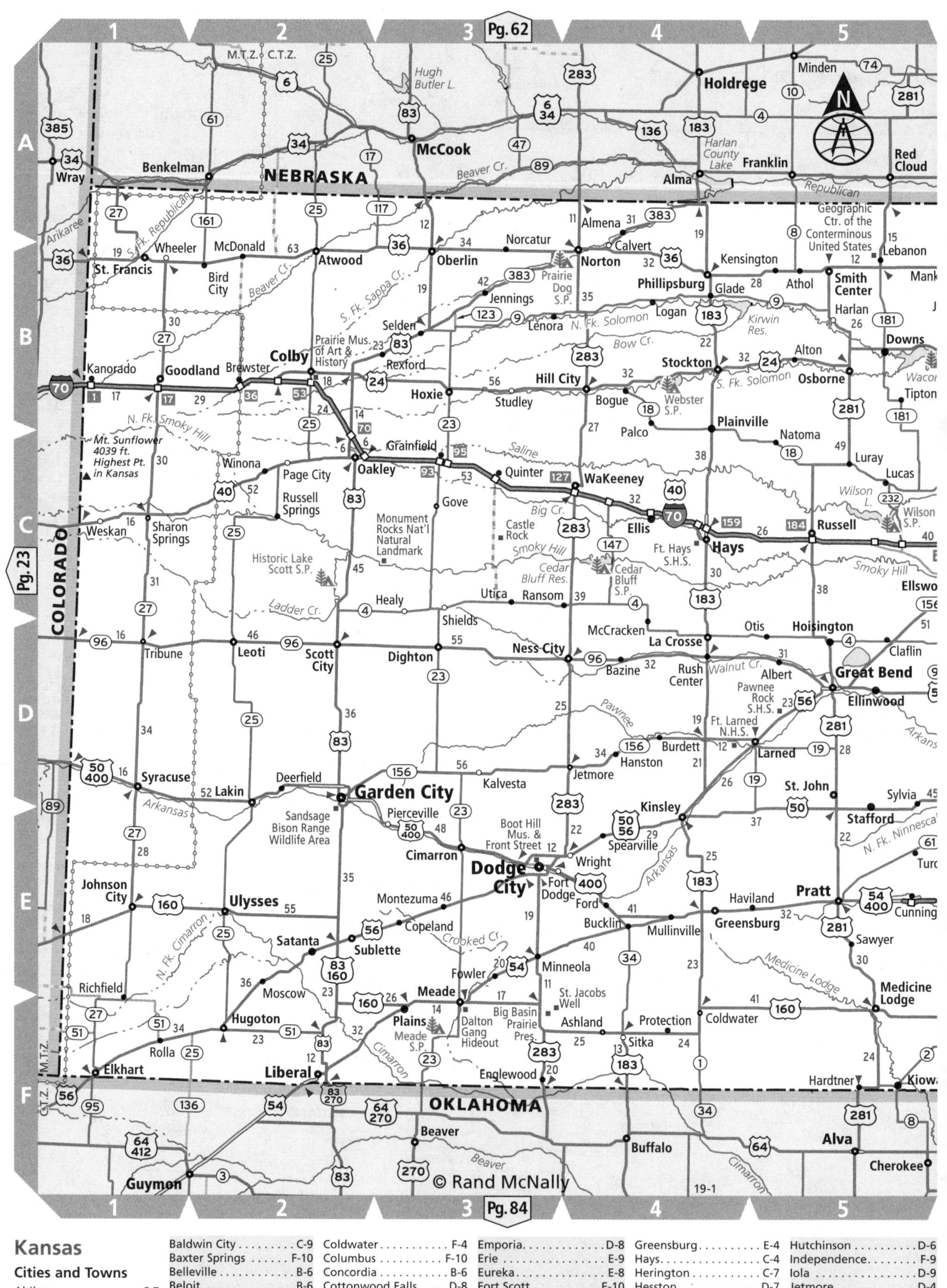

Pg. 23

Pg. 84

Kansas

Cities and Towns

Abilene C-7
Alma C-8
Anthony F-6
Arkansas City F-7
Ashland F-4
Atchison B-9
Atwood B-2
Augusta E-7
Baldwin City C-9
Baxter Springs F-10
Belleville B-6
Beloit B-6
Burlington D-9
Caney F-8
Chanute E-9
Cherryvale F-9
Cimarron E-3
Clay Center B-7
Coffeyville F-9
Colby B-2
Coldwater F-4
Columbus F-10
Concordia B-6
Cottonwood Falls D-8
Council Grove C-8
Derby E-7
Dighton D-3
Dodge City E-3
El Dorado E-7
Elkhart F-1
Ellinwood D-5
Ellsworth C-6
Emporia D-8
Erie E-9
Eureka E-8
Fort Scott E-10
Fredonia E-9
Frontenac E-10
Garden City D-2
Garnett D-9
Girard E-10
Goodland B-1
Gove C-3
Great Bend D-5
Greensburg E-4
Hays C-4
Herington C-7
Hesston D-7
Hiawatha A-9
Hill City B-4
Hillsboro D-7
Hoisington D-5
Holton B-9
Howard E-8
Hoxie B-3
Hugoton F-2
Hutchinson D-6
Independence F-9
Iola D-9
Jetmore D-4
Johnson City E-1
Junction City C-7
Kansas City C-10
Kingman E-6
Kinsley E-4
La Crosse D-4
Lakin D-2
Larned D-5

NOTE: Maps are not always in alphabetical order.
See Page 1 for map location in this atlas.

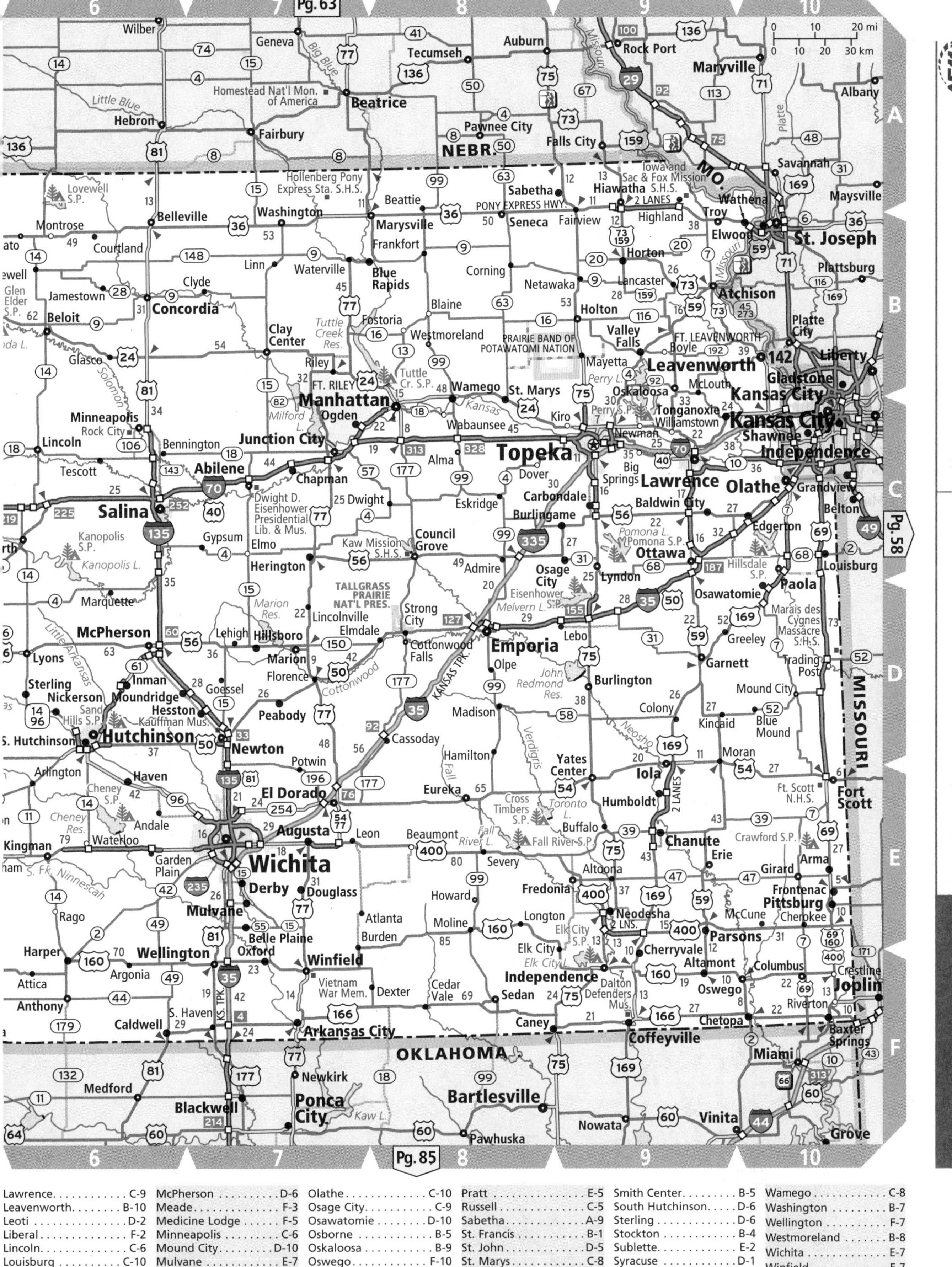

Road Conditions & Construction
511
(800) 585-7623, (785) 296-3585
www.kandrive.org, www.ksdot.org

Tourism Information
Kansas Tourism Office
(800) 252-6727, (785) 296-2009
www.travelks.com

Travel planning & on-the-road resources

Lawrence C-9	McPherson D-6	Olathe C-10	Pratt E-5	Smith Center B-5	Wamego C-8
Leavenworth B-10	Meade F-3	Osage City C-9	Russell C-5	South Hutchinson D-6	Washington B-7
Leoti D-2	Medicine Lodge F-5	Osawatomie D-10	Sabetha A-9	Sterling D-6	Wellington F-7
Liberal F-2	Minneapolis C-6	Osborne B-5	St. Francis B-1	Stockton B-4	Westmoreland B-8
Lincoln C-6	Mound City D-10	Oskaloosa B-9	St. John D-5	Sublette E-2	Wichita E-7
Louisburg C-10	Mulvane E-7	Oswego F-10	St. Marys C-8	Syracuse D-1	Winfield F-7
Lyndon C-9	Neodesha E-9	Ottawa C-9	Salina C-6	Tonganoxie C-9	Yates Center E-9
Lyons D-6	Ness City D-4	Paola C-10	Scott City D-2	Topeka C-9	
Manhattan C-8	Newton D-7	Parsons E-9	Sedan F-8	Tribune D-1	
Mankato B-6	Norton B-4	Phillipsburg B-4	Seneca B-8	Troy B-9	
Marion D-7	Oakley C-2	Pittsburg E-10	Sharon Springs C-1	Ulysses E-2	
Marysville B-8	Oberlin B-3	Plainville B-4	Shawnee C-10	WaKeeney C-4	

Kentucky state facts

Nickname: The Bluegrass State
Capital: Frankfort, C-9

Population: 4,339,367 (rank: 26th)
Largest city: Louisville, 597,337, C-8

Land area: 39,486 sq. mi. (rank: 37th)
Highest point: Black Mountain, 4,145 ft., E-12

Pg. 37 Pg. 39 more map Pg. 46 Pg. 59

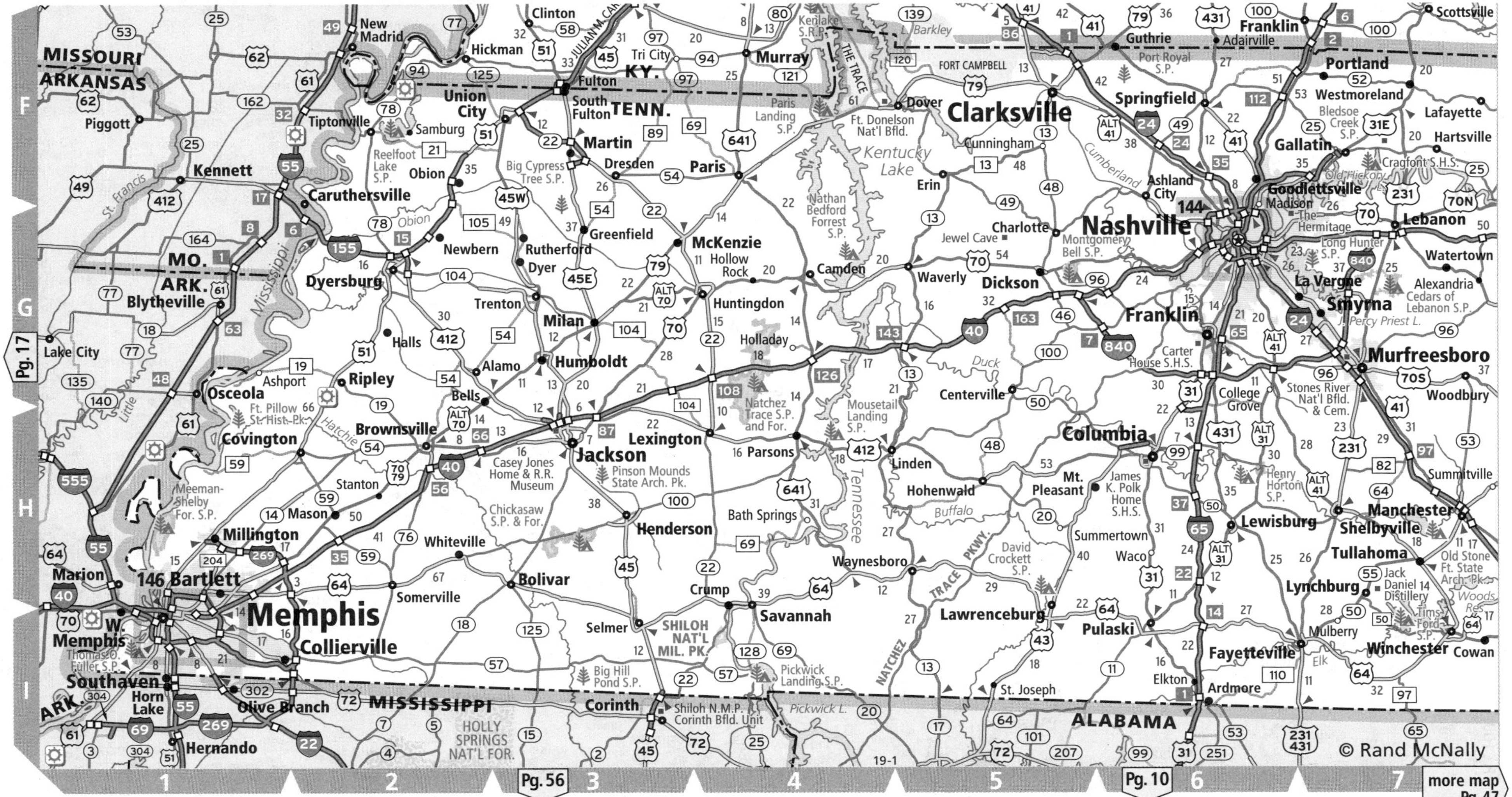

more map Pg. 47

© Rand McNally

Kentucky

Cities and Towns

City	Grid
Albany	F-9
Alexandria	A-10
Ashland	B-13
Barbourville	E-11
Bardstown	C-8
Beaver Dam	D-6
Benton	E-4
Berea	D-10
Bowling Green	E-7
Cadiz	E-5
Campbellsville	D-9
Carrollton	B-9
Central City	D-6
Columbia	E-9
Corbin	E-10
Cumberland	E-12
Cynthiana	B-10
Danville	D-9
Dawson Springs	E-5
Eddyville	E-4
Elizabethtown	D-8
Eminence	B-9
Falmouth	B-10
Flemingsburg	B-11
Florence	A-10
Fort Thomas	A-10
Frankfort	C-9
Franklin	F-7
Fulton	F-3
Georgetown	C-10
Glasgow	E-8
Greensburg	E-8
Greenville	E-6
Hardinsburg	C-7
Harlan	E-12
Harrodsburg	D-9
Hartford	D-6
Hazard	E-12
Henderson	C-5
Hickman	F-2
Hopkinsville	E-5
Horse Cave	E-8
Irvine	D-11
Jackson	D-12
Jeffersontown	C-8
Jenkins	E-13
La Grange	B-8
Lancaster	D-10
Lawrenceburg	C-9
Lebanon	D-9
Leitchfield	D-7
Lexington	C-10
London	E-11
Louisville	C-8
Madisonville	D-5
Marion	D-4
Mayfield	E-3
Middlesboro	F-11
Middletown	C-8
Monticello	E-9
Morehead	C-11
Morganfield	D-4
Morgantown	E-6
Mount Sterling	C-11
Mount Vernon	D-10
Mount Washington	C-8
Murray	F-4
Nicholasville	C-10
Owensboro	D-6
Paducah	E-3
Paintsville	C-12
Paris	C-10
Pikeville	D-13
Pineville	E-11
Prestonsburg	D-13
Princeton	E-4
Providence	D-5
Radcliff	C-8
Richmond	D-10
Russell Springs	E-9
Russellville	E-6
Scottsville	F-7
Shelbyville	C-9
Shepherdsville	C-8
Shively	C-8
Somerset	E-10
Springfield	D-9
Stanford	D-10
Stanton	C-11
Tompkinsville	F-8
Versailles	C-9
West Liberty	C-12
Williamsburg	F-10
Williamstown	B-10
Wilmore	C-10
Winchester	C-10

Travel planning & on-the-road resources

Tourism Information
Kentucky Department of Travel & Tourism
(800) 225-8747
www.kentuckytourism.com

Road Conditions & Construction
511
(866) 737-3767
www.drive.ky.gov, transportation.ky.gov

Tennessee state facts

Nickname: The Volunteer State
Capital: Nashville, G-6
Population: 6,346,105 (rank: 17th)
Largest city: Memphis, 646,889, I-1
Land area: 41,235 sq. mi. (rank: 34th)
Highest point: Clingmans Dome, 6,643 ft., H-11

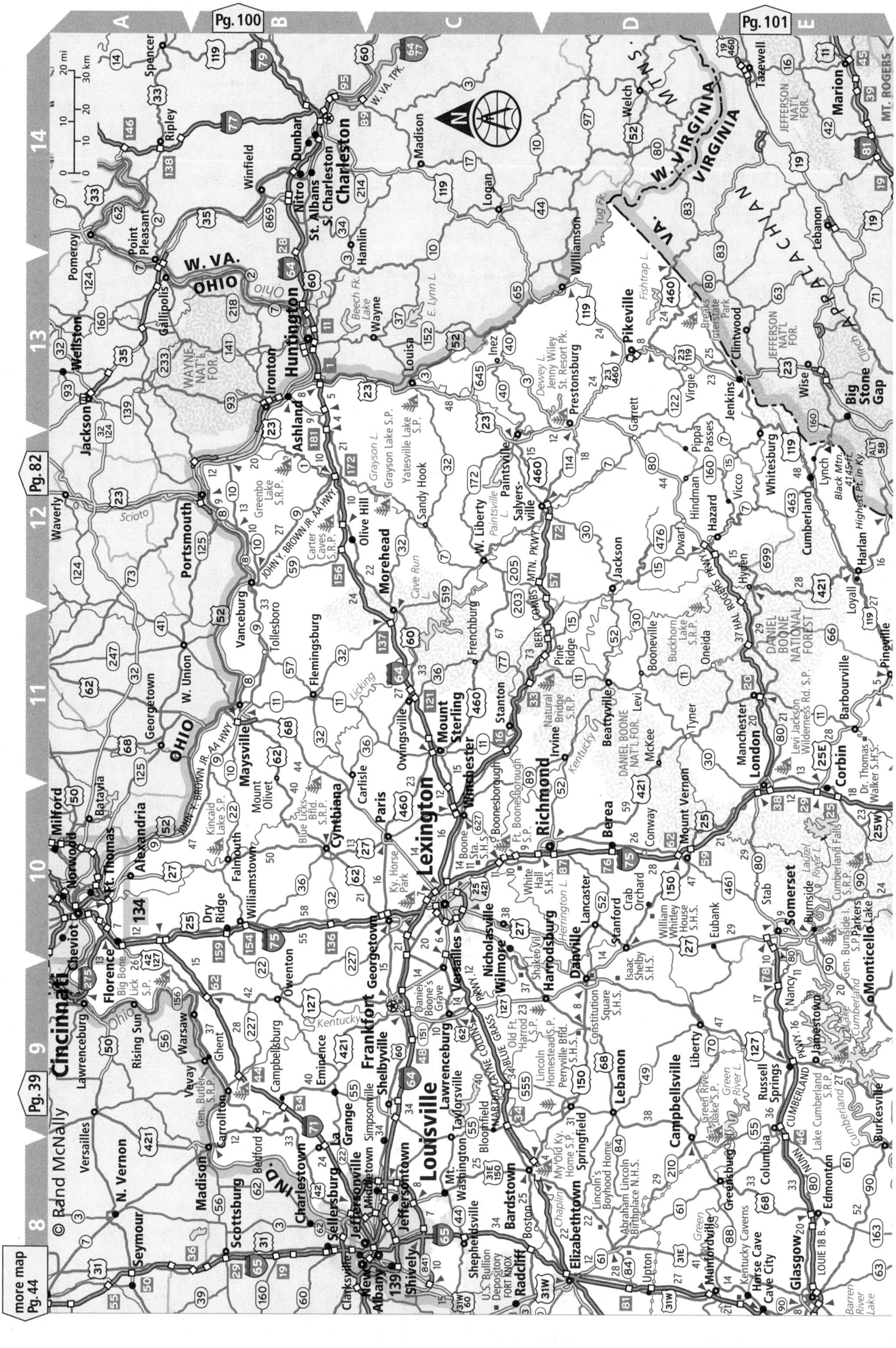

more map Pg. 44
Pg. 39
Pg. 82
Pg. 100
Pg. 101

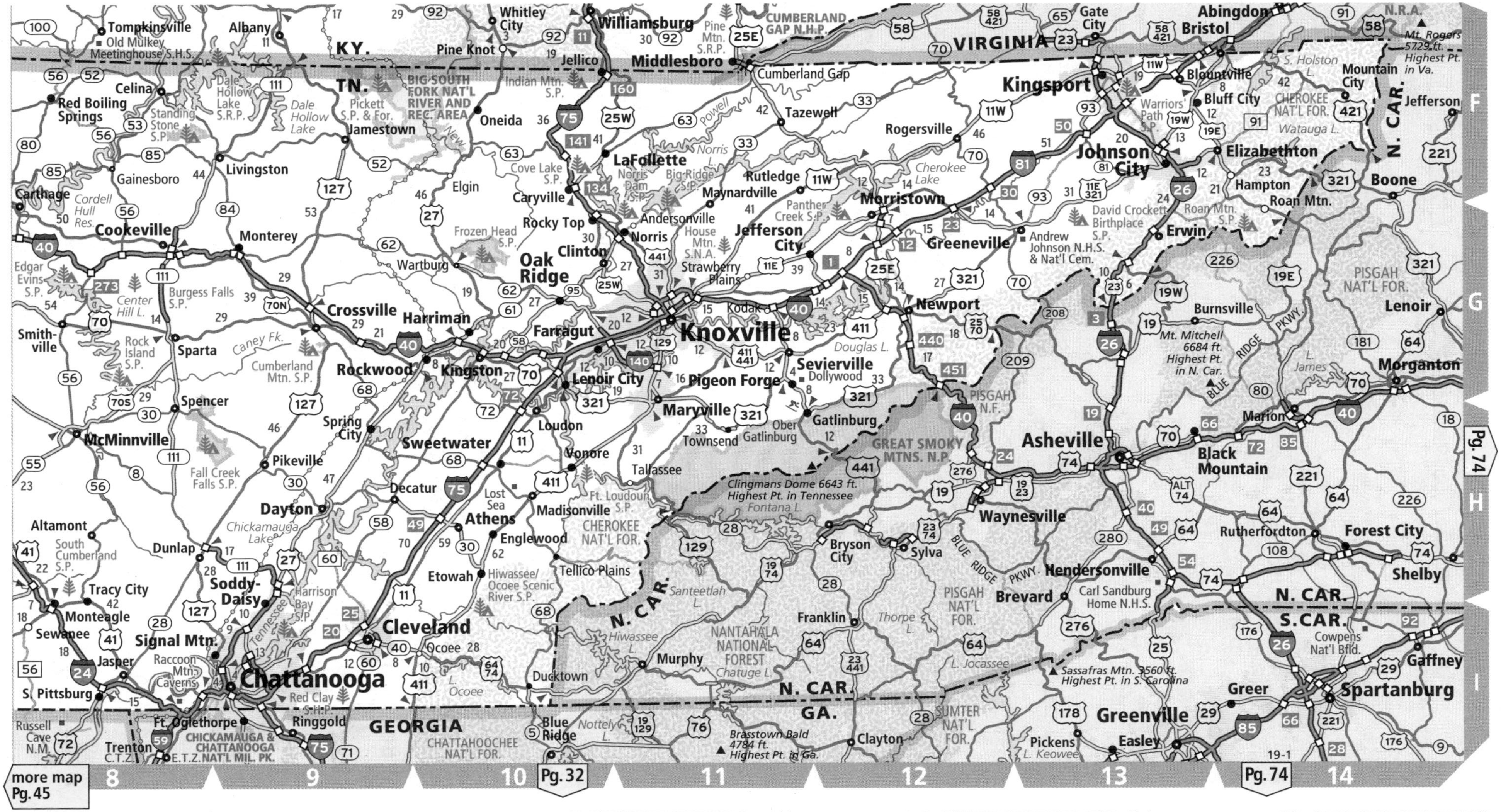

NOTE: Maps are not always in alphabetical order. See Page 1 for map location in this atlas.

more map Pg. 45

Pg. 32

Pg. 74

Tennessee

Cities and Towns

Ashland City F-6
Athens H-10
Bartlett H-1
Bolivar H-3
Bristol F-14
Brownsville H-2
Camden G-4
Centerville G-5
Chattanooga I-9
Clarksville F-5
Cleveland I-9
Clinton G-10
Collierville I-1
Columbia H-6
Cookeville G-8
Covington H-2
Crossville G-9
Dayton H-9
Dickson G-5
Dunlap H-8
Dyersburg G-2
Elizabethton F-14
Erwin G-13
Etowah H-10
Farragut G-10
Fayetteville I-7
Franklin G-6
Gallatin F-7
Gatlinburg H-11
Goodlettsville F-6
Greeneville G-13
Harriman G-10
Henderson H-3
Hohenwald H-5
Humboldt G-3
Huntingdon G-4
Jackson H-3
Jefferson City G-11
Johnson City F-13
Kingsport F-13
Kingston G-10
Knoxville G-11
La Vergne G-7
Lafayette F-7
LaFollette F-10
Lawrenceburg H-5
Lebanon G-7
Lenoir City G-10
Lewisburg H-6
Lexington H-4
Livingston F-9
Loudon H-10
Lynchburg H-7
Madison G-6
Madisonville H-10
Manchester H-7
Martin F-3
Maryville G-11
McKenzie G-3
McMinnville H-8
Memphis I-1
Milan G-3
Millington H-1
Morristown G-12
Mount Pleasant H-5
Murfreesboro G-7
Nashville G-6
Newport G-12
Oak Ridge G-10
Oneida F-10
Paris F-4
Pigeon Forge G-11
Portland F-7
Pulaski I-6
Ripley G-2
Rockwood G-10
Rogersville F-12
Savannah H-4
Selmer I-3
Sevierville G-11
Shelbyville H-7
Signal Mountain I-9
Smithville G-8
Smyrna G-7
Soddy-Daisy H-9
Sparta G-8
Springfield F-6
Sweetwater H-10
Tallassee H-11
Tellico Plains H-10
Trenton G-3
Tullahoma H-7
Union City F-3
Waverly G-5
Whiteville H-2
Winchester I-7

Travel planning & on-the-road resources

Tourism Information
Tennessee Dept. of Tourist Development
(615) 741-2159
www.tnvacation.com

Road Conditions & Construction
511
(877) 244-0065
www.tn511.com, www.tn.gov/tdot

Louisiana

Cities and Towns

City	Grid
Abbeville	F-4
Alexandria	D-4
Amite	E-7
Arcadia	A-3
Baldwin	F-5
Bastrop	A-5
Baton Rouge	E-6
Benton	A-2
Bogalusa	D-8
Bossier City	A-2
Breaux Bridge	E-5
Broussard	F-4
Bunkie	D-4
Cameron	F-2
Chalmette	F-7
Clinton	D-6
Colfax	C-3
Columbia	B-4
Coushatta	B-2
Covington	E-7
Crowley	E-4
Delhi	B-5
Denham Springs	E-6
DeQuincy	E-2
DeRidder	D-2
Donaldsonville	F-6
Edgard	F-7
Eunice	E-4
Farmerville	A-4
Ferriday	C-5
Franklin	F-5
Franklinton	D-7
Gramercy	F-6
Greensburg	D-6
Greenwood	B-1
Gretna	F-7
Hahnville	F-7
Hammond	E-7
Harrisonburg	C-5
Haynesville	A-3
Homer	A-3
Houma	G-6
Iowa	E-3
Jackson	D-6
Jeanerette	F-5
Jena	C-4
Jennings	E-3
Jonesboro	B-3
Jonesville	C-5
Kaplan	F-4
Lafayette	E-4
Lake Arthur	F-3
Lake Charles	E-3
Lake Providence	A-6
Laplace	F-7
Leesville	D-3
Livingston	E-6
Mamou	E-4
Mandeville	E-7
Mansfield	B-2
Many	C-2
Marksville	D-4
Metairie	F-7
Minden	A-3
Monroe	A-4
Morgan City	F-6
Napoleonville	F-6
Natchitoches	C-3
New Iberia	F-5
New Orleans	F-7
New Roads	E-5
Oak Grove	A-5
Oakdale	D-3
Oberlin	E-3
Opelousas	E-4
Patterson	F-5
Plaquemine	E-6
Ponchatoula	E-7
Port Allen	E-6
Port Sulphur	G-8
Raceland	F-7
Rayne	E-4
Rayville	B-5
Ruston	A-3
St. Francisville	D-5
St. Joseph	C-6
St. Martinville	F-5
Scott	E-4
Shreveport	A-2
Simmesport	D-5
Slidell	E-8
Springhill	A-2
Sulphur	E-2
Tallulah	B-6
Thibodaux	F-6
Vidalia	C-5
Ville Platte	E-4
Vivian	A-2
Walker	E-6
Welsh	E-3
West Monroe	A-4
Winnfield	C-3
Winnsboro	B-5

Louisiana state facts

Nickname: The Pelican State
Capital: Baton Rouge, E-6

Population: 4,533,372 (rank: 25th)
Largest city: New Orleans, 343,829, F-7

Land area: 43,204 sq. mi. (rank: 33rd)
Highest point: Driskill Mountain, 535 ft., B-3

Pg. 16

Pg. 96

NOTE: Maps are not always in alphabetical order.
See Page 1 for map location in this atlas.

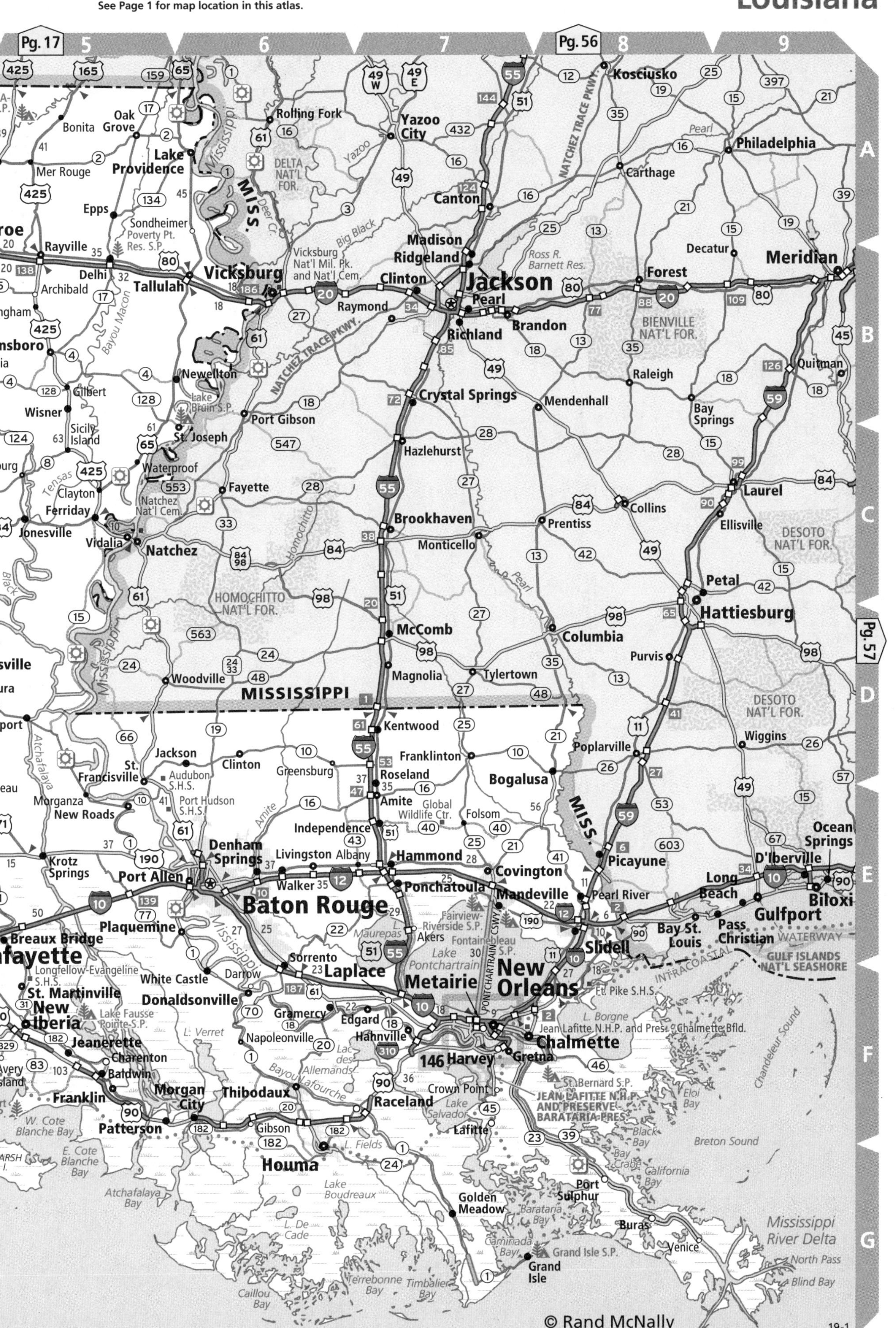

Road Conditions & Construction
511
(877) 452-3683
www.511la.org, www.dotd.la.gov

Tourism Information
Louisiana Office of Tourism
(800) 677-4082, (225) 635-0090
www.louisianatravel.com

Travel planning & on-the-road resources

Maine state facts

Nickname: The Pine Tree State
Capital: Augusta, G-2

Population: 1,328,361 (rank: 41st)
Largest city: Portland, 66,194, H-2

Land area: 30,843 sq. mi. (rank: 39th)
Highest point: Mount Katahdin, 5,268 ft., D-4

Maine

Cities and Towns

Andover . . . F-1
Ashland . . . C-4
Auburn . . . H-2
Augusta . . . G-2
Bailey Island . . . H-2
Bangor . . . F-4
Bar Harbor . . . G-5
Bath . . . H-2
Belfast . . . G-3
Bethel . . . G-1
Biddeford . . . I-1
Bingham . . . F-2
Blue Hill . . . G-4
Boothbay Harbor . . . H-3
Brewer . . . F-4
Bridgewater . . . C-5
Bridgton . . . H-1
Brownville Junction . . . E-3
Brunswick . . . H-2
Bucksport . . . G-4
Calais . . . E-6
Camden . . . G-3
Caribou . . . B-5
Castine . . . G-4
Cherryfield . . . G-5
Corinna . . . F-3
Cornish . . . H-1
Damariscotta . . . H-3
Danforth . . . D-5
Deer Isle . . . G-4
Dexter . . . F-3
Dixfield . . . G-1
Dover-Foxcroft . . . E-3
Eagle Lake . . . B-4
East Corinth . . . F-3
East Millinocket . . . E-4
Eastport . . . F-6
Ellsworth . . . G-4
Fairfield . . . G-3
Falmouth . . . H-2
Farmington . . . F-2
Fort Fairfield . . . B-5
Fort Kent . . . A-4
Freeport . . . H-2
Friendship . . . H-3
Fryeburg . . . H-1
Gardiner . . . G-2
Gorham . . . H-1
Gray . . . H-2
Greenville . . . E-3
Guilford . . . E-3
Hampden . . . F-4
Harrington . . . G-5
Harrison . . . H-1
Houlton . . . D-5
Howland . . . E-4
Jackman . . . E-2
Jonesport . . . G-5
Kennebunk . . . I-1
Kennebunkport . . . I-1
Kingfield . . . F-2
Kittery . . . J-1
Lewiston . . . H-2
Limestone . . . B-5
Lincoln . . . E-4
Livermore Falls . . . G-2
Lubec . . . F-6
Machias . . . F-6
Madison . . . F-2
Mars Hill . . . C-5

Pg. 125
Pg. 126

Mattawamkeag . . . E-4
Medway . . . E-4
Mexico . . . G-1
Milbridge . . . G-5
Millinocket . . . D-4
Milo . . . E-4
Monson . . . E-3
Monticello . . . C-5
Naples . . . H-1
Newport . . . F-3
Norridgewock . . . F-2
North Anson . . . F-2
North Berwick . . . I-1
North Bridgton . . . H-1
North Windham . . . H-1
Northeast Harbor . . . G-4
Norway . . . G-1
Ogunquit . . . I-1
Old Orchard Beach . . . I-1
Old Town . . . F-4
Orono . . . F-4
Patten . . . D-4
Phillips . . . F-2
Pittsfield . . . F-3
Poland . . . H-1
Port Clyde . . . H-3
Portage . . . B-4
Portland . . . H-2
Presque Isle . . . B-5
Princeton . . . E-6
Rangeley . . . F-1
Rockland . . . H-3
Rockwood . . . D-2
Rumford . . . G-1
Saco . . . I-1
Sanford . . . I-1
Scarborough . . . I-2
Searsport . . . G-4
Sebago Lake . . . H-1
Sherman Station . . . D-4
Skowhegan . . . F-2
Solon . . . F-2
South China . . . G-3
South Paris . . . G-1
South Portland . . . H-2
Southwest Harbor . . . G-4
Standish . . . H-1
Stonington . . . G-4
Stratton . . . E-1
Thomaston . . . H-3
Turner . . . G-2
Union . . . G-3
Unity . . . G-3
Van Buren . . . A-5
Vinalhaven . . . H-4
Waldoboro . . . H-3
Washburn . . . B-5
Waterville . . . G-3
Wells . . . I-1
West Enfield . . . E-4
West Scarborough . . . I-1
Westbrook . . . H-2
Wilton . . . G-2
Winslow . . . G-3
Winterport . . . F-4
Winthrop . . . G-2
Woodland . . . E-6
Yarmouth . . . H-2
York Beach . . . I-1
York Harbor . . . I-1
York Village . . . I-1

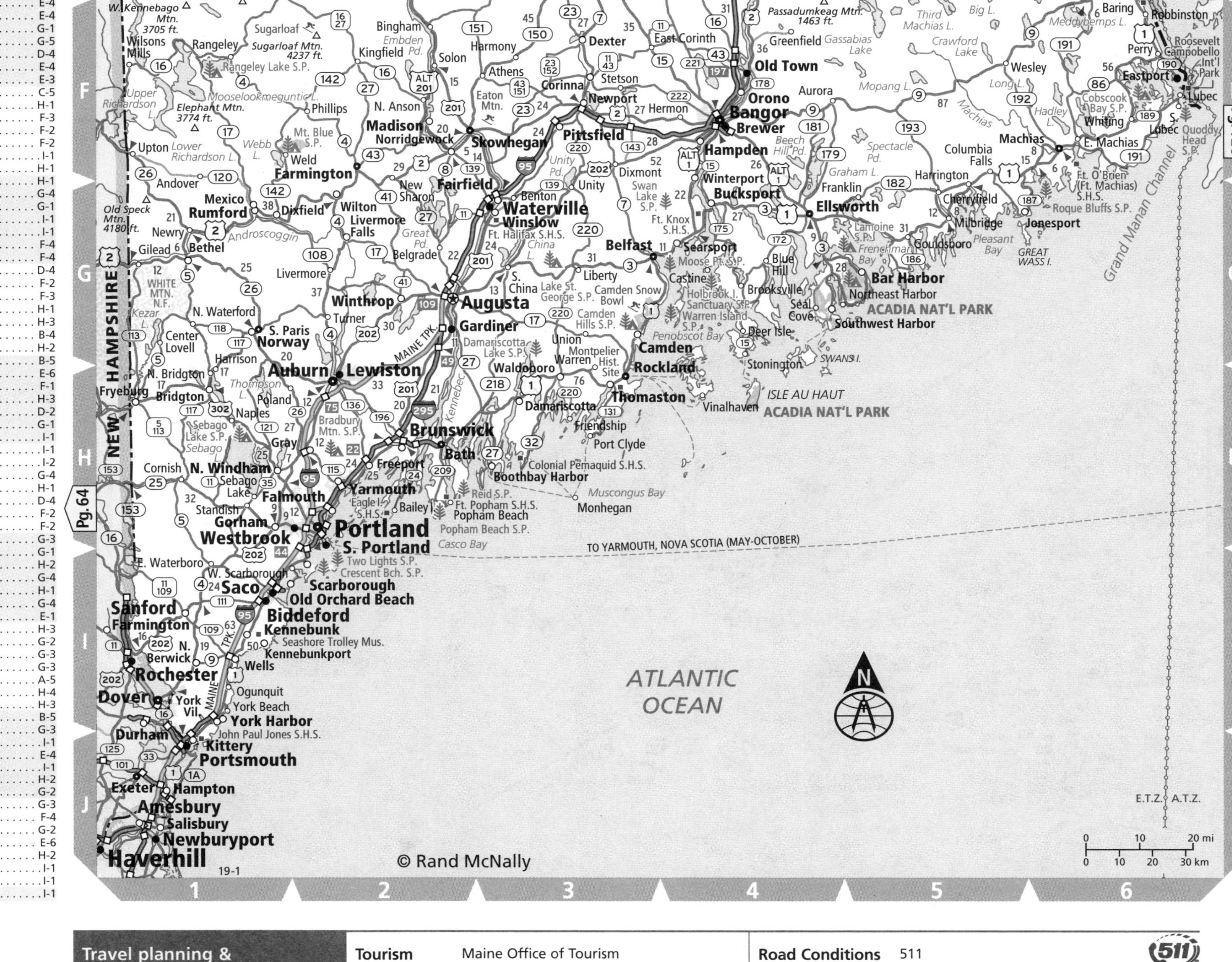

Travel planning & on-the-road resources

Tourism Information
Maine Office of Tourism
(888) 624-6345, (877) 624-6331
www.visitmaine.com

Road Conditions & Construction
511
(207) 624-3000, (800) 675-7453
www.maine.gov/mdot

Michigan state facts

Nickname: The Great Lake State
Capital: Lansing, H-4
Population: 9,883,640 (rank: 8th)
Largest city: Detroit, 713,777, I-6
Land area: 56,539 sq. mi. (rank: 22nd)
Highest point: Mount Arvon, 1,979 ft., B-6

Michigan

Cities and Towns

Adrian J-4
Albion I-4
Allegan I-2
Alma G-4
Alpena D-5
Ann Arbor I-5
Atlanta E-4
Bad Axe F-6
Baldwin F-2
Battle Creek I-3
Bay City G-4
Bellaire E-3
Benton Harbor I-2
Benton Heights I-2
Bertrand J-2
Bessemer B-5
Beulah E-2
Big Rapids G-3
Birch Run G-5
Brighton I-5
Buchanan J-2
Burton H-5
Cadillac F-3
Caro G-5
Cassopolis J-2
Cement City I-4
Centreville J-3
Charlevoix D-3
Charlotte I-3
Cheboygan D-4
Chelsea I-4
Coldwater J-3
Corunna H-4
Crystal Falls B-6
Davison H-5
Dearborn I-5
Detroit I-6
Dimondale H-4
Dowagiac I-2
Eagle River A-6
Eaton Rapids I-4
Escanaba C-1
Fenton H-5
Flint H-5
Frankenmuth G-5
Fremont G-2
Gaylord E-4
Gladstone C-1
Gladwin F-4
Grand Haven H-2
Grand Ledge H-4
Grand Rapids H-2
Grayling E-3
Greenville H-3
Harrison F-3
Harrisville E-5
Hart G-2
Hastings H-3
Hillsdale J-4
Holland H-2
Holly H-5
Houghton A-6
Howell H-5
Hudsonville H-2
Ionia H-3
Iron Mountain C-6
Ironwood B-5
Ishpeming B-6
Ithaca G-4
Jackson I-4

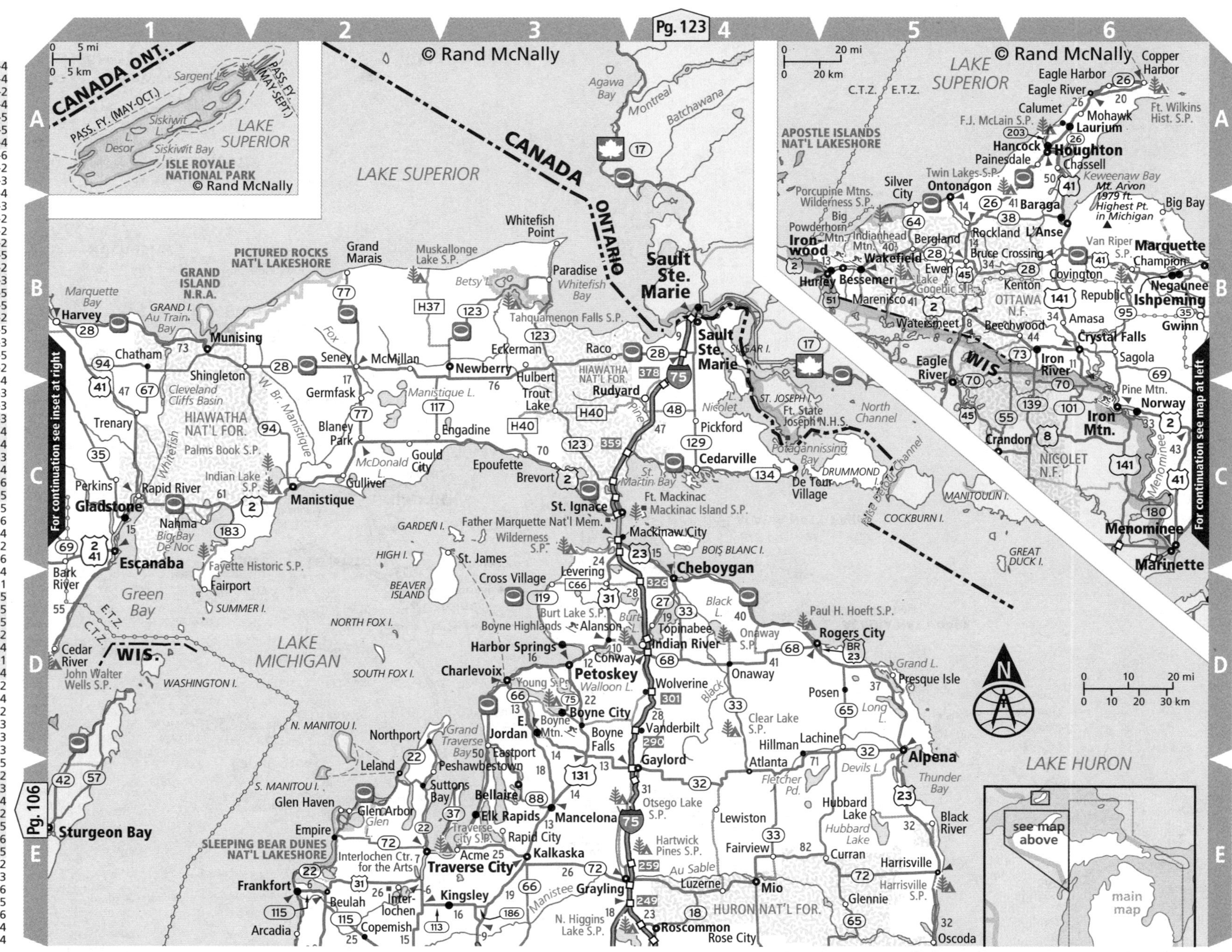

Kalamazoo I-3
Kalkaska E-3
L'Anse B-6
Lake City F-3
Lansing H-4
Lapeer H-5
Leland E-2
Livonia I-5
Ludington F-2
Mackinaw City C-3
Manistee F-2
Manistique C-2
Marine City H-6
Marquette B-6
Marshall I-3
Marysville H-6
Mason H-4
Menominee C-6
Michigan Center I-4
Midland G-4
Milan I-5
Mio E-4
Monroe J-5
Mount Clemens H-6
Mount Pleasant G-3
Munising B-1
Muskegon G-2
Muskegon Heights H-2
Negaunee B-6
New Baltimore H-6
Newberry B-3
Niles J-2
Novi I-5
Ontonagon B-5
Owosso H-4
Paw Paw I-2
Petoskey D-3
Pontiac H-5
Port Huron H-6
Portage I-3
Reed City F-3
Richmond H-6
Rockford H-3
Rogers City D-4
Roscommon E-4
Saginaw G-4
St. Clair H-6
St. Ignace C-3
St. Johns H-4
St. Joseph I-1
St. Louis G-4
Saline I-5
Sandusky G-6
Sault Ste. Marie B-4
South Haven I-2
Standish F-4
Stanton G-3
Sturgis J-3
Tawas City F-5
Tecumseh I-4
Three Rivers J-2
Traverse City E-2
Trenton I-5
Warren I-6
Waterford H-5
West Branch F-4
Westland I-5
Wyandotte I-5
Wyoming H-2
Ypsilanti I-5
Zeeland H-2

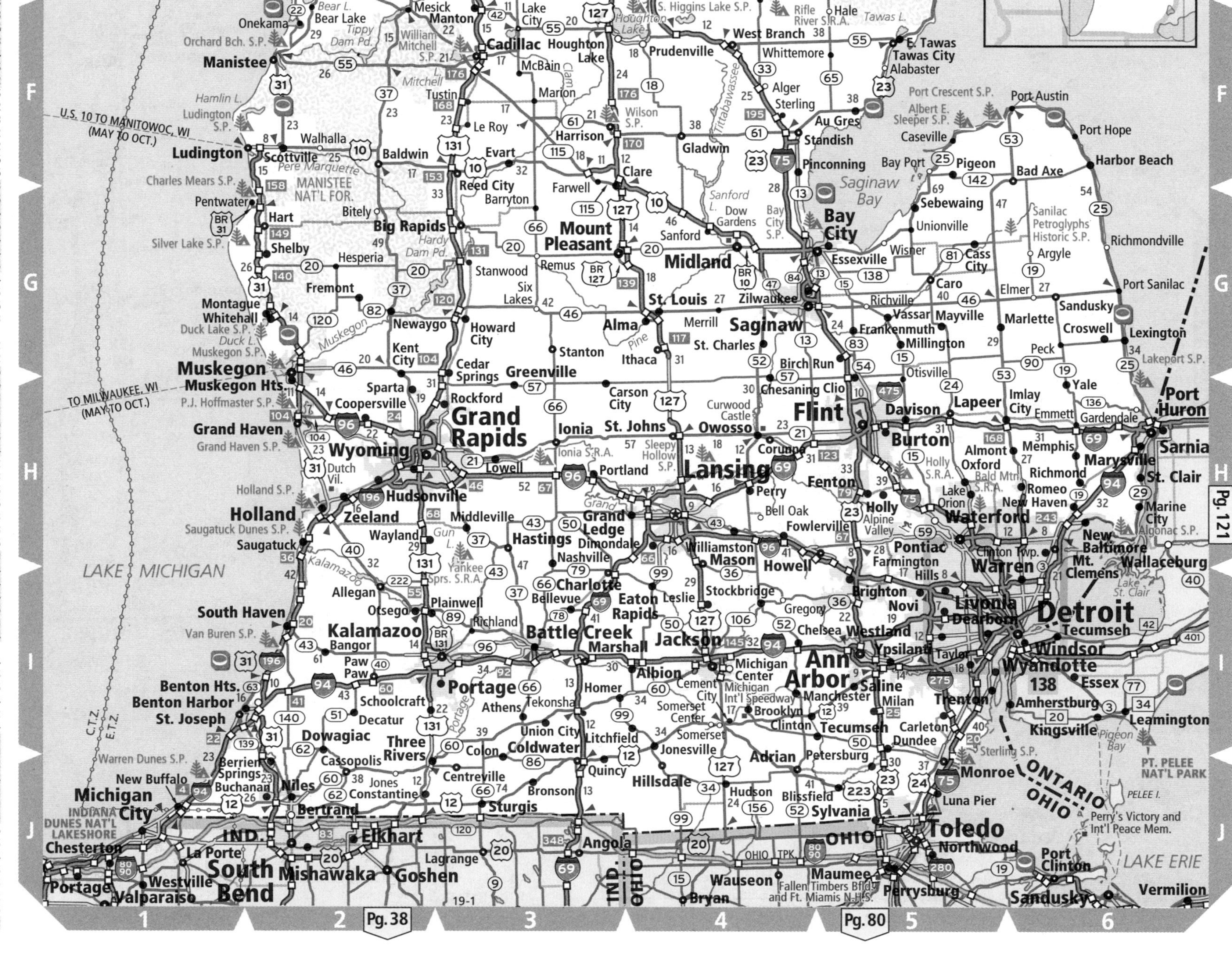

Travel planning & on-the-road resources

Tourism Information — Travel Michigan, (888) 784-7328, www.michigan.org

Road Conditions & Construction — (800) 381-8477, (517) 373-2090, www.michigan.gov/drive

Minnesota state facts

Nickname: The North Star State
Capital: St. Paul, H-5

Population: 5,303,925 (rank: 21st)
Largest city: Minneapolis, 382,578, H-4

Land area: 79,627 sq. mi. (rank: 14th)
Highest point: Eagle Mountain, 2,301 ft., A-5

Minnesota

Cities and Towns

Ada E-1
Aitkin F-4
Albert Lea J-4
Alexandria G-2
Anoka H-4
Appleton H-2
Austin J-5
Bagley D-2
Baudette C-3
Baxter F-3
Becker G-4
Belle Plaine H-4
Bemidji D-3
Benson G-2
Big Lake G-4
Blaine H-4
Bloomington H-4
Blue Earth J-3
Brainerd F-3
Breckenridge F-1
Buffalo H-4
Caledonia J-6
Cambridge G-4
Cannon Falls I-5
Chaska H-4
Chatfield J-5
Chisholm D-5
Cloquet E-5
Cohasset E-4
Cokato H-3
Crookston D-1
Crosby F-4
Delano H-4
Detroit Lakes E-2
Duluth E-5
East Grand Forks D-1
Eden Prairie H-4
Elbow Lake G-2
Elk River G-4
Ely D-6
Eveleth D-5
Fairmont J-3
Faribault I-4
Farmington H-4
Fergus Falls F-2
Foley G-4
Forest Lake H-5
Gaylord I-3
Glencoe H-3
Glenwood G-2
Grand Marais B-6
Grand Rapids E-4
Granite Falls H-2
Hallock C-1
Hastings H-5
Hibbing D-5
Hutchinson H-3
International Falls C-4
Ivanhoe I-1
Jackson J-3
Jordan H-4
Kasson I-5
La Crescent J-6
Lake City I-5
Lake Crystal I-3
Lakeville H-4
Le Sueur I-4
Litchfield H-3
Little Falls G-3
Long Prairie G-3

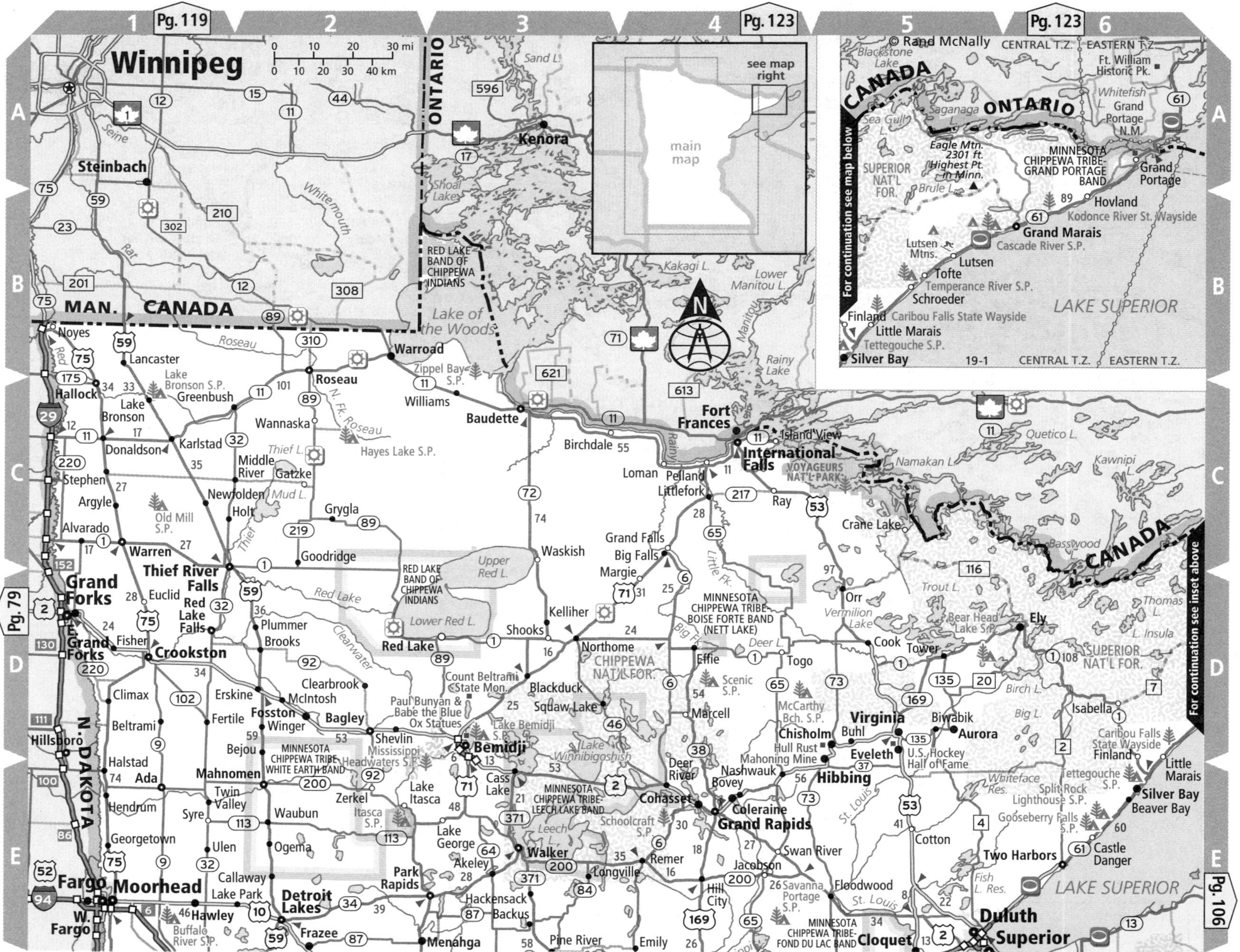

Luverne . . . J-1
Madelia . . . I-3
Madison . . . H-1
Mahnomen . . . E-2
Mankato . . . I-4
Marshall . . . I-2
Milaca . . . G-4
Minneapolis . . . H-4
Montevideo . . . H-2
Montgomery . . . I-4
Monticello . . . G-4
Moorhead . . . E-1
Moose Lake . . . F-5
Mora . . . G-4
Morris . . . G-2
New Prague . . . I-4
New Ulm . . . I-3
North Branch . . . G-5
Northfield . . . I-4
Olivia . . . H-3
Ortonville . . . G-1
Owatonna . . . I-4
Park Rapids . . . E-3
Paynesville . . . G-3
Pelican Rapids . . . F-2
Perham . . . F-2
Pine City . . . G-5
Pine Island . . . I-5
Pipestone . . . I-1
Plainview . . . I-5
Preston . . . J-6
Princeton . . . G-4
Raymond . . . H-2
Red Lake Falls . . . D-1
Red Wing . . . I-5
Redwood Falls . . . I-2
Rochester . . . I-5
Roseau . . . B-2
St. Cloud . . . G-3
St. James . . . I-3
St. Joseph . . . G-3
St. Paul . . . H-5
St. Peter . . . I-4
Sandstone . . . F-5
Sauk Centre . . . G-3
Sauk Rapids . . . G-3
Shakopee . . . H-4
Slayton . . . I-2
Sleepy Eye . . . I-3
Spring Valley . . . J-5
Staples . . . F-3
Stewartville . . . J-5
Stillwater . . . H-5
Thief River Falls . . . C-1
Tracy . . . I-2
Two Harbors . . . E-6
Virginia . . . D-5
Wabasha . . . I-6
Wadena . . . F-2
Walker . . . E-3
Warren . . . C-1
Waseca . . . I-4
Wells . . . J-4
Wheaton . . . G-1
White Bear Lake . . . H-5
Willmar . . . H-3
Windom . . . J-2
Winona . . . I-6
Worthington . . . J-2
Zimmerman . . . G-4
Zumbrota . . . I-5

Pg. 79
Pg. 93
Pg. 106
Pg. 40
WISCONSIN
SOUTH DAKOTA
IOWA
N.D.
S.D.
Minneapolis
St. Paul
St. Cloud
Rochester
Mankato
Bloomington
Eden Prairie
Blaine
Wahpeton
Breckenridge
Fergus Falls
Alexandria
Morris
Willmar
Montevideo
Marshall
Worthington
Sioux Falls
Brookings
Watertown
Owatonna
Faribault
Northfield
Winona
La Crosse
Eau Claire
Red Wing
Albert Lea
Austin
Brainerd
Little Falls
New Ulm
Hutchinson
Redwood Falls
© Rand McNally
19-1

Mississippi state facts

Nickname: The Magnolia State
Capital: Jackson, F-3

Population: 2,967,297 (rank: 31st)
Largest city: Jackson, 173,514, F-3

Land area: 46,923 sq. mi. (rank: 31st)
Highest point: Woodall Mountain, 806 ft., B-6

Mississippi

Cities and Towns

Aberdeen C-5
Ackerman D-5
Amory C-6
Ashland B-4
Baldwyn B-5
Batesville B-3
Bay St. Louis J-4
Bay Springs G-4
Belmont B-6
Belzoni D-3
Biloxi J-5
Booneville B-5
Brandon F-3
Brookhaven G-3
Brooksville D-5
Bruce C-4
Calhoun City C-4
Canton F-3
Carthage E-4
Centreville H-2
Charleston C-3
Clarksdale C-2
Cleveland C-2
Clinton F-3
Coffeeville C-4
Collins G-4
Columbia H-4
Columbus D-6
Como B-3
Corinth A-5
Crystal Springs G-3
D'Iberville I-5
De Kalb E-5
Decatur F-5
Drew C-2
Durant E-3
Edwards F-2
Ellisville G-5
Eupora D-4
Fayette G-2
Flora F-3
Florence F-3
Forest F-4
Fulton C-6
Gautier J-5
Greenville D-2
Greenwood D-3
Grenada C-4
Gulfport J-5
Hattiesburg H-4
Hazlehurst G-3
Hernando B-3
Hollandale E-2
Holly Springs B-4
Horn Lake A-3
Houston C-5
Indianola D-2
Itta Bena D-3
Iuka B-6
Jackson F-3
Kosciusko E-4
Lambert C-3
Laurel G-5
Leakesville H-6
Leland D-2
Lexington E-3
Liberty H-2
Long Beach J-5
Louisville E-5
Lucedale I-5

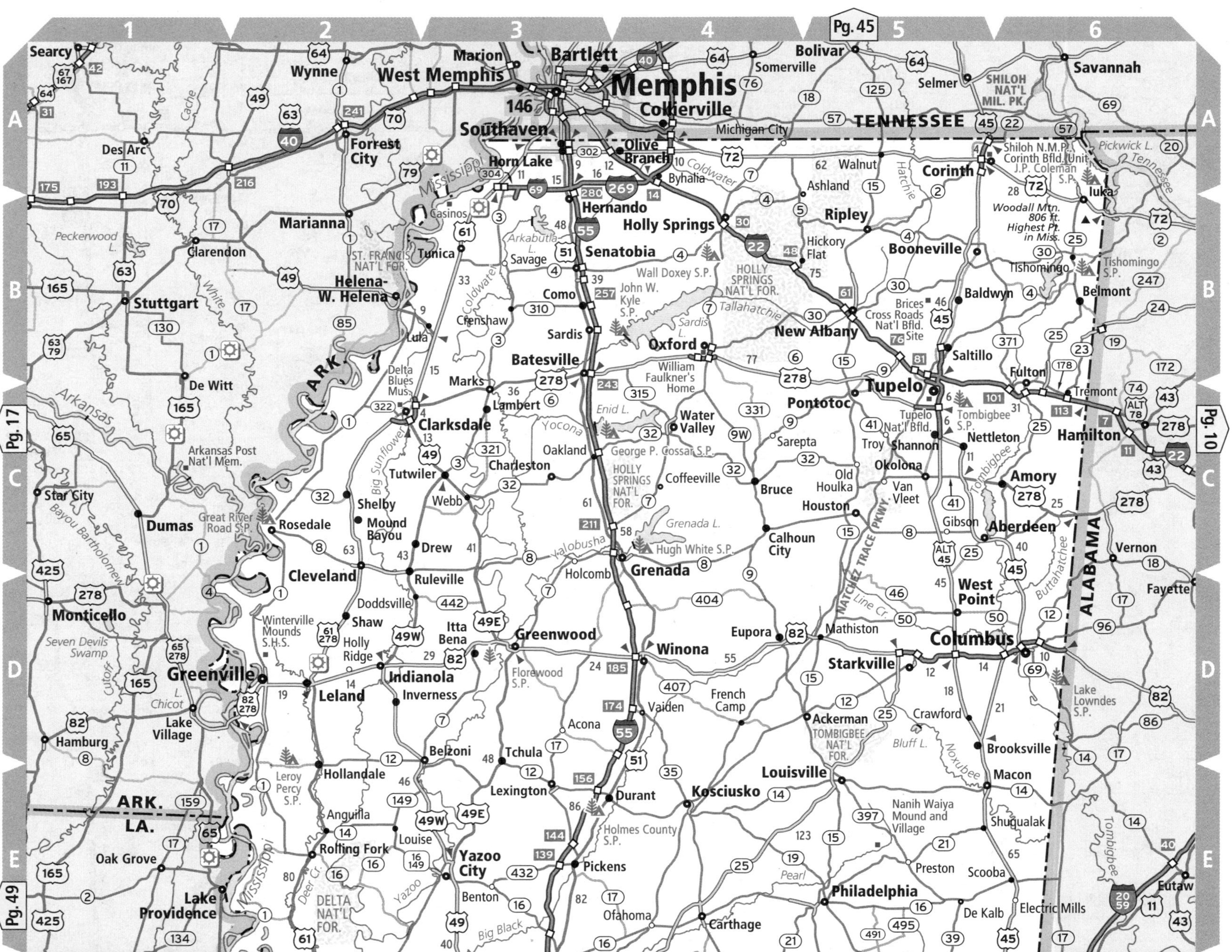

Lumberton H-4
Macon E-5
Madison F-3
Magee G-4
Magnolia H-3
Marks C-3
McComb H-3
Meadville H-2
Mendenhall G-3
Meridian F-5
Monticello G-3
Morton F-4
Moss Point J-6
Mound Bayou C-2
Natchez G-1
Nettleton C-5
New Albany B-5
Newton F-5
Ocean Springs I-5
Okolona C-5
Olive Branch A-4
Oxford B-4
Pascagoula J-6
Pass Christian J-4
Pearl F-3
Petal H-4
Philadelphia E-5
Picayune I-4
Pickens E-3
Pontotoc C-5
Poplarville I-4
Port Gibson G-2
Prentiss G-3
Purvis H-4
Quitman G-5
Raleigh G-4
Raymond F-3
Richland F-3
Ridgeland F-3
Ripley B-5
Rolling Fork E-2
Rosedale C-2
Ruleville C-2
Saltillo B-5
Sardis B-3
Saucier I-5
Senatobia B-3
Shannon C-5
Shaw D-2
Shelby C-2
Southaven A-3
Starkville D-5
Summit H-3
Taylorsville G-4
Tchula D-3
Tunica B-3
Tupelo C-5
Tutwiler C-3
Tylertown H-3
Union F-5
Vaiden D-4
Vancleave I-5
Vicksburg F-2
Water Valley C-4
Waynesboro G-5
Wesson G-3
West Point D-5
Wiggins I-5
Winona D-4
Woodville H-1
Yazoo City E-3

Pg. 11

Pg. 49

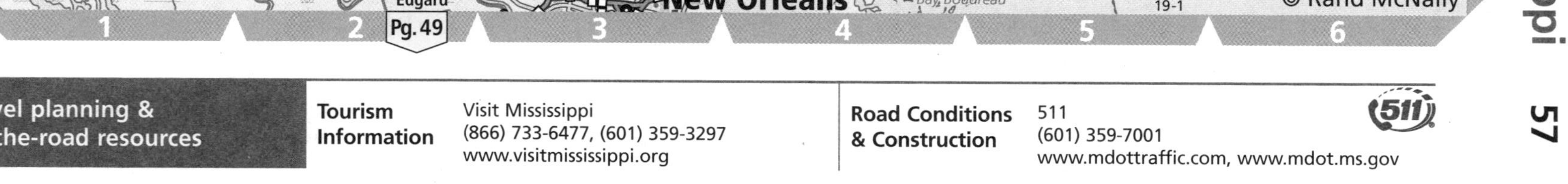

Travel planning & on-the-road resources

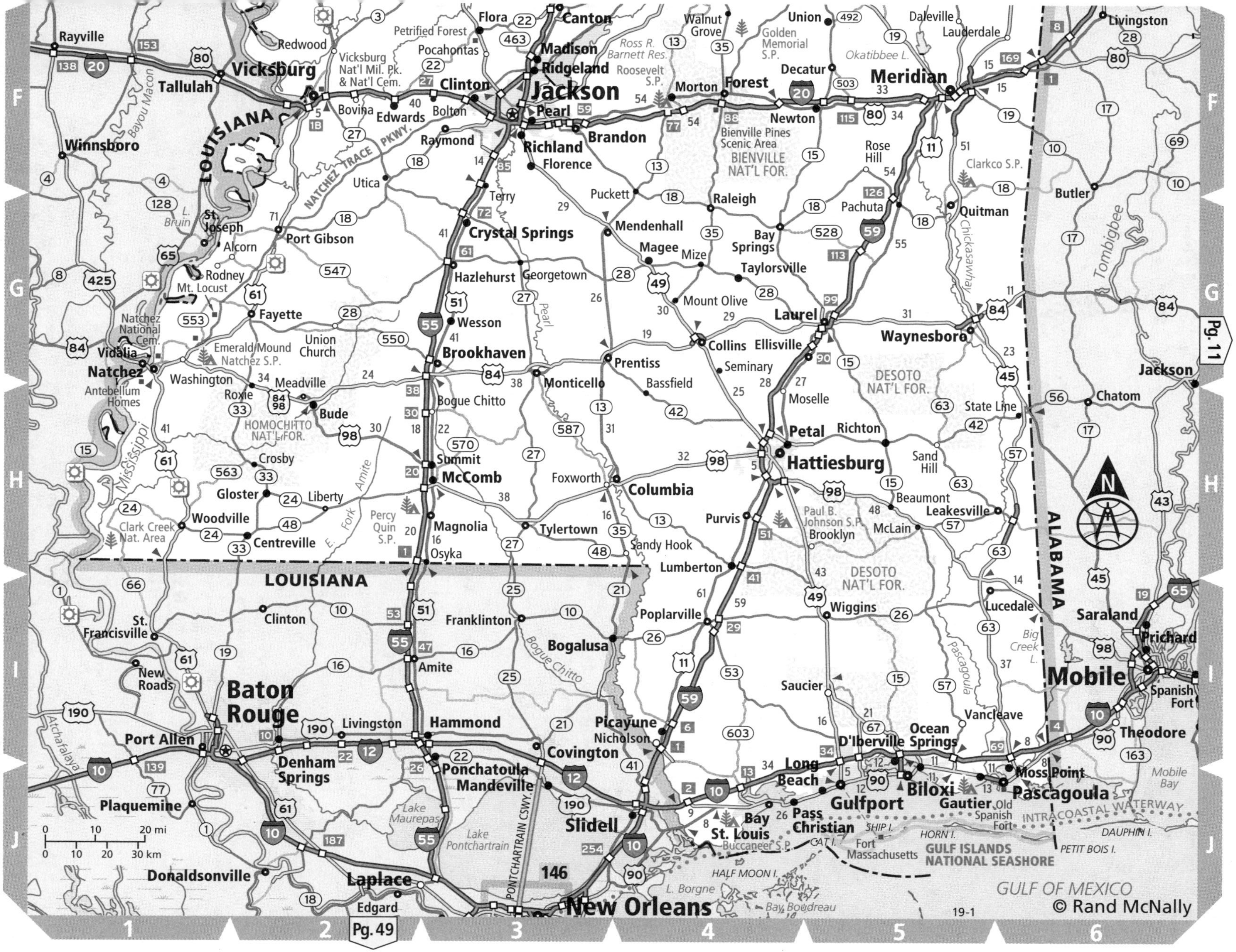

Tourism Information	Visit Mississippi (866) 733-6477, (601) 359-3297 www.visitmississippi.org	**Road Conditions & Construction**	511 (601) 359-7001 www.mdottraffic.com, www.mdot.ms.gov

Missouri

Cities and Towns

Aurora F-3
Belton C-2
Blue Springs C-3
Bolivar E-4
Bonne Terre E-7
Boonville C-4
Bowling Green B-6
Branson F-4
Brookfield B-4
Butler D-2
California D-4
Cameron B-3
Cape Girardeau E-8
Carrollton B-3
Carthage F-2
Caruthersville G-8
Centralia C-5
Charleston F-8
Chillicothe B-3
Clinton D-3
Columbia C-5
Crystal City D-7
De Soto D-7
Dexter F-8
El Dorado Springs E-3
Eldon D-4
Eureka D-7
Excelsior Springs B-3
Farmington E-7
Festus D-7
Fredericktown E-7
Fulton C-5
Gladstone C-2
Grandview C-2
Hannibal B-6
Harrisonville C-2
Hollister F-4
Independence C-2
Jackson E-8
Jefferson City D-5
Joplin F-2
Kansas City C-2
Kearney B-2
Kennett G-7
Kirksville A-4
Kirkwood D-7
Lamar E-3
Lebanon E-4
Lexington C-3
Liberty C-2
Louisiana B-6
Macon B-5
Malden F-8
Marshall C-4
Marshfield E-4
Maryville A-2
Mexico C-5
Moberly B-5
Monett F-3
Mount Vernon F-3
Mountain Grove F-5
Neosho F-2
Nevada E-2
New Madrid F-8
Nixa F-4
Odessa C-3
Osage Beach D-4
Ozark F-4
Pacific D-7
Park Hills E-7
Perryville E-8
Platte City B-2
Pleasant Hill C-3
Poplar Bluff F-7
Republic F-3
Richmond C-3
Rolla E-5
St. Charles C-7
St. Clair D-6
St. James D-6
St. Joseph B-2
St. Louis C-7
Ste. Genevieve D-7
Salem E-6
Savannah B-2
Scott City F-8
Sedalia C-4
Sikeston F-8
Springfield F-4
Sullivan D-6
Trenton A-3
Troy C-6
Union D-6
Vandalia C-6
Villa Ridge D-6
Warrensburg C-3
Warrenton C-6
Washington D-6
Waynesville E-5
Webb City F-2
Weldon Spring C-7
Wentzville C-6
West Plains F-5

Missouri state facts

Nickname: The Show Me State
Capital: Jefferson City, D-5

Population: 5,988,927 (rank: 18th)
Largest city: Kansas City, 459,787, C-2

Land area: 68,741 sq. mi. (rank: 18th)
Highest point: Taum Sauk Mtn., 1,772 ft., E-7

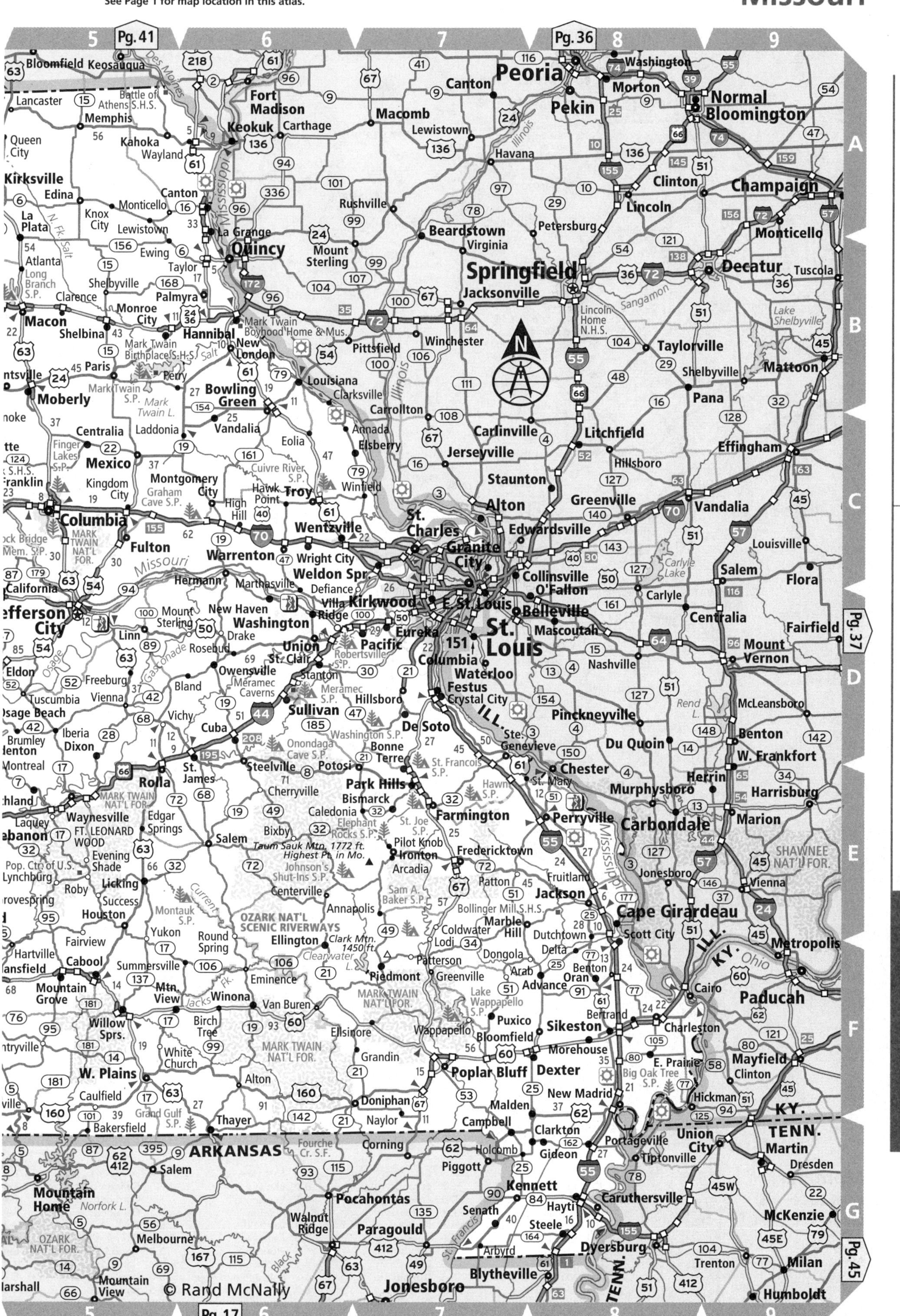

Road Conditions & Construction
(888) 275-6636
(573) 751-2551
www.modot.org

Tourism Information
Missouri Division of Tourism
(573) 751-4133, (800) 519-2100
www.visitmo.com

Travel planning & on-the-road resources

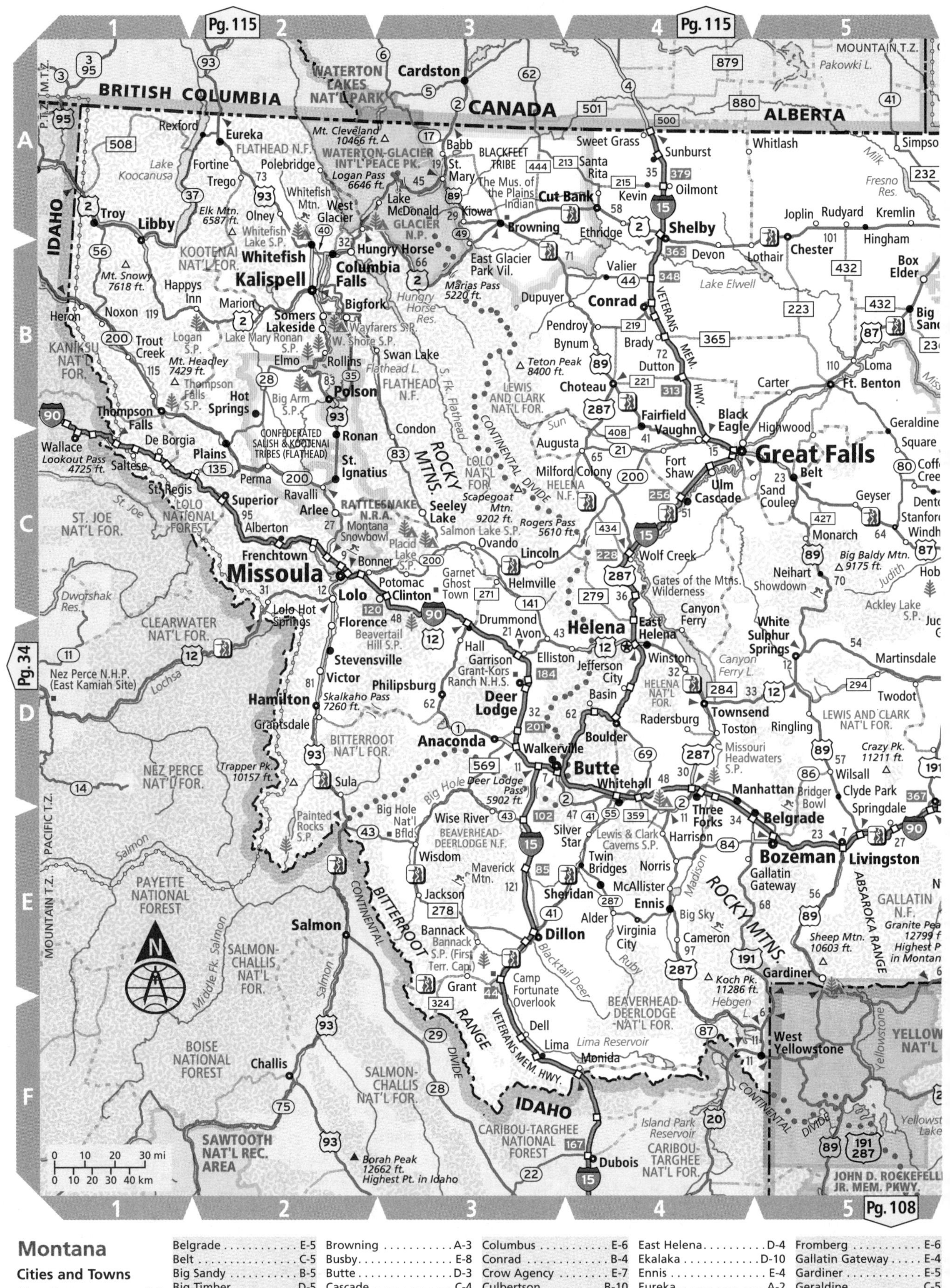

Montana

Cities and Towns

Absarokee . . . E-6
Alberton . . . C-2
Anaconda . . . D-3
Arlee . . . C-2
Ashland . . . E-8
Augusta . . . C-4
Baker . . . D-10
Ballantine . . . D-7
Belgrade . . . E-5
Belt . . . C-5
Big Sandy . . . B-5
Big Timber . . . D-5
Bigfork . . . B-2
Billings . . . E-7
Black Eagle . . . C-4
Boulder . . . D-4
Box Elder . . . B-5
Bozeman . . . E-5
Bridger . . . E-6
Broadus . . . E-9
Browning . . . A-3
Busby . . . E-8
Butte . . . D-3
Cascade . . . C-4
Chester . . . A-5
Chinook . . . A-6
Choteau . . . B-4
Circle . . . C-9
Clinton . . . C-3
Clyde Park . . . D-5
Colstrip . . . D-8
Columbia Falls . . . B-2
Columbus . . . E-6
Conrad . . . B-4
Crow Agency . . . E-7
Culbertson . . . B-10
Cut Bank . . . A-4
Deer Lodge . . . D-3
Denton . . . C-5
Dillon . . . E-3
Drummond . . . D-3
Dutton . . . B-4
East Glacier Park Village . . . B-3
East Helena . . . D-4
Ekalaka . . . D-10
Ennis . . . E-4
Eureka . . . A-2
Fairfield . . . B-4
Fairview . . . B-10
Florence . . . D-2
Forsyth . . . D-8
Fort Belknap Agency . . B-6
Fort Benton . . . B-5
Frazer . . . B-8
Frenchtown . . . C-2
Fromberg . . . E-6
Gallatin Gateway . . . E-4
Gardiner . . . E-5
Geraldine . . . C-5
Glasgow . . . B-8
Glendive . . . C-10
Great Falls . . . C-4
Hamilton . . . D-2
Hardin . . . E-7
Harlem . . . A-6
Harlowton . . . D-6
Havre . . . A-6

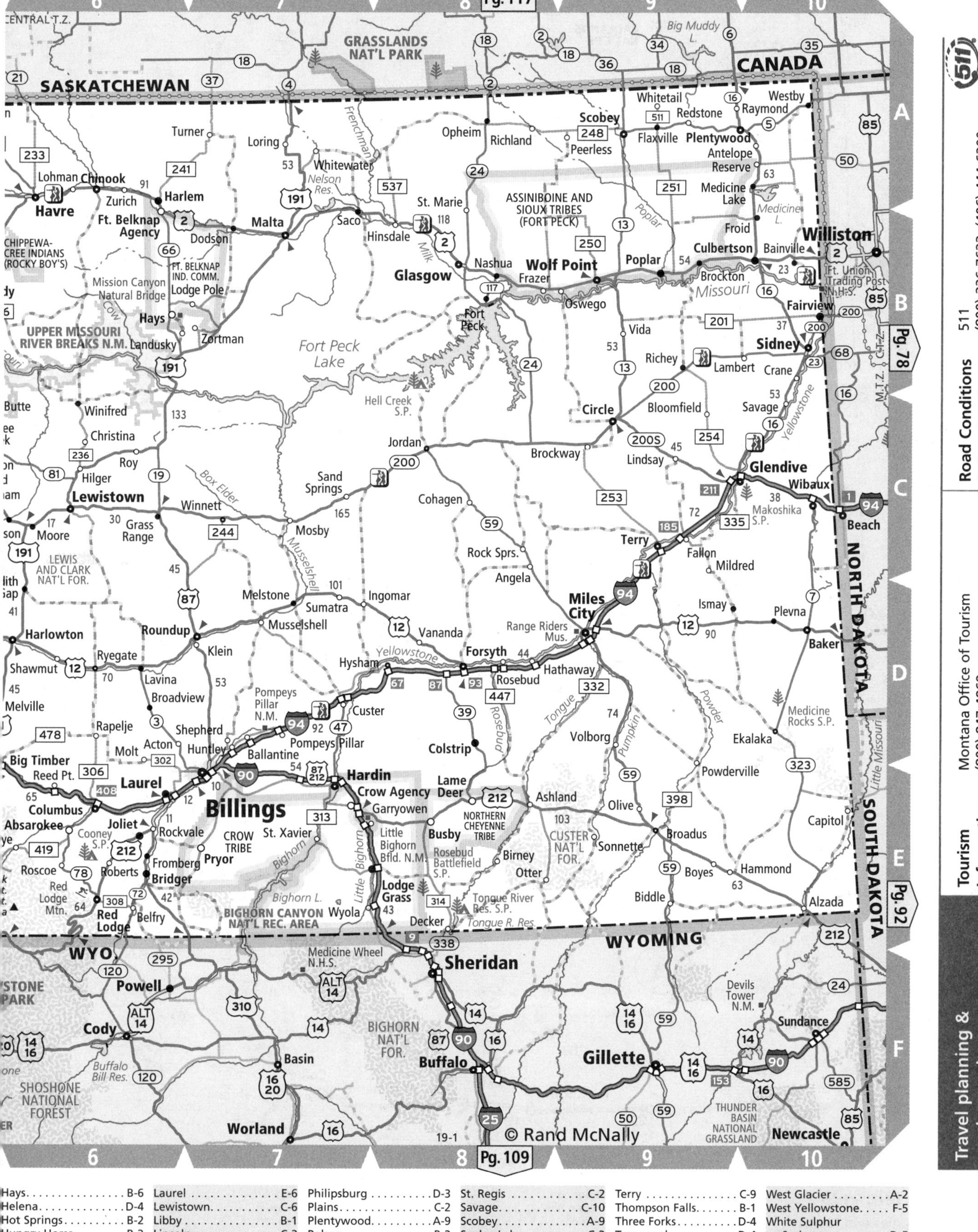

511
511
(800) 226-7623, (406) 444-6200
www.mdt511.com, www.mdt.mt.gov
Road Conditions & Construction

Tourism Information
Montana Office of Tourism
(800) 847-4868
www.visitmt.com

Travel planning & on-the-road resources

Hays . . . B-6
Helena . . . D-4
Hot Springs . . . B-2
Hungry Horse . . . B-2
Huntley . . . D-7
Hysham . . . D-8
Jefferson City . . . D-4
Joliet . . . E-6
Jordan . . . C-8
Kalispell . . . B-2
Lakeside . . . B-2
Lame Deer . . . E-8
Laurel . . . E-6
Lewistown . . . C-6
Libby . . . B-1
Lincoln . . . C-3
Livingston . . . E-5
Lodge Grass . . . E-8
Lolo . . . C-2
Malta . . . B-7
Manhattan . . . D-4
Miles City . . . D-9
Missoula . . . C-2
Nashua . . . B-8
Philipsburg . . . D-3
Plains . . . C-2
Plentywood . . . A-9
Polson . . . B-2
Poplar . . . B-9
Pryor . . . E-7
Red Lodge . . . E-6
Roberts . . . E-6
Ronan . . . C-2
Roundup . . . D-7
Ryegate . . . D-6
St. Ignatius . . . C-2
St. Regis . . . C-2
Savage . . . C-10
Scobey . . . A-9
Seeley Lake . . . C-3
Shelby . . . A-4
Sheridan . . . E-4
Sidney . . . B-10
Somers . . . B-2
Stanford . . . C-5
Stevensville . . . D-2
Sunburst . . . A-4
Superior . . . C-2
Terry . . . C-9
Thompson Falls . . . B-1
Three Forks . . . D-4
Townsend . . . D-4
Troy . . . A-1
Twin Bridges . . . E-4
Ulm . . . C-4
Valier . . . B-4
Vaughn . . . C-4
Victor . . . D-2
Virginia City . . . E-4
Walkerville . . . D-3
West Glacier . . . A-2
West Yellowstone . . . F-5
White Sulphur Springs . . . D-5
Whitefish . . . B-2
Whitehall . . . D-4
Wibaux . . . C-10
Winnett . . . C-7
Wolf Point . . . B-9

Nebraska state facts

Nickname: The Cornhusker State
Capital: Lincoln, D-9

Population: 1,826,341 (rank: 38th)
Largest city: Omaha, 408,958, D-9

Land area: 76,824 sq. mi. (rank: 15th)
Highest point: Panorama Point, 5,424 ft., D-1

Nebraska

Cities and Towns

Ainsworth B-5
Albion C-7
Alliance B-2
Alma E-6
Arapahoe E-5
Arthur C-3
Ashland D-9
Atkinson B-6
Auburn E-10
Aurora D-7
Bartlett C-7
Bassett B-6
Bayard C-2
Beatrice E-9
Beaver City E-5
Bellevue D-9
Benkelman E-3
Blair C-9
Bloomfield B-8
Brewster C-5
Bridgeport C-2
Broken Bow C-5
Burwell C-6
Butte A-6
Cambridge E-5
Center B-7
Central City D-7
Chadron A-2
Chappell D-2
Clay Center E-7
Columbus C-8
Cozad D-5
Crawford B-2
Creighton B-7
Crete D-8
Dakota City B-9
David City D-8
Eagle D-9
Elwood E-5
Fairbury E-8
Falls City E-10
Franklin E-6
Fremont C-9
Friend D-8
Fullerton C-7
Geneva E-8
Genoa C-8
Gering C-1
Gibbon D-6
Gordon A-3
Gothenburg D-5
Grand Island D-7
Grant D-3
Greeley C-7
Harrisburg C-1
Harrison B-1
Hartington B-8
Hastings E-7
Hayes Center E-4
Hebron E-8
Hemingford B-2
Holdrege E-6
Hyannis C-3
Imperial E-3
Kearney D-6
Kimball D-1
Laurel B-8
Lexington D-5

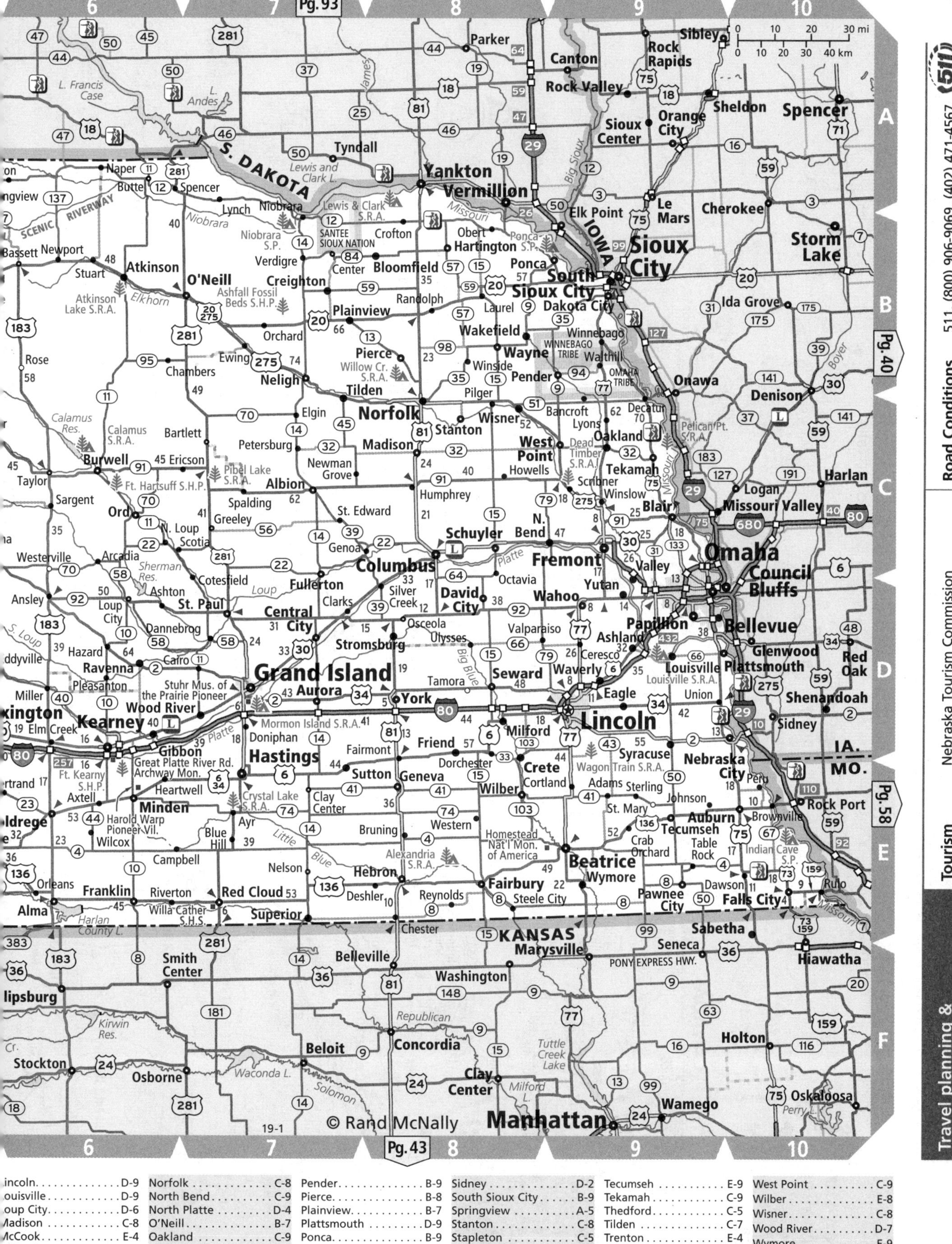

Road Conditions & Construction
511, (800) 906-9069, (402) 471-4567
www.511.nebraska.gov
www.dot.nebraska.gov

Tourism Information
Nebraska Tourism Commission
(402) 471-3796
www.visitnebraska.com

Travel planning & on-the-road resources

incoln. D-9
ouisville. D-9
oup City. D-6
Aadison C-8
AcCook. E-4
Ailford D-8
Ainden E-6
Aitchell. C-1
Aullen. C-4
lebraska City D-10
leligh B-7
lelson E-7
Norfolk C-8
North Bend. C-9
North Platte D-4
O'Neill B-7
Oakland C-9
Ogallala. D-3
Omaha D-9
Ord C-6
Osceola D-8
Oshkosh C-3
Papillion D-9
Pawnee City E-9
Pender. B-9
Pierce. B-8
Plainview. B-7
Plattsmouth D-9
Ponca. B-9
Ravenna D-6
Red Cloud E-7
Rushville B-3
St. Paul D-7
Schuyler. C-8
Scottsbluff. C-1
Seward D-8
Sidney D-2
South Sioux City. B-9
Springview A-5
Stanton C-8
Stapleton C-5
Stockville. E-5
Stromsburg D-8
Superior E-7
Sutherland D-4
Sutton E-7
Syracuse D-9
Taylor C-6
Tecumseh E-9
Tekamah C-9
Thedford. C-5
Tilden C-7
Trenton E-4
Tryon C-4
Valentine. A-5
Valley. D-9
Wahoo D-9
Wakefield B-8
Waverly. D-9
Wayne. B-8
West Point C-9
Wilber. E-8
Wisner. C-8
Wood River. D-7
Wymore E-9
York. D-8
Yutan. D-9

New Hampshire state facts

Nickname: The Granite State
Capital: Concord, H-5
Population: 1,316,470 (rank: 42nd)
Largest city: Manchester, 109,565, H-5
Land area: 8,953 sq. mi. (rank: 44th)
Highest point: Mt. Washington, 6,288 ft., D-6

Travel planning & on-the-road resources

Tourism Information N.H. Div. of Travel & Tourism Dev. (603) 271-2665 www.visitnh.gov

Road Conditions & Construction 511, (603) 271-3734 www.nhtmc.com www.nh.gov/dot

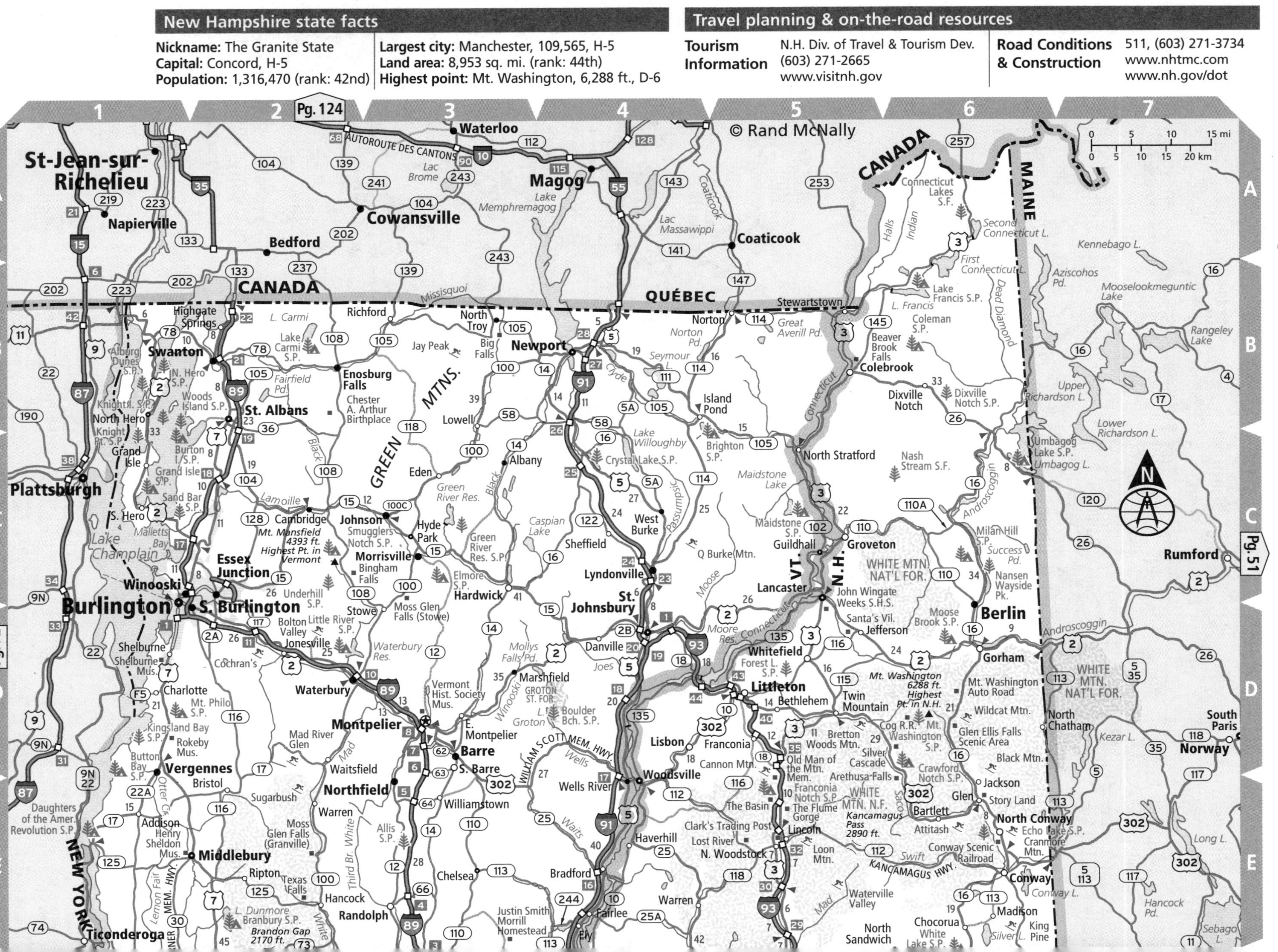

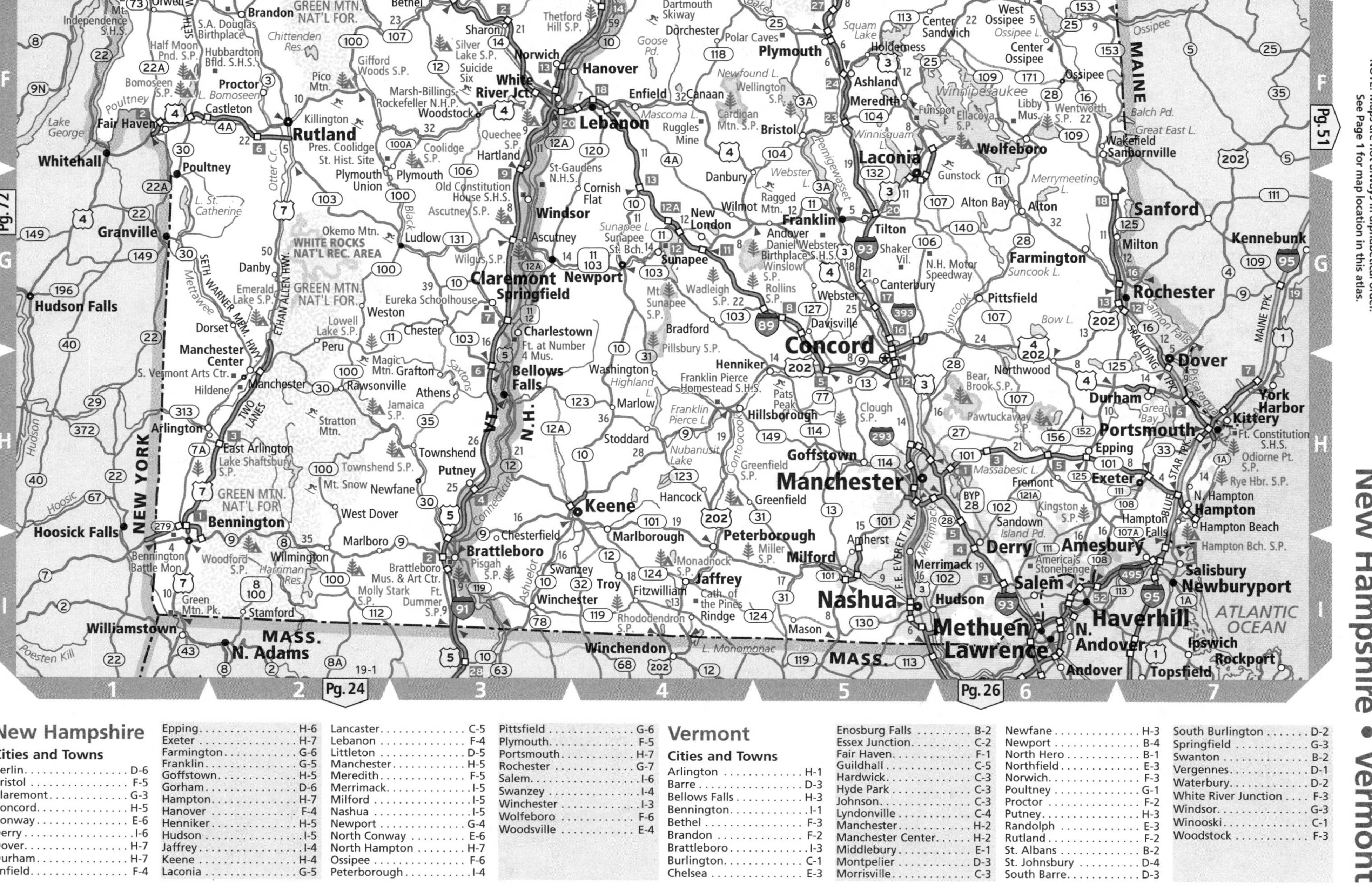

New Hampshire

Cities and Towns

Berlin D-6
Bristol F-5
Claremont G-3
Concord H-5
Conway E-6
Derry I-6
Dover H-7
Durham H-7
Enfield F-4
Epping H-6
Exeter H-7
Farmington G-6
Franklin G-5
Goffstown H-5
Gorham D-6
Hampton H-7
Hanover F-4
Henniker H-5
Hudson I-5
Jaffrey I-4
Keene H-4
Laconia G-5
Lancaster C-5
Lebanon F-4
Littleton D-5
Manchester H-5
Meredith F-5
Merrimack I-5
Milford I-5
Nashua I-5
Newport G-4
North Conway E-6
North Hampton H-7
Ossipee F-6
Peterborough I-4
Pittsfield G-6
Plymouth F-5
Portsmouth H-7
Rochester G-7
Salem I-6
Swanzey I-4
Winchester I-3
Wolfeboro F-6
Woodsville E-4

Vermont

Cities and Towns

Arlington H-1
Barre D-3
Bellows Falls H-3
Bennington I-1
Bethel F-3
Brandon F-2
Brattleboro I-3
Burlington C-1
Chelsea E-3
Enosburg Falls B-2
Essex Junction C-2
Fair Haven F-1
Guildhall C-5
Hardwick C-3
Hyde Park C-3
Johnson C-3
Lyndonville C-4
Manchester H-2
Manchester Center H-2
Middlebury E-1
Montpelier D-3
Morrisville C-3
Newfane H-3
Newport B-4
North Hero B-1
Northfield E-3
Norwich F-3
Poultney G-1
Proctor F-2
Putney H-3
Randolph E-3
Rutland F-2
St. Albans B-2
St. Johnsbury D-4
South Barre D-3
South Burlington D-2
Springfield G-3
Swanton B-2
Vergennes D-1
Waterbury D-2
White River Junction F-3
Windsor G-3
Winooski C-1
Woodstock F-3

Vermont state facts

Nickname: The Green Mtn. State
Capital: Montpelier, D-3
Population: 625,741 (rank: 49th)
Largest city: Burlington, 42,417, C-1
Land area: 9,217 sq. mi. (rank: 43rd)
Highest point: Mt. Mansfield, 4,393 ft., C-2

Travel planning & on-the-road resources

Tourism Information
Vt. Dept. of Tourism & Mktg.
(800) 837-6668, (802) 828-3237
www.vermontvacation.com

Road Conditions & Construction
511
511
www.vtrans.vermont.gov

New Jersey state facts

Nickname: The Garden State
Capital: Trenton, E-3

Population: 8,791,894 (rank: 11th)
Largest city: Newark, 277,140, C-5

Land area: 7,354 sq. mi. (rank: 46th)
Highest point: High Point, 1,803 ft., A-4

New Jersey

Cities and Towns

Absecon H-4
Asbury Park E-5
Atlantic City H-4
Atlantic Highlands D-5
Audubon F-2
Avalon I-3
Beachwood F-5
Belleville C-5
Belvidere C-2
Berlin G-3
Bernardsville C-4
Blackwood G-2
Boonton C-4
Bordentown E-3
Bound Brook D-4
Bridgeton H-2
Brigantine H-4
Browns Mills F-4
Budd Lake C-3
Buena H-3
Burlington F-3
Caldwell C-5
Camden F-2
Cape May J-3
Cape May Court House I-3
Clifton C-5
Clinton D-3
Cranbury E-4
Denville C-4
Dover C-4
Eatontown E-5
Edison D-4
Egg Harbor City H-4
Elizabeth D-5
Elmer H-2
Ewing E-3
Flemington D-3
Folsom H-3
Forked River G-5
Franklin B-4
Freehold E-5
Glassboro G-2
Hackensack C-5
Hackettstown C-3
Hamburg B-4
Hammonton G-3
High Bridge D-3
Highland Park D-4
Highlands E-5
Hightstown E-4
Hopatcong B-4
Hope C-3
Hopewell E-3
Jamesburg E-4
Keansburg D-5
Kinnelon B-4
Lakehurst F-5
Lakewood F-5
Lambertville E-3
Lawrenceville E-3
Lebanon D-3
Linden D-5
Little Silver E-5
Long Branch E-6
Madison C-4
Mahwah B-5
Malaga H-2
Manahawkin G-5
Manville D-4
Margate City I-4

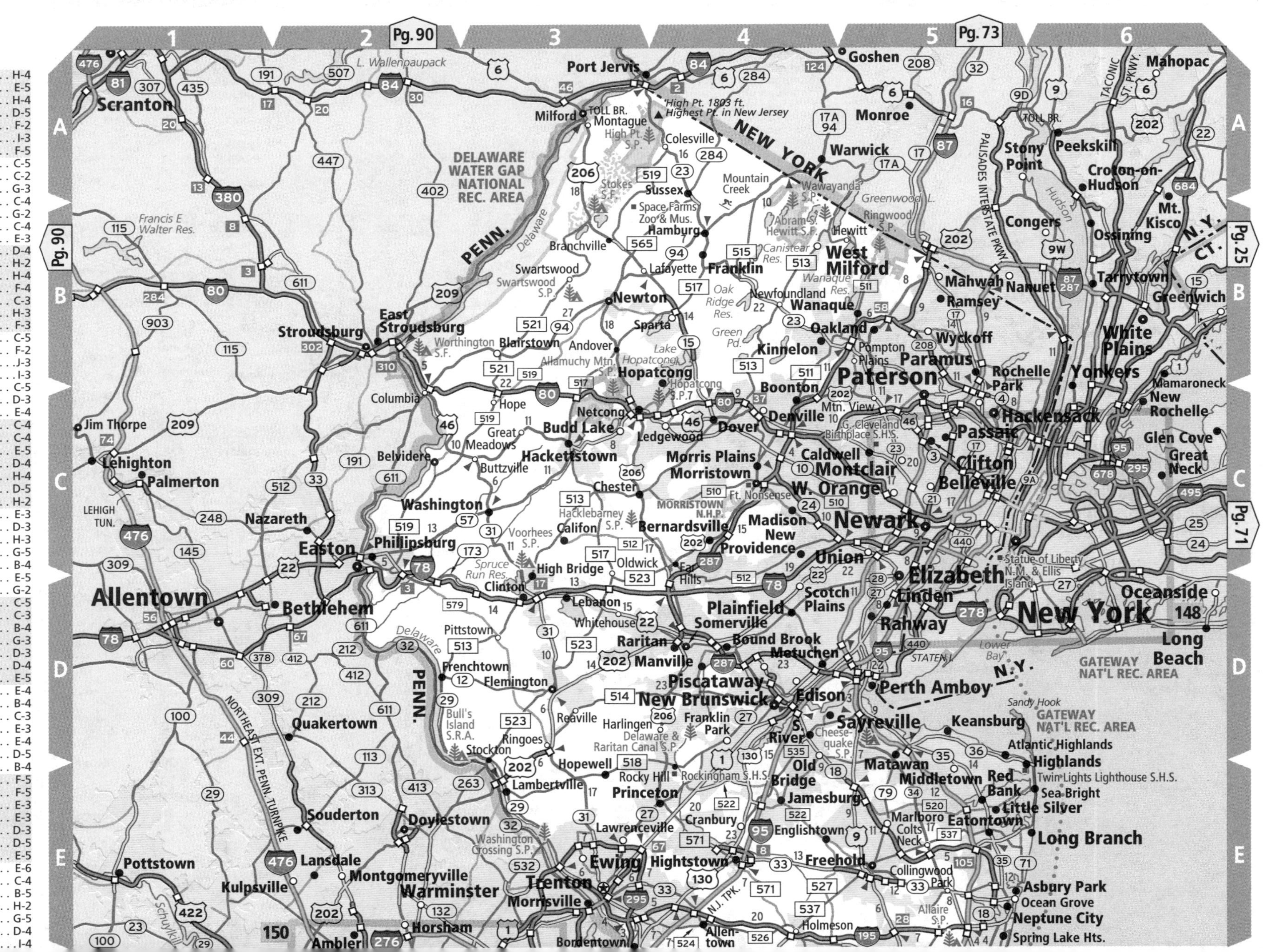

Marlton	F-3
Matawan	D-5
Mays Landing	H-3
Medford	F-3
Metuchen	D-4
Middletown	E-5
Millville	H-2
Montclair	C-5
Morris Plains	C-4
Morristown	C-4
Mount Holly	F-3
Neptune City	E-5
Netcong	C-3
New Brunswick	D-4
New Egypt	F-4
New Providence	C-4
Newark	C-5
Newton	B-3
Oakland	B-5
Ocean City	I-4
Ocean Grove	E-5
Old Bridge	D-4
Paramus	B-5
Passaic	C-5
Paterson	C-5
Paulsboro	G-2
Penns Grove	G-1
Pennsville	G-1
Perth Amboy	D-5
Phillipsburg	C-2
Piscataway	D-4
Plainfield	D-4
Pleasantville	H-4
Point Pleasant	F-5
Princeton	E-4
Rahway	D-5
Ramsey	B-5
Raritan	D-4
Red Bank	E-5
Rio Grande	J-3
Rochelle Park	C-5
Salem	H-1
Sayreville	D-4
Scotch Plains	D-4
Sea Girt	F-5
Sea Isle City	I-3
Seaside Heights	F-5
Seaside Park	F-5
Somerdale	G-3
Somers Point	I-4
Somerville	D-4
South River	D-4
Spring Lake Heights	E-5
Sussex	A-4
Toms River	F-5
Trenton	E-3
Tuckerton	H-4
Union	C-5
Ventnor City	I-4
Villas	J-3
Vineland	H-2
Wanaque	B-5
Washington	C-3
West Milford	B-4
West Orange	C-5
Wildwood	J-3
Williamstown	G-3
Woodbury	G-2
Woodstown	G-2
Wyckoff	B-5

Pg. 91

Pg. 29

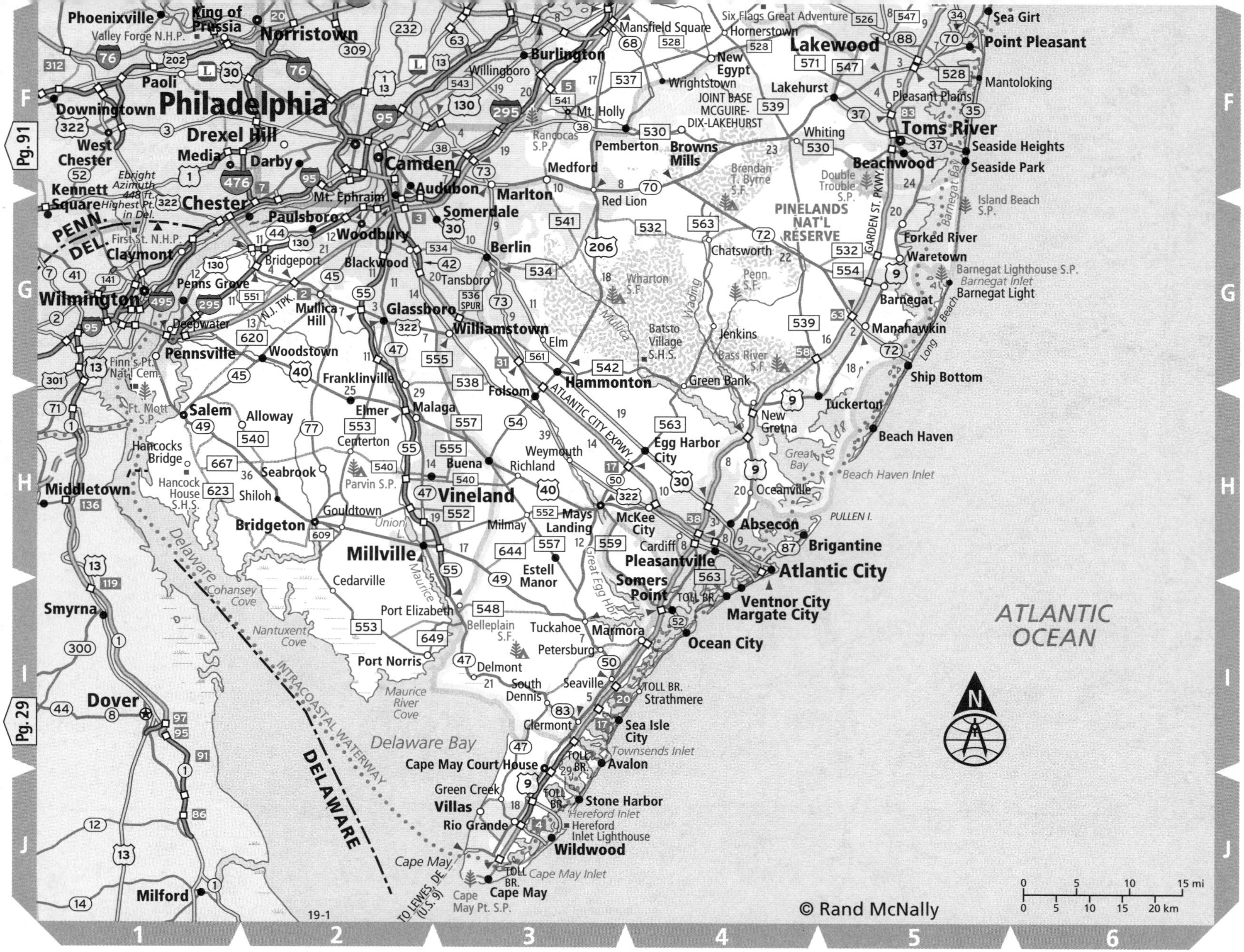

Travel planning & on-the-road resources

Tourism Information
New Jersey Division of Travel and Tourism
(609) 599-6540
www.visitnj.org

Road Conditions & Construction
511, (866) 511-6538
www.511.nj.org
www.state.nj.us/transportation

New Mexico state facts

Nickname: Land of Enchantment
Capital: Santa Fe, C-4

Population: 2,059,179 (rank: 36th)
Largest city: Albuquerque, 545,852, D-3

Land area: 121,298 sq. mi. (rank: 5th)
Highest point: Wheeler Peak, 13,161 ft., B-5

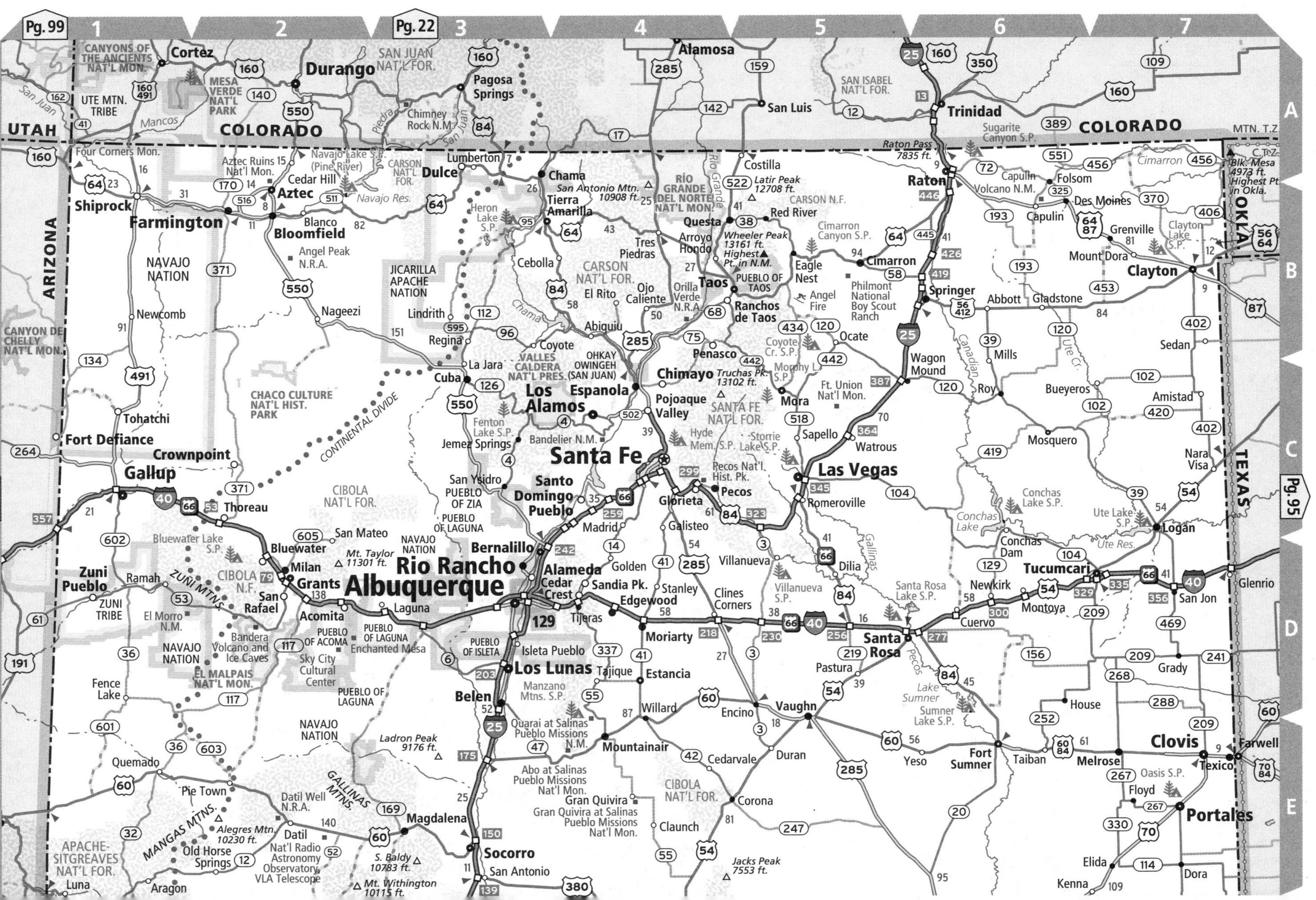

NOTE: Maps are not always in alphabetical order.
See Page 1 for map location in this atlas.

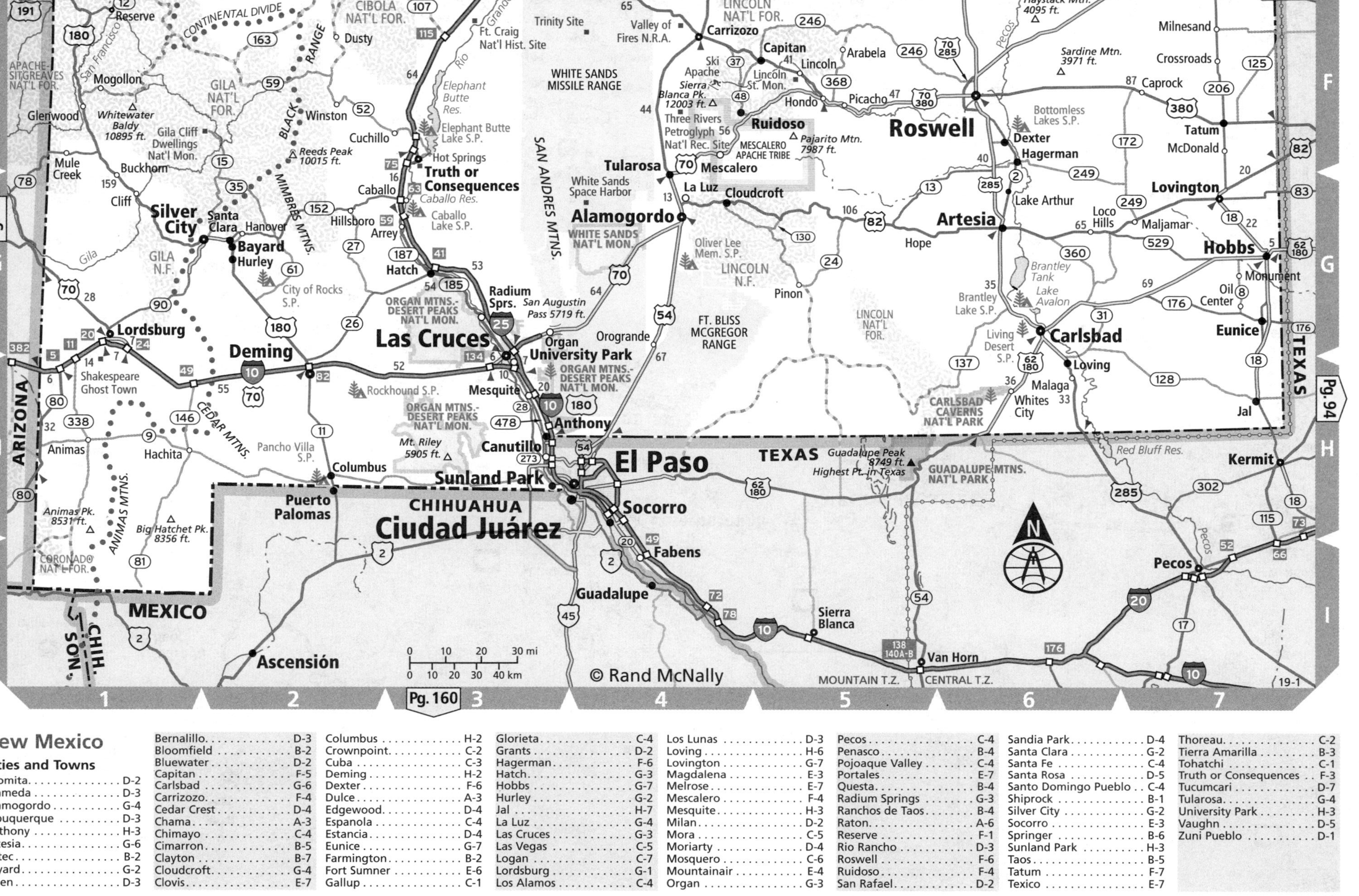

New Mexico

Cities and Towns

Acomita . . . D-2	Bernalillo . . . D-3	Columbus . . . H-2	Glorieta . . . C-4	Los Lunas . . . D-3	Pecos . . . C-4	Sandia Park . . . D-4	Thoreau . . . C-2
Alameda . . . D-3	Bloomfield . . . B-2	Crownpoint . . . C-2	Grants . . . D-2	Loving . . . H-6	Penasco . . . B-4	Santa Clara . . . G-2	Tierra Amarilla . . . B-3
Alamogordo . . . G-4	Bluewater . . . D-2	Cuba . . . C-3	Hagerman . . . F-6	Lovington . . . G-7	Pojoaque Valley . . . C-4	Santa Fe . . . C-4	Tohatchi . . . C-1
Albuquerque . . . D-3	Capitan . . . F-5	Deming . . . H-2	Hatch . . . G-3	Magdalena . . . E-3	Portales . . . E-7	Santa Rosa . . . D-5	Truth or Consequences . . F-3
Anthony . . . H-3	Carlsbad . . . G-6	Dexter . . . F-6	Hobbs . . . G-7	Melrose . . . E-7	Questa . . . B-4	Santo Domingo Pueblo . . C-4	Tucumcari . . . D-7
Artesia . . . G-6	Carrizozo . . . F-4	Dulce . . . A-3	Hurley . . . G-2	Mescalero . . . F-4	Radium Springs . . . G-3	Shiprock . . . B-1	Tularosa . . . G-4
Aztec . . . B-2	Cedar Crest . . . D-4	Edgewood . . . D-4	Jal . . . H-7	Mesquite . . . H-3	Ranchos de Taos . . . B-4	Silver City . . . G-2	University Park . . . H-3
Bayard . . . G-2	Chama . . . A-3	Espanola . . . C-4	La Luz . . . G-4	Milan . . . D-2	Raton . . . A-6	Socorro . . . E-3	Vaughn . . . D-5
Belen . . . D-3	Chimayo . . . C-4	Estancia . . . D-4	Las Cruces . . . G-3	Mora . . . C-5	Reserve . . . F-1	Springer . . . B-6	Zuni Pueblo . . . D-1
	Cimarron . . . B-5	Eunice . . . G-7	Las Vegas . . . C-5	Moriarty . . . D-4	Rio Rancho . . . D-3	Sunland Park . . . H-3	
	Clayton . . . B-7	Farmington . . . B-2	Logan . . . C-7	Mosquero . . . C-6	Roswell . . . F-6	Taos . . . B-5	
	Cloudcroft . . . G-4	Fort Sumner . . . E-6	Lordsburg . . . G-1	Mountainair . . . E-4	Ruidoso . . . F-4	Tatum . . . F-7	
	Clovis . . . E-7	Gallup . . . C-1	Los Alamos . . . C-4	Organ . . . G-3	San Rafael . . . D-2	Texico . . . E-7	

Travel planning & on-the-road resources

Tourism Information
New Mexico Tourism Department
(505) 827-7400
www.newmexico.org

Road Conditions & Construction
511
(800) 432-4269, (505) 827-5100
www.nmroads.com, www.dot.state.nm.us

New York state facts

Nickname: The Empire State
Capital: Albany, F-11

Population: 19,378,102 (rank: 3rd)
Largest city: New York, 8,175,133, J-1

Land area: 47,126 sq. mi. (rank: 30th)
Highest point: Mount Marcy, 5,344 ft., C-11

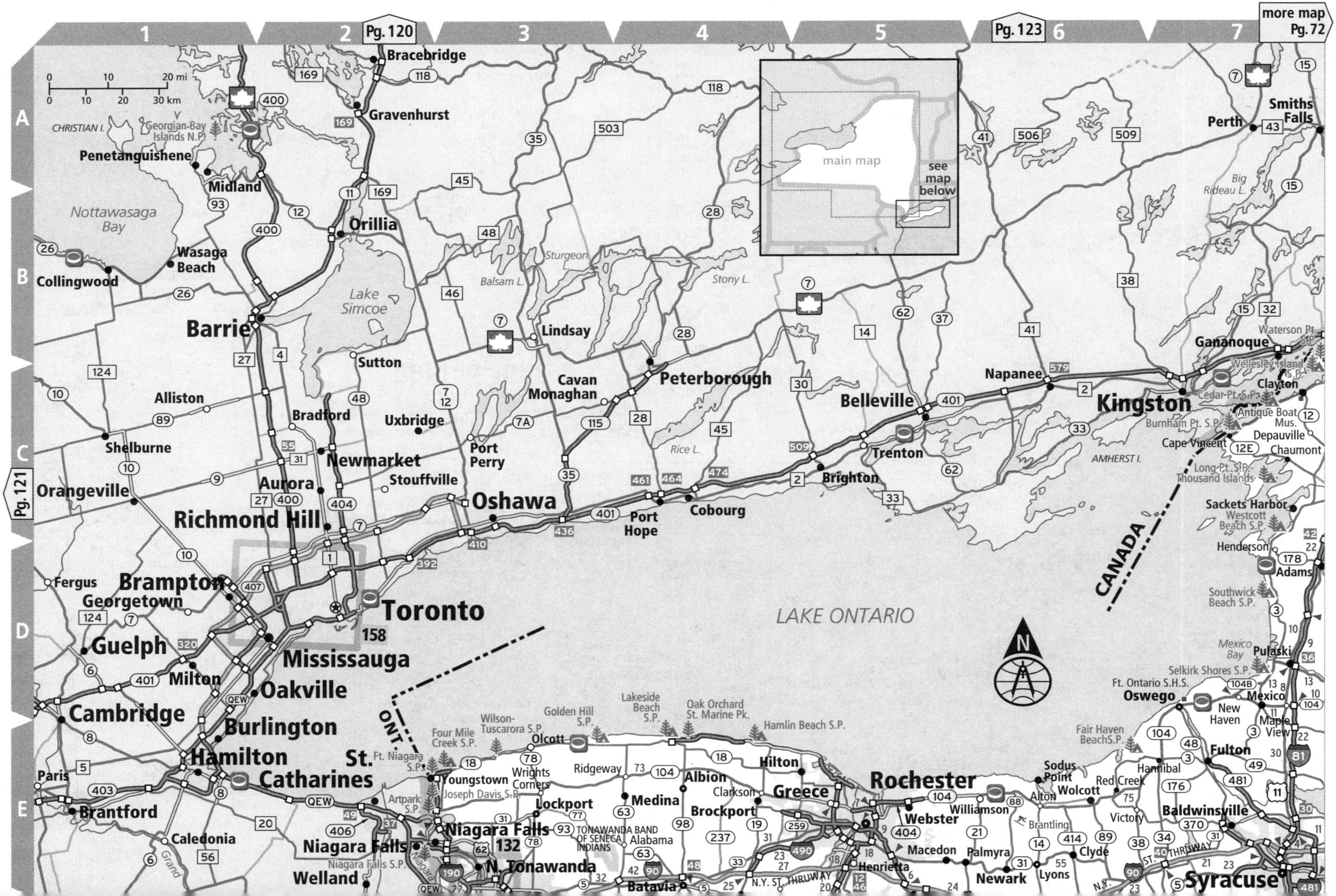

more map Pg. 72
Pg. 120
Pg. 123
Pg. 121

Travel planning & on-the-road resources
Tourism Information
New York State Division of Tourism
(800) 225-5697
www.iloveny.com
Road Conditions & Construction
511, (888) 465-1169
www.511ny.org, www.dot.ny.gov
Thruway: (800) 847-8929, www.thruway.ny.gov
more map Pg. 73
Pg. 90
Pg. 121
Pg. 88
Pg. 66
For continuation see map on pg. 73
© Rand McNally
ATLANTIC OCEAN
Long Island Sound
LAKE ERIE
ONTARIO
CANADA
PENNSYLVANIA
0 10 20 mi
0 10 20 30 km
Buffalo
Erie
Jamestown
Olean
Salamanca
Hornell
Corning
Elmira
Ithaca
Cortland
Auburn
Geneva
Canandaigua
Bath
Dunkirk
Fredonia
Bradford
Sayre
Williamsport
New York
Yonkers
Newark
Stamford
Bridgeport
Central Islip
Riverhead
Montauk
Southampton
FIRE ISLAND NAT'L SEASHORE
ALLEGHENY NAT'L REC. AREA

New York state facts

Nickname: The Empire State	**Population:** 19,378,102 (rank: 3rd)	**Land area:** 47,126 sq. mi. (rank: 30th)
Capital: Albany, F-11	**Largest city:** New York, 8,175,133, J-1	**Highest point:** Mount Marcy, 5,344 ft.,C-11

more map Pg. 70
Pg. 123
Pg. 124
Pg. 64

New York

Cities and Towns

Adams . . . D-7
Adams Center . . . D-8
Addison . . . G-5
Albany . . . F-11
Albion . . . E-4
Alexandria Bay . . . B-8
Alfred . . . G-5
Amagansett . . . I-5
Amenia . . . H-12
Amherst . . . E-3
Amsterdam . . . F-11
Andover . . . G-5
Arcade . . . F-3
Arkport . . . G-5
Armonk . . . J-11
Attica . . . F-4
Auburn . . . F-7
Avon . . . F-5
Bainbridge . . . G-8
Baldwinsville . . . E-7
Ballston Spa . . . E-11
Batavia . . . E-4
Bath . . . G-5
Bay Shore . . . J-3
Beacon . . . I-11
Belfast . . . G-4
Bellmore . . . J-2
Belmont . . . G-4
Binghamton . . . G-8
Bolivar . . . H-4
Bolton Landing . . . D-11
Boonville . . . D-9
Brewster . . . I-12
Brockport . . . E-4
Brocton . . . G-2
Buffalo . . . F-3
Cadyville . . . B-11
Cairo . . . G-11
Cambridge . . . E-12
Camden . . . E-8
Canajoharie . . . F-10
Canandaigua . . . F-5
Canastota . . . E-8
Candor . . . G-7
Canisteo . . . G-5
Canton . . . B-9
Carthage . . . C-8
Catskill . . . G-11
Cayuta . . . G-6
Cazenovia . . . F-8
Centerport . . . I-2
Central Islip . . . I-3
Champlain . . . A-12
Chestertown . . . D-11
Claverack . . . G-11
Clayton . . . C-7
Clinton . . . E-9
Clyde . . . E-6
Cobleskill . . . F-10
Cohocton . . . G-5
Cohoes . . . F-11
Congers . . . H-1
Cooperstown . . . F-9
Corinth . . . E-11
Corning . . . G-6
Cornwall-on-Hudson . . . I-11
Cortland . . . F-7
Croton Falls . . . I-12
Croton-on-Hudson . . . I-11
Crown Point . . . C-12
Le Roy . . . E-4
Liberty . . . H-10
Little Falls . . . E-9
Little Valley . . . G-3
Livingston Manor . . . H-9
Livonia . . . F-5
Loch Sheldrake . . . H-10
Lockport . . . E-3
Long Beach . . . J-2
Lowville . . . D-8
Lyons . . . E-6
Macedon . . . E-5
Mahopac . . . I-11
Malone . . . A-10
Mamaroneck . . . J-11
Manchester . . . F-5
Massena . . . A-9
Mattituck . . . I-4
Mayville . . . G-2
McGraw . . . F-7
Mechanicville . . . F-11
Medina . . . E-4
Mexico . . . D-7
Middleburgh . . . F-10
Middletown . . . I-10
Millbrook . . . H-11
Millerton . . . H-12
Monroe . . . I-11
Montauk . . . I-5
Monticello . . . H-10
Montour Falls . . . G-6
Moravia . . . F-7
Mount Kisco . . . I-11
Mount Morris . . . F-4
Naples . . . F-5
New Berlin . . . F-9
New Hartford . . . E-9
New Lebanon . . . G-12
New Paltz . . . H-11
New Rochelle . . . J-11
New Windsor . . . I-11
New York . . . J-1
New York Mills . . . E-9
Newark . . . E-6
Newburgh . . . I-11
Niagara Falls . . . E-3
North Tonawanda . . . E-3
Northville . . . E-11
Norwich . . . F-8
Norwood . . . A-9
Nunda . . . F-4
Oakdale . . . I-3
Oceanside . . . J-2
Ogdensburg . . . B-8
Olcott . . . E-3
Old Forge . . . D-9
Olean . . . H-3
Oneida . . . E-8
Oneonta . . . G-9
Orchard Park . . . F-3
Ossining . . . J-11
Oswego . . . D-7
Owego . . . G-7
Oxford . . . G-8
Oyster Bay . . . I-2
Painted Post . . . G-6
Palmyra . . . E-5
Pawling . . . I-12
Peekskill . . . I-11
Penn Yan . . . F-6
Perry . . . F-4
Plattsburgh . . . B-12
Port Henry . . . C-12
Port Jefferson . . . I-3

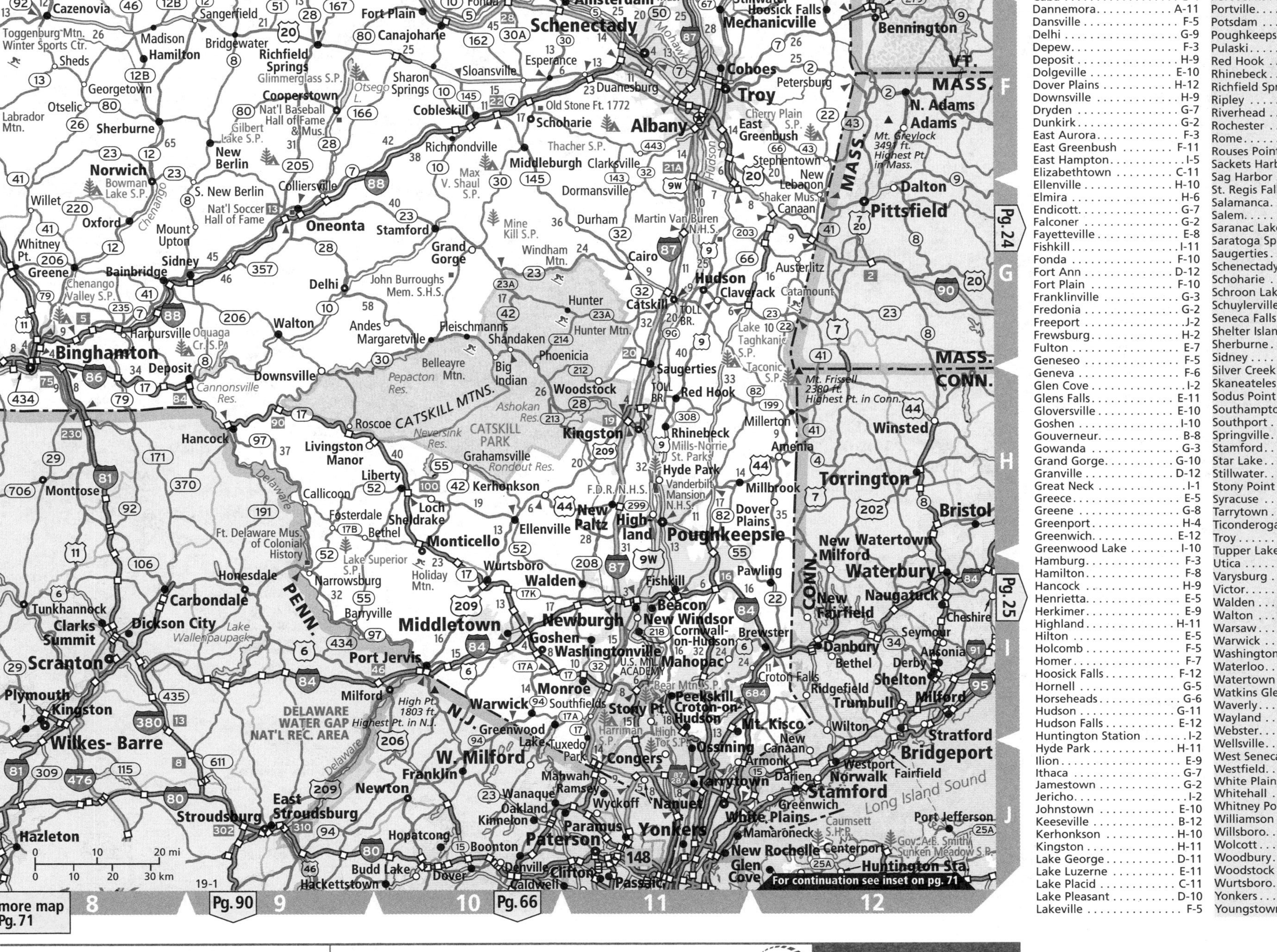

Cuba . . . G-4
Dannemora . . . A-11
Dansville . . . F-5
Delhi . . . G-9
Depew . . . F-3
Deposit . . . H-9
Dolgeville . . . E-10
Dover Plains . . . H-12
Downsville . . . H-9
Dryden . . . G-7
Dunkirk . . . G-2
East Aurora . . . F-3
East Greenbush . . . F-11
East Hampton . . . I-5
Elizabethtown . . . C-11
Ellenville . . . H-10
Elmira . . . H-6
Endicott . . . G-7
Falconer . . . G-2
Fayetteville . . . E-8
Fishkill . . . I-11
Fonda . . . F-10
Fort Ann . . . D-12
Fort Plain . . . F-10
Franklinville . . . G-3
Fredonia . . . G-2
Freeport . . . J-2
Frewsburg . . . H-2
Fulton . . . E-7
Geneseo . . . F-5
Geneva . . . F-6
Glen Cove . . . I-2
Glens Falls . . . E-11
Gloversville . . . E-10
Goshen . . . I-10
Gouverneur . . . B-8
Gowanda . . . G-3
Grand Gorge . . . G-10
Granville . . . D-12
Great Neck . . . I-1
Greece . . . E-5
Greene . . . G-8
Greenport . . . H-4
Greenwich . . . E-12
Greenwood Lake . . . I-10
Hamburg . . . F-3
Hamilton . . . F-8
Hancock . . . H-9
Henrietta . . . E-5
Herkimer . . . E-9
Highland . . . H-11
Hilton . . . E-5
Holcomb . . . F-5
Homer . . . F-7
Hoosick Falls . . . F-12
Hornell . . . G-5
Horseheads . . . G-6
Hudson . . . G-11
Hudson Falls . . . E-12
Huntington Station . . . I-2
Hyde Park . . . H-11
Ilion . . . E-9
Ithaca . . . G-7
Jamestown . . . G-2
Jericho . . . I-2
Johnstown . . . E-10
Keeseville . . . B-12
Kerhonkson . . . H-10
Kingston . . . H-11
Lake George . . . D-11
Lake Luzerne . . . E-11
Lake Placid . . . C-11
Lake Pleasant . . . D-10
Lakeville . . . F-5
Port Jervis . . . I-10
Portville . . . H-4
Potsdam . . . B-9
Poughkeepsie . . . H-11
Pulaski . . . D-7
Red Hook . . . H-11
Rhinebeck . . . H-11
Richfield Springs . . . F-9
Ripley . . . G-1
Riverhead . . . I-4
Rochester . . . E-5
Rome . . . E-8
Rouses Point . . . A-12
Sackets Harbor . . . C-7
Sag Harbor . . . I-5
St. Regis Falls . . . B-10
Salamanca . . . G-3
Salem . . . E-12
Saranac Lake . . . B-11
Saratoga Springs . . . E-11
Saugerties . . . G-11
Schenectady . . . F-11
Schoharie . . . F-10
Schroon Lake . . . C-11
Schuylerville . . . E-12
Seneca Falls . . . F-6
Shelter Island . . . I-4
Sherburne . . . F-8
Sidney . . . G-9
Silver Creek . . . F-2
Skaneateles . . . F-7
Sodus Point . . . E-6
Southampton . . . I-4
Southport . . . H-6
Springville . . . G-3
Stamford . . . G-10
Star Lake . . . C-9
Stillwater . . . F-11
Stony Point . . . I-11
Syracuse . . . E-7
Tarrytown . . . J-11
Ticonderoga . . . C-12
Troy . . . F-11
Tupper Lake . . . C-10
Utica . . . E-9
Varysburg . . . F-4
Victor . . . E-5
Walden . . . I-11
Walton . . . G-9
Warsaw . . . F-4
Warwick . . . I-10
Washingtonville . . . I-11
Waterloo . . . F-6
Watertown . . . C-8
Watkins Glen . . . G-6
Waverly . . . H-7
Wayland . . . F-5
Webster . . . E-5
Wellsville . . . G-4
West Seneca . . . F-3
Westfield . . . G-2
White Plains . . . J-11
Whitehall . . . D-12
Whitney Point . . . G-8
Williamson . . . E-6
Willsboro . . . B-12
Wolcott . . . E-6
Woodbury . . . I-2
Woodstock . . . H-11
Wurtsboro . . . I-10
Yonkers . . . J-11
Youngstown . . . E-2

Tourism Information N.Y. State Division of Tourism (800) 225-5697 www.iloveny.com

Road Conditions & Construction 511, (888) 465-1169 www.511ny.org, www.dot.ny.gov Thruway: (800) 847-8929, www.thruway.ny.gov

511

Travel planning & on-the-road resources

North Carolina state facts

Nickname: The Tar Heel State
Capital: Raleigh, C-8

Population: 9,535,483 (rank: 10th)
Largest city: Charlotte, 731,424, D-5

Land area: 48,618 sq. mi. (rank: 29th)
Highest point: Mount Mitchell, 6,684 ft., C-3

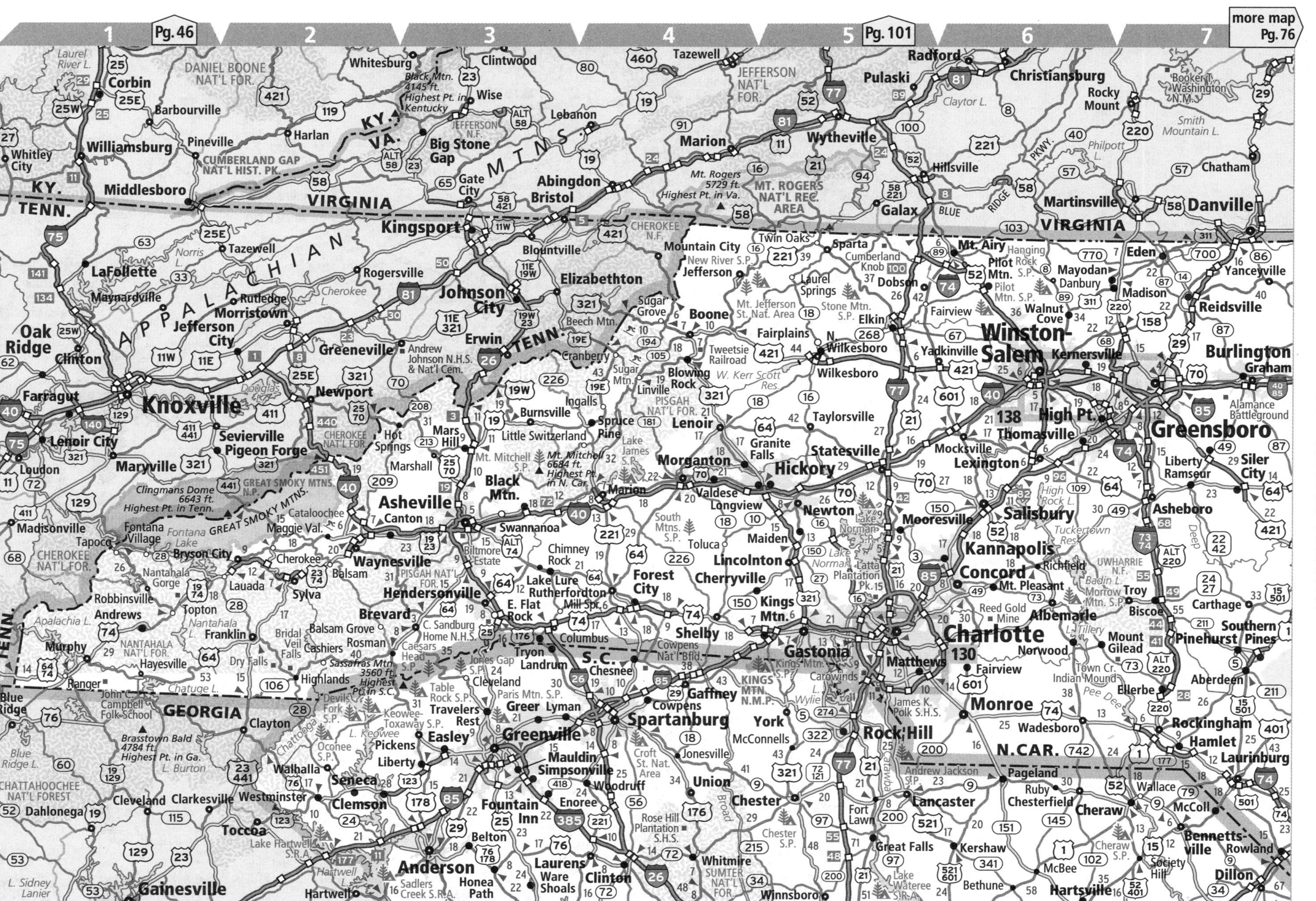

Travel planning & on-the-road resources

Tourism Information
Visit North Carolina
(800) 847-4862
www.visitnc.com

Road Conditions & Construction
511, (877) 511-4662
www.ncdot.gov/travel/511
www.ncdot.gov

South Carolina state facts

Nickname: The Palmetto State
Capital: Columbia, F-5
Population: 4,625,364 (rank: 24th)
Largest city: Columbia, 129,272, F-5
Land area: 30,061 sq. mi. (rank: 40th)
Highest point: Sassafras Mtn., 3,560 ft., D-3

more map Pg. 74
Pg. 103

North Carolina

Cities and Towns

Aberdeen . . . D-7
Ahoskie . . . B-11
Albemarle . . . D-6
Apex . . . C-8
Asheboro . . . C-7
Asheville . . . C-3
Bayboro . . . D-11
Beaufort . . . E-11
Benson . . . D-8
Black Mountain . . . C-3
Bolivia . . . F-9
Boone . . . B-4
Brevard . . . D-3
Bryson City . . . D-2
Burgaw . . . E-9
Burlington . . . C-7
Burnsville . . . C-3
Canton . . . C-2
Carolina Beach . . . F-9
Carthage . . . D-7
Cary . . . C-8
Chapel Hill . . . C-8
Charlotte . . . D-5
Cherokee . . . D-2
Cherryville . . . D-5
Clayton . . . C-9
Clinton . . . D-9
Columbia . . . C-12
Columbus . . . D-3
Concord . . . D-6
Currituck . . . B-12
Danbury . . . B-6
Dobson . . . B-5
Dunn . . . D-8
Durham . . . C-8
East Flat Rock . . . D-3
Eden . . . B-7
Edenton . . . C-11
Elizabeth City . . . B-12
Elizabethtown . . . E-8
Elkin . . . B-5
Enfield . . . B-10
Erwin . . . D-8
Fairview . . . D-6
Farmville . . . C-10
Fayetteville . . . D-8
Forest City . . . D-4
Franklin . . . D-2
Fuquay-Varina . . . C-8
Garner . . . C-8
Gastonia . . . D-5
Goldsboro . . . D-9
Graham . . . C-7
Granite Falls . . . C-4
Greensboro . . . C-7
Greenville . . . C-10
Hamlet . . . E-7
Harbinger . . . B-12
Havelock . . . E-11
Hayesville . . . D-1
Henderson . . . B-9
Hendersonville . . . D-3
Hertford . . . B-11
Hickory . . . C-5
High Point . . . C-6
Hillsborough . . . C-8
Hope Mills . . . D-8
Jackson . . . B-10
Jacksonville . . . E-10
Jefferson . . . B-4
Wallace . . . E-9
Warrenton . . . B-9
Warsaw . . . D-9
Washington . . . C-11
Waynesville . . . D-2
Whiteville . . . F-8
Wilkesboro . . . B-5
Williamston . . . C-11
Wilmington . . . F-9
Wilson . . . C-9
Windsor . . . C-11
Winston-Salem . . . C-6
Winterville . . . C-10
Winton . . . B-11
Wrightsville Beach . . . F-10
Yadkinville . . . B-6
Yanceyville . . . B-7
Zebulon . . . C-9

South Carolina

Cities and Towns

Abbeville . . . F-3
Aiken . . . G-4
Allendale . . . H-5
Anderson . . . E-3
Andrews . . . G-7
Awendaw . . . H-7
Bamberg . . . G-5
Barnwell . . . G-4
Batesburg-Leesville . . . F-4
Beaufort . . . I-5
Beech Island . . . G-4
Belton . . . E-3
Bennettsville . . . E-7
Bishopville . . . F-6
Blackville . . . G-5
Branchville . . . G-5
Calhoun Falls . . . F-3
Camden . . . F-6
Centerville . . . H-6
Charleston . . . H-7
Cheraw . . . E-7
Chesnee . . . D-4
Chester . . . E-5
Chesterfield . . . E-6
Clemson . . . E-2
Clinton . . . E-4
Columbia . . . F-5
Conway . . . F-8
Cowpens . . . D-4
Darlington . . . F-7
Denmark . . . G-5
Dillon . . . E-7
Easley . . . E-3
Eastover . . . F-5
Edgefield . . . F-4
Elgin . . . F-5
Enoree . . . E-4
Estill . . . H-5
Fairfax . . . H-5
Florence . . . F-7
Folly Beach . . . H-7
Fort Lawn . . . E-5
Fountain Inn . . . E-3
Gaffney . . . D-4
Garden City Beach . . . G-8
Georgetown . . . G-7
Goose Creek . . . H-6
Great Falls . . . E-5
Greenville . . . E-3
Greenwood . . . F-3
Greer . . . D-3
Hampton . . . H-5

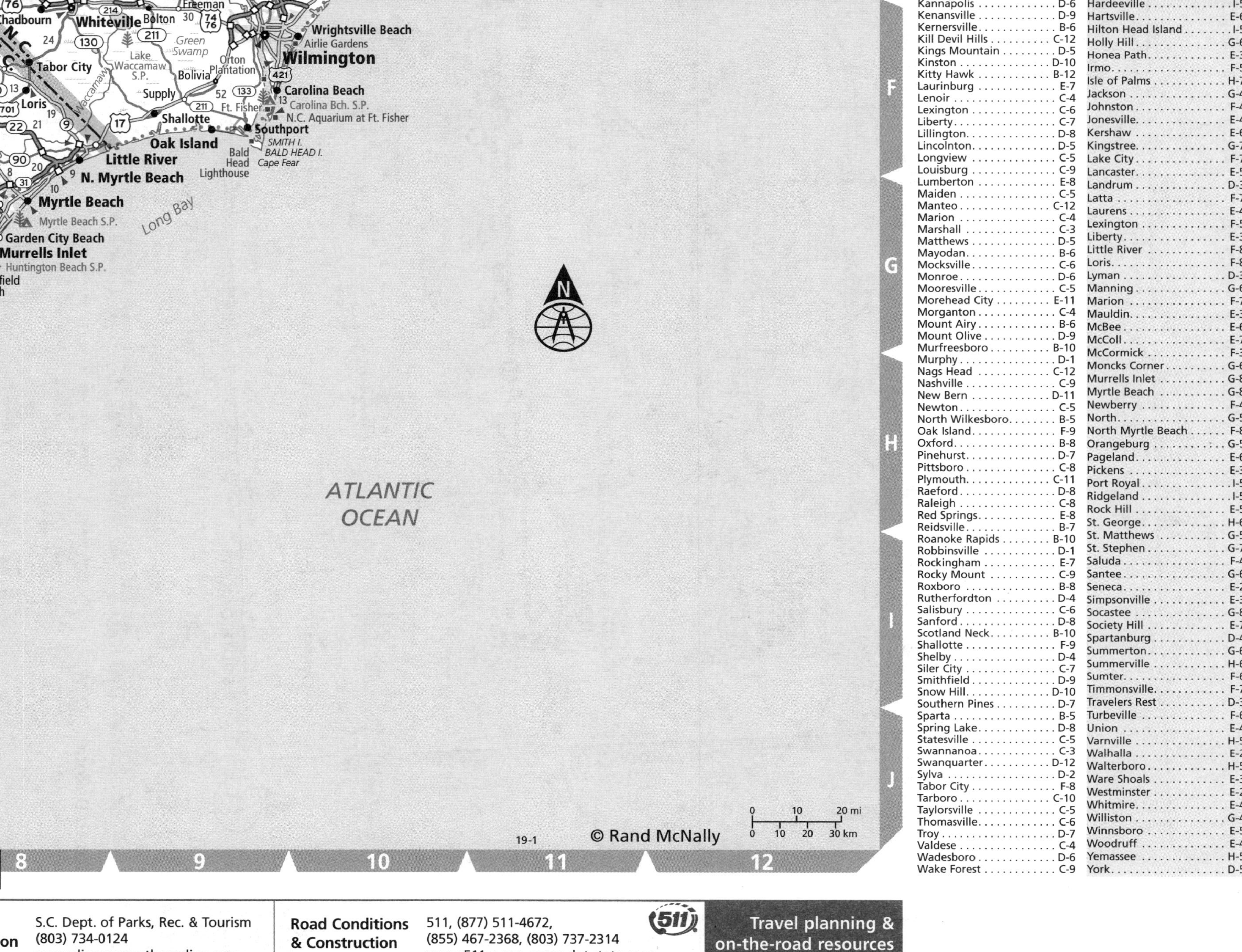

more map Pg. 75

Kannapolis D-6
Kenansville D-9
Kernersville B-6
Kill Devil Hills C-12
Kings Mountain D-5
Kinston D-10
Kitty Hawk B-12
Laurinburg E-7
Lenoir C-4
Lexington C-6
Liberty C-7
Lillington D-8
Lincolnton D-5
Longview C-5
Louisburg C-9
Lumberton E-8
Maiden C-5
Manteo C-12
Marion C-4
Marshall C-3
Matthews D-5
Mayodan B-6
Mocksville C-6
Monroe D-6
Mooresville C-5
Morehead City E-11
Morganton C-4
Mount Airy B-6
Mount Olive D-9
Murfreesboro B-10
Murphy D-1
Nags Head C-12
Nashville C-9
New Bern D-11
Newton C-5
North Wilkesboro B-5
Oak Island F-9
Oxford B-8
Pinehurst D-7
Pittsboro C-8
Plymouth C-11
Raeford D-8
Raleigh C-8
Red Springs E-8
Reidsville B-7
Roanoke Rapids B-10
Robbinsville D-1
Rockingham E-7
Rocky Mount C-9
Roxboro B-8
Rutherfordton D-4
Salisbury C-6
Sanford D-8
Scotland Neck B-10
Shallotte F-9
Shelby D-4
Siler City C-7
Smithfield D-9
Snow Hill D-10
Southern Pines D-7
Sparta B-5
Spring Lake D-8
Statesville C-5
Swannanoa C-3
Swanquarter D-12
Sylva D-2
Tabor City F-8
Tarboro C-10
Taylorsville C-5
Thomasville C-6
Troy D-7
Valdese C-4
Wadesboro D-6
Wake Forest C-9

Hardeeville I-5
Hartsville E-6
Hilton Head Island I-5
Holly Hill G-6
Honea Path E-3
Irmo F-5
Isle of Palms H-7
Jackson G-4
Johnston F-4
Jonesville E-4
Kershaw E-6
Kingstree G-7
Lake City F-7
Lancaster E-5
Landrum D-3
Latta F-7
Laurens E-4
Lexington F-5
Liberty E-3
Little River F-8
Loris F-8
Lyman D-3
Manning G-6
Marion F-7
Mauldin E-3
McBee E-6
McColl E-7
McCormick F-3
Moncks Corner G-6
Murrells Inlet G-8
Myrtle Beach G-8
Newberry F-4
North G-5
North Myrtle Beach F-8
Orangeburg G-5
Pageland E-6
Pickens E-3
Port Royal I-5
Ridgeland I-5
Rock Hill E-5
St. George H-6
St. Matthews G-5
St. Stephen G-7
Saluda F-4
Santee G-6
Seneca E-2
Simpsonville E-3
Socastee G-8
Society Hill E-7
Spartanburg D-4
Summerton G-6
Summerville H-6
Sumter F-6
Timmonsville F-7
Travelers Rest D-3
Turbeville F-6
Union E-4
Varnville H-5
Walhalla E-2
Walterboro H-5
Ware Shoals E-3
Westminster E-2
Whitmire E-4
Williston G-4
Winnsboro E-5
Woodruff E-4
Yemassee H-5
York D-5

Tourism Information S.C. Dept. of Parks, Rec. & Tourism
(803) 734-0124
www.discoversouthcarolina.com

Road Conditions & Construction 511, (877) 511-4672,
(855) 467-2368, (803) 737-2314
www.511sc.org, www.dot.state.sc.us

511

Travel planning & on-the-road resources

Land area: 69,000 sq. mi. (rank: 17th)
Highest point: White Butte, 3,506 ft., E-2

Population: 672,591 (rank: 48th)
Largest city: Fargo, 105,549, D-10

Nickname: The Peace Garden State
Capital: Bismarck, E-5

North Dakota state facts

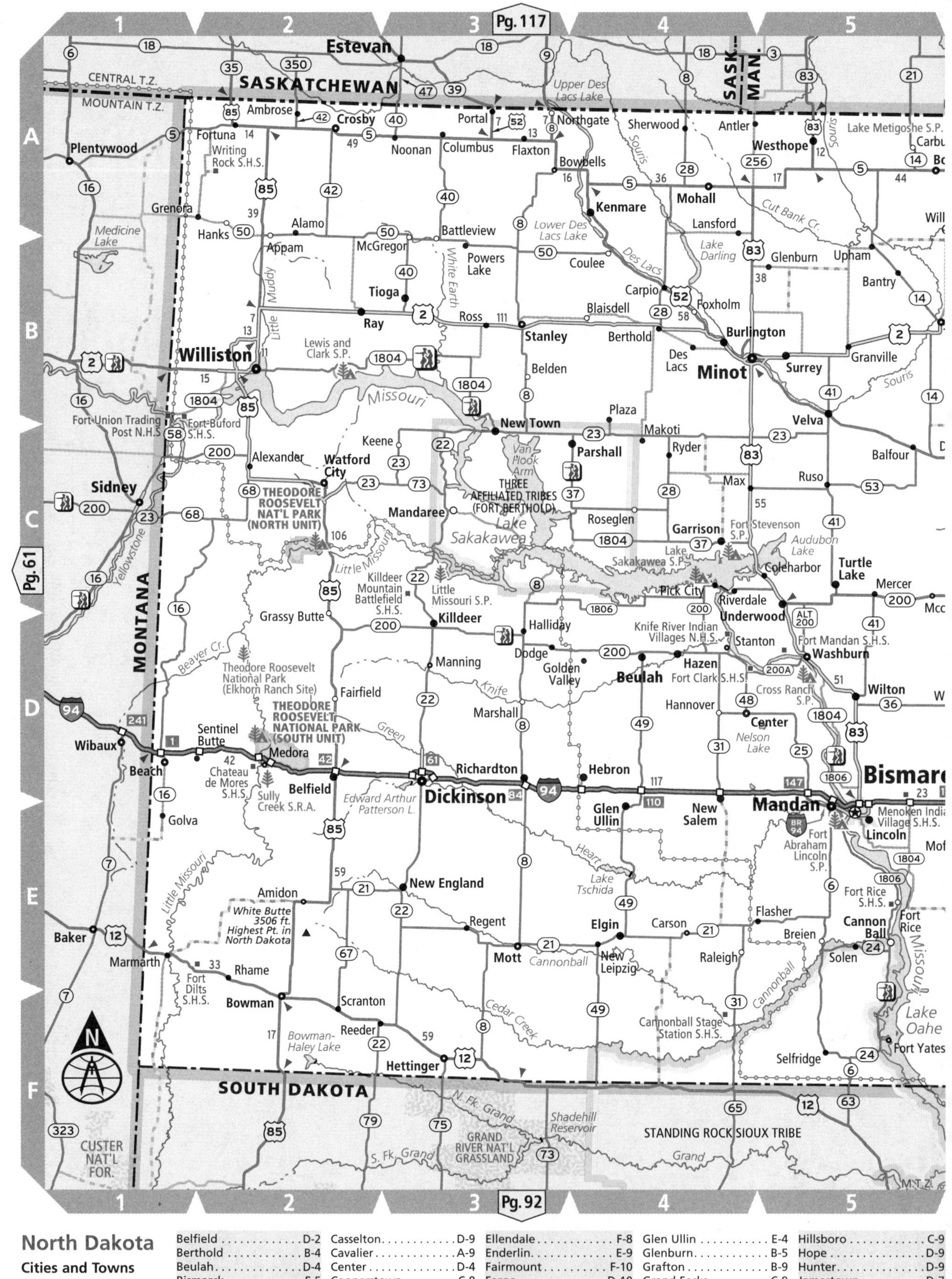

North Dakota

Cities and Towns

- Abercrombie . . . E-10
- Amidon . . . E-2
- Anamoose . . . C-6
- Aneta . . . C-8
- Arthur . . . D-9
- Ashley . . . F-7
- Beach . . . D-1
- Belcourt . . . A-6
- Belfield . . . D-2
- Berthold . . . B-4
- Beulah . . . D-4
- Bismarck . . . E-5
- Bottineau . . . A-5
- Bowbells . . . A-3
- Bowman . . . F-2
- Burlington . . . B-4
- Cando . . . B-7
- Cannon Ball . . . E-5
- Carrington . . . C-7
- Carson . . . E-4
- Casselton . . . D-9
- Cavalier . . . A-9
- Center . . . D-4
- Cooperstown . . . C-8
- Crosby . . . A-2
- Devils Lake . . . B-7
- Dickinson . . . D-3
- Drake . . . C-6
- Drayton . . . B-9
- Dunseith . . . A-6
- Edgeley . . . E-7
- Elgin . . . E-4
- Ellendale . . . F-8
- Enderlin . . . E-9
- Fairmount . . . F-10
- Fargo . . . D-10
- Fessenden . . . C-6
- Finley . . . C-8
- Flasher . . . E-5
- Forman . . . F-9
- Fort Totten . . . C-7
- Fort Yates . . . F-5
- Gackle . . . E-7
- Garrison . . . C-4
- Glen Ullin . . . E-4
- Glenburn . . . B-5
- Grafton . . . B-9
- Grand Forks . . . C-9
- Granville . . . B-5
- Gwinner . . . F-9
- Hankinson . . . F-10
- Harvey . . . C-6
- Hatton . . . C-9
- Hazen . . . D-4
- Hebron . . . D-4
- Hettinger . . . F-3
- Hillsboro . . . C-9
- Hope . . . D-9
- Hunter . . . D-9
- Jamestown . . . D-7
- Kenmare . . . A-4
- Killdeer . . . D-3
- Kindred . . . E-9
- Kulm . . . E-7
- Lakota . . . B-8
- Lamoure . . . E-8
- Langdon . . . A-8
- Larimore . . . C-9

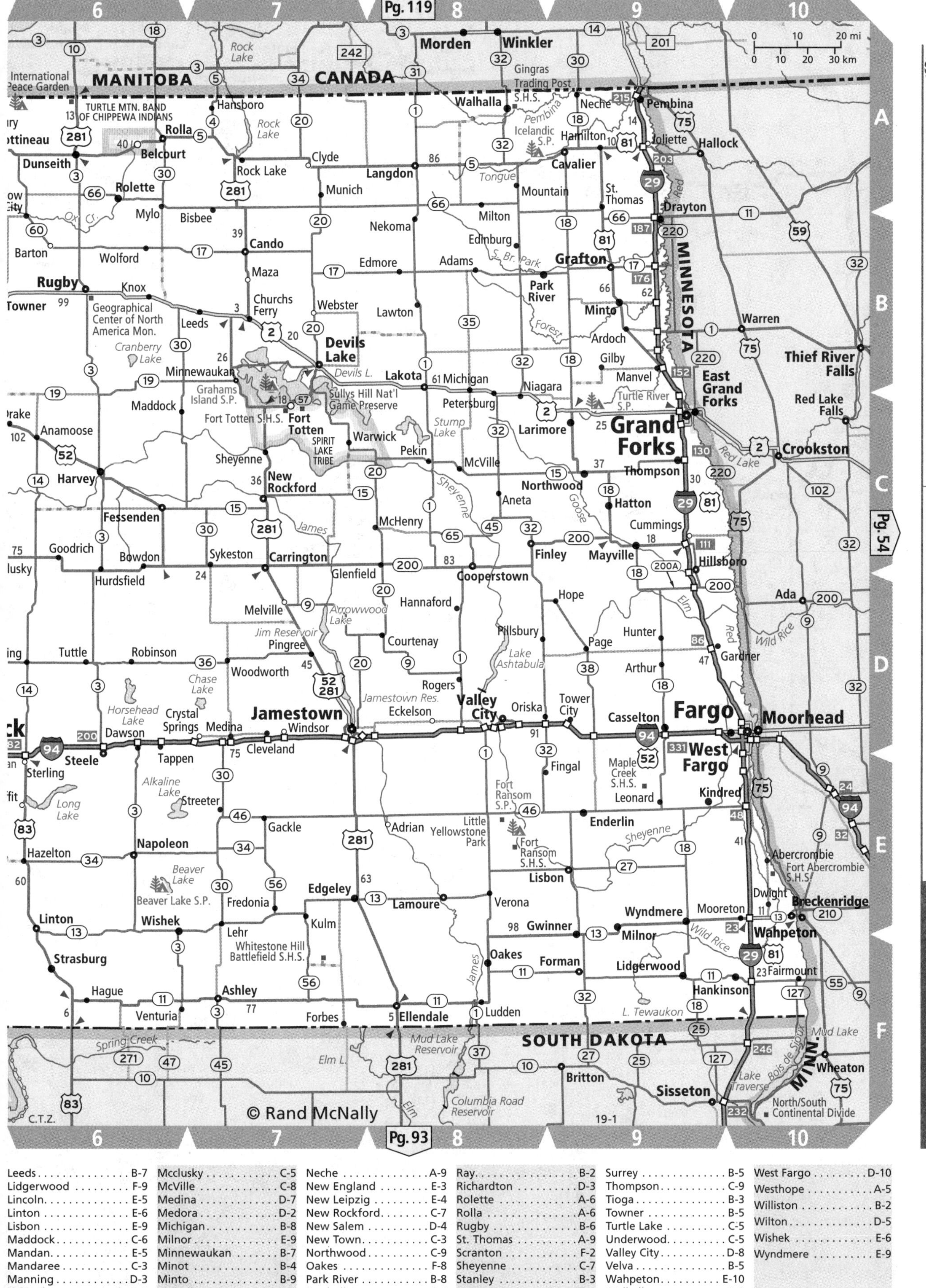

511
Road Conditions & Construction
511, (855) 637-6237
www.dot.nd.gov
www.dot.nd.gov/travel-info-v2

Tourism Information
North Dakota Tourism Division
(800) 435-5663, (701) 328-2525
www.ndtourism.com

Travel planning & on-the-road resources

Leeds B-7
Lidgerwood F-9
Lincoln E-5
Linton E-6
Lisbon E-9
Maddock C-6
Mandan E-5
Mandaree C-3
Manning D-3
Manvel B-9
Max C-4
Mayville C-9
Mcclusky C-5
McVille C-8
Medina D-7
Medora D-2
Michigan B-8
Milnor E-9
Minnewaukan B-7
Minot B-4
Minto B-9
Mohall A-4
Mott E-3
Napoleon E-6
Neche A-9
New England E-3
New Leipzig E-4
New Rockford C-7
New Salem D-4
New Town C-3
Northwood C-9
Oakes F-8
Park River B-8
Parshall C-4
Pembina A-9
Powers Lake B-3
Ray B-2
Richardton D-3
Rolette A-6
Rolla A-6
Rugby B-6
St. Thomas A-9
Scranton F-2
Sheyenne C-7
Stanley B-3
Stanton D-4
Steele D-6
Strasburg F-6
Surrey B-5
Thompson C-9
Tioga B-3
Towner B-5
Turtle Lake C-5
Underwood C-5
Valley City D-8
Velva B-5
Wahpeton E-10
Walhalla A-8
Washburn D-5
Watford City C-2
West Fargo D-10
Westhope A-5
Williston B-2
Wilton D-5
Wishek E-6
Wyndmere E-9

Ohio state facts

Nickname: The Buckeye State
Capital: Columbus, G-5

Population: 11,536,504 (rank: 7th)
Largest city: Columbus, 787,033, G-5

Land area: 40,861 sq. mi. (rank: 35th)
Highest point: Campbell Hill, 1,550 ft., F-3

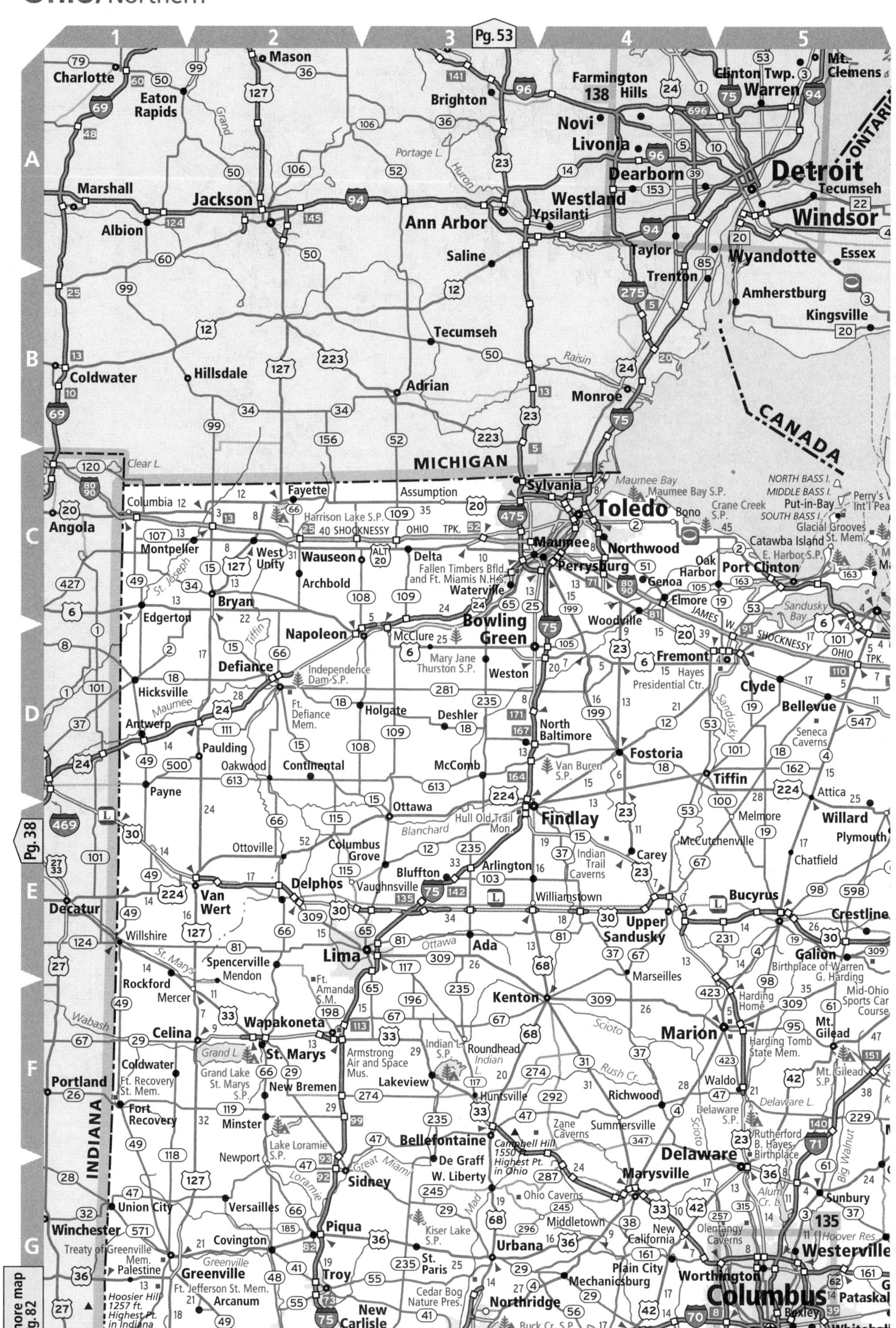

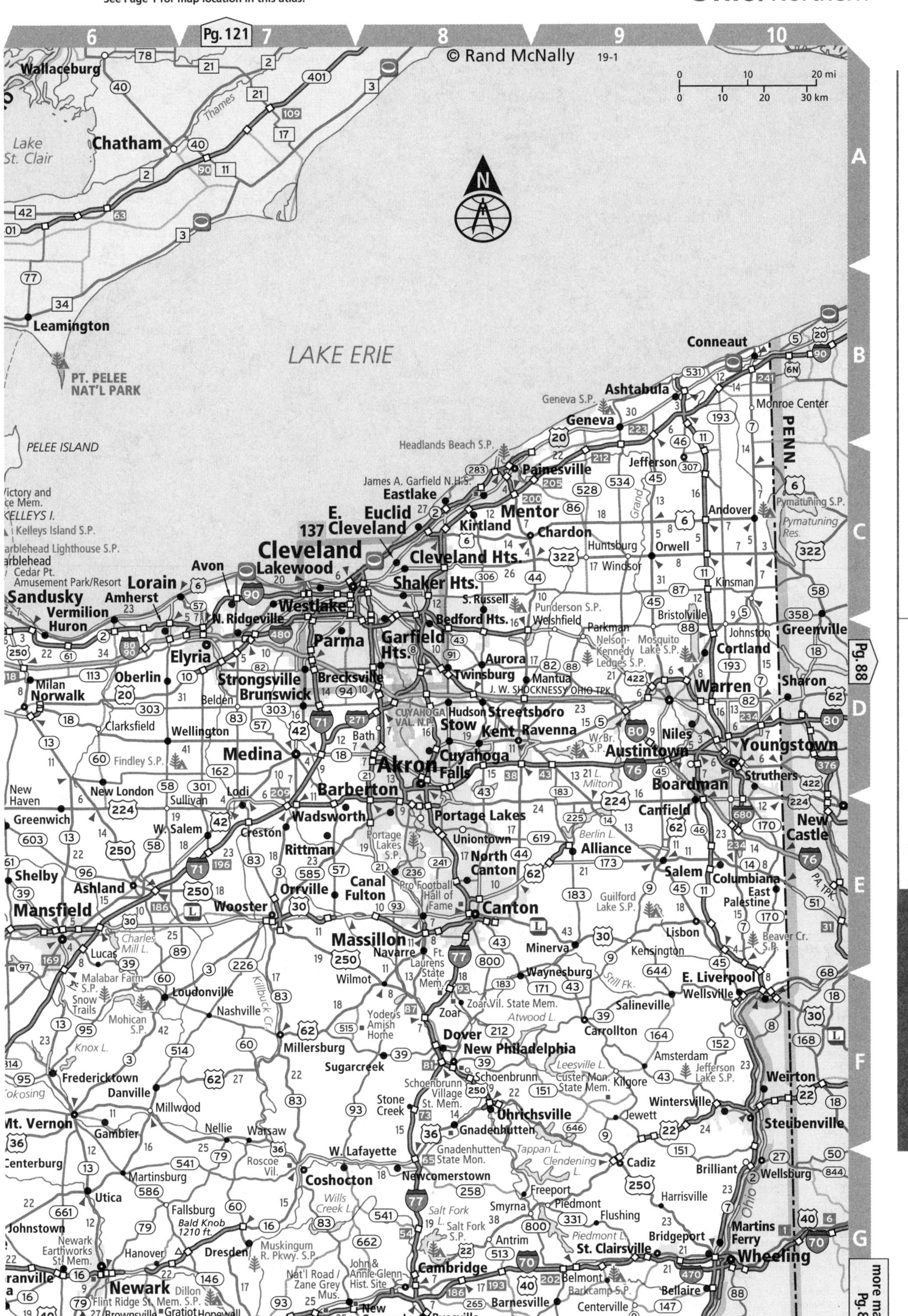

Road Conditions & Construction
(614) 466-7170, www.dot.state.oh.us, www.buckeyetraffic.org
Turnpike: (440) 234-2030, (440) 234-2081
Turnpike: www.ohioturnpike.org

Tourism Information
Tourism Ohio
(800) 282-5393
www.ohio.org

Travel planning & on-the-road resources

Ohio state facts

Nickname: The Buckeye State
Capital: Columbus, G-5
Population: 11,536,504 (rank: 7th)
Largest city: Columbus, 787,033, G-5
Land area: 40,861 sq. mi. (rank: 35th)
Highest point: Campbell Hill, 1,550 ft., F-3

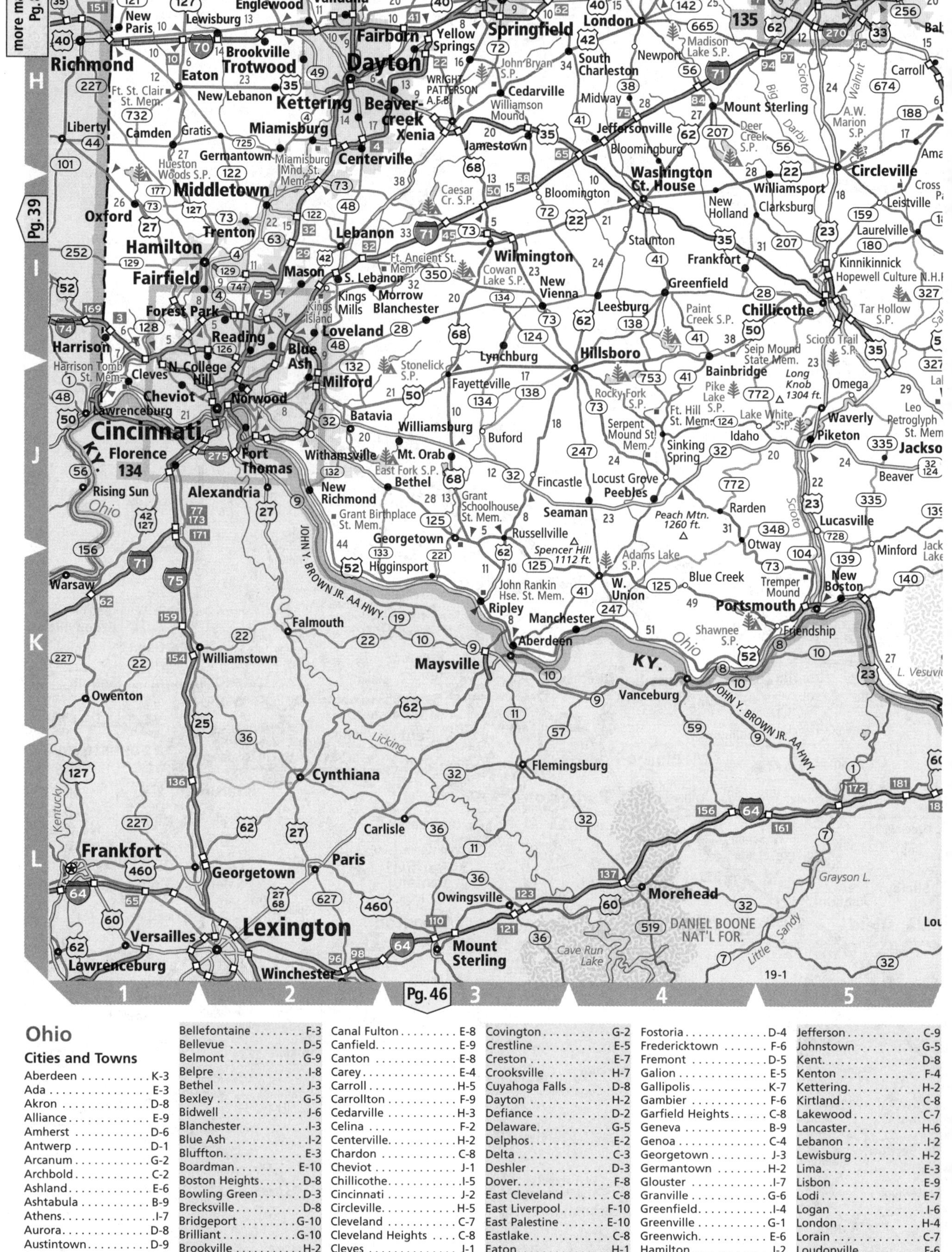

Ohio

Cities and Towns

Aberdeen K-3
Ada E-3
Akron D-8
Alliance E-9
Amherst D-6
Antwerp D-1
Arcanum G-2
Archbold C-2
Ashland E-6
Ashtabula B-9
Athens I-7
Aurora D-8
Austintown D-9
Avon D-7
Baltimore H-6
Barberton E-8
Barnesville G-9
Batavia J-2
Beavercreek H-3
Bedford Heights D-8
Bellaire G-9
Bellefontaine F-3
Bellevue D-5
Belmont G-9
Belpre I-8
Bethel J-3
Bexley G-5
Bidwell J-6
Blanchester I-3
Blue Ash I-2
Bluffton E-3
Boardman E-10
Boston Heights D-8
Bowling Green D-3
Brecksville D-8
Bridgeport G-10
Brilliant G-10
Brookville H-2
Brunswick D-7
Bryan C-2
Bucyrus E-5
Byesville G-8
Cadiz G-9
Caldwell H-8
Cambridge G-8
Camden H-1
Canal Fulton E-8
Canfield E-9
Canton E-8
Carey E-4
Carroll H-5
Carrollton F-9
Cedarville H-3
Celina F-2
Centerville H-2
Chardon C-8
Cheviot J-1
Chillicothe I-5
Cincinnati J-2
Circleville H-5
Cleveland C-7
Cleveland Heights C-8
Cleves J-1
Clyde D-5
Coldwater F-1
Columbiana E-10
Columbus G-5
Columbus Grove E-3
Conneaut B-10
Cortland D-9
Coshocton G-7
Covington G-2
Crestline E-5
Creston E-7
Crooksville H-7
Cuyahoga Falls D-8
Dayton H-2
Defiance D-2
Delaware G-5
Delphos E-2
Delta C-3
Deshler D-3
Dover F-8
East Cleveland C-8
East Liverpool F-10
East Palestine E-10
Eastlake C-8
Eaton H-1
Edgerton C-1
Elyria D-7
Englewood H-2
Euclid C-8
Fairborn H-3
Fairfield I-2
Findlay E-3
Forest Park I-2
Fostoria D-4
Fredericktown F-6
Fremont D-5
Galion E-5
Gallipolis K-7
Gambier F-6
Garfield Heights C-8
Geneva B-9
Genoa C-4
Georgetown J-3
Germantown H-2
Glouster I-7
Granville G-6
Greenfield I-4
Greenville G-1
Greenwich E-6
Hamilton I-2
Harrison I-1
Hicksville D-1
Hillsboro J-4
Hudson D-8
Huron D-6
Ironton K-5
Jackson J-6
Jamestown H-3
Jefferson C-9
Johnstown G-5
Kent D-8
Kenton F-4
Kettering H-2
Kirtland C-8
Lakewood C-7
Lancaster H-6
Lebanon I-2
Lewisburg H-2
Lima E-3
Lisbon E-9
Lodi E-7
Logan I-6
London H-4
Lorain C-7
Loudonville F-6
Loveland I-2
Lucasville J-5
Manchester K-4
Mansfield E-6
Mantua D-8
Marietta I-8
Marion F-5
Martins Ferry G-10

NOTE: Maps are not always in alphabetical order.
See Page 1 for map location in this atlas.

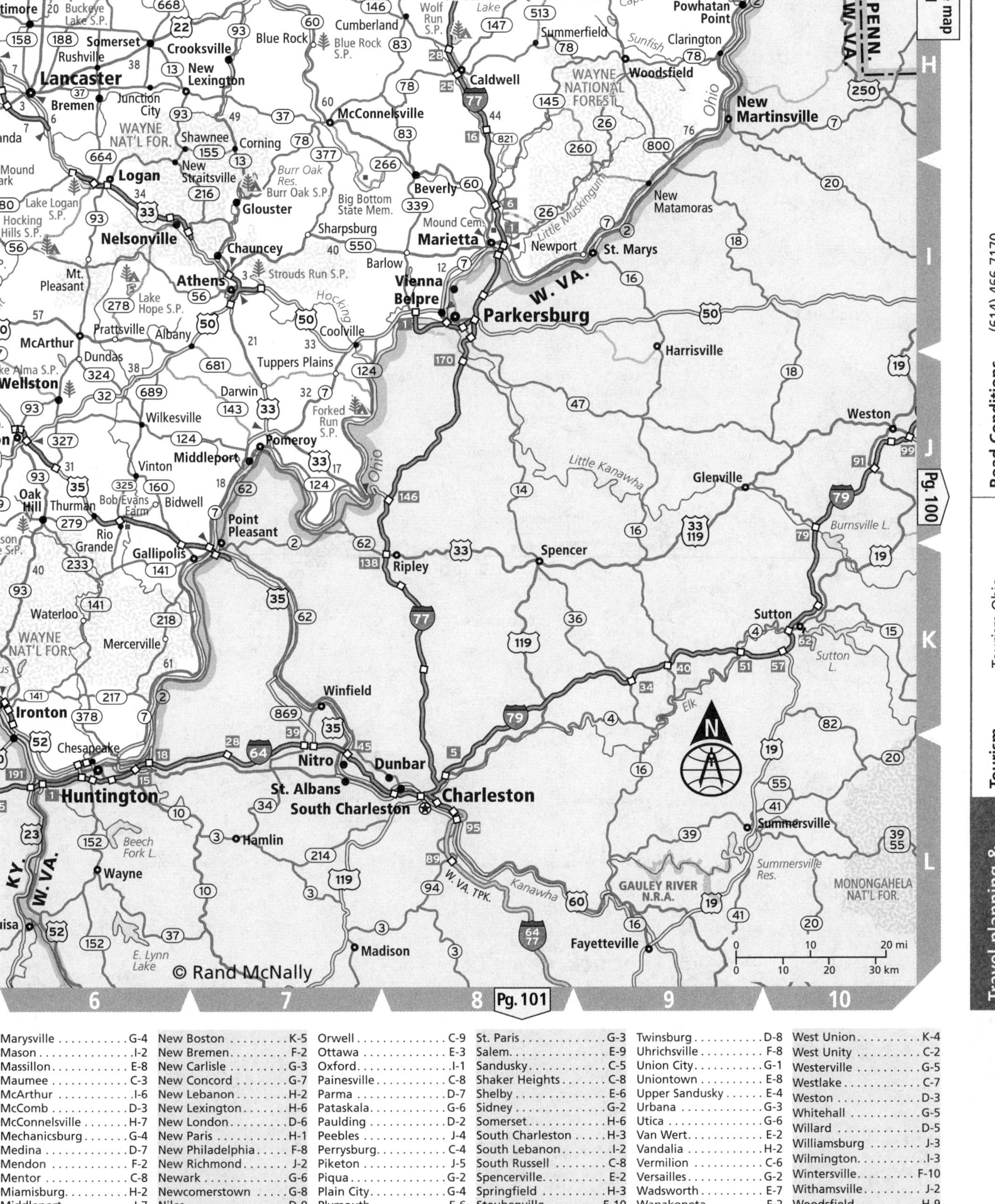

Travel planning & on-the-road resources

Tourism Information
Tourism Ohio
(800) 282-5393
www.ohio.org

Road Conditions & Construction
(614) 466-7170
www.dot.state.oh.us, www.buckeyetraffic.org
Cincinnati metro area: 511

Marysville G-4
Mason I-2
Massillon E-8
Maumee C-3
McArthur I-6
McComb D-3
McConnelsville H-7
Mechanicsburg G-4
Medina D-7
Mendon F-2
Mentor C-8
Miamisburg H-2
Middleport J-7
Middletown I-2
Milford J-2
Millersburg F-7
Minerva E-9
Minster F-2
Montpelier C-2
Mount Gilead F-5
Mount Orab J-3
Mount Sterling H-4
Mount Vernon F-6
Napoleon D-3
Nelsonville I-6
New Boston K-5
New Bremen F-2
New Carlisle G-3
New Concord G-7
New Lebanon H-2
New Lexington H-6
New London D-6
New Paris H-1
New Philadelphia F-8
New Richmond J-2
Newark G-6
Newcomerstown G-8
Niles D-9
North Baltimore D-3
North Canton E-8
North College Hill I-2
North Ridgeville D-7
Northridge G-3
Northwood C-4
Norwalk D-6
Norwood J-2
Oak Harbor C-5
Oak Hill J-6
Oberlin D-6
Orrville E-7
Orwell C-9
Ottawa E-3
Oxford I-1
Painesville C-8
Parma D-7
Pataskala G-6
Paulding D-2
Peebles J-4
Perrysburg C-4
Piketon J-5
Piqua G-2
Plain City G-4
Plymouth E-6
Pomeroy J-7
Port Clinton C-5
Portage Lakes E-8
Portsmouth K-5
Powhatan Point H-9
Ravenna D-8
Reading I-2
Richwood F-4
Ripley K-3
Rittman E-7
St. Clairsville G-9
St. Marys F-2
St. Paris G-3
Salem E-9
Sandusky C-5
Shaker Heights C-8
Shelby E-6
Sidney G-2
Somerset H-6
South Charleston H-3
South Lebanon I-2
South Russell C-8
Spencerville E-2
Springfield H-3
Steubenville F-10
Stow D-8
Streetsboro D-8
Strongsville D-7
Struthers D-10
Sugarcreek F-8
Sunbury G-5
Sylvania C-3
Tiffin D-4
Toledo C-4
Trenton I-2
Trotwood H-2
Troy G-2
Twinsburg D-8
Uhrichsville F-8
Union City G-1
Uniontown E-8
Upper Sandusky E-4
Urbana G-3
Utica G-6
Van Wert E-2
Vandalia H-2
Vermilion C-6
Versailles G-2
Wadsworth E-7
Wapakoneta F-2
Warren D-9
Washington Court House I-4
Waterville C-3
Wauseon C-3
Waverly J-5
Wellington D-6
Wellston J-6
Wellsville F-10
West Lafayette G-7
West Liberty G-3
West Salem E-7
West Union K-4
West Unity C-2
Westerville G-5
Westlake C-7
Weston D-3
Whitehall G-5
Willard D-5
Williamsburg J-3
Wilmington I-3
Wintersville F-10
Withamsville J-2
Woodsfield H-9
Woodville C-4
Wooster E-7
Worthington G-5
Xenia H-3
Yellow Springs H-3
Youngstown D-10
Zanesville H-7

Oklahoma state facts

Nickname: The Sooner State
Capital: Oklahoma City, C-7

Population: 3,751,351 (rank: 28th)
Largest city: Oklahoma City, 579,999, C-7

Land area: 68,595 sq. mi. (rank: 19th)
Highest point: Black Mesa, 4,973 ft., A-1

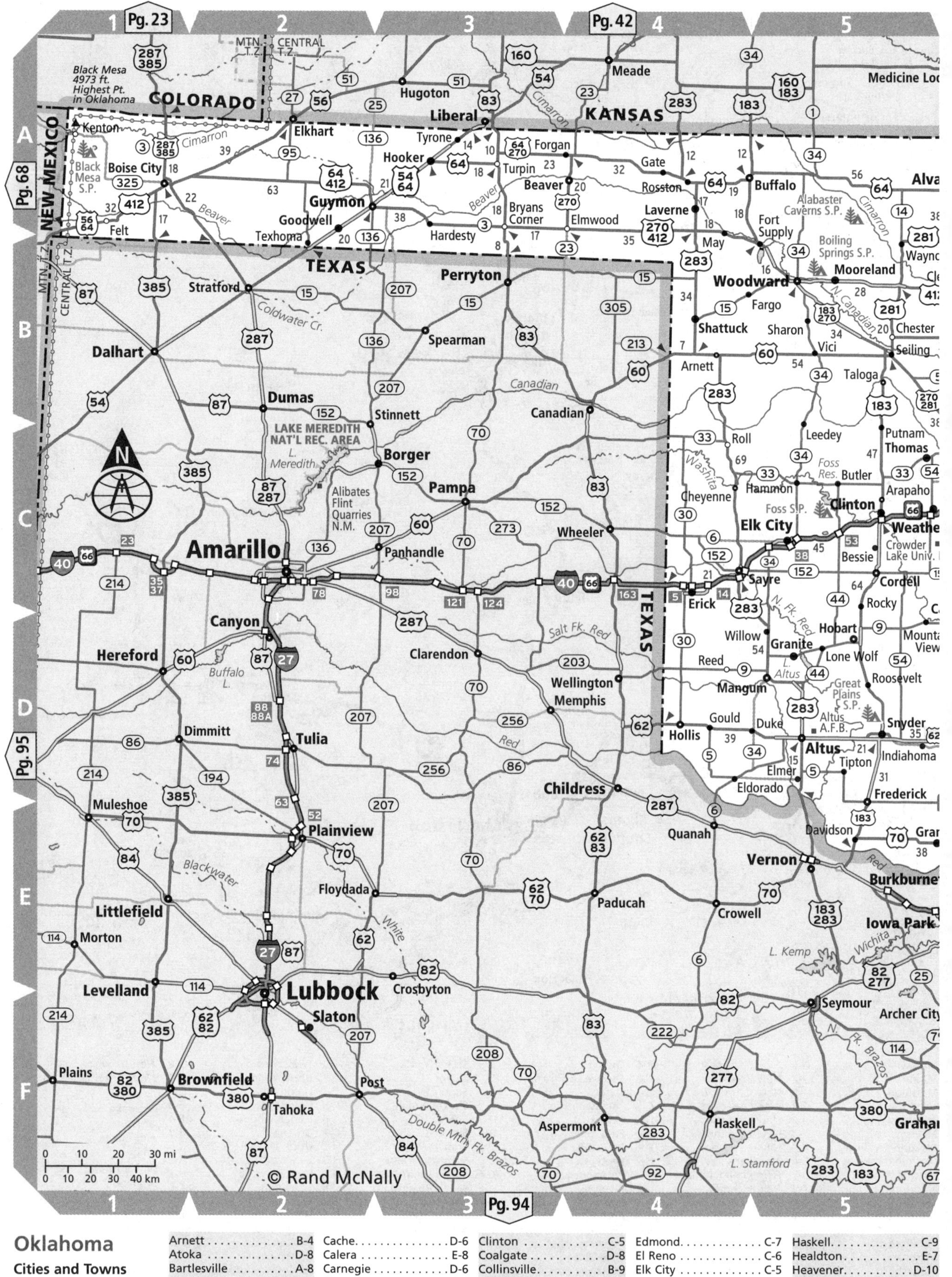

Oklahoma

Cities and Towns

Ada D-8
Altus D-5
Alva A-6
Anadarko D-6
Antlers E-9
Apache D-6
Arapaho C-5
Ardmore E-7
Arnett B-4
Atoka D-8
Bartlesville A-8
Beaver A-4
Bixby B-9
Blackwell A-7
Blanchard C-7
Boise City A-1
Bristow C-8
Broken Arrow B-9
Broken Bow E-10
Buffalo A-4
Cache D-6
Calera E-8
Carnegie D-6
Chandler C-7
Checotah C-9
Chelsea B-9
Cherokee A-6
Cheyenne C-4
Chickasha D-6
Chouteau B-9
Claremore B-9
Cleveland B-8
Clinton C-5
Coalgate D-8
Collinsville B-9
Commerce A-10
Cordell C-5
Coweta B-9
Cushing B-8
Davis D-7
Dewey A-8
Drumright B-8
Duncan D-6
Durant E-8
Edmond C-7
El Reno C-6
Elk City C-5
Enid B-6
Eufaula C-9
Fairview B-6
Frederick D-5
Granite D-5
Grove A-10
Guthrie B-7
Guymon A-2
Harrah C-7
Haskell C-9
Healdton E-7
Heavener D-10
Hennessey B-6
Henryetta C-8
Hinton C-6
Hobart D-5
Holdenville D-8
Hollis D-4
Hominy B-8
Hooker A-3
Hugo E-9

NOTE: Maps are not always in alphabetical order.
See Page 1 for map location in this atlas.

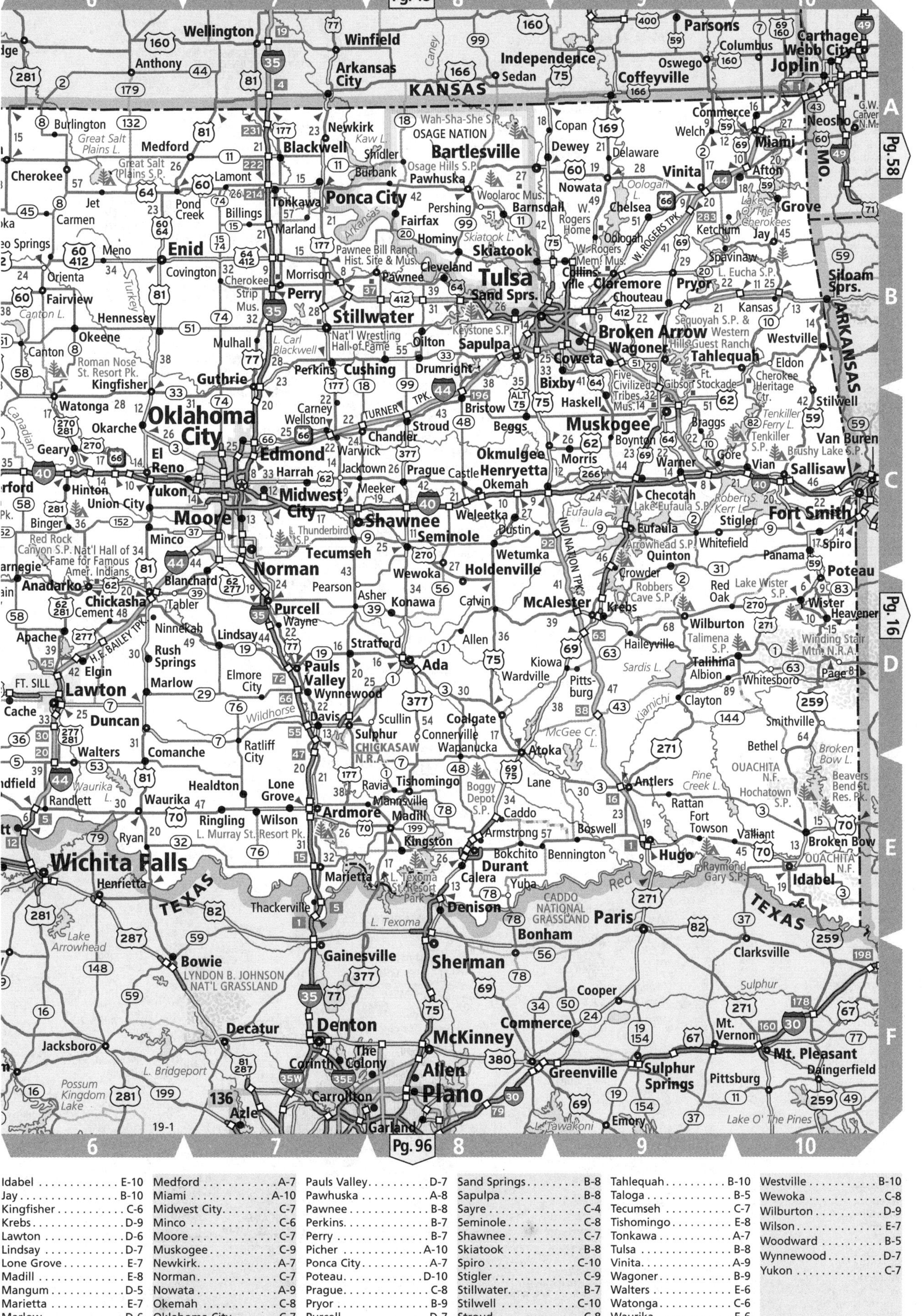

Idabel . . . E-10	Medford . . . A-7	Pauls Valley . . . D-7	Sand Springs . . . B-8	Tahlequah . . . B-10	Westville . . . B-10
Jay . . . B-10	Miami . . . A-10	Pawhuska . . . A-8	Sapulpa . . . B-8	Taloga . . . B-5	Wewoka . . . C-8
Kingfisher . . . C-6	Midwest City . . . C-7	Pawnee . . . B-8	Sayre . . . C-4	Tecumseh . . . C-7	Wilburton . . . D-9
Krebs . . . D-9	Minco . . . C-6	Perkins . . . B-7	Seminole . . . C-8	Tishomingo . . . E-8	Wilson . . . E-7
Lawton . . . D-6	Moore . . . C-7	Perry . . . B-7	Shawnee . . . C-7	Tonkawa . . . A-7	Woodward . . . B-5
Lindsay . . . D-7	Muskogee . . . C-9	Picher . . . A-10	Skiatook . . . B-8	Tulsa . . . B-8	Wynnewood . . . D-7
Lone Grove . . . E-7	Newkirk . . . A-7	Ponca City . . . A-7	Spiro . . . C-10	Vinita . . . A-9	Yukon . . . C-7
Madill . . . E-8	Norman . . . C-7	Poteau . . . D-10	Stigler . . . C-9	Wagoner . . . B-9	
Mangum . . . D-5	Nowata . . . A-9	Prague . . . C-8	Stillwater . . . B-7	Walters . . . E-6	
Marietta . . . E-7	Okemah . . . C-8	Pryor . . . B-9	Stilwell . . . C-10	Watonga . . . C-6	
Marlow . . . D-6	Oklahoma City . . . C-7	Purcell . . . D-7	Stroud . . . C-8	Waurika . . . E-6	
McAlester . . . D-9	Okmulgee . . . C-8	Sallisaw . . . C-10	Sulphur . . . D-7	Weatherford . . . C-5	

Road Conditions & Construction
(844) 465-4997, (405) 522-2800
www.okroads.org
www.okladot.state.ok.us

Tourism Information
Oklahoma Tourism Department
(800) 652-6552
www.travelok.com

Travel planning & on-the-road resources

Oregon

Cities and Towns

Albany C-2
Amity C-2
Ashland G-3
Astoria A-2
Athena B-7
Baker City C-8
Bandon E-1
Beaverton B-3
Bend D-4
Boardman B-6
Brookings G-1
Bunker Hill E-1
Burns E-7
Cannon Beach A-2
Canyon City D-7
Canyonville F-2
Cave Junction G-2
Central Point G-2
Clatskanie A-2
Condon B-5
Coos Bay E-1
Coquille E-1
Corvallis C-2
Cottage Grove E-2
Dallas C-2
Eagle Point F-3
Elgin B-8
Enterprise B-8
Estacada B-3
Eugene D-2
Florence D-1
Fossil C-5
Gladstone B-3
Glide E-2
Gold Beach F-1
Grants Pass F-2
Heppner B-6
Hermiston B-6
Hillsboro B-3
Hood River B-4
Jacksonville G-2
John Day D-7
Junction City D-2
Klamath Falls G-4
La Grande B-8
La Pine E-4
Lakeside E-1
Lakeview G-5
Lebanon C-3
Lincoln City C-1
Madras C-4
McMinnville B-2
Medford G-3
Mill City C-3
Milton-Freewater A-7
Molalla C-3
Monmouth C-2
Moro B-5
Myrtle Creek F-2
Myrtle Point F-1
Newberg B-3
Newport C-1
North Bend E-1
Nyssa D-9
Oakridge E-3
Ontario D-9
Oregon City B-3
Pendleton B-7
Philomath C-2
Phoenix G-3
Pilot Rock B-7
Portland B-3
Prineville D-5
Rainier A-3
Redmond D-4
Reedsport E-1
Rockaway Beach B-2
Roseburg E-2
St. Helens B-3
Salem C-2
Sandy B-3
Scappoose B-3
Seaside A-2
Silverton C-3
Springfield D-2
Stayton C-3
Sublimity C-3
Sutherlin E-2
Sweet Home D-3
The Dalles B-4
Tigard B-3
Tillamook B-2
Toledo C-2
Umatilla A-6
Union B-8
Vale D-9
Veneta D-2
Vernonia A-2
Waldport D-1
Warm Springs C-4
Warrenton A-2
Winston E-2
Woodburn C-3

Oregon state facts

Nickname: The Beaver State
Capital: Salem, C-2

Population: 3,831,074 (rank: 27th)
Largest city: Portland, 583,776, B-3

Land area: 95,988 sq. mi. (rank: 10th)
Highest point: Mount Hood, 11,239 ft., B-4

Pg. 104

Pg. 18

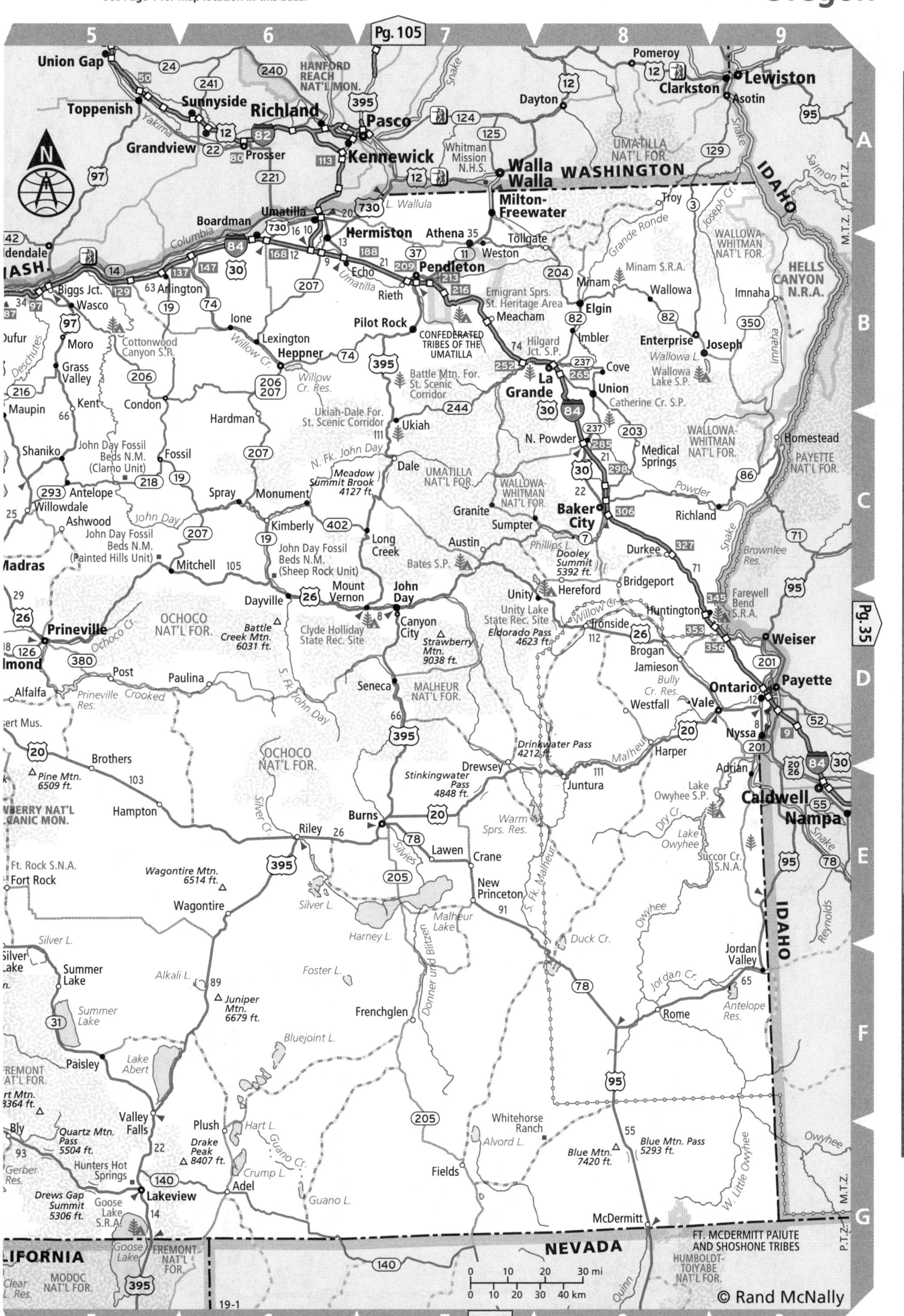

Road Conditions & Construction
511, (800) 977-6368
(888) 275-6368, (503) 588-2941
www.tripcheck.com, www.oregon.gov/odot

Tourism Information
Travel Oregon
(800) 547-7842
www.traveloregon.com

Travel planning & on-the-road resources

Pennsylvania state facts

Nickname: The Keystone State
Capital: Harrisburg, G-9
Population: 12,702,379 (rank: 6th)
Largest city: Philadelphia, 1,526,006, H-13
Land area: 44,743 sq. mi. (rank: 32nd)
Highest point: Mount Davis, 3,213 ft., I-4

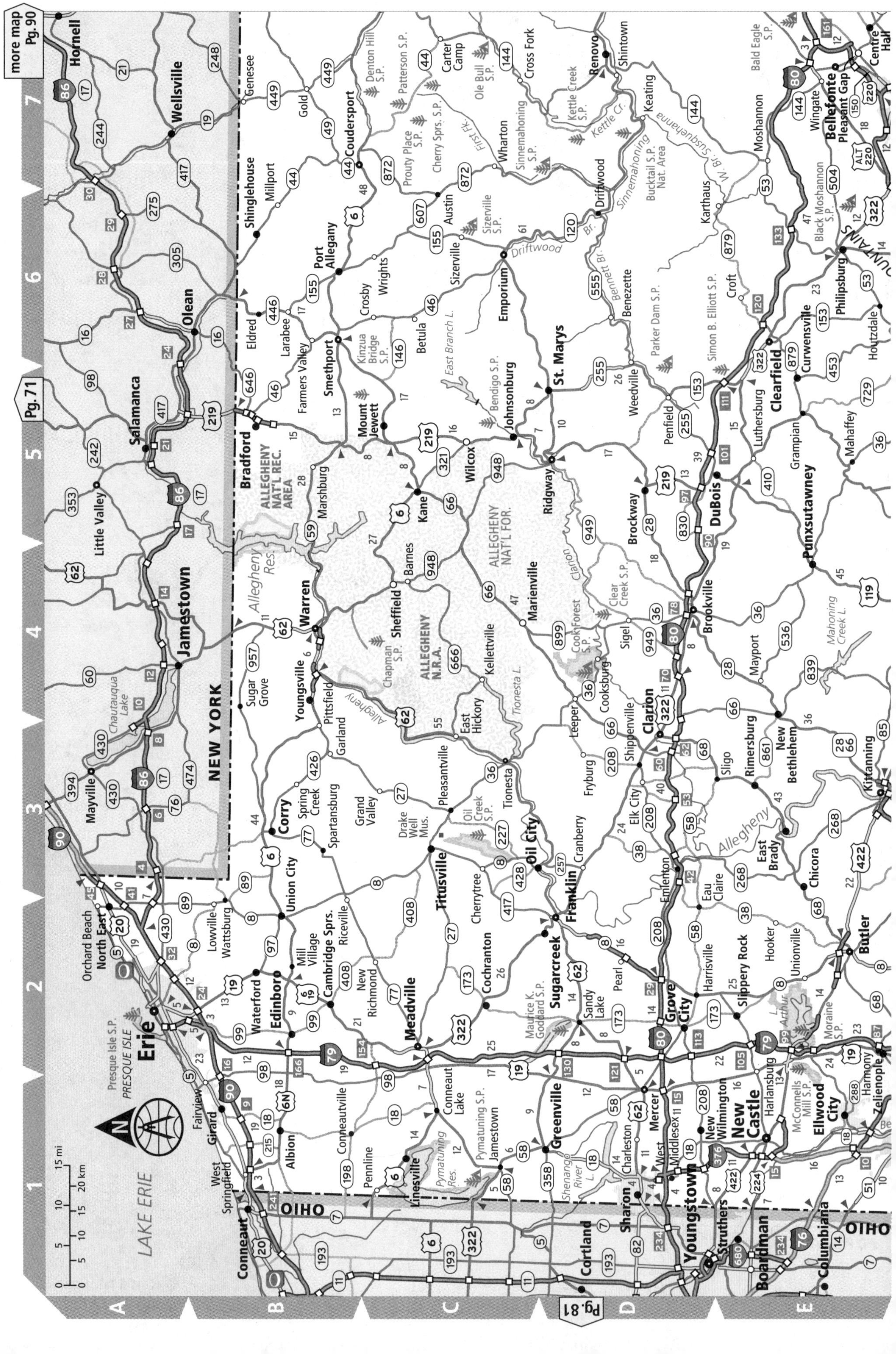

more map Pg. 90

Pg. 71

Pg. 81

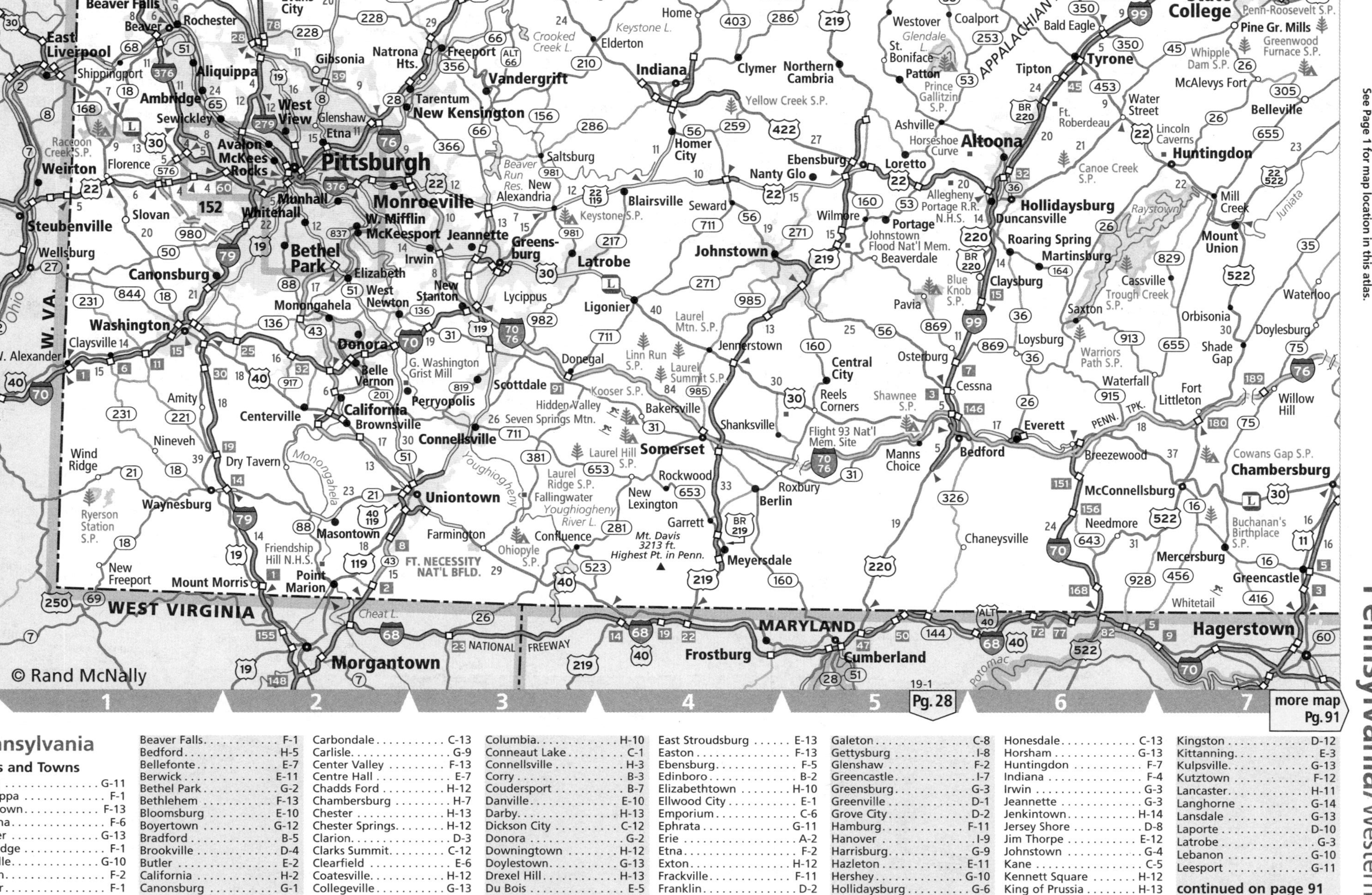

Pennsylvania

Cities and Towns

Akron . . . G-11
Aliquippa . . . F-1
Allentown . . . F-13
Altoona . . . F-6
Ambler . . . G-13
Ambridge . . . F-1
Annville . . . G-10
Avalon . . . F-2
Beaver . . . F-1
Beaver Falls . . . F-1
Bedford . . . H-5
Bellefonte . . . E-7
Berwick . . . E-11
Bethel Park . . . G-2
Bethlehem . . . F-13
Bloomsburg . . . E-10
Boyertown . . . G-12
Bradford . . . B-5
Brookville . . . D-4
Butler . . . E-2
California . . . H-2
Canonsburg . . . G-1
Carbondale . . . C-13
Carlisle . . . G-9
Center Valley . . . F-13
Centre Hall . . . E-7
Chadds Ford . . . H-12
Chambersburg . . . H-7
Chester . . . H-13
Chester Springs . . . H-12
Clarion . . . D-3
Clarks Summit . . . C-12
Clearfield . . . E-6
Coatesville . . . H-12
Collegeville . . . G-13
Columbia . . . H-10
Conneaut Lake . . . C-1
Connellsville . . . H-3
Corry . . . B-3
Coudersport . . . B-7
Danville . . . E-10
Darby . . . H-13
Dickson City . . . C-12
Donora . . . G-2
Downingtown . . . H-12
Doylestown . . . G-13
Drexel Hill . . . H-13
Du Bois . . . E-5
East Stroudsburg . . . E-13
Easton . . . F-13
Ebensburg . . . F-5
Edinboro . . . B-2
Elizabethtown . . . H-10
Ellwood City . . . E-1
Emporium . . . C-6
Ephrata . . . G-11
Erie . . . A-2
Etna . . . F-2
Exton . . . H-12
Frackville . . . F-11
Franklin . . . D-2
Galeton . . . C-8
Gettysburg . . . I-8
Glenshaw . . . F-2
Greencastle . . . I-7
Greensburg . . . G-3
Greenville . . . D-1
Grove City . . . D-2
Hamburg . . . F-11
Hanover . . . I-9
Harrisburg . . . G-9
Hazleton . . . E-11
Hershey . . . G-10
Hollidaysburg . . . G-6
Honesdale . . . C-13
Horsham . . . G-13
Huntingdon . . . F-7
Indiana . . . F-4
Irwin . . . G-3
Jeannette . . . G-3
Jenkintown . . . H-14
Jersey Shore . . . D-8
Jim Thorpe . . . E-12
Johnstown . . . G-4
Kane . . . C-5
Kennett Square . . . H-12
King of Prussia . . . H-13
Kingston . . . D-12
Kittanning . . . E-3
Kulpsville . . . G-13
Kutztown . . . F-12
Lancaster . . . H-11
Langhorne . . . G-14
Lansdale . . . G-13
Laporte . . . D-10
Latrobe . . . G-3
Lebanon . . . G-10
Leesport . . . G-11
continued on page 91

Travel planning & on-the-road resources

Tourism Information	Pennsylvania Tourism Office (800) 847-4872 www.visitpa.com	**Road Conditions & Construction**	511, (888) 783-6783 (800) 349-7623, (717) 787-2838 www.511pa.com, www.penndot.gov

Pennsylvania state facts

Nickname: The Keystone State
Capital: Harrisburg, G-9
Population: 12,702,379 (rank: 6th)
Largest city: Philadelphia, 1,526,006, H-13
Land area: 44,743 sq. mi. (rank: 32nd)
Highest point: Mount Davis, 3,213 ft., I-4

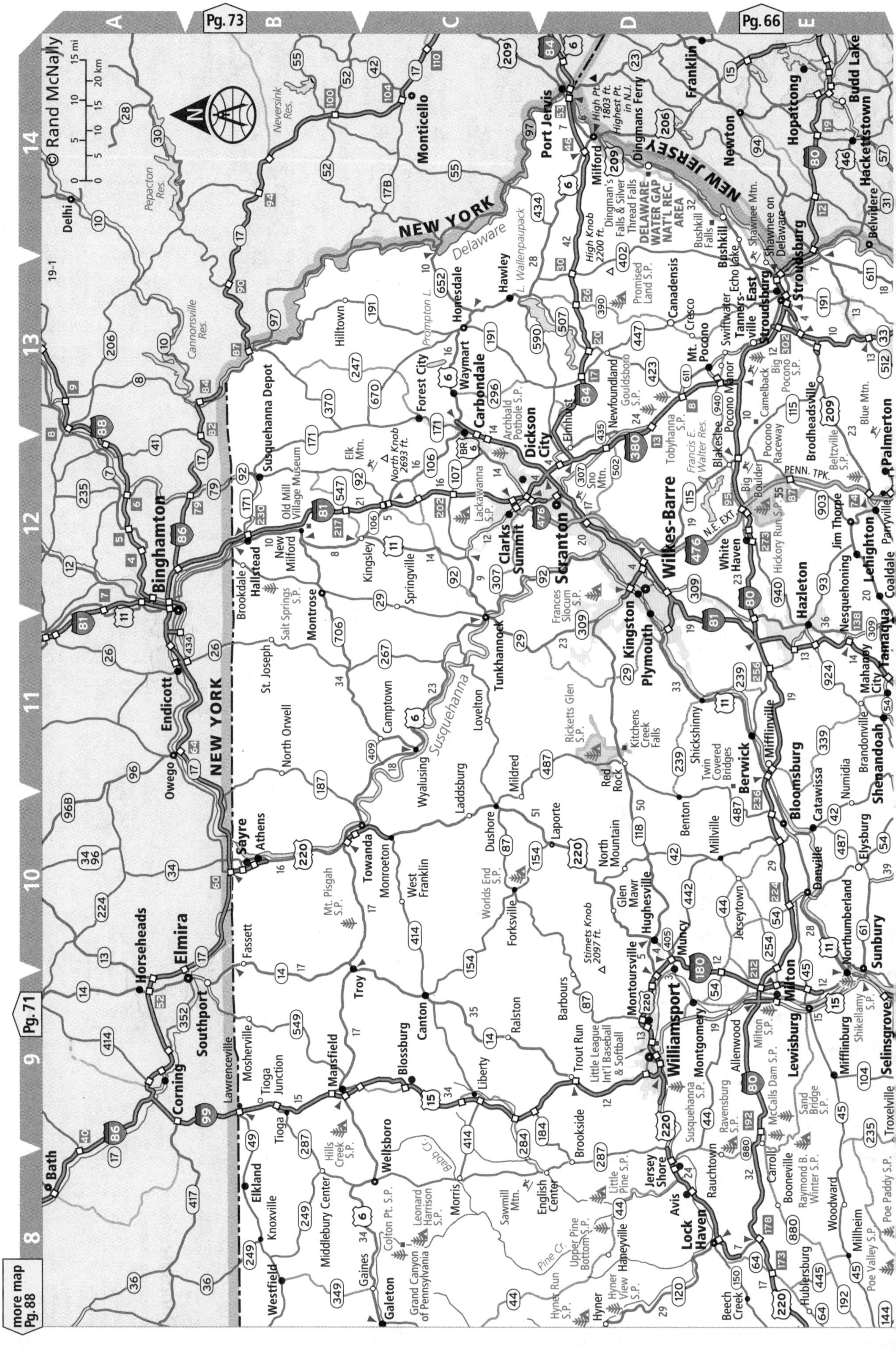

more map Pg.88
Pg.73
Pg.66
Pg.71

more map Pg. 89

continued from page 89

Lehighton E-12
Lewisburg E-9
Lewistown F-8
Lititz H-11
Littlestown I-9
Lock Haven D-8
Lower Burrell F-2
Mahanoy City E-11
Manheim G-10
Mansfield B-9
McConnellsburg H-7
McKees Rocks F-2
McKeesport G-2
Meadville C-2
Mechanicsburg G-9
Media H-13
Mercer D-1
Middleburg F-9
Middletown G-10
Mifflintown F-8
Milford D-14
Milton E-9
Monongahela G-2
Monroeville G-2
Montgomeryville G-13
Montoursville D-9
Montrose B-12
Morrisville G-14
Mount Carmel F-10
Mount Joy H-10
Munhall G-2
Nazareth F-13
New Bloomfield G-9
New Castle E-1
New Holland H-11
Norristown H-13
North East A-2
Northern Cambria F-5
Oil City C-3
Orwigsburg F-11
Oxford I-11
Palmerton E-12
Paoli H-13
Parryville E-12
Philadelphia H-13
Phoenixville H-13
Pittsburgh F-2
Plains D-12
Plymouth D-11
Pottstown G-12
Pottsville F-11
Punxsutawney E-4
Quakertown G-13
Reading G-12
Red Lion H-10
Ridgway D-5
Rochester F-1
St. Marys D-5
Sayre B-10
Schuylkill Haven F-11
Scottdale H-3
Scranton D-12
Selinsgrove F-9
Sellersville G-13
Sewickley F-1
Shamokin F-10
Sharon D-1
Shenandoah E-11
Shippensburg H-8
Smethport B-6
Somerset H-4
Souderton G-13
State College F-7
Stroudsburg E-13
Sugarcreek D-2
Sunbury E-10
Tamaqua F-11
Tarentum F-3
Tionesta C-3
Titusville C-3
Towanda C-10
Tunkhannock C-11
Tyrone F-6
Uniontown H-3
Valley Forge H-13
Vandergrift F-3
Warminster G-14
Warren B-4
Washington G-1
Waynesboro I-8
Waynesburg H-1
Wellsboro C-8
West Chester H-12
West Mifflin G-2
West View F-2
West York H-10
Whitehall G-2
Wilkes-Barre D-12
Williamsport D-9
Willow Street H-11
York H-10
Zelienople E-2

Travel planning & on-the-road resources

Tourism Information
Pennsylvania Tourism Office
(800) 847-4872
www.visitpa.com

Road Conditions & Construction
511, (888) 783-6783
(800) 349-7623, (717) 787-2838
www.511pa.com, www.penndot.gov

Land area: 75,811 sq. mi. (rank: 16th)
Highest point: Black Elk Peak, 7,242 ft., D-2

Population: 814,180 (rank: 46th)
Largest city: Sioux Falls, 153,888, E-10

Nickname: The Mount Rushmore State
Capital: Pierre, C-5

South Dakota state facts

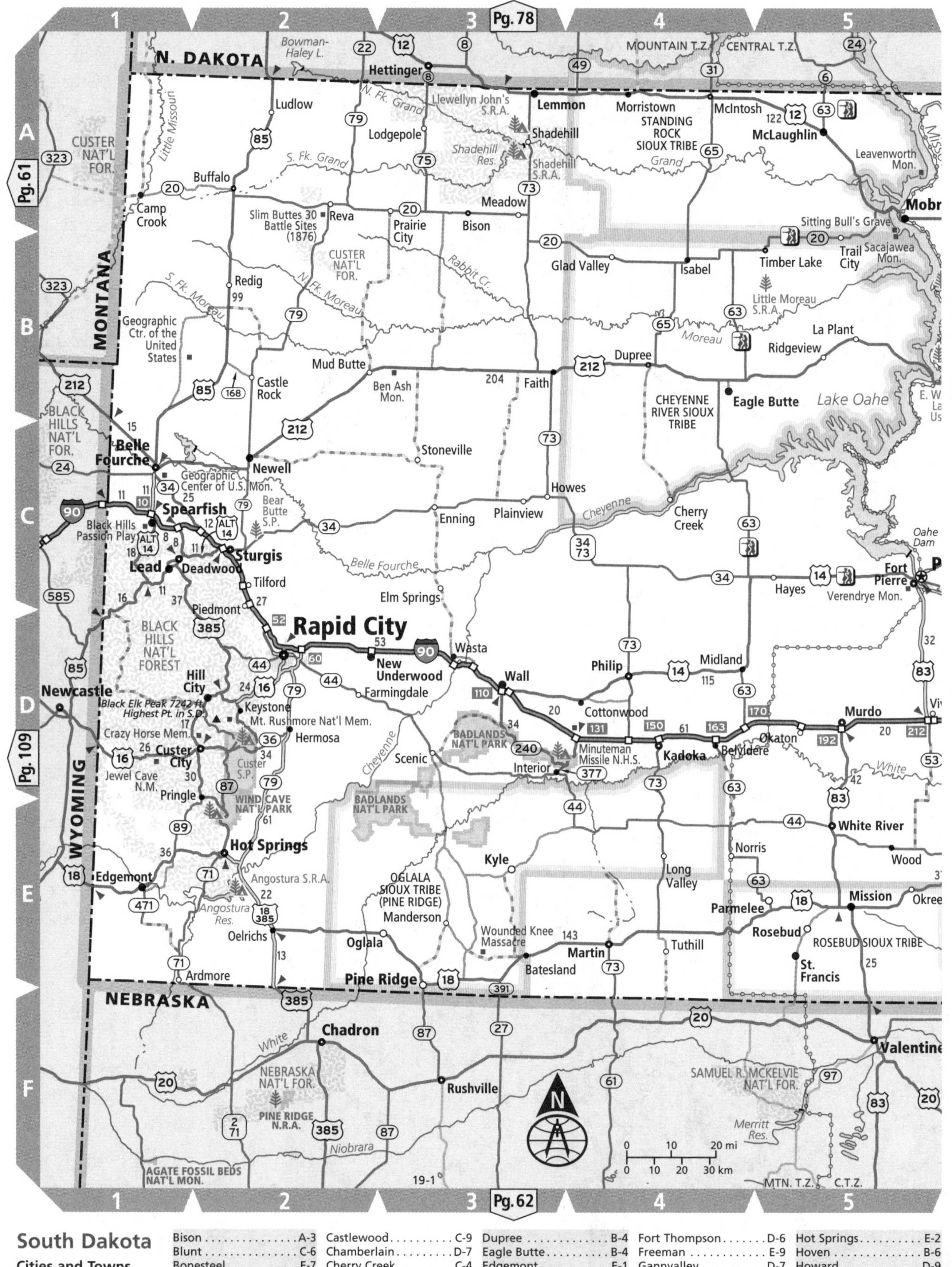

South Dakota

Cities and Towns

Aberdeen B-8
Alexandria D-8
Arlington C-9
Armour E-8
Avon F-8
Belle Fourche C-1
Beresford E-10
Big Stone City. B-10
Bison A-3
Blunt C-6
Bonesteel E-7
Bowdle B-6
Bridgewater E-9
Bristol B-8
Britton. A-8
Brookings C-10
Bryant C-9
Buffalo A-2
Burke. E-7
Canton E-10
Castlewood. C-9
Chamberlain D-7
Cherry Creek. C-4
Clark B-8
Clear Lake. C-10
Colman D-10
Colome E-6
Custer D-2
De Smet C-9
Deadwood C-1
Dell Rapids D-10
Doland B-8
Dupree B-4
Eagle Butte. B-4
Edgemont. E-1
Elk Point F-10
Elkton C-10
Estelline. C-9
Ethan. E-8
Eureka. A-6
Faith B-3
Faulkton B-7
Flandreau D-10
Fort Pierre. C-5
Fort Thompson. D-6
Freeman E-9
Gannvalley D-7
Gettysburg B-6
Gregory. E-6
Groton. B-8
Harrisburg. E-10
Hecla A-8
Hermosa D-2
Herreid A-6
Highmore C-6
Hill City D-2
Hot Springs. E-2
Hoven B-6
Howard. D-9
Huron C-8
Ipswich B-7
Kadoka D-4
Kennebec D-6
Keystone. D-2
Kimball D-7
Kyle. E-3
Lake Andes E-8
Lake Preston. C-9

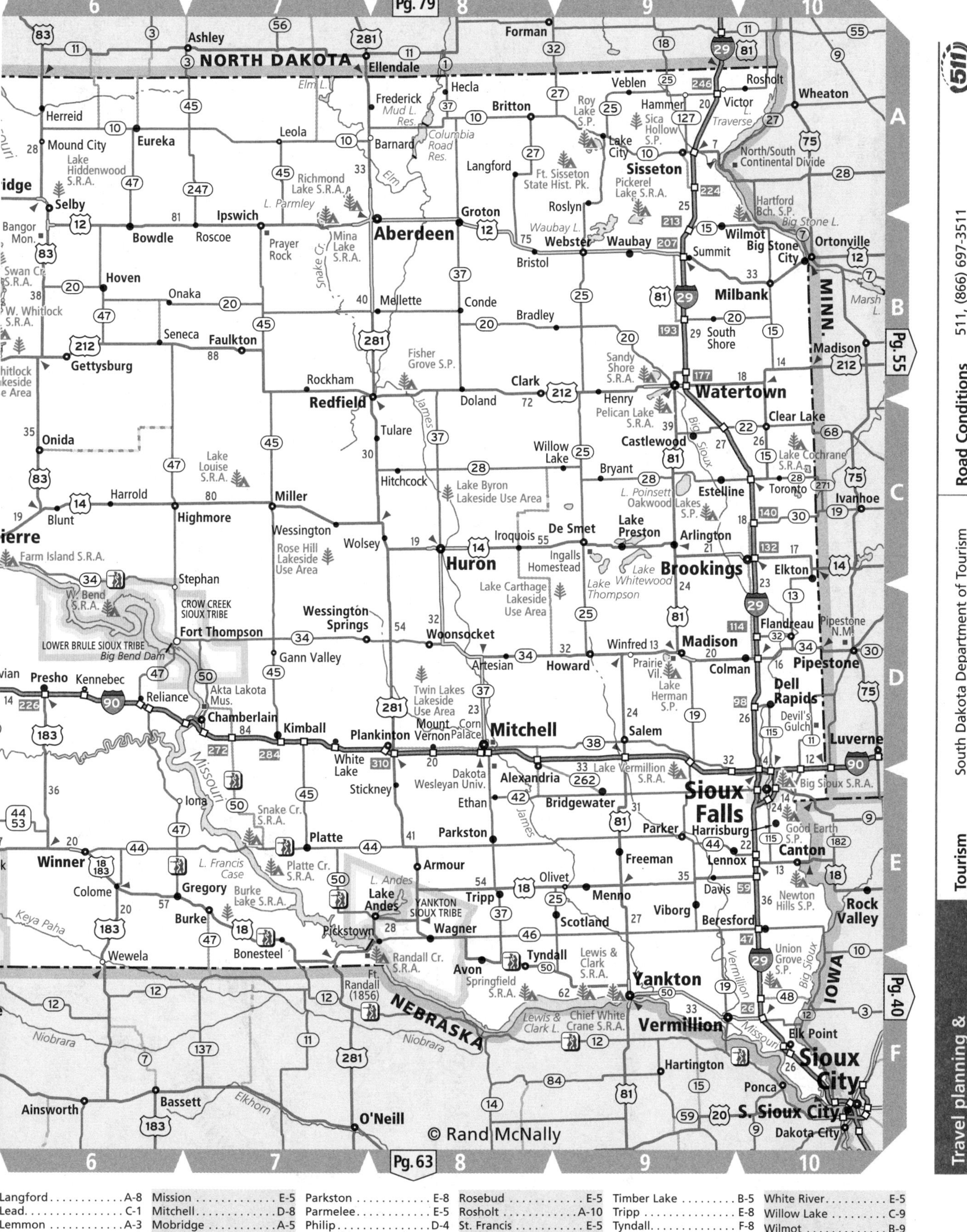

Road Conditions & Construction

511, (866) 697-3511
www.safetravelusa.com/sd
www.sddot.com

Tourism Information

South Dakota Department of Tourism
(800) 732-5682; www.travelsd.com
www.travelsouthdakota.com

Travel planning & on-the-road resources

Langford A-8
Lead C-1
Lemmon A-3
Lennox E-9
Leola A-7
Madison D-9
Martin E-4
McIntosh A-4
McLaughlin A-5
Menno E-9
Milbank B-10
Miller C-7
Mission E-5
Mitchell D-8
Mobridge A-5
Mound City A-6
Mount Vernon D-8
Murdo D-5
New Underwood D-2
Newell C-2
Oglala E-3
Olivet E-9
Onida C-6
Parker E-9
Parkston E-8
Parmelee E-5
Philip D-4
Piedmont C-2
Pierre C-5
Pine Ridge E-3
Plankinton D-8
Platte E-7
Presho D-6
Rapid City D-2
Redfield B-8
Roscoe B-7
Rosebud E-5
Rosholt A-10
St. Francis E-5
Salem D-9
Scotland E-9
Selby A-6
Sioux Falls E-10
Sisseton A-9
Spearfish C-1
Stickney E-8
Sturgis C-2
Summit B-9
Timber Lake B-5
Tripp E-8
Tyndall F-8
Vermillion F-9
Viborg E-9
Wagner E-8
Wall D-3
Watertown B-9
Waubay B-9
Webster B-9
Wessington Springs D-7
White Lake D-7
White River E-5
Willow Lake C-9
Wilmot B-9
Winner E-6
Wolsey C-8
Woonsocket D-8
Yankton F-9

Texas state facts

Nickname: The Lone Star State
Capital: Austin, E-9

Population: 25,145,561 (rank: 2nd)
Largest city: Houston, 2,099,451, F-11

Land area: 261,231 sq. mi. (rank: 2nd)
Highest point: Guadalupe Peak, 8,749 ft., C-2

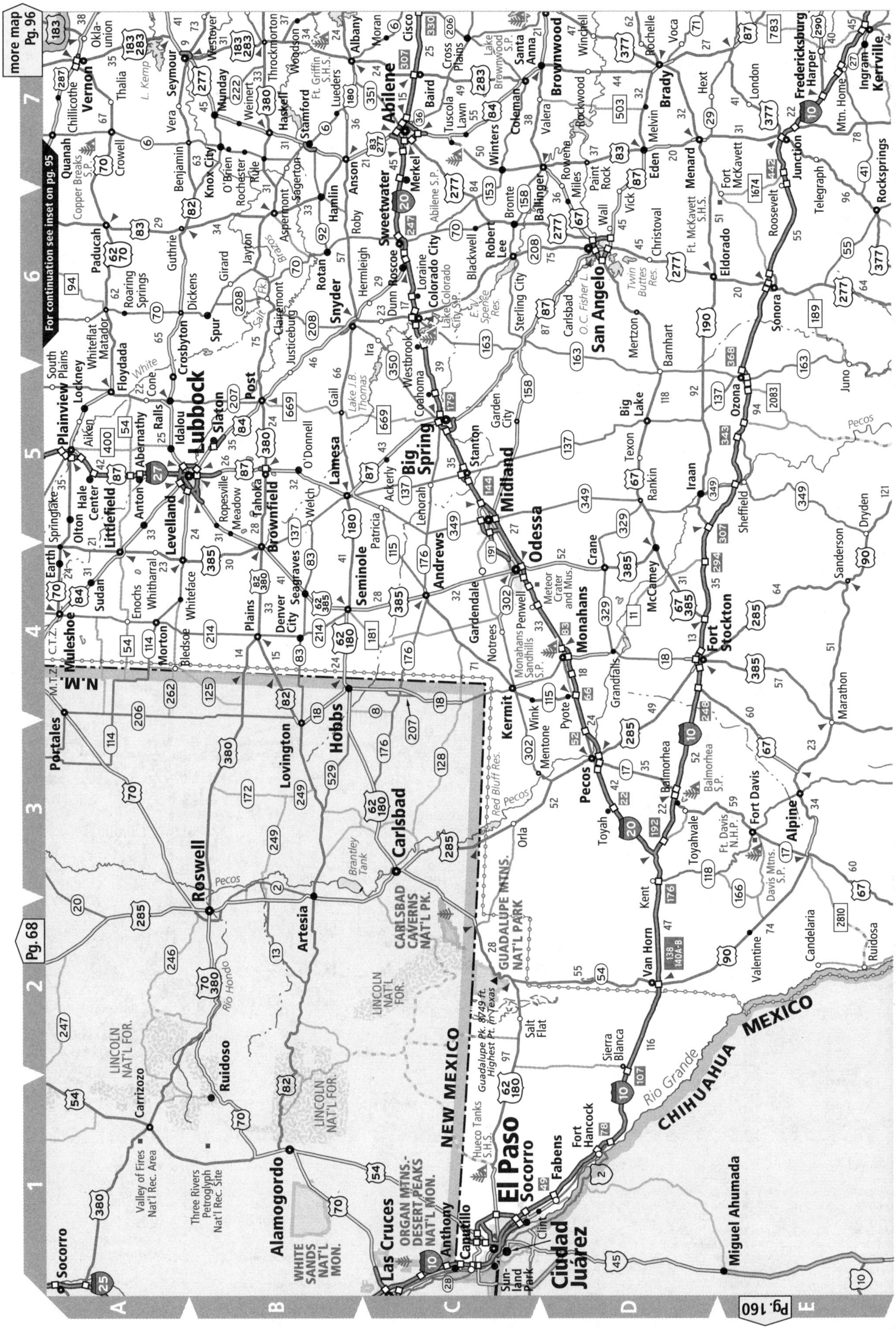

more map Pg. 96

For continuation see inset on pg. 95

Pg. 68

Pg. 160

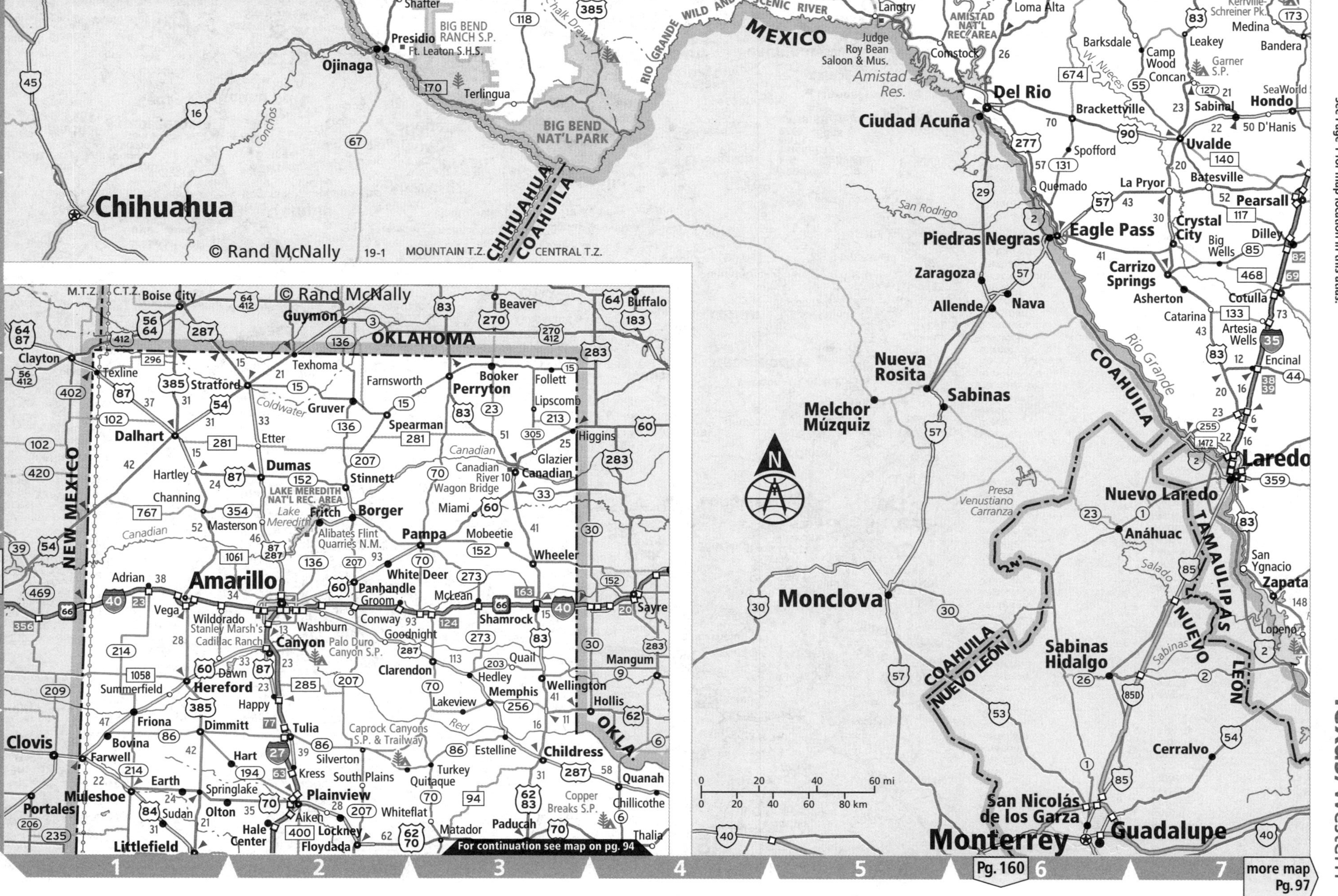

Travel planning & on-the-road resources

Tourism Information
Texas Tourism
(800) 452-9292
www.traveltexas.com

Road Conditions & Construction
(800) 452-9292, (512) 463-8588
www.txdot.gov
www.drivetexas.org

Nickname: The Lone Star State	Population: 25,145,561 (rank: 2nd)	Land area: 261,231 sq. mi. (rank: 2nd)	Texas state facts
Capital: Austin, E-9	Largest city: Houston, 2,099,451, F-11	Highest point: Guadalupe Peak, 8,749 ft., C-2	

more map Pg. 94

Texas

Cities and Towns

Abilene C-7
Albany B-7
Alice H-8
Allen B-10
Alpine E-3
Alvin F-11
Amarillo I-2
Anahuac F-12
Anderson E-10
Andrews C-4
Angleton F-11
Anson B-7
Archer City A-8
Arlington B-9
Aspermont B-6
Athens C-10
Austin E-9
Baird C-7
Ballinger D-7
Bandera F-7
Bastrop E-9
Bay City F-10
Baytown F-11
Beaumont E-12
Beeville G-9
Bellville E-10
Belton D-9
Benjamin B-7
Big Lake D-5
Big Spring C-5
Boerne F-8
Bonham A-10
Borger H-2
Brackettville F-6
Brady D-7
Breckenridge B-8
Brownfield B-4
Brownsville J-9
Brownwood D-7
Bryan E-10
Burnet E-8
Caldwell E-10
Cameron D-9
Canadian H-3
Canton C-10
Canyon I-2
Carrizo Springs G-7
Carthage C-12
Cedar Park E-9
Center C-12
Centerville D-10
Channing H-1
Childress J-3
Clarendon I-3
Clarksville A-11
Cleburne C-9
Coldspring E-11
Coleman C-7
College Station E-10
Colorado City C-6
Columbus F-10
Comanche C-8
Conroe E-11
Cooper B-11
Copperas Cove D-9
Corinth B-9
Corpus Christi H-9
Corsicana C-10
Cotulla G-7
Crane D-4
Johnson City E-8
Jourdanton G-8
Junction E-7
Karnes City G-9
Kaufman C-10
Kermit C-4
Kerrville E-7
Killeen D-9
Kingsville H-9
Kingwood E-11
Kountze E-12
La Grange E-10
La Porte F-11
Lake Jackson F-11
Lamesa B-5
Lampasas D-8
Laredo H-7
Leakey F-7
Levelland A-4
Liberty E-12
Linden B-12
Lipscomb H-3
Littlefield A-4
Livingston E-11
Llano E-8
Lockhart F-9
Longview C-11
Lubbock B-5
Lufkin D-12
Madisonville D-10
Marlin D-9
Marshall C-12
Matador A-6
McAllen J-8
McKinney B-10
Memphis I-3
Menard D-7
Mentone C-3
Mercedes J-9
Meridian C-9
Mertzon D-6
Miami H-3
Midland C-5
Mineral Wells B-8
Mission J-8
Monahans D-4
Montague A-9
Morton A-4
Mount Pleasant B-11
Mount Vernon B-11
Muleshoe J-1
Nacogdoches D-12
New Braunfels F-8
Odessa C-4
Orange E-12
Ozona E-5
Paducah A-6
Paint Rock D-7
Palestine C-11
Palo Pinto B-8
Pampa I-3
Panhandle I-2
Paris A-11
Pearsall G-7
Pecos D-3
Perryton H-3
Pharr J-8
Pittsburg B-11
Plains B-4
Plainview J-2
Plano B-10
Port Arthur E-12
Port Lavaca G-10
Post B-5

Pg. 85
Pg. 16
Pg. 48

NOTE: Maps are not always in alphabetical order.
See Page 1 for map location in this atlas.

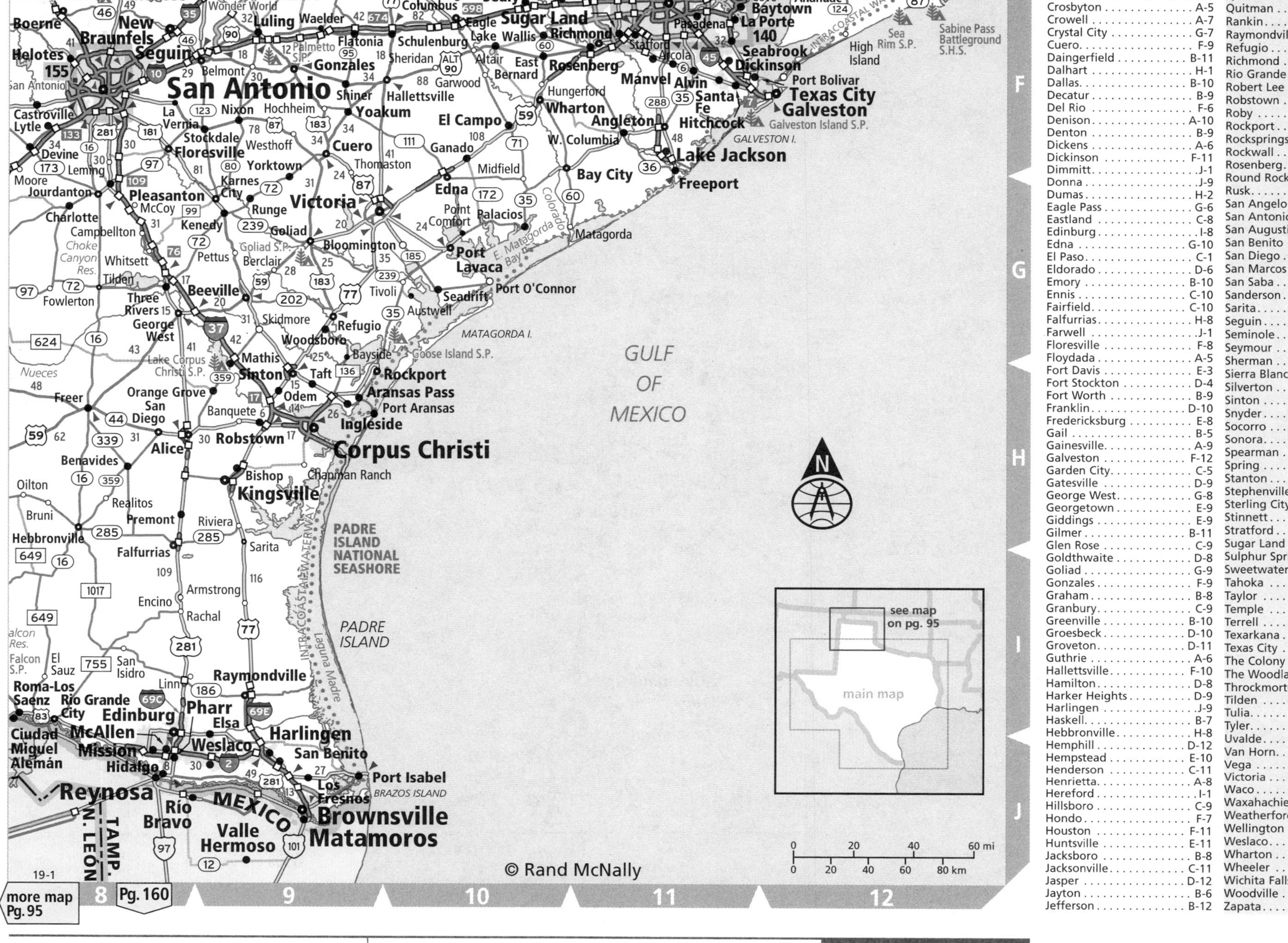

Crockett D-11
Crosbyton A-5
Crowell A-7
Crystal City G-7
Cuero F-9
Daingerfield B-11
Dalhart H-1
Dallas B-10
Decatur B-9
Del Rio F-6
Denison A-10
Denton B-9
Dickens A-6
Dickinson F-11
Dimmitt J-1
Donna J-9
Dumas H-2
Eagle Pass G-6
Eastland C-8
Edinburg I-8
Edna G-10
El Paso C-1
Eldorado D-6
Emory B-10
Ennis C-10
Fairfield C-10
Falfurrias H-8
Farwell J-1
Floresville F-8
Floydada A-5
Fort Davis E-3
Fort Stockton D-4
Fort Worth B-9
Franklin D-10
Fredericksburg E-8
Gail B-5
Gainesville A-9
Galveston F-12
Garden City C-5
Gatesville D-9
George West G-8
Georgetown E-9
Giddings E-9
Gilmer B-11
Glen Rose C-9
Goldthwaite D-8
Goliad G-9
Gonzales F-9
Graham B-8
Granbury C-9
Greenville B-10
Groesbeck D-10
Groveton D-11
Guthrie A-6
Hallettsville F-10
Hamilton D-8
Harker Heights D-9
Harlingen J-9
Haskell B-7
Hebbronville H-8
Hemphill D-12
Hempstead E-10
Henderson C-11
Henrietta A-8
Hereford I-1
Hillsboro C-9
Hondo F-7
Houston F-11
Huntsville E-11
Jacksboro B-8
Jacksonville C-11
Jasper D-12
Jayton B-6
Jefferson B-12
Quanah J-4
Quitman B-11
Rankin D-5
Raymondville I-9
Refugio G-9
Richmond F-11
Rio Grande City I-8
Robert Lee C-6
Robstown H-9
Roby B-6
Rockport H-9
Rocksprings E-6
Rockwall B-10
Rosenberg F-11
Round Rock E-9
Rusk C-11
San Angelo D-6
San Antonio F-8
San Augustine D-12
San Benito J-9
San Diego H-8
San Marcos F-9
San Saba D-8
Sanderson E-4
Sarita H-9
Seguin F-9
Seminole B-4
Seymour A-7
Sherman A-10
Sierra Blanca D-2
Silverton J-2
Sinton H-9
Snyder B-6
Socorro C-1
Sonora E-6
Spearman H-2
Spring E-11
Stanton C-5
Stephenville C-8
Sterling City C-6
Stinnett H-2
Stratford H-2
Sugar Land F-11
Sulphur Springs B-11
Sweetwater C-6
Tahoka B-5
Taylor E-9
Temple D-9
Terrell B-10
Texarkana B-12
Texas City F-11
The Colony B-9
The Woodlands E-11
Throckmorton B-7
Tilden G-8
Tulia J-2
Tyler C-11
Uvalde F-7
Van Horn D-2
Vega I-1
Victoria G-9
Waco D-9
Waxahachie C-9
Weatherford B-9
Wellington I-3
Weslaco J-9
Wharton F-10
Wheeler I-3
Wichita Falls A-8
Woodville D-12
Zapata I-7

Tourism Information Texas Tourism
(800) 452-9292
www.traveltex.com

Road Conditions & Construction (800) 452-9292, (512) 463-8588
www.txdot.gov
www.drivetexas.org

Travel planning & on-the-road resources

Utah state facts

Nickname: The Beehive State
Capital: Salt Lake City, C-4

Population: 2,763,885 (rank: 34th)
Largest city: Salt Lake City, 186,440, C-4

Land area: 82,169 sq. mi. (rank: 12th)
Highest point: Kings Peak, 13,528 ft., C-5

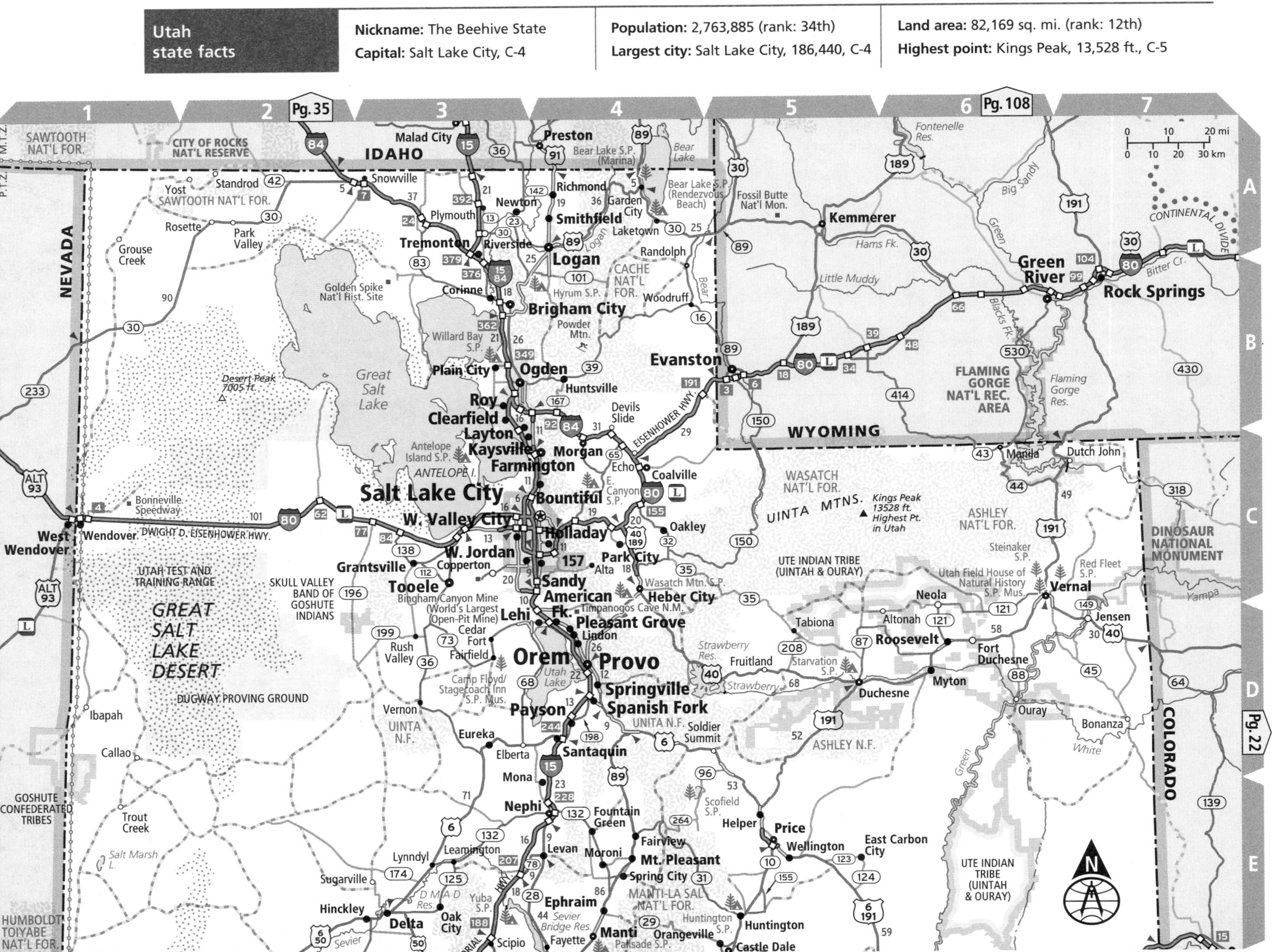

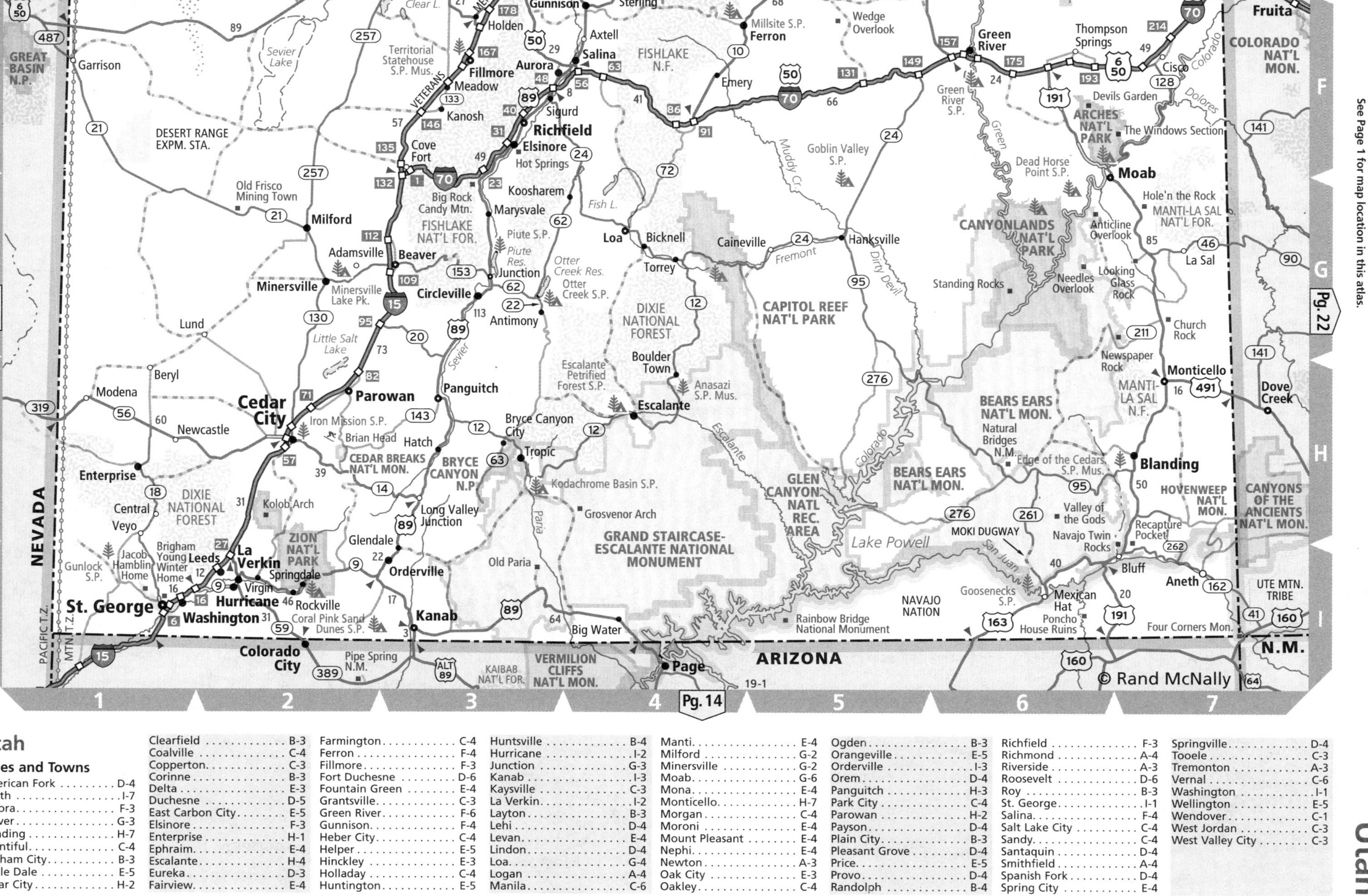

Utah

Cities and Towns

American Fork D-4
Aneth I-7
Aurora F-3
Beaver G-3
Blanding H-7
Bountiful C-4
Brigham City B-3
Castle Dale E-5
Cedar City H-2
Clearfield B-3
Coalville C-4
Copperton C-3
Corinne B-3
Delta E-3
Duchesne D-5
East Carbon City E-5
Elsinore F-3
Enterprise H-1
Ephraim E-4
Escalante H-4
Eureka D-3
Fairview E-4
Farmington C-4
Ferron F-4
Fillmore F-3
Fort Duchesne D-6
Fountain Green E-4
Grantsville C-3
Green River F-6
Gunnison F-4
Heber City C-4
Helper E-5
Hinckley E-3
Holladay C-4
Huntington E-5
Huntsville B-4
Hurricane I-2
Junction G-3
Kanab I-3
Kaysville C-3
La Verkin I-2
Layton B-3
Lehi D-4
Levan E-4
Lindon D-4
Loa G-4
Logan A-4
Manila C-6
Manti E-4
Milford G-2
Minersville G-2
Moab G-6
Mona E-4
Monticello H-7
Morgan C-4
Moroni E-4
Mount Pleasant E-4
Nephi E-4
Newton A-3
Oak City E-3
Oakley C-4
Ogden B-3
Orangeville E-5
Orderville I-3
Orem D-4
Panguitch H-3
Park City C-4
Parowan H-2
Payson D-4
Plain City B-3
Pleasant Grove D-4
Price E-5
Provo D-4
Randolph B-4
Richfield F-3
Richmond A-4
Riverside A-3
Roosevelt D-6
Roy B-3
St. George I-1
Salina F-4
Salt Lake City C-4
Sandy C-4
Santaquin D-4
Smithfield A-4
Spanish Fork D-4
Spring City E-4
Springville D-4
Tooele C-3
Tremonton A-3
Vernal C-6
Washington I-1
Wellington E-5
Wendover C-1
West Jordan C-3
West Valley City C-3

Travel planning & on-the-road resources

Tourism Information
Utah Office of Tourism
(800) 200-1160, (800) 882-4386, (801) 538-1900
www.visitutah.com

Road Conditions & Construction
511, (866) 511-8824, (801) 887-3700, (801) 965-4000; www.udot.utah.gov, www.utahcommuterlink.com

Virginia state facts

Nickname: Old Dominion
Capital: Richmond, G-11
Population: 8,001,024 (rank: 12th)
Largest city: Virginia Beach, 437,994, H-13
Land area: 39,490 sq. mi. (rank: 36th)
Highest point: Mount Rogers, 5,729 ft., I-4

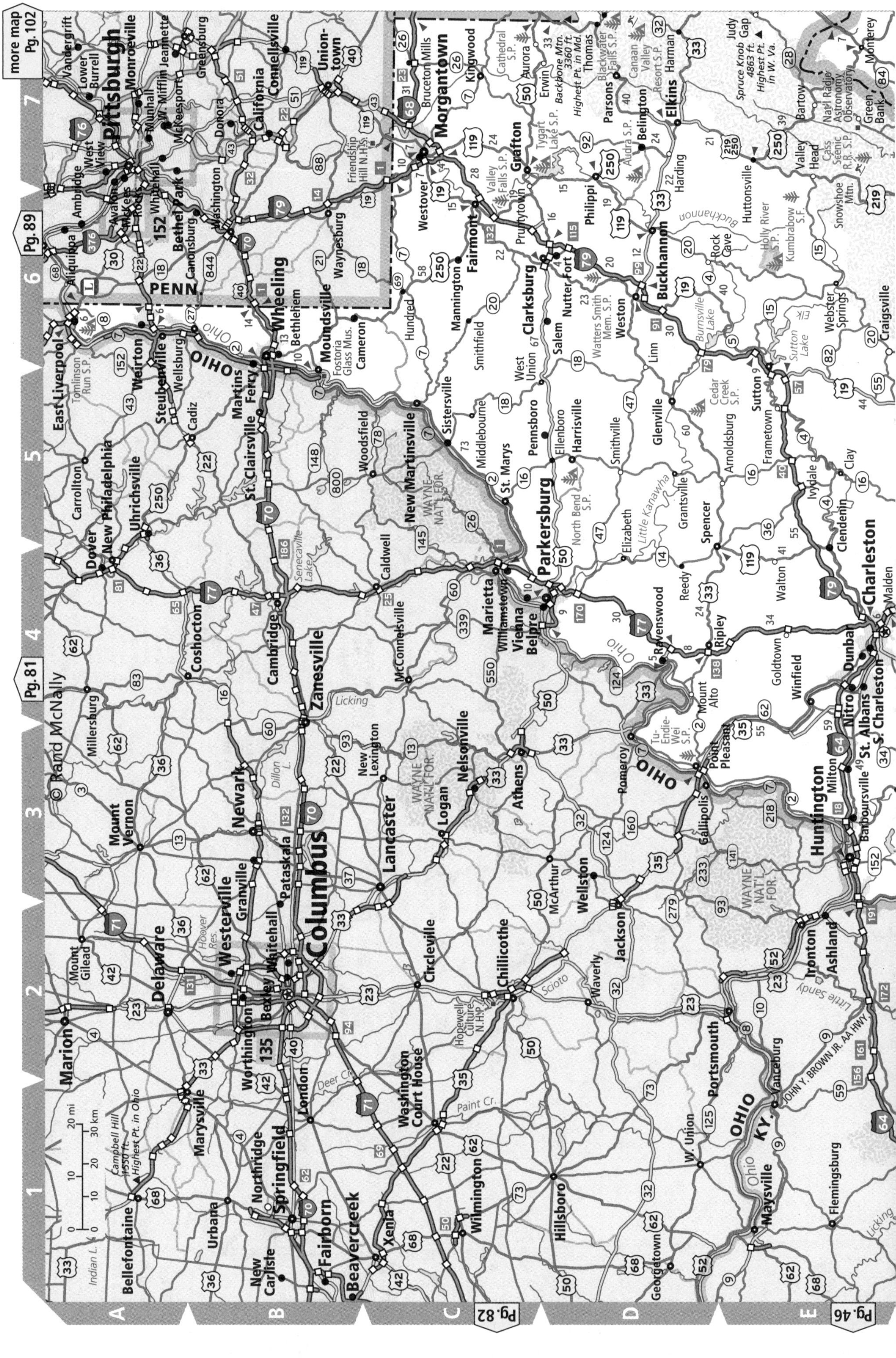

more map Pg. 102
Pg. 89
Pg. 81
Pg. 82
Pg. 46

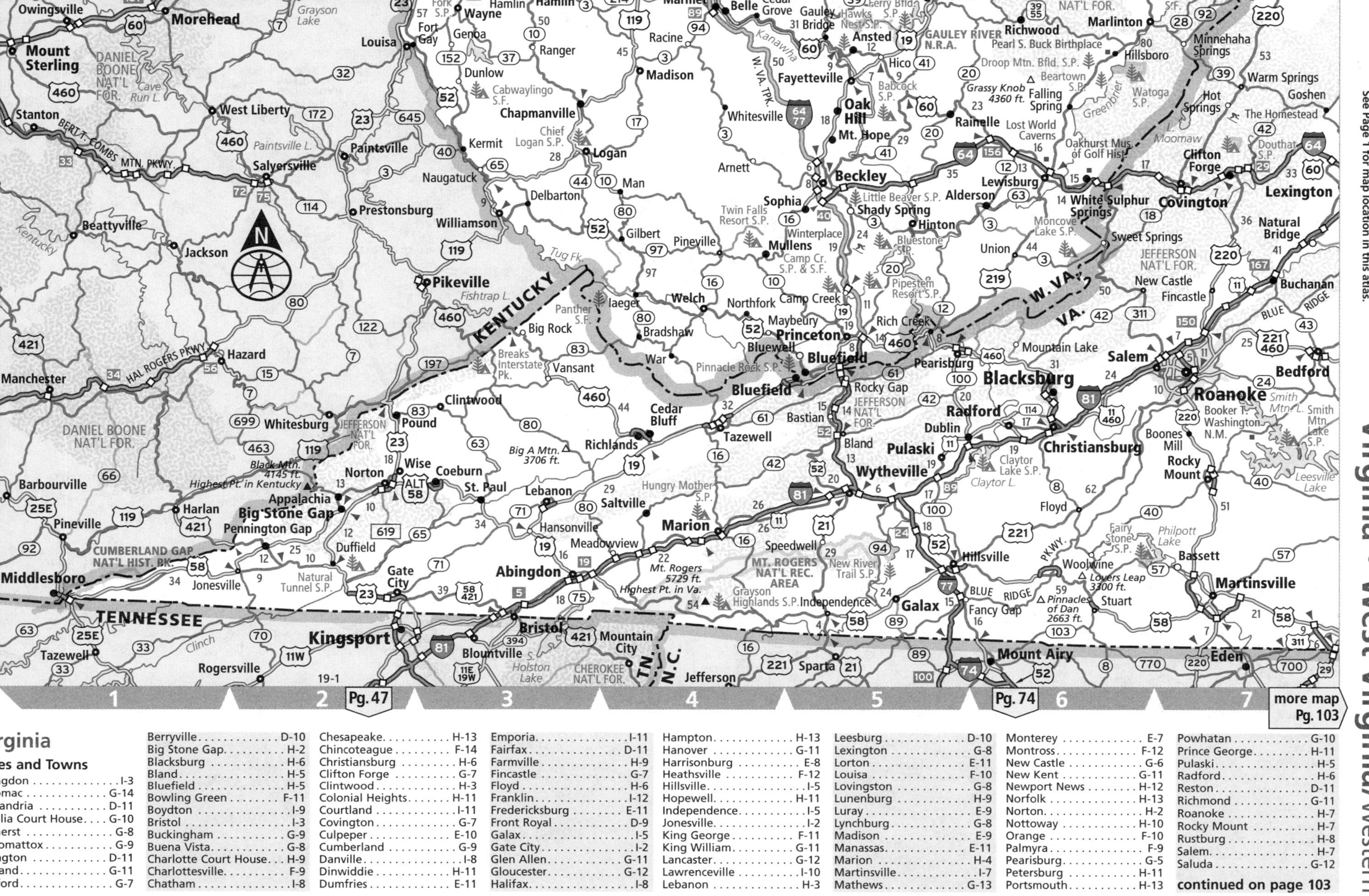

Virginia

Cities and Towns

Abingdon I-3
Accomac G-14
Alexandria D-11
Amelia Court House G-10
Amherst G-8
Appomattox G-9
Arlington D-11
Ashland G-11
Bedford G-7
Berryville D-10
Big Stone Gap H-2
Blacksburg H-6
Bland H-5
Bluefield H-5
Bowling Green F-11
Boydton I-9
Bristol I-3
Buckingham G-9
Buena Vista G-8
Charlotte Court House H-9
Charlottesville F-9
Chatham I-8
Chesapeake H-13
Chincoteague F-14
Christiansburg H-6
Clifton Forge G-7
Clintwood H-3
Colonial Heights H-11
Courtland I-11
Covington G-7
Culpeper E-10
Cumberland G-9
Danville I-8
Dinwiddie H-11
Dumfries E-11
Emporia I-11
Fairfax D-11
Farmville H-9
Fincastle G-7
Floyd H-6
Franklin I-12
Fredericksburg E-11
Front Royal D-9
Galax I-5
Gate City I-2
Glen Allen G-11
Gloucester G-12
Halifax I-8
Hampton H-13
Hanover G-11
Harrisonburg E-8
Heathsville F-12
Hillsville I-5
Hopewell H-11
Independence I-5
Jonesville I-2
King George F-11
King William G-11
Lancaster G-12
Lawrenceville I-10
Lebanon H-3
Leesburg D-10
Lexington G-8
Lorton E-11
Louisa F-10
Lovingston G-8
Lunenburg H-9
Luray E-9
Lynchburg G-8
Madison E-9
Manassas E-11
Marion H-4
Martinsville I-7
Mathews G-13
Monterey E-7
Montross F-12
New Castle G-6
New Kent G-11
Newport News H-12
Norfolk H-13
Norton H-2
Nottoway H-10
Orange F-10
Palmyra F-9
Pearisburg G-5
Petersburg H-11
Portsmouth H-13
Powhatan G-10
Prince George H-11
Pulaski H-5
Radford H-6
Reston D-11
Richmond G-11
Roanoke H-7
Rocky Mount H-7
Rustburg H-8
Salem H-7
Saluda G-12

continued on page 103

Travel planning & on-the-road resources

Tourism Information
Virginia Tourism
(800) 847-4882
www.virginia.org

Road Conditions & Construction
511, (866) 695-1182, (800) 367-7623
www.511virginia.org
www.virginiadot.org/travel

West Virginia state facts

Nickname: The Mountain State
Capital: Charleston, E-4

Population: 1,852,994 (rank: 37th)
Largest city: Charleston, 51,400, E-4

Land area: 24,038 sq. mi. (rank: 41st)
Highest point: Spruce Knob, 4,863 ft., E-7

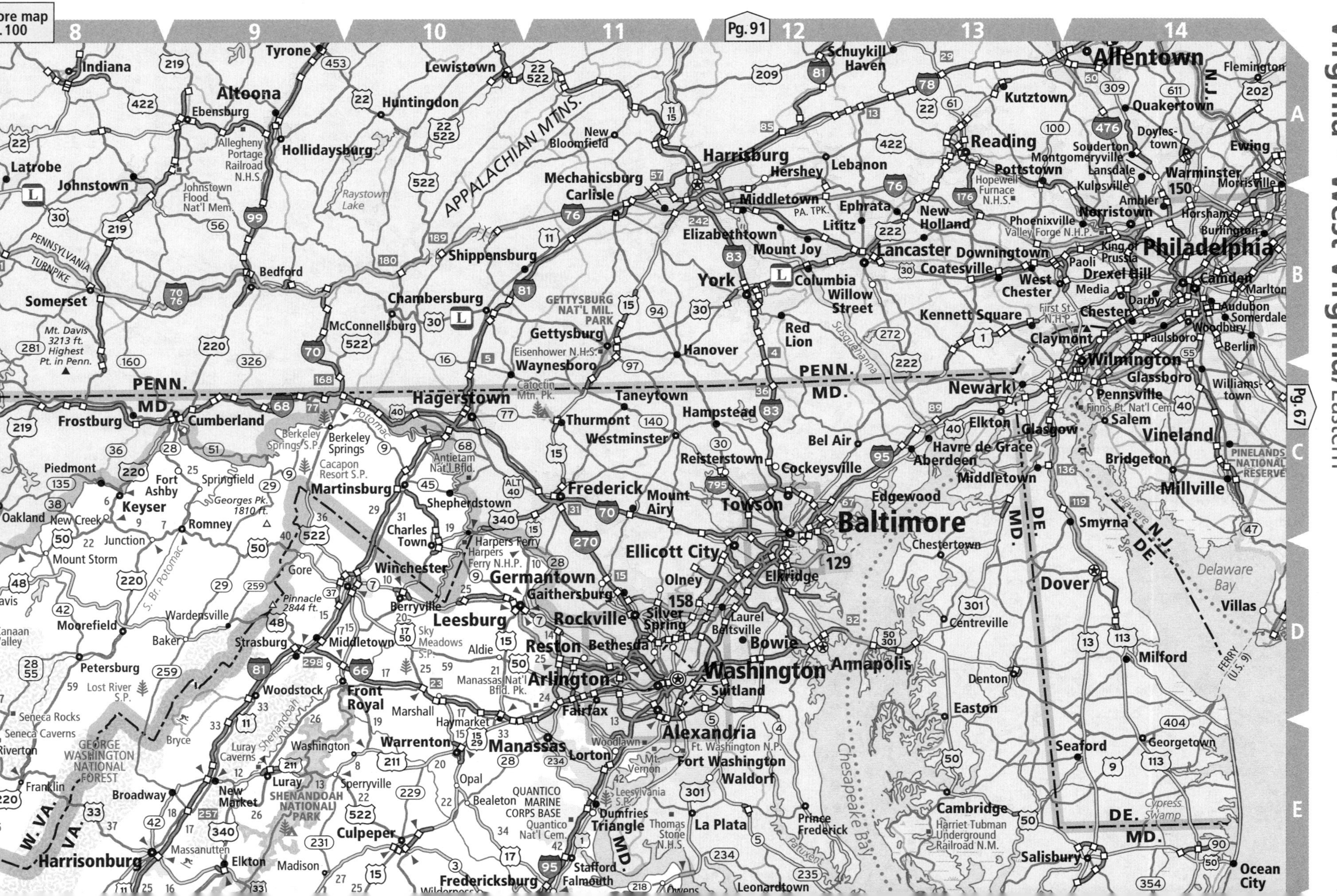

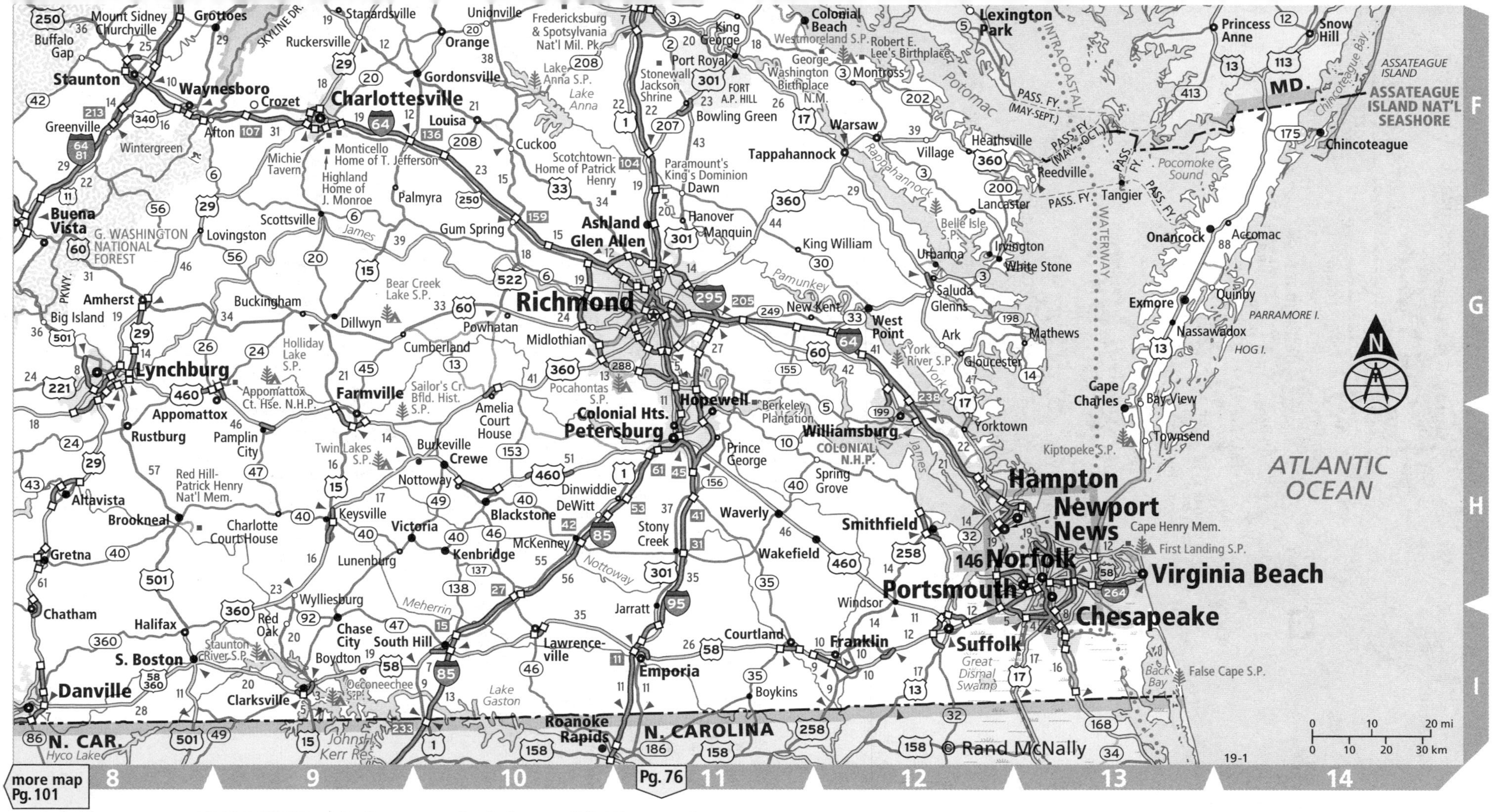

more map Pg. 101

Pg. 76

8 9 10 11 12 13 14

© Rand McNally

continued from page 101

Smithfield H-12
South Boston I-8
South Hill I-10
Stafford E-11
Stanardsville F-9
Staunton F-8
Stuart I-6
Suffolk I-12
Tappahannock F-12
Tazewell H-4
Triangle E-11
Virginia Beach H-13
Warm Springs F-7
Warrenton E-10
Warsaw F-12
Washington E-10
Waynesboro F-8
Williamsburg H-12
Winchester D-10
Wise H-2
Woodbridge E-11
Woodstock D-9
Wytheville H-5
Yorktown H-12

West Virginia

Cities and Towns

Barboursville E-3
Beckley G-5
Berkeley Springs C-9
Bethlehem B-6
Bluefield H-5
Buckhannon D-6
Charles Town D-10
Charleston E-4
Clay E-5
Delbarton G-3
Dunbar E-4
Elizabeth D-4
Elkins D-7
Fairmont C-6
Fayetteville F-5
Franklin E-8
Glenville D-5
Grafton C-7
Grantsville D-5
Hamlin F-3
Harrisville D-5
Hico F-5
Hinton G-5
Huntington E-3
Keyser C-8
Kingwood C-7
Lewisburg G-6
Logan F-3
Madison F-4
Marlinton F-6
Martinsburg C-10
Middlebourne C-5
Milton E-3
Moorefield D-8
Morgantown C-7
Moundsville B-5
New Martinsville C-5
Nitro E-4
Nutter Fort D-6
Oak Hill F-5
Parsons D-7
Petersburg D-8
Philippi D-7
Pineville G-4
Point Pleasant D-3
Princeton G-5
Ravenswood D-4
Richwood F-6
Ripley D-4
Romney C-9
St. Albans E-4
St. Marys C-5
South Charleston E-4
Spencer D-4
Summersville F-5
Sutton E-6
Union G-6
Vienna C-4
Wayne F-3
Webster Springs E-6
Weirton A-6
Welch G-4
Wellsburg B-6
West Union D-5
Weston D-6
Wheeling B-6
White Sulphur Springs G-6
Williamson G-3
Williamstown C-4
Winfield E-4

Travel planning & on-the-road resources

Tourism Information	West Virginia Division of Tourism (800) 225-5982, (304) 558-2200 gotowv.com, www.wvtourism.com	**Road Conditions & Construction**	511, (877) 982-7623 www.wv511.org www.transportation.wv.gov

Washington state facts

Nickname: The Evergreen State
Capital: Olympia, D-3

Population: 6,724,540 (rank: 13th)
Largest city: Seattle, 608,660, C-4

Land area: 66,455 sq. mi. (rank: 20th)
Highest point: Mount Rainier, 14,411 ft., D-4

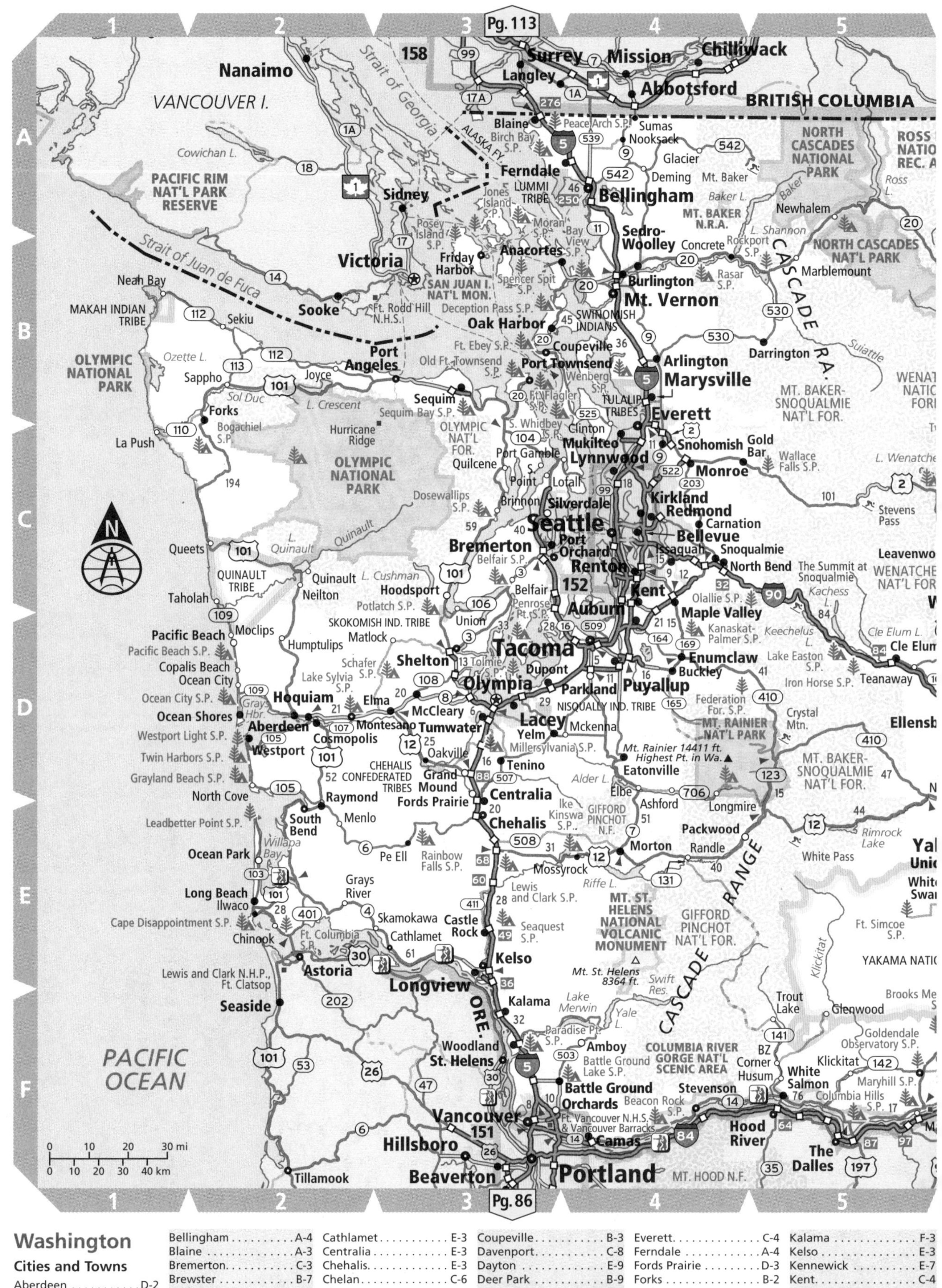

Washington

Cities and Towns

Aberdeen D-2
Amboy. F-4
Anacortes B-4
Arlington B-4
Asotin E-10
Auburn D-4
Battle Ground. F-3
Bellevue C-4
Bellingham A-4
Blaine A-3
Bremerton. C-3
Brewster B-7
Bridgeport B-7
Buckley D-4
Burbank E-7
Burlington. B-4
Camas F-4
Carnation C-4
Cashmere C-6
Castle Rock E-3
Cathlamet. E-3
Centralia E-3
Chehalis. E-3
Chelan. C-6
Cheney C-9
Chewelah B-9
Clarkston. E-10
Cle Elum D-5
Colfax D-9
Colville B-9
Connell E-8
Cosmopolis D-2
Coupeville. B-3
Davenport. C-8
Dayton E-9
Deer Park B-9
Dupont D-3
East Wenatchee C-6
Eatonville D-4
Ellensburg D-6
Elma D-3
Entiat. C-6
Enumclaw D-4
Ephrata D-7
Everett. C-4
Ferndale A-4
Fords Prairie D-3
Forks B-2
Friday Harbor B-3
Gold Bar C-4
Goldendale F-5
Grand Mound. D-3
Grandview E-6
Granger. E-6
Hoquiam D-2
Issaquah C-4
Kalama F-3
Kelso E-3
Kennewick E-7
Kent. C-4
Kettle Falls A-8
Kirkland C-4
Lacey D-3
Leavenworth. C-6
Longview E-3
Lynnwood C-4
Mabton E-6
Maple Valley. C-4

NOTE: Maps are not always in alphabetical order.
See Page 1 for map location in this atlas.

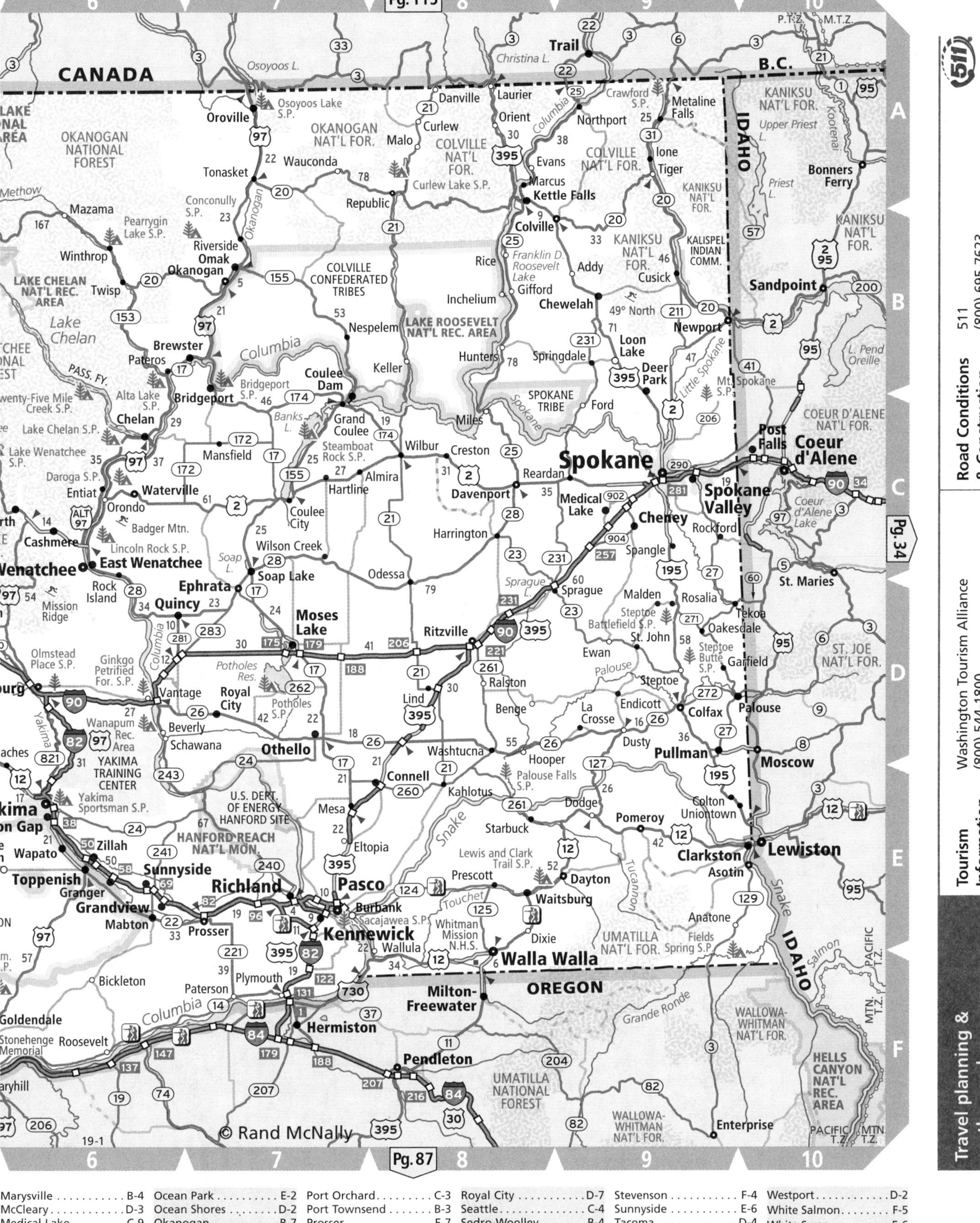

Road Conditions & Construction

511
(800) 695-7623
www.wsdot.wa.gov/traffic

Tourism Information

Washington Tourism Alliance
(800) 544-1800
www.experiencewa.com

Travel planning & on-the-road resources

Marysville B-4
McCleary D-3
Medical Lake C-9
Monroe C-4
Montesano D-2
Morton E-4
Moses Lake D-7
Mount Vernon B-4
Mukilteo C-4
Newport B-9
North Bend C-4
Oak Harbor B-3
Ocean Park E-2
Ocean Shores D-2
Okanogan B-7
Olympia D-3
Omak B-7
Orchards F-3
Oroville A-7
Othello D-7
Parkland D-4
Pasco E-7
Pomeroy E-9
Port Angeles B-3
Port Orchard C-3
Port Townsend B-3
Prosser E-7
Pullman D-9
Puyallup D-4
Quincy D-6
Raymond E-2
Redmond C-4
Renton C-4
Republic A-8
Richland E-7
Ritzville D-8
Royal City D-7
Seattle C-4
Sedro-Woolley B-4
Sequim B-3
Shelton D-3
Silverdale C-3
Snohomish C-4
Snoqualmie C-4
Soap Lake C-7
South Bend E-2
Spokane C-9
Spokane Valley C-9
Stevenson F-4
Sunnyside E-6
Tacoma D-4
Tenino D-3
Toppenish E-6
Tumwater D-3
Union Gap E-6
Vancouver F-3
Walla Walla F-8
Wapato E-6
Waterville C-6
Wenatchee C-6
Westport D-2
White Salmon F-5
White Swan E-6
Woodland F-3
Yakima E-6
Yelm D-3
Zillah E-6

Wisconsin state facts

Nickname: The Badger State
Capital: Madison, G-4

Population: 5,686,986 (rank: 20th)
Largest city: Milwaukee, 594,833, G-6

Land area: 54,158 sq. mi. (rank: 25th)
Highest point: Timms Hill, 1,951 ft., D-4

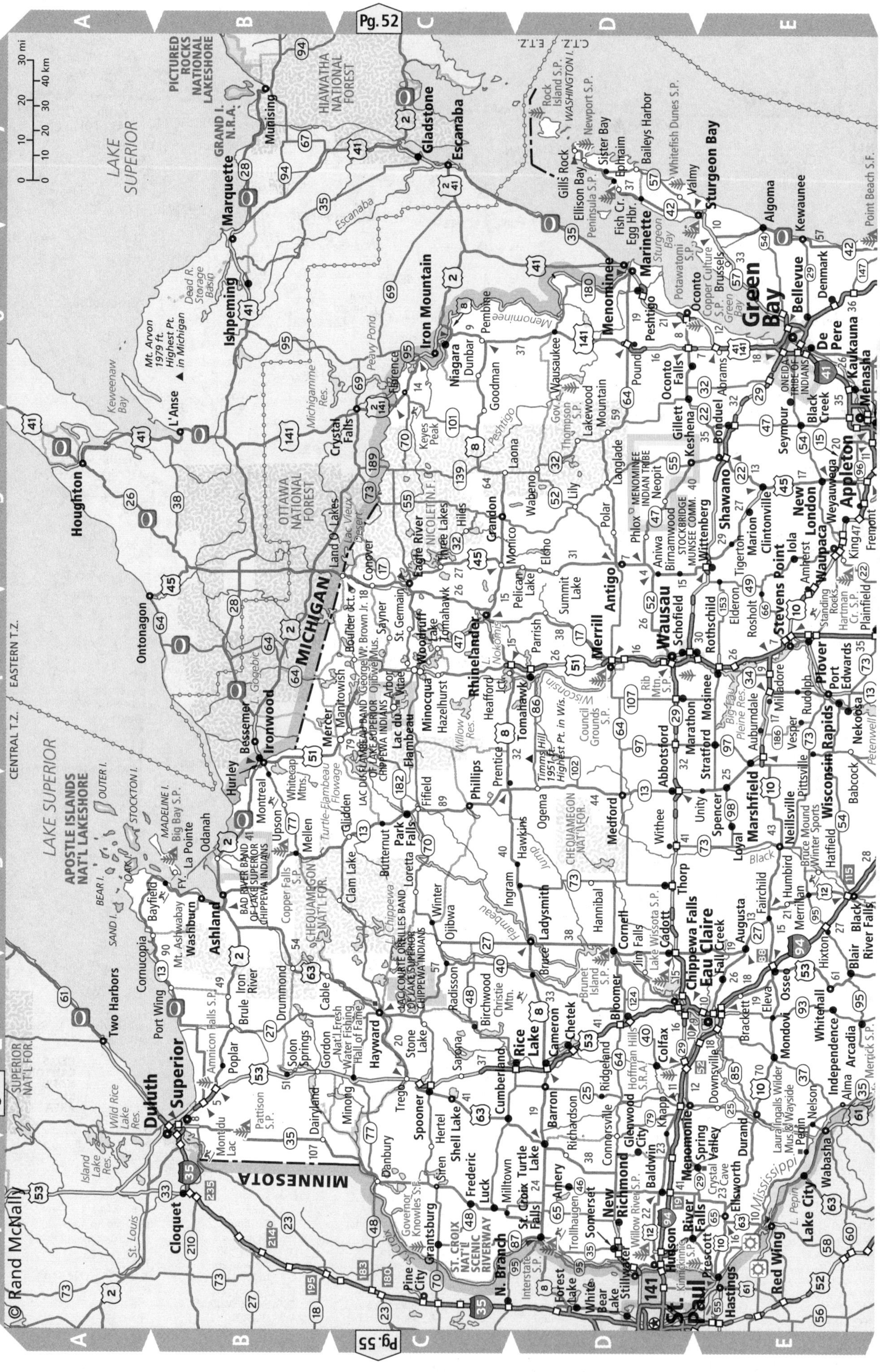

Pg. 52
Pg. 54
Pg. 55

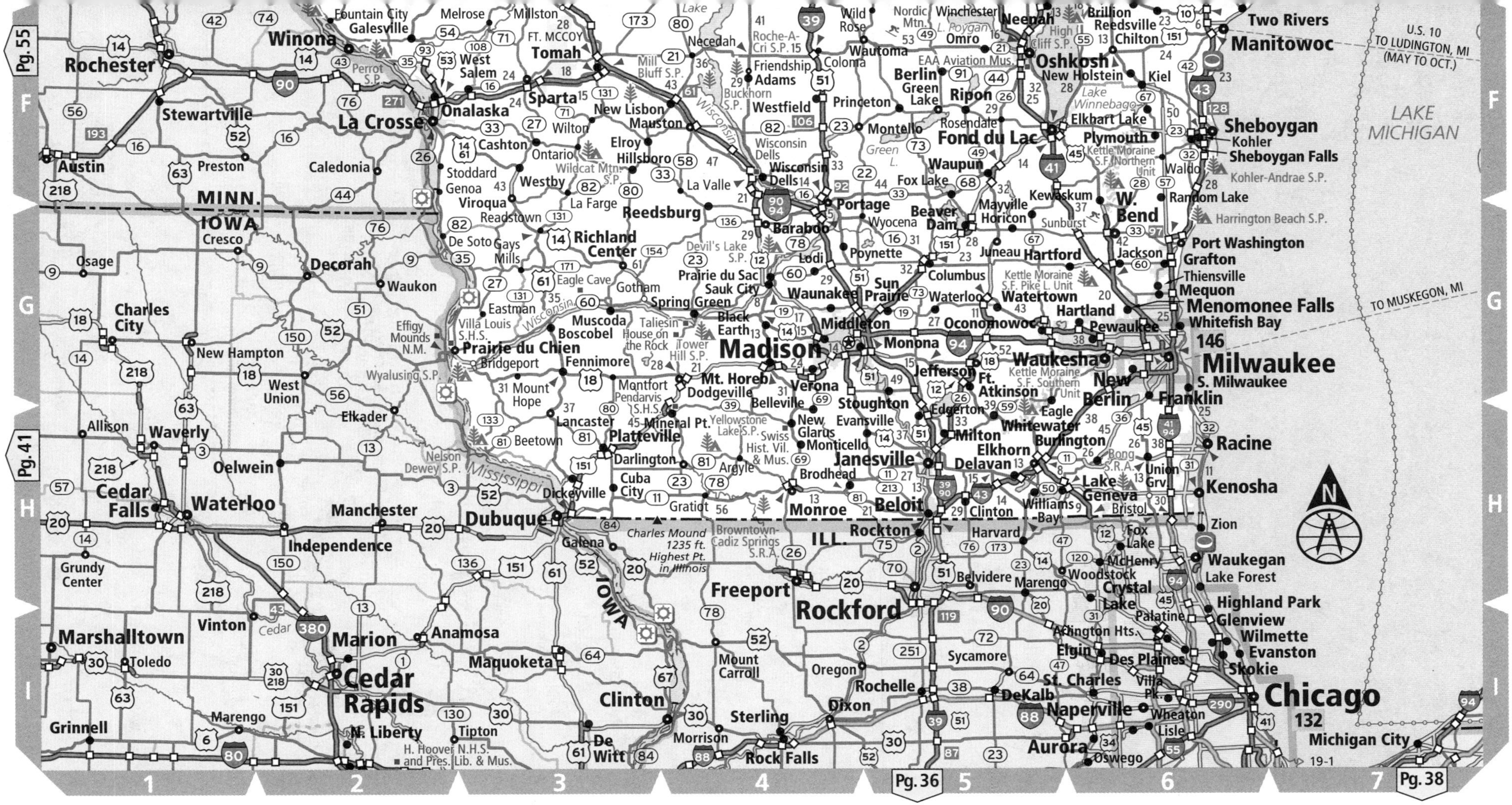

NOTE: Maps are not always in alphabetical order.
See Page 1 for map location in this atlas.

Wisconsin

Cities and Towns

City	Grid
Antigo	D-5
Appleton	E-5
Arbor Vitae	C-4
Ashland	B-3
Baraboo	G-4
Barron	D-2
Beaver Dam	G-5
Bellevue	E-6
Beloit	H-5
Black River Falls	E-3
Bonduel	E-5
Chilton	F-6
Chippewa Falls	D-2
Darlington	H-4
De Pere	E-6
Dodgeville	G-4
Eau Claire	E-2
Elkhorn	H-5
Ellsworth	E-1
Fond du Lac	F-5
Fort Atkinson	G-5
Franklin	G-6
Grafton	G-6
Green Bay	E-6
Hartford	G-6
Hayward	C-2
Hudson	D-1
Janesville	H-5
Jefferson	G-5
Juneau	G-5
Kaukauna	E-6
Kenosha	H-6
Kewaunee	E-6
La Crosse	F-2
Ladysmith	D-3
Lancaster	H-3
Madison	G-4
Manitowoc	F-6
Marinette	D-6
Marshfield	E-4
Mauston	F-4
Medford	D-3
Menasha	E-5
Menomonee Falls	G-6
Menomonie	D-2
Mequon	G-6
Merrill	D-4
Middleton	G-4
Milwaukee	G-6
Monroe	H-4
Neenah	F-5
Neillsville	E-3
New Berlin	G-6
New Richmond	D-1
Oconomowoc	G-5
Oconto	D-6
Onalaska	F-2
Oshkosh	F-5
Peshtigo	D-6
Pewaukee	G-6
Plover	E-4
Port Washington	G-6
Portage	G-4
Prairie du Chien	G-2
Racine	H-6
Rhinelander	C-4
Rice Lake	D-2
Richland Center	G-3
River Falls	D-1
Rothschild	E-4
Sauk City	G-4
Shawano	E-5
Sheboygan	F-6
South Milwaukee	G-6
Sparta	F-3
Stevens Point	E-4
Stoughton	G-5
Sturgeon Bay	E-7
Sun Prairie	G-5
Superior	B-2
Thiensville	G-6
Two Rivers	F-6
Viroqua	F-3
Washburn	B-3
Watertown	G-5
Waukesha	G-6
Waupaca	E-5
Waupun	F-5
Wausau	D-4
Wautoma	F-5
West Bend	G-6
Whitefish Bay	G-6
Whitewater	H-5
Wisconsin Dells	F-4
Wisconsin Rapids	E-4

Travel planning & on-the-road resources

Tourism Information
Wisconsin Department of Tourism
(800) 432-8747, (608) 266-2161
www.travelwisconsin.com

Road Conditions & Construction
511
(866) 511-9472
www.511wi.gov

Wyoming

Cities and Towns

Afton D-1
Albin F-9
Alpine C-1
Baggs G-5
Bairoil E-5
Bar Nunn D-6
Basin B-4
Beulah A-9
Big Horn A-6
Big Piney D-2
Bondurant C-2
Buffalo B-6
Burlington B-4
Burns F-9
Carpenter G-9
Casper D-6
Centennial F-7
Cheyenne F-8
Chugwater F-8
Clearmont A-6
Cody A-3
Cokeville E-1
Daniel D-2
Dayton A-5
Deaver A-4
Diamondville F-2
Douglas D-7
Dubois C-3
Eden E-3
Edgerton C-6
Elk Mountain F-6
Evanston F-1
Evansville D-6
Farson E-3
Fort Bridger F-2
Fort Laramie E-8
Fort Washakie D-4
Freedom D-1
Garland A-4
Gillette B-7
Glendo D-8
Granger F-2
Green River F-3
Greybull B-4
Guernsey E-8
Hanna E-6
Horse Creek F-8
Hudson D-4
Hulett A-8
Jackson C-1
Jeffrey City D-5
Kaycee C-6
Kemmerer E-2
Kinnear D-4
La Barge E-2
LaGrange F-9
Lander D-4
Laramie F-7
Linch C-6
Lingle E-9
Lovell A-4
Lucerne C-4
Lusk D-8
Lyman F-2
Manderson B-5
Manville D-8
Marbleton D-2
McFadden F-7
Medicine Bow E-6
Meeteetse B-4
Midwest C-6
Moorcroft B-8
Moose C-2
Mountain View F-2
Newcastle B-9
Opal F-2
Osage B-8
Pavillion C-4
Pine Bluffs F-9
Pinedale D-2
Powell A-4
Ranchester A-5
Rawlins F-5
Riverton D-4
Rock River F-7
Rock Springs F-3
Saratoga F-6
Sheridan A-6
Shoshoni C-4
Sinclair F-5
Smoot D-1
Sundance B-8
Superior F-3
Ten Sleep B-5
Teton Village C-1
Thayne D-1
Thermopolis C-4
Torrington E-9
Upton B-8
Wamsutter F-5
Wheatland E-8
Worland B-5
Wright C-7

Wyoming state facts

Nickname: The Equality State
Capital: Cheyenne, F-8

Population: 563,626 (rank: 50th)
Largest city: Cheyenne, 59,466, F-8

Land area: 97,093 sq. mi. (rank: 9th)
Highest point: Gannett Peak, 13,804 ft., C-3

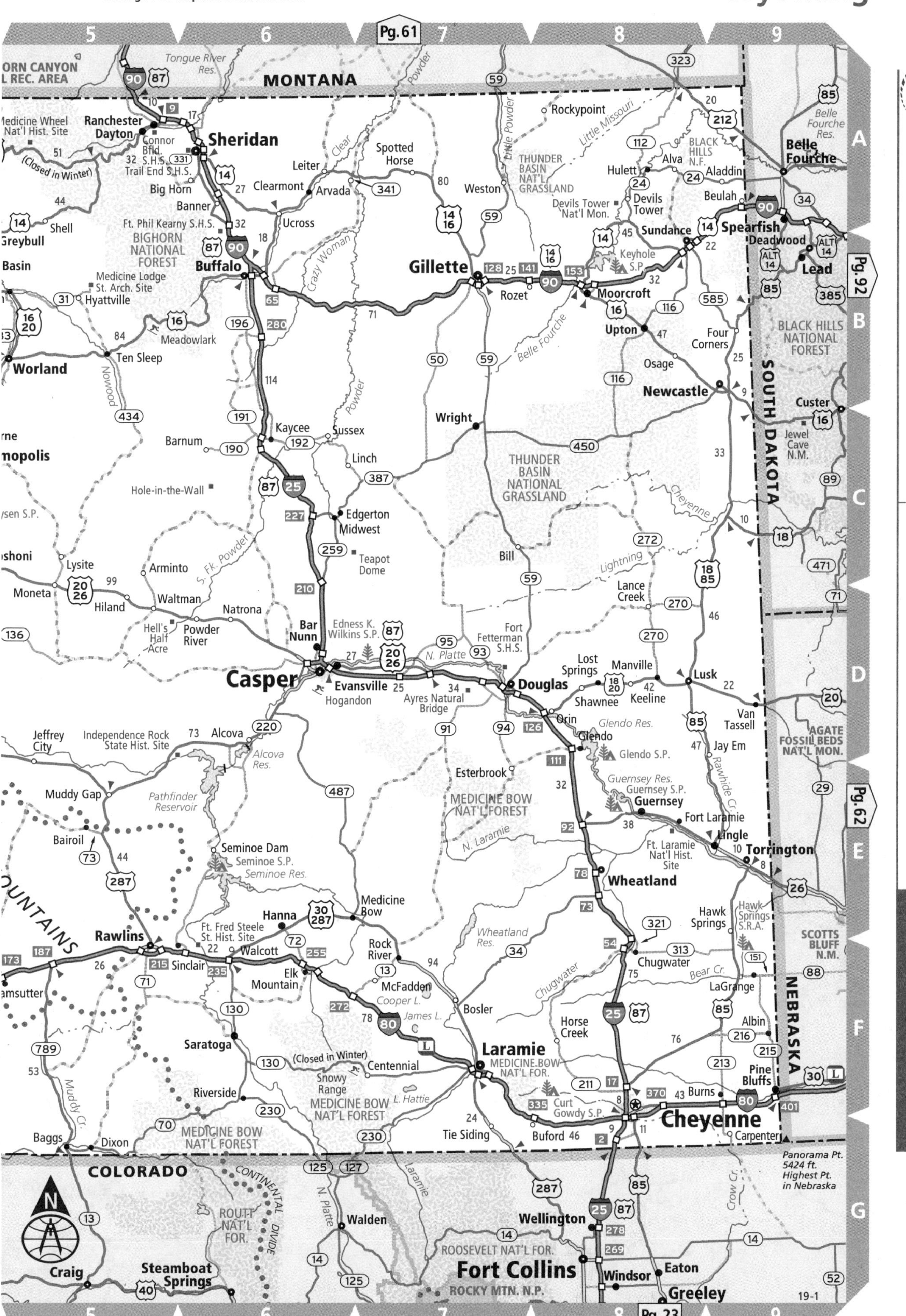

Tourism Information
Wyoming Office of Tourism
(800) 225-5996, (307) 777-7777
www.wyomingtourism.org

Road Conditions & Construction
511
(888) 996-7623
www.wyoroad.info

Travel planning & on-the-road resources

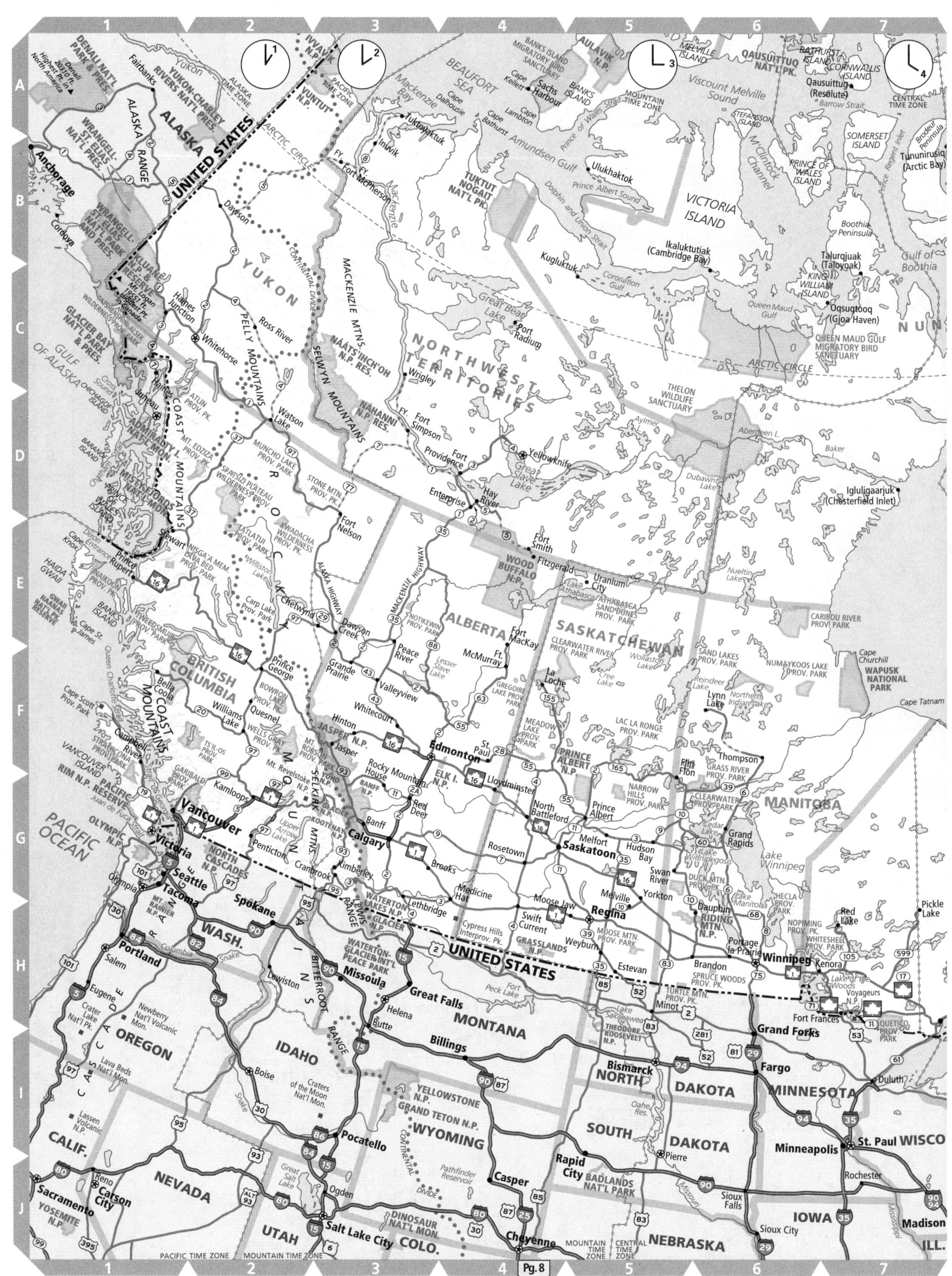
YUKON
NORTHWEST TERRITORIES
BRITISH COLUMBIA
ALBERTA
SASKATCHEWAN
MANITOBA
ALASKA
UNITED STATES
PACIFIC OCEAN
Edmonton
Calgary
Vancouver
Victoria
Saskatoon
Regina
Winnipeg
Whitehorse
Yellowknife
Seattle
Spokane
Portland
WASH.
OREGON
IDAHO
MONTANA
WYOMING
NORTH DAKOTA
SOUTH DAKOTA
MINNESOTA
NEVADA
UTAH
COLO.
NEBRASKA
IOWA
CALIF.
Pg. 8

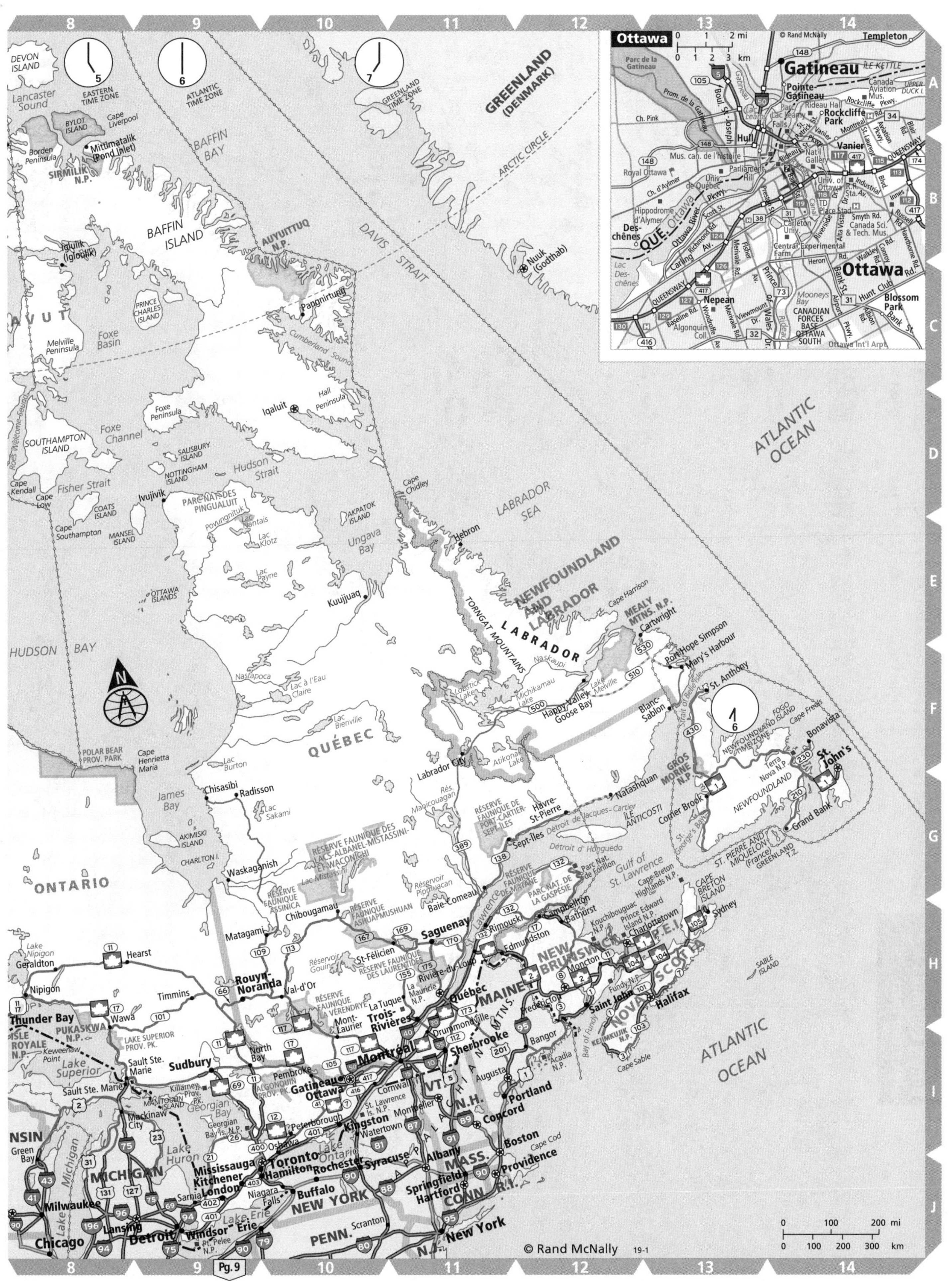

British Columbia provincial facts

Capital: Victoria, I-6

Population: 4,400,057 (rank: 3rd)

Largest city: Vancouver, 603,502, H-6

Land area: 357,216 sq. mi. (rank: 4th)

Highest point: Mt. Fairweather, 15,300 ft.

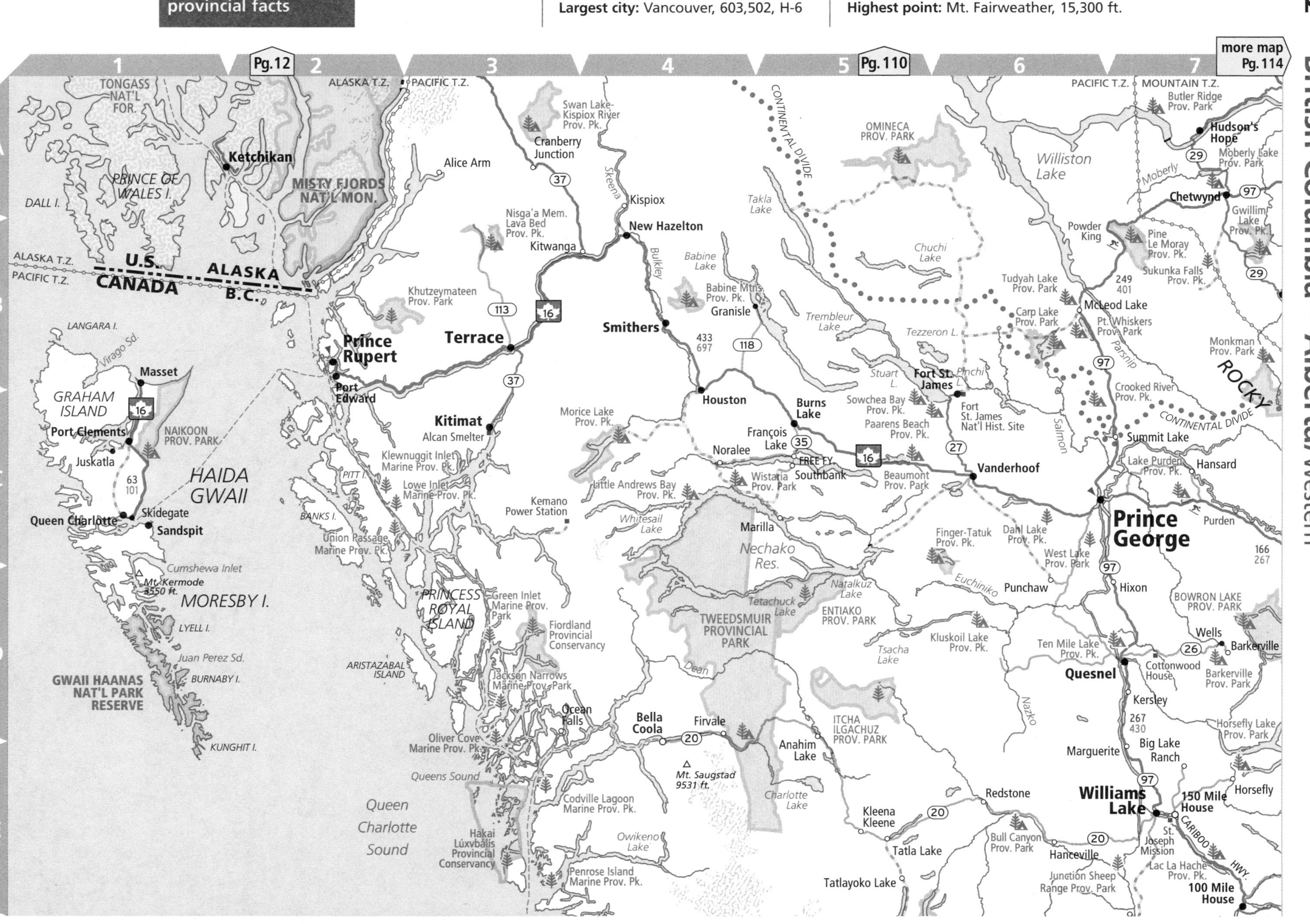

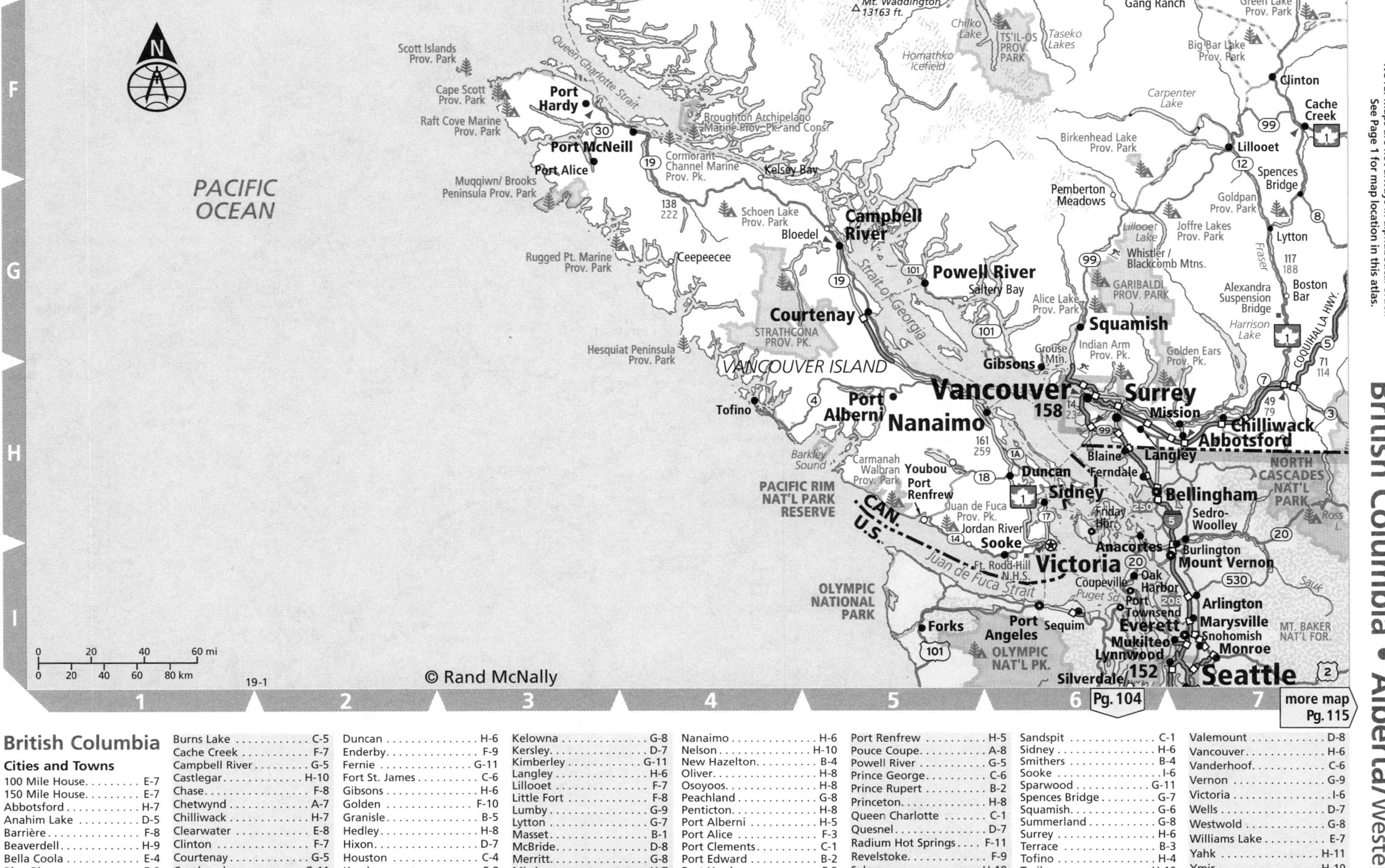

British Columbia

Cities and Towns

100 Mile House . . . E-7
150 Mile House . . . E-7
Abbotsford . . . H-7
Anahim Lake . . . D-5
Barrière . . . F-8
Beaverdell . . . H-9
Bella Coola . . . E-4
Blue River . . . E-9
Boston Bar . . . G-7
Burns Lake . . . C-5
Cache Creek . . . F-7
Campbell River . . . G-5
Castlegar . . . H-10
Chase . . . F-8
Chetwynd . . . A-7
Chilliwack . . . H-7
Clearwater . . . E-8
Clinton . . . F-7
Courtenay . . . G-5
Cranbrook . . . G-11
Creston . . . H-10
Duncan . . . H-6
Enderby . . . F-9
Fernie . . . G-11
Fort St. James . . . C-6
Gibsons . . . H-6
Golden . . . F-10
Granisle . . . B-5
Hedley . . . H-8
Hixon . . . D-7
Houston . . . C-4
Kamloops . . . F-8
Kaslo . . . G-10
Kelowna . . . G-8
Kersley . . . D-7
Kimberley . . . G-11
Langley . . . H-6
Lillooet . . . F-7
Little Fort . . . F-8
Lumby . . . G-9
Lytton . . . G-7
Masset . . . B-1
McBride . . . D-8
Merritt . . . G-8
Mission . . . H-7
Nakusp . . . G-9
Nanaimo . . . H-6
Nelson . . . H-10
New Hazelton . . . B-4
Oliver . . . H-8
Osoyoos . . . H-8
Peachland . . . G-8
Penticton . . . H-8
Port Alberni . . . H-5
Port Alice . . . F-3
Port Clements . . . C-1
Port Edward . . . B-2
Port Hardy . . . F-3
Port McNeill . . . F-4
Port Renfrew . . . H-5
Pouce Coupe . . . A-8
Powell River . . . G-5
Prince George . . . C-6
Prince Rupert . . . B-2
Princeton . . . H-8
Queen Charlotte . . . C-1
Quesnel . . . D-7
Radium Hot Springs . . . F-11
Revelstoke . . . F-9
Salmo . . . H-10
Salmon Arm . . . F-9
Sandspit . . . C-1
Sidney . . . H-6
Smithers . . . B-4
Sooke . . . I-6
Sparwood . . . G-11
Spences Bridge . . . G-7
Squamish . . . G-6
Summerland . . . G-8
Surrey . . . H-6
Terrace . . . B-3
Tofino . . . H-4
Trail . . . H-10
Tumbler Ridge . . . B-8
Valemount . . . D-8
Vancouver . . . H-6
Vanderhoof . . . C-6
Vernon . . . G-9
Victoria . . . I-6
Wells . . . D-7
Westwold . . . G-8
Williams Lake . . . E-7
Yahk . . . H-11
Ymir . . . H-10
Youbou . . . H-5

Travel planning & on-the-road resources

Tourism Information
Destination British Columbia
(604) 660-2861
www.hellobc.com

Road Conditions & Construction
(800) 550-4997
www.drivebc.ca

Alberta provincial facts

Capital: Edmonton, C-12
Population: 3,645,257 (rank: 4th)
Largest city: Calgary, 1,096,833, F-12
Land area: 248,000 sq. mi. (rank: 6th)
Highest point: Mount Columbia, 12,294 ft., E-10

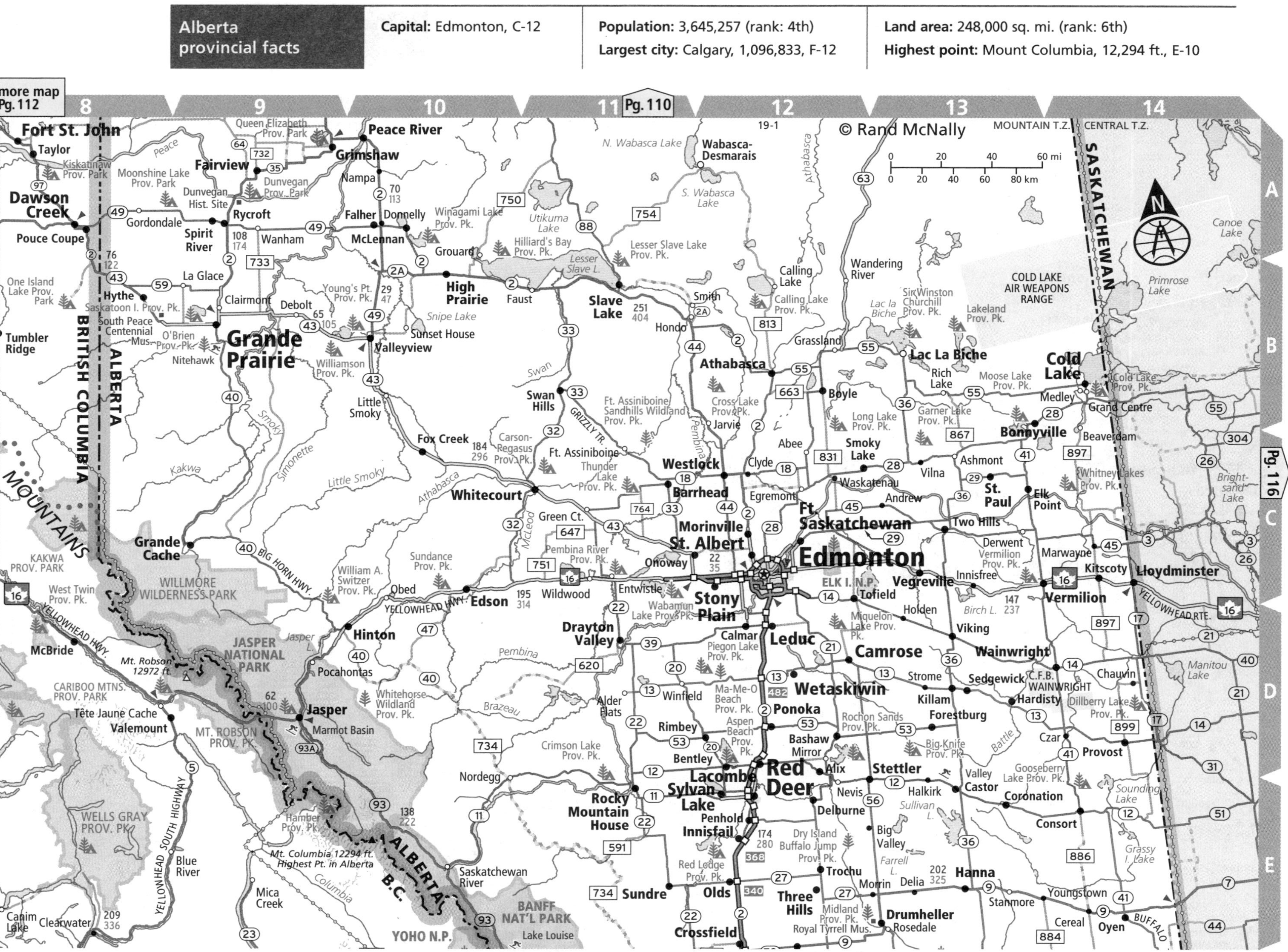

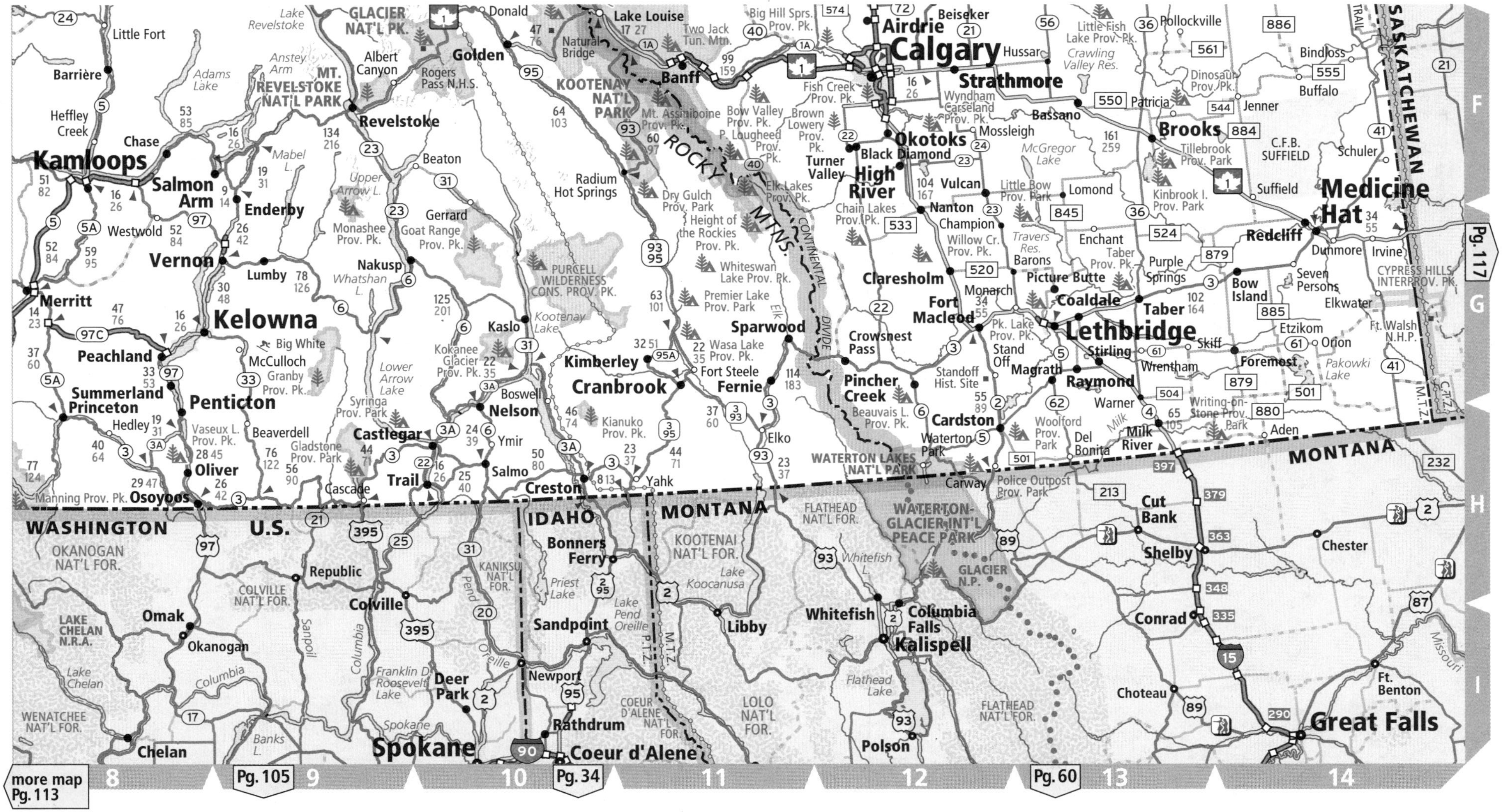

Pg. 117

more map Pg. 113

Pg. 105

Pg. 34

Pg. 60

Alberta

Cities and Towns

Airdrie . . . F-12
Alix . . . D-12
Athabasca . . . B-12
Banff . . . F-11
Barrhead . . . C-11
Bassano . . . F-13
Beiseker . . . E-12
Bentley . . . D-12
Black Diamond . . . F-12
Bonnyville . . . B-13
Bow Island . . . G-14
Boyle . . . B-12
Brooks . . . F-13
Calgary . . . F-12
Calmar . . . D-12
Camrose . . . D-12
Cardston . . . H-12
Castor . . . E-13
Claresholm . . . G-12
Coaldale . . . G-13
Cold Lake . . . B-14
Coronation . . . E-13
Crossfield . . . E-12
Crowsnest Pass . . . G-12
Drayton Valley . . . D-11
Drumheller . . . E-13
Dunmore . . . G-14
Edmonton . . . C-12
Edson . . . C-10
Elk Point . . . C-13
Falher . . . A-10
Forestburg . . . D-13
Fort Macleod . . . G-12
Fort Saskatchewan . . . C-12
Fox Creek . . . C-10
Grande Cache . . . C-9
Grande Prairie . . . B-9
Hanna . . . E-13
High Prairie . . . B-10
High River . . . F-12
Hinton . . . D-10
Hythe . . . B-8
Innisfail . . . E-12
Jasper . . . D-9
Killam . . . D-13
Lac La Biche . . . B-13
Lacombe . . . D-12
Leduc . . . D-12
Lethbridge . . . G-13
Lloydminster . . . C-14
Magrath . . . G-13
McLennan . . . A-10
Medicine Hat . . . G-14
Morinville . . . C-12
Nanton . . . G-12
Okotoks . . . F-12
Olds . . . E-12
Onoway . . . C-12
Oyen . . . E-14
Penhold . . . E-12
Picture Butte . . . G-13
Pincher Creek . . . G-12
Ponoka . . . D-12
Provost . . . D-14
Raymond . . . G-13
Red Deer . . . E-12
Redcliff . . . G-14
Rimbey . . . D-12
Rocky Mountain House . . . E-11
St. Albert . . . C-12
St. Paul . . . C-13
Sedgewick . . . D-13
Slave Lake . . . B-11
Smoky Lake . . . C-12
Stettler . . . E-13
Stirling . . . G-13
Stony Plain . . . C-12
Sundre . . . E-11
Swan Hills . . . B-11
Sylvan Lake . . . E-12
Taber . . . G-13
Three Hills . . . E-12
Tofield . . . C-12
Trochu . . . E-12
Turner Valley . . . F-12
Two Hills . . . C-13
Valleyview . . . B-10
Vegreville . . . C-13
Vermilion . . . C-14
Viking . . . D-13
Vulcan . . . F-12
Wainwright . . . D-14
Westlock . . . C-12
Wetaskiwin . . . D-12
Whitecourt . . . C-11

Travel planning & on-the-road resources

Tourism Information
Travel Alberta
(800) 252-3782
www.travelalberta.com, travelalberta.us

Road Conditions & Construction
511, (877) 262-4997
(888) 799-1522, (855) 391-9743
www.ama.ab.ca, 511.alberta.ca

Saskatchewan provincial facts

Capital: Regina, H-5

Population: 1,033,381 (rank: 6th)
Largest city: Saskatoon, 222,189, F-4

Land area: 228,445 sq. mi. (rank: 7th)
Highest point: Cypress Hills, 4,817 ft., I-1

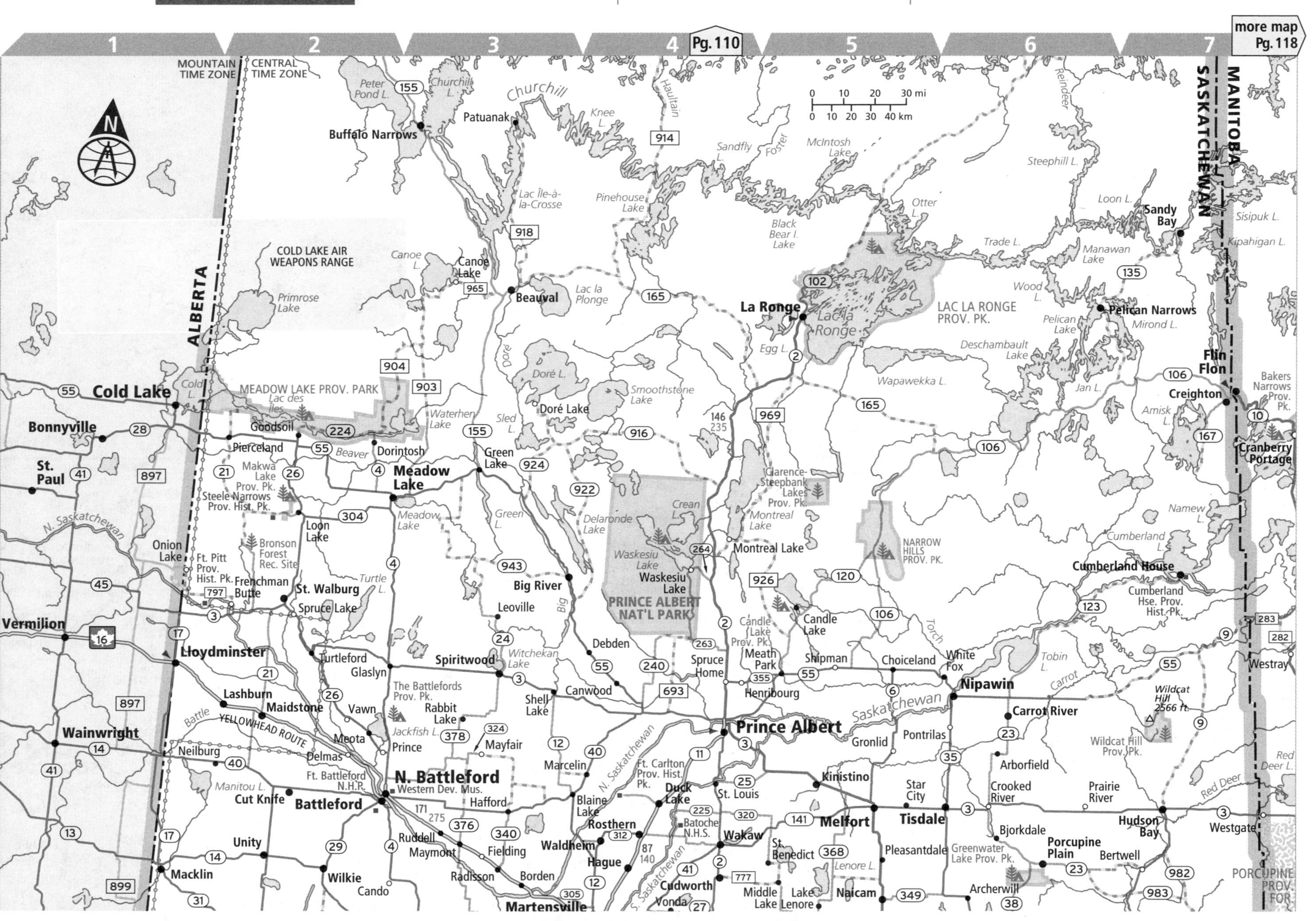

Road Conditions & Construction

(888) 335-7623
Saskatoon area: (306) 933-8333
Regina area: (306) 787-7623, www.saskatchewan.ca/residents/transportation/highways/highway-hotline

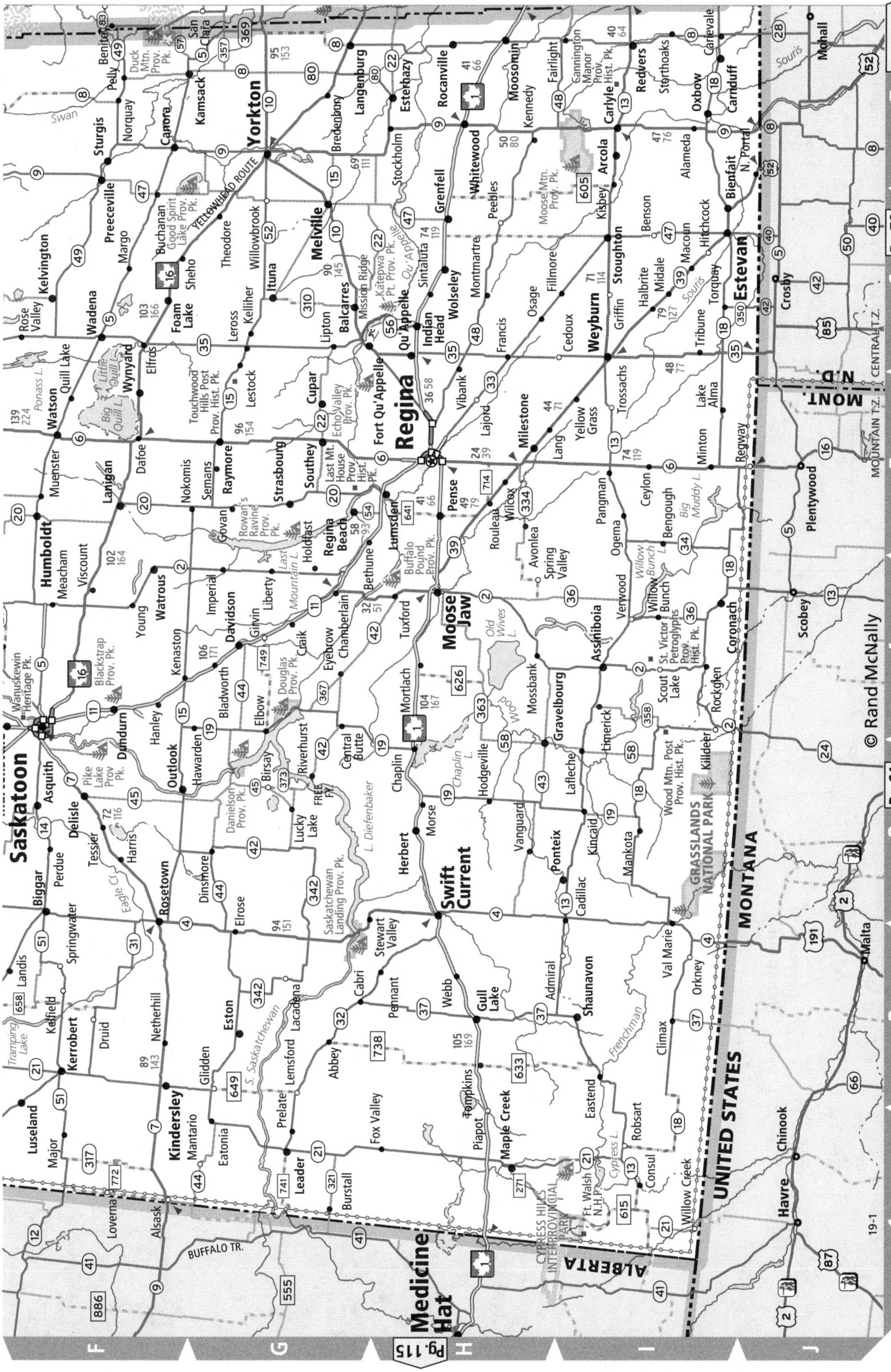

Tourism Information

Tourism Saskatchewan
(877) 237-2273, (306) 787-9600
www.tourismsaskatchewan.com
www.sasktourism.com

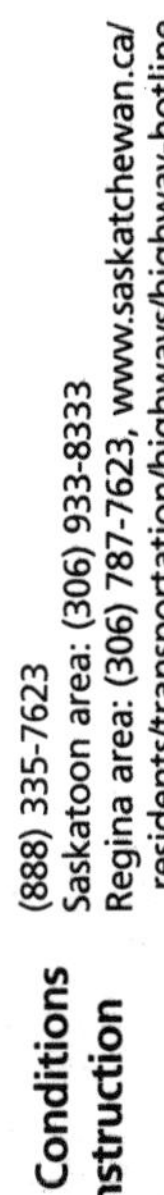

Travel planning & on-the-road resources

Manitoba provincial facts

Capital: Winnipeg, H-11	**Population:** 1,208,268 (rank: 5th)	**Land area:** 213,729 sq. mi. (rank: 8th)
	Largest city: Winnipeg, 663,617, H-11	**Highest point:** Baldy Mountain, 2,730 ft., G-8

more map Pg. 116

Pg. 110

Saskatchewan

Cities and Towns

Place	Grid
Arcola	I-7
Asquith	F-3
Assiniboia	I-4
Avonlea	H-5
Balcarres	G-6
Battleford	E-2
Beauval	B-3
Bethune	G-5
Bienfait	I-6
Big River	D-3
Biggar	F-3
Blaine Lake	E-3
Buffalo Narrows	A-3
Cabri	G-2
Canora	F-7
Canwood	D-4
Carlyle	I-7
Carnduff	I-7
Carrot River	D-6
Central Butte	G-4
Choiceland	D-5
Coronach	I-4
Craik	G-4
Creighton	C-7
Cudworth	E-4
Cumberland House	D-7
Cupar	G-5
Cut Knife	E-2
Davidson	G-4
Debden	D-4
Delisle	F-3
Duck Lake	E-4
Dundurn	F-4
Eastend	I-2
Eatonia	G-1
Elrose	G-2
Esterhazy	H-7
Estevan	I-6
Eston	G-2
Foam Lake	F-6
Fort Qu'Appelle	G-6
Glaslyn	D-2
Gravelbourg	H-3
Green Lake	C-3
Grenfell	H-6
Gull Lake	H-2
Hafford	E-3
Hague	E-4
Hanley	F-4
Herbert	H-3
Hudson Bay	E-7
Humboldt	F-5
Indian Head	H-6
Ituna	G-6
Kamsack	G-7
Kelvington	F-6
Kerrobert	F-2
Kindersley	F-2
Kinistino	E-5
La Ronge	B-5
Lafleche	I-3
Langenburg	G-7
Lanigan	F-5
Lashburn	D-2
Leader	G-1
Leoville	D-3
Lloydminster	D-1
Lucky Lake	G-3
Lumsden	H-5
Luseland	F-2

Manitoba

Cities and Towns

Place	Grid
Amaranth	H-10
Angusville	H-8
Arborg	G-11
Ashern	G-10
Austin	H-9
Baldur	I-9
Beausejour	H-11
Belmont	I-9
Benito	F-7
Berens River	E-11
Binscarth	H-8
Birch River	E-8
Birtle	H-8
Boissevain	I-9
Bowsman	F-8
Brandon	I-9
Camperville	F-8
Carberry	I-9
Carman	I-10
Cartwright	I-9
Cormorant	C-8
Cranberry Portage	C-7
Crystal City	I-9
Darlingford	I-10
Dauphin	G-9
Deloraine	I-8
Douglas	H-9
Duck Bay	F-8
Elkhorn	H-8
Elm Creek	I-10
Elphinstone	H-8
Emerson	I-11
Erickson	H-9
Eriksdale	G-10
Ethelbert	G-8
Fisher Branch	G-10
Flin Flon	C-7
Gilbert Plains	G-8
Gimli	G-11
Gladstone	H-9
Glenboro	I-9
Glenella	H-9
Grand Rapids	E-9
Grandview	G-8
Gretna	I-11
Gypsumville	F-10
Hamiota	H-8
Hartney	I-8
Holland	I-9
Inglis	G-8
Inwood	H-11
Kenville	F-8
Killarney	I-9
La Broquerie	I-11
Lac du Bonnet	H-12
Langruth	H-10
Letellier	I-11
Lockport	H-11
Lowe Farm	I-11
Lundar	G-10
MacGregor	H-10
Mafeking	E-8
Manigotagan	G-11
Manitou	I-10
Matheson Island	F-11
McCreary	G-9
Melita	I-8
Miniota	H-8
Minitonas	F-8
Minnedosa	H-9

Macklin . . . E-1
Maidstone . . . D-2
Maple Creek . . . H-1
Martensville . . . F-4
Meadow Lake . . . C-2
Melfort . . . E-5
Melville . . . G-6
Midale . . . I-6
Milestone . . . H-5
Montmartre . . . H-6
Moose Jaw . . . H-4
Moosomin . . . H-7
Muenster . . . F-5
Naicam . . . E-5
Neilburg . . . E-1
Nipawin . . . D-6
Nokomis . . . G-5
Norquay . . . F-7
North Battleford . . . E-2
Outlook . . . F-3
Oxbow . . . I-7
Pelican Narrows . . . B-6
Pense . . . H-5
Perdue . . . F-3
Pierceland . . . C-2
Ponteix . . . I-3
Porcupine Plain . . . E-6
Preeceville . . . F-7
Prince Albert . . . D-4
Qu'Appelle . . . H-6
Quill Lake . . . F-5
Radisson . . . E-3
Raymore . . . G-5
Redvers . . . I-7
Regina . . . H-5
Regina Beach . . . G-5
Rocanville . . . H-7
Rockglen . . . I-4
Rosetown . . . F-3
Rosthern . . . E-4
Rouleau . . . H-5
Saint Louis . . . E-4
Saint Walburg . . . D-2
Sandy Bay . . . B-7
Saskatoon . . . F-4
Shaunavon . . . I-2
Southey . . . G-5
Spiritwood . . . D-3
Star City . . . E-5
Stoughton . . . I-6
Strasbourg . . . G-5
Sturgis . . . F-7
Swift Current . . . H-3
Theodore . . . G-6
Tisdale . . . E-6
Turtleford . . . D-2
Unity . . . E-2
Vibank . . . H-6
Wadena . . . F-6
Wakaw . . . E-4
Waldheim . . . E-4
Watrous . . . F-4
Watson . . . F-5
Weyburn . . . I-6
White Fox . . . D-6
Whitewood . . . H-7
Wilkie . . . E-2
Wolseley . . . H-6
Wynyard . . . F-5
Yellow Grass . . . I-5
Yorkton . . . G-7
Moose Lake . . . D-8
Moosehorn . . . G-10
Morden . . . I-10
Morris . . . I-11
Neepawa . . . H-9
Newdale . . . H-8
Ninette . . . I-9
Niverville . . . I-11
Norway House . . . D-10
Oak River . . . H-8
Oakburn . . . H-8
Oakville . . . H-10
Ochre River . . . G-9
Petersfield . . . H-11
Pierson . . . I-8
Pilot Mound . . . I-10
Pine Falls . . . H-11
Pine River . . . F-8
Pipestone . . . I-8
Plum Coulee . . . I-10
Plumas . . . H-9
Poplar Point . . . H-10
Portage la Prairie . . . H-10
Rathwell . . . I-10
Rennie . . . H-12
Reston . . . I-8
Richer . . . I-11
Rivers . . . H-8
Riverton . . . G-11
Roblin . . . G-8
Roland . . . I-10
Rorketon . . . G-9
Rossburn . . . H-8
Russell . . . G-8
Saint Claude . . . I-10
Saint Jean Baptiste . . . I-11
Saint Laurent . . . H-10
Saint Malo . . . I-11
Saint-Georges . . . H-12
Saint-Pierre-Jolys . . . I-11
Sainte Agathe . . . I-11
Sainte Anne . . . I-11
Sainte Rose du Lac . . . G-9
Sanford . . . I-11
Selkirk . . . H-11
Shoal Lake . . . H-8
Sifton . . . G-8
Snow Lake . . . B-8
Somerset . . . I-10
Souris . . . I-8
Sprague . . . I-12
Steinbach . . . I-11
Swan River . . . F-8
Teulon . . . H-11
The Pas . . . D-8
Thompson . . . A-10
Treherne . . . I-10
Tyndall . . . H-11
Victoria Beach . . . G-11
Virden . . . I-8
Vita . . . I-11
Wabowden . . . B-9
Warren . . . H-11
Wawanesa . . . I-9
Whitemouth . . . H-12
Winkler . . . I-10
Winnipeg . . . H-11
Winnipeg Beach . . . H-11
Winnipegosis . . . F-9
Woodridge . . . I-12

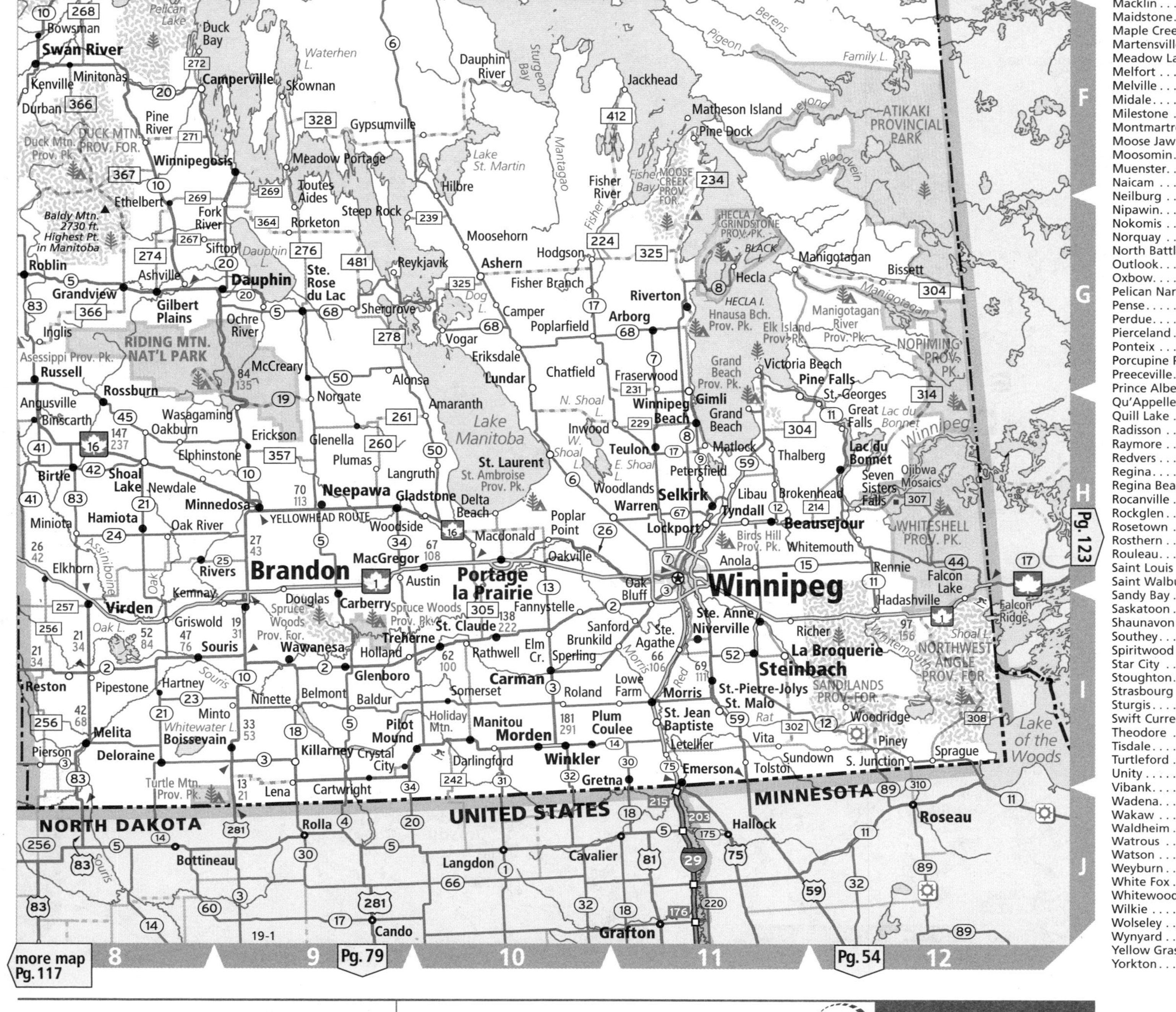

Tourism Information Travel Manitoba
(800) 665-0040, (204) 927-7800
www.travelmanitoba.com

Road Conditions & Construction 511
(877) 627-6237, (204) 945-3704
www.manitoba.ca/roadinfo

Travel planning & on-the-road resources

Ontario provincial facts

Capital: Toronto, G-6

Population: 12,851,821 (rank: 1st)
Largest city: Toronto, 2,615,060, G-6

Land area: 354,342 sq. mi. (rank: 5th)
Highest point: Ishpatina Ridge, 2,275 ft., J-12

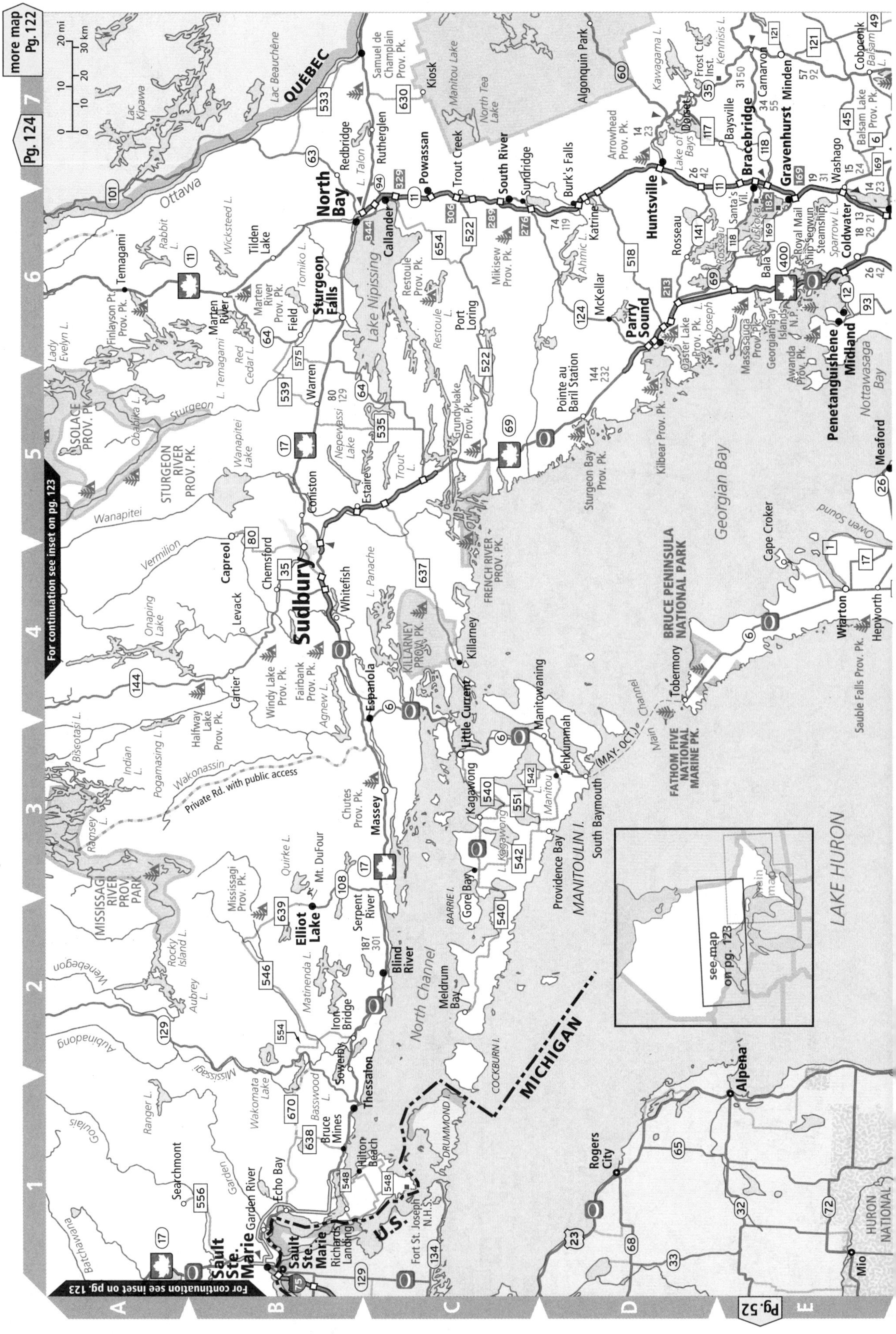

0 10 20 mi
0 10 20 30 km

more map Pg. 122
Pg. 124
For continuation see inset on pg. 123
For continuation see inset on pg. 123
see map on pg. 123
Pg. 52

NOTE: Maps are not always in alphabetical order.
See Page 1 for map location in this atlas.

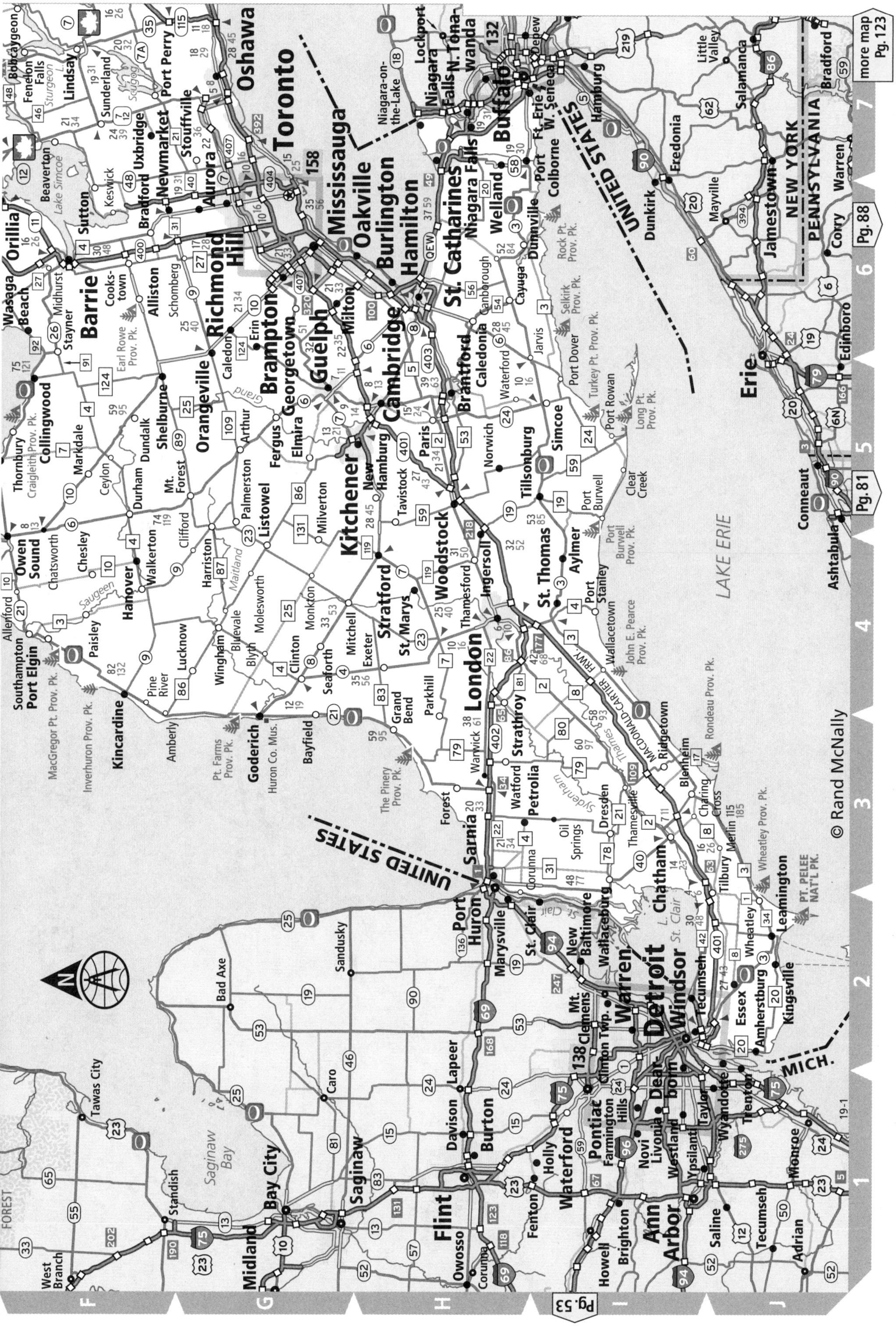

more map Pg. 123

Pg. 88

Pg. 81

Pg. 53

LAKE ERIE

Travel planning & on-the-road resources

Tourism Information
Ont. Tourism Marketing Partnership Corp.
(800) 668-2746
www.ontariotravel.net

Road Conditions & Construction
511, (800) 268-4686
Toronto area: (416) 235-4686
www.mto.gov.on.ca/english/traveller

Capital: Toronto, G-6

Population: 12,851,821 (rank: 1st)
Largest city: Toronto, 2,615,060, G-6

Land area: 354,342 sq. mi. (rank: 5th)
Highest point: Ishpatina Ridge, 2,275 ft., J-12

Ontario provincial facts

more map Pg. 120

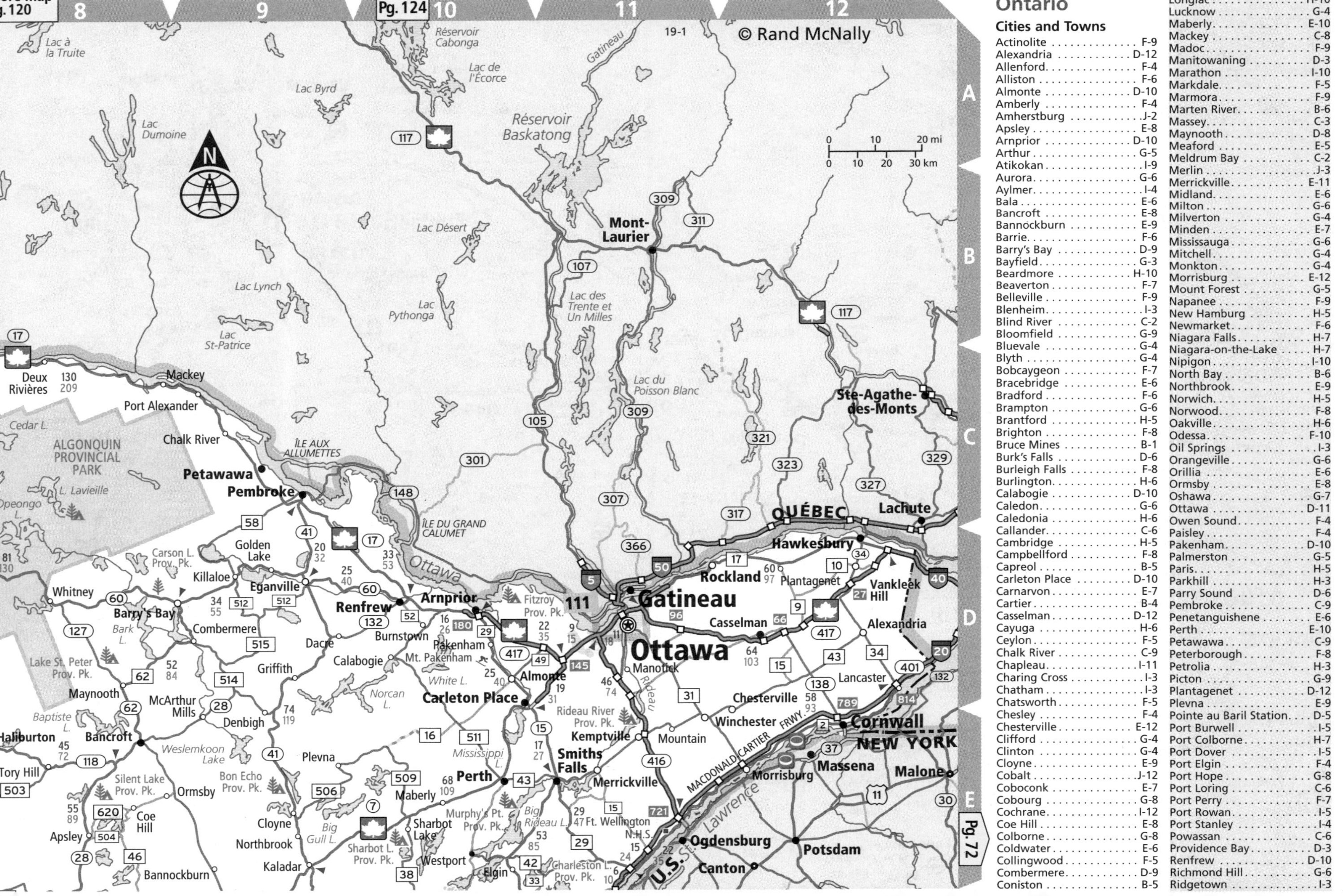

Ontario

Cities and Towns

Actinolite . . . F-9
Alexandria . . . D-12
Allenford . . . F-4
Alliston . . . F-6
Almonte . . . D-10
Amberly . . . F-4
Amherstburg . . . J-2
Apsley . . . E-8
Arnprior . . . D-10
Arthur . . . G-5
Atikokan . . . I-9
Aurora . . . G-6
Aylmer . . . I-4
Bala . . . E-6
Bancroft . . . E-8
Bannockburn . . . E-9
Barrie . . . F-6
Barry's Bay . . . D-9
Bayfield . . . G-3
Beardmore . . . H-10
Beaverton . . . F-7
Belleville . . . F-9
Blenheim . . . I-3
Blind River . . . C-2
Bloomfield . . . G-9
Bluevale . . . G-4
Blyth . . . G-4
Bobcaygeon . . . F-7
Bracebridge . . . E-6
Bradford . . . F-6
Brampton . . . G-6
Brantford . . . H-5
Brighton . . . F-8
Bruce Mines . . . B-1
Burk's Falls . . . D-6
Burleigh Falls . . . F-8
Burlington . . . H-6
Calabogie . . . D-10
Caledon . . . G-6
Caledonia . . . H-6
Callander . . . C-6
Cambridge . . . H-5
Campbellford . . . F-8
Capreol . . . B-5
Carleton Place . . . D-10
Carnarvon . . . E-7
Cartier . . . B-4
Casselman . . . D-12
Cayuga . . . H-6
Ceylon . . . F-5
Chalk River . . . C-9
Chapleau . . . I-11
Charing Cross . . . I-3
Chatham . . . I-3
Chatsworth . . . F-5
Chesley . . . F-4
Chesterville . . . E-12
Clifford . . . G-4
Clinton . . . G-4
Cloyne . . . E-9
Cobalt . . . J-12
Coboconk . . . E-7
Cobourg . . . G-8
Cochrane . . . I-12
Coe Hill . . . E-8
Colborne . . . G-8
Coldwater . . . E-6
Collingwood . . . F-5
Combermere . . . D-9
Coniston . . . B-5
Longlac . . . H-10
Lucknow . . . G-4
Maberly . . . E-10
Mackey . . . C-8
Madoc . . . F-9
Manitowaning . . . D-3
Marathon . . . I-10
Markdale . . . F-5
Marmora . . . F-9
Marten River . . . B-6
Massey . . . C-3
Maynooth . . . D-8
Meaford . . . E-5
Meldrum Bay . . . C-2
Merlin . . . J-3
Merrickville . . . E-11
Midland . . . E-6
Milton . . . G-6
Milverton . . . G-4
Minden . . . E-7
Mississauga . . . G-6
Mitchell . . . G-4
Monkton . . . G-4
Morrisburg . . . E-12
Mount Forest . . . G-5
Napanee . . . F-9
New Hamburg . . . H-5
Newmarket . . . F-6
Niagara Falls . . . H-7
Niagara-on-the-Lake . . . H-7
Nipigon . . . I-10
North Bay . . . B-6
Northbrook . . . E-9
Norwich . . . H-5
Norwood . . . F-8
Oakville . . . H-6
Odessa . . . F-10
Oil Springs . . . I-3
Orangeville . . . G-6
Orillia . . . E-6
Ormsby . . . E-8
Oshawa . . . G-7
Ottawa . . . D-11
Owen Sound . . . F-4
Paisley . . . F-4
Pakenham . . . D-10
Palmerston . . . G-5
Paris . . . H-5
Parkhill . . . H-3
Parry Sound . . . D-6
Pembroke . . . C-9
Penetanguishene . . . E-6
Perth . . . E-10
Petawawa . . . C-9
Peterborough . . . F-8
Petrolia . . . H-3
Picton . . . G-9
Plantagenet . . . D-12
Plevna . . . E-9
Pointe au Baril Station . . . D-5
Port Burwell . . . I-5
Port Colborne . . . H-7
Port Dover . . . I-5
Port Elgin . . . F-4
Port Hope . . . G-8
Port Loring . . . C-6
Port Perry . . . F-7
Port Rowan . . . I-5
Port Stanley . . . I-4
Powassan . . . C-6
Providence Bay . . . D-3
Renfrew . . . D-10
Richmond Hill . . . G-6
Ridgetown . . . I-3

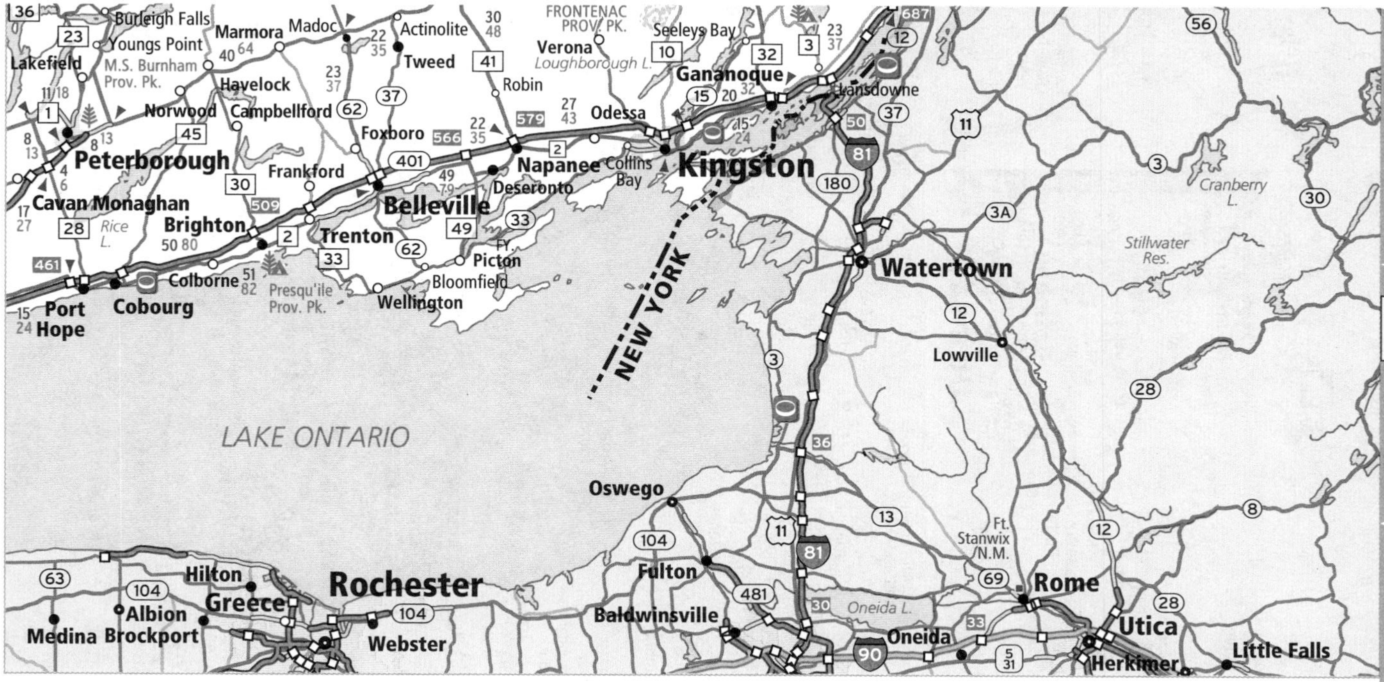

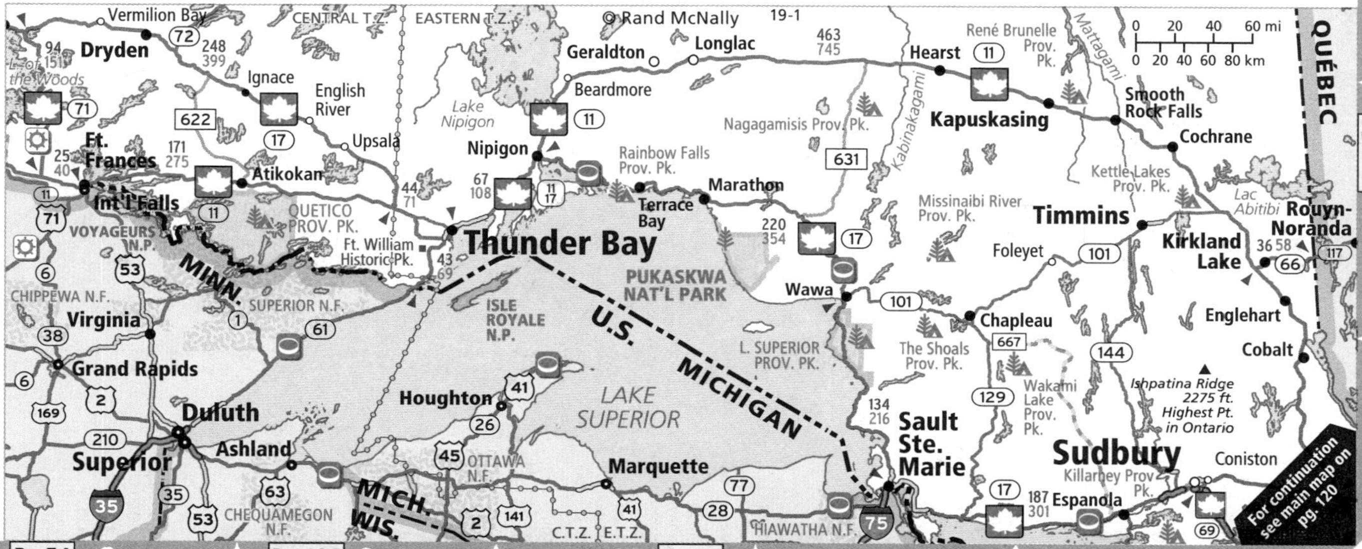

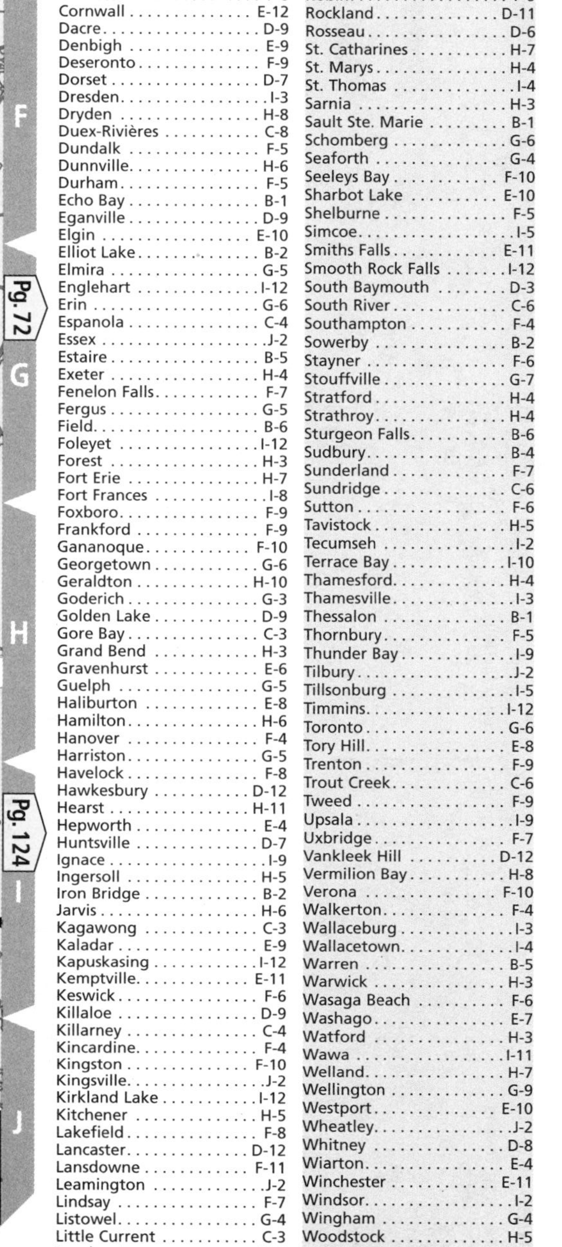

Cookstown . . . F-6
Cornwall . . . E-12
Dacre . . . D-9
Denbigh . . . E-9
Deseronto . . . F-9
Dorset . . . D-7
Dresden . . . I-3
Dryden . . . H-8
Duex-Rivières . . . C-8
Dundalk . . . F-5
Dunnville . . . H-6
Durham . . . F-5
Echo Bay . . . B-1
Eganville . . . D-9
Elgin . . . E-10
Elliot Lake . . . B-2
Elmira . . . G-5
Englehart . . . I-12
Erin . . . G-6
Espanola . . . C-4
Essex . . . J-2
Estaire . . . B-5
Exeter . . . H-4
Fenelon Falls . . . F-7
Fergus . . . G-5
Field . . . B-6
Foleyet . . . I-12
Forest . . . H-3
Fort Erie . . . H-7
Fort Frances . . . I-8
Foxboro . . . F-9
Frankford . . . F-9
Gananoque . . . F-10
Georgetown . . . G-6
Geraldton . . . H-10
Goderich . . . G-3
Golden Lake . . . D-9
Gore Bay . . . C-3
Grand Bend . . . H-3
Gravenhurst . . . E-6
Guelph . . . G-5
Haliburton . . . E-8
Hamilton . . . H-6
Hanover . . . F-4
Harriston . . . G-5
Havelock . . . F-8
Hawkesbury . . . D-12
Hearst . . . H-11
Hepworth . . . E-4
Huntsville . . . D-7
Ignace . . . I-9
Ingersoll . . . H-5
Iron Bridge . . . B-2
Jarvis . . . H-6
Kagawong . . . C-3
Kaladar . . . E-9
Kapuskasing . . . I-12
Kemptville . . . E-11
Keswick . . . F-6
Killaloe . . . D-9
Killarney . . . C-4
Kincardine . . . F-4
Kingston . . . F-10
Kingsville . . . J-2
Kirkland Lake . . . I-12
Kitchener . . . H-5
Lakefield . . . F-8
Lancaster . . . D-12
Lansdowne . . . F-11
Leamington . . . J-2
Lindsay . . . F-7
Listowel . . . G-4
Little Current . . . C-3
London . . . H-4
Robin . . . F-9
Rockland . . . D-11
Rosseau . . . D-6
St. Catharines . . . H-7
St. Marys . . . H-4
St. Thomas . . . I-4
Sarnia . . . H-3
Sault Ste. Marie . . . B-1
Schomberg . . . G-6
Seaforth . . . G-4
Seeleys Bay . . . F-10
Sharbot Lake . . . E-10
Shelburne . . . F-5
Simcoe . . . I-5
Smiths Falls . . . E-11
Smooth Rock Falls . . . I-12
South Baymouth . . . D-3
South River . . . C-6
Southampton . . . F-4
Sowerby . . . B-2
Stayner . . . F-6
Stouffville . . . G-7
Stratford . . . H-4
Strathroy . . . H-4
Sturgeon Falls . . . B-6
Sudbury . . . B-4
Sunderland . . . F-7
Sundridge . . . C-6
Sutton . . . F-6
Tavistock . . . H-5
Tecumseh . . . I-2
Terrace Bay . . . I-10
Thamesford . . . H-4
Thamesville . . . I-3
Thessalon . . . B-1
Thornbury . . . F-5
Thunder Bay . . . I-9
Tilbury . . . J-2
Tillsonburg . . . I-5
Timmins . . . I-12
Toronto . . . G-6
Tory Hill . . . E-8
Trenton . . . F-9
Trout Creek . . . C-6
Tweed . . . F-9
Upsala . . . I-9
Uxbridge . . . F-7
Vankleek Hill . . . D-12
Vermilion Bay . . . H-8
Verona . . . F-10
Walkerton . . . F-4
Wallaceburg . . . I-3
Wallacetown . . . I-4
Warren . . . B-5
Warwick . . . H-3
Wasaga Beach . . . F-6
Washago . . . E-7
Watford . . . H-3
Wawa . . . I-11
Welland . . . H-7
Wellington . . . G-9
Westport . . . E-10
Wheatley . . . J-2
Whitney . . . D-8
Wiarton . . . E-4
Winchester . . . E-11
Windsor . . . I-2
Wingham . . . G-4
Woodstock . . . H-5
Youngs Point . . . F-8

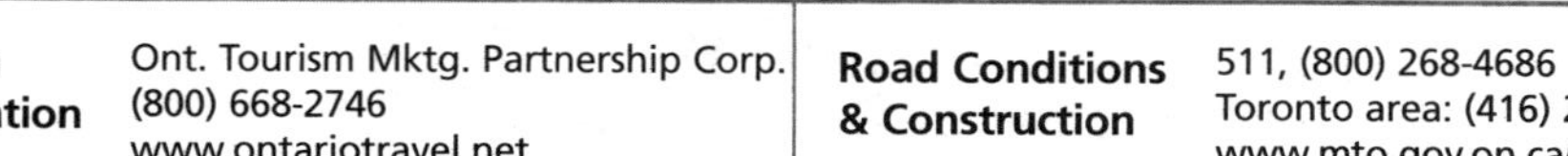

Tourism Information Ont. Tourism Mktg. Partnership Corp.
(800) 668-2746
www.ontariotravel.net

Road Conditions & Construction 511, (800) 268-4686
Toronto area: (416) 235-4686
www.mto.gov.on.ca/english/traveller

Travel planning & on-the-road resources

Québec

Cities and Towns

Place	Grid
Acton Vale	F-4
Alma	B-5
Amos	B-2
Asbestos	F-5
Baie-Comeau	G-8
Baie-St-Paul	C-7
Beauceville	E-6
Bécancour	E-5
Berthierville	E-4
Black Lake	F-6
Bromptonville	F-5
Cap-St-Ignace	D-7
Chandler	G-9
Chicoutimi	B-6
Châteauguay	G-3
Coaticook	G-5
Cowansville	G-4
Dégelis	C-9
Delisle	A-5
Dolbeau-Mistassini	A-5
Donnacona	E-5
Drummondville	F-4
Forestville	A-8
Gaspé	G-9
Gatineau	F-1
Granby	F-4
Grand-Mère	E-4
Havre-St-Pierre	F-9
Joliette	E-3
Jonquière	B-6
La Malbaie	C-7
La Pocatière	C-7
La Sarre	A-2
La Tuque	C-4
Lac-Mégantic	F-6
Lachute	F-2
Laval	F-3
Lebel-sur-Quévillon	A-3
Lévis	D-6
Longueuil	F-3
Louiseville	E-4
Magog	G-5
Malartic	B-2
Maniwaki	C-3
Matane	G-8
Mont-Joli	B-9
Mont-Laurier	E-1
Mont-Tremblant	E-2
Montmagny	D-7
Montréal	F-3
Napierville	G-3
Nicolet	E-4
Notre-Dame-des-Pins	E-6
Plessisville	E-5
Pohénègamook	C-8
Port-Cartier	F-8
Princeville	E-5
Québec	D-6
Repentigny	F-3
Richmond	F-5
Rimouski	B-9
Rivière-du-Loup	C-8
Roberval	B-5
Rouyn-Noranda	B-2
Saguenay	B-6
St-Alexis-des-Monts	E-4
St-Eustache	F-3
St-Félicien	A-5
St-Georges	E-6
St-Henri	D-6
St-Hyacinthe	F-4
St-Jacques	F-3
St-Jean-Port-Joli	D-7
St-Jean-sur-Richelieu	G-4
St-Jérôme	F-3
St-Joseph-de-Beauce	E-6
St-Nicéphore	F-5
St-Pamphile	D-7
St-Raymond	D-5
St-Sauveur	F-3
Ste-Agathe-des-Monts	E-2
Ste-Anne-de-Beaupré	D-6
Ste-Anne-des-Monts	G-8
Ste-Claire	E-6
Ste-Julie	E-5
Ste-Marie	E-6
Salaberry-de-Valleyfield	G-3
Senneterre	B-3
Sept-Îles	F-8
Shawinigan	E-4
Sherbrooke	G-5
Sorel-Tracy	E-4
Témiscaming	C-2
Thetford Mines	E-6
Trois-Pistoles	B-8
Trois-Rivières	E-4
Val-d'Or	B-2
Varennes	F-3
Vaudreuil-Dorion	F-3
Victoriaville	E-5
Warwick	F-5
Waterloo	G-4
Windsor	F-5

Québec provincial facts

Capital: Québec, D-6

Population: 7,903,001 (rank: 2nd)
Largest city: Montréal, 1,649,519, F-3

Land area: 527,079 sq. mi. (rank: 2nd)
Highest point: Mont d'Iberville, 5,420 ft.

© Rand McNally

Pg. 111 · Pg. 123 · Pg. 122 · Pg. 72 · Pg. 64
For continuation see main map below
For continuation see inset above

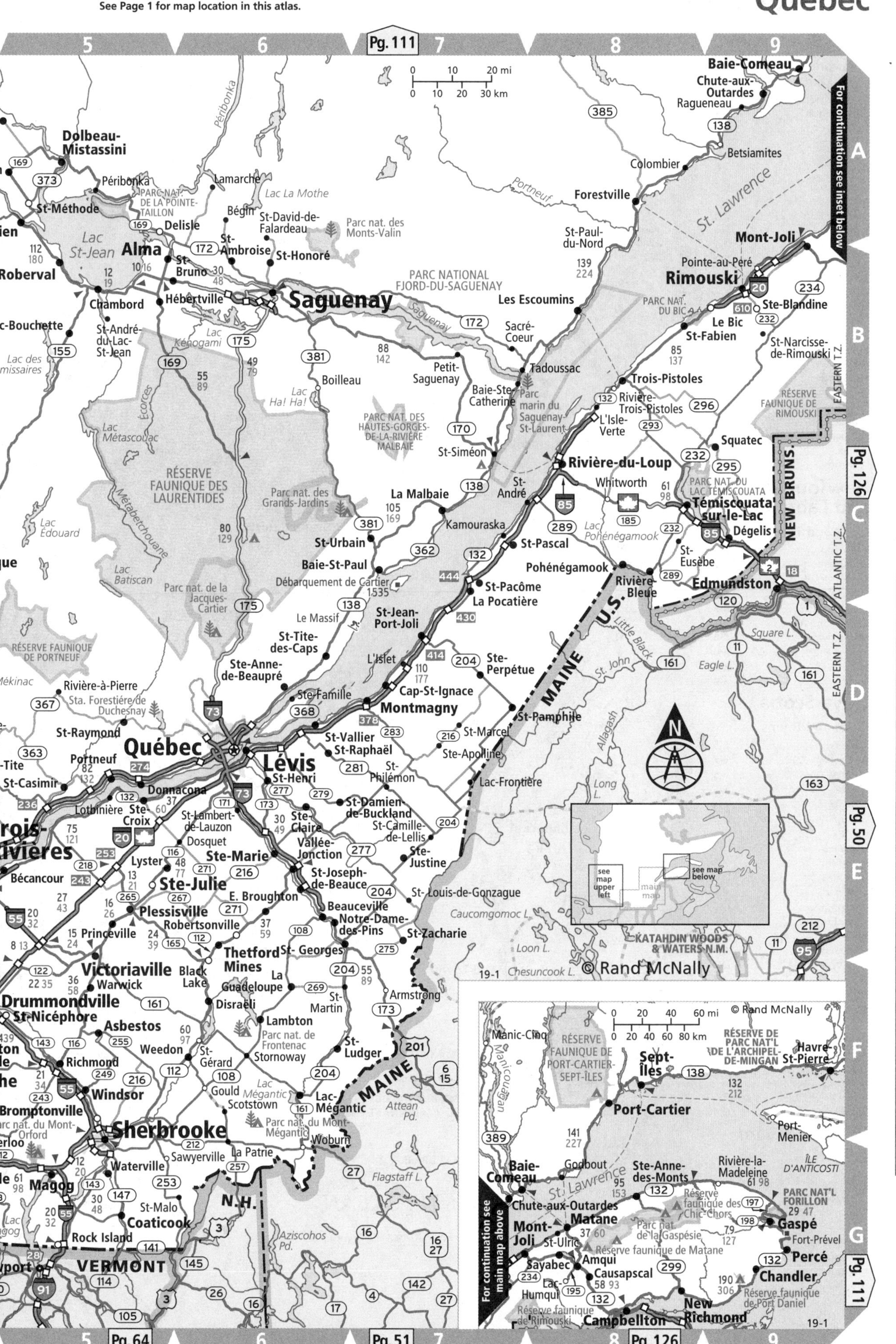

Road Conditions & Construction
511, (888) 355-0511
www.quebec511.gouv.qc.ca/en

Tourism Information
Tourisme Québec
(877) 266-5687, (514) 873-2015
www.bonjourquebec.com

Travel planning & on-the-road resources

Provincial facts

NEW BRUNSWICK
Population: 751,171 (rank: 8th)
Largest city: Saint John, 70,063, E-4
Land area: 27,587 sq. mi. (rank: 11th)

NEWFOUNDLAND & LABRADOR
Population: 514,536 (rank: 9th)
Largest city: St. John's, 106,172, B-9
Land area: 144,353 sq. mi. (rank: 10th)

NOVA SCOTIA
Population: 921,727 (rank: 7th)
Largest city: Halifax, 390,096, F-6
Land area: 20,594 sq. mi. (rank: 12th)

PRINCE EDWARD ISLAND
Population: 140,204 (rank: 10th)
Largest city: Charlottetown, 34,562, D-6
Land area: 2,185 sq. mi. (rank: 13th)

New Brunswick

Cities and Towns

Bathurst C-4
Bouctouche D-5
Campbellton B-3
Cap-Pele D-5
Caraquet B-5
Dalhousie B-4
Dieppe D-5
Edmundston C-2
Fredericton D-3
Grand Falls (Grand Sault) . C-3
Hampton E-4
Memramcook D-5
Minto D-4
Miramichi C-4
Moncton D-5
Oromocto E-4
Perth-Andover C-3
Sackville E-5
St. Andrews E-3
Saint John E-4
St. Stephen E-3
St-Quentin C-3
Salisbury D-5
Shediac D-5
Shippagan B-5
Sussex E-4
Woodstock D-3

Newfoundland and Labrador

Cities and Towns

Bonavista B-9
Channel-Port aux Basques . B-7
Corner Brook B-8
Deer Lake B-8
Gander B-8
Grand Falls-Windsor B-8
Marystown C-8
Mount Pearl B-9
St. John's B-9
Torbay B-9

Nova Scotia

Cities and Towns

Amherst E-5
Antigonish E-7
Bridgewater F-5
Chester F-5
Digby F-4
Glace Bay D-9
Halifax F-6
Hebron G-4
Ingonish D-8
Inverness D-8
Kentville F-5
Liverpool G-5
Lunenburg F-5
Middleton F-5
New Glasgow E-7
New Waterford D-9
Pictou E-7
Port Hawkesbury E-8
Shelburne G-4
Springhill E-5
Sydney D-9
Sydney Mines D-9
Truro E-6
Windsor F-5
Wolfville E-5
Yarmouth G-4

Prince Edward Island

Cities and Towns

Alberton C-5
Charlottetown D-6
Cornwall D-6
Georgetown D-7
Kensington D-6
Montague D-7
Port Borden D-6
Souris D-7
Summerside D-6
Tignish C-6

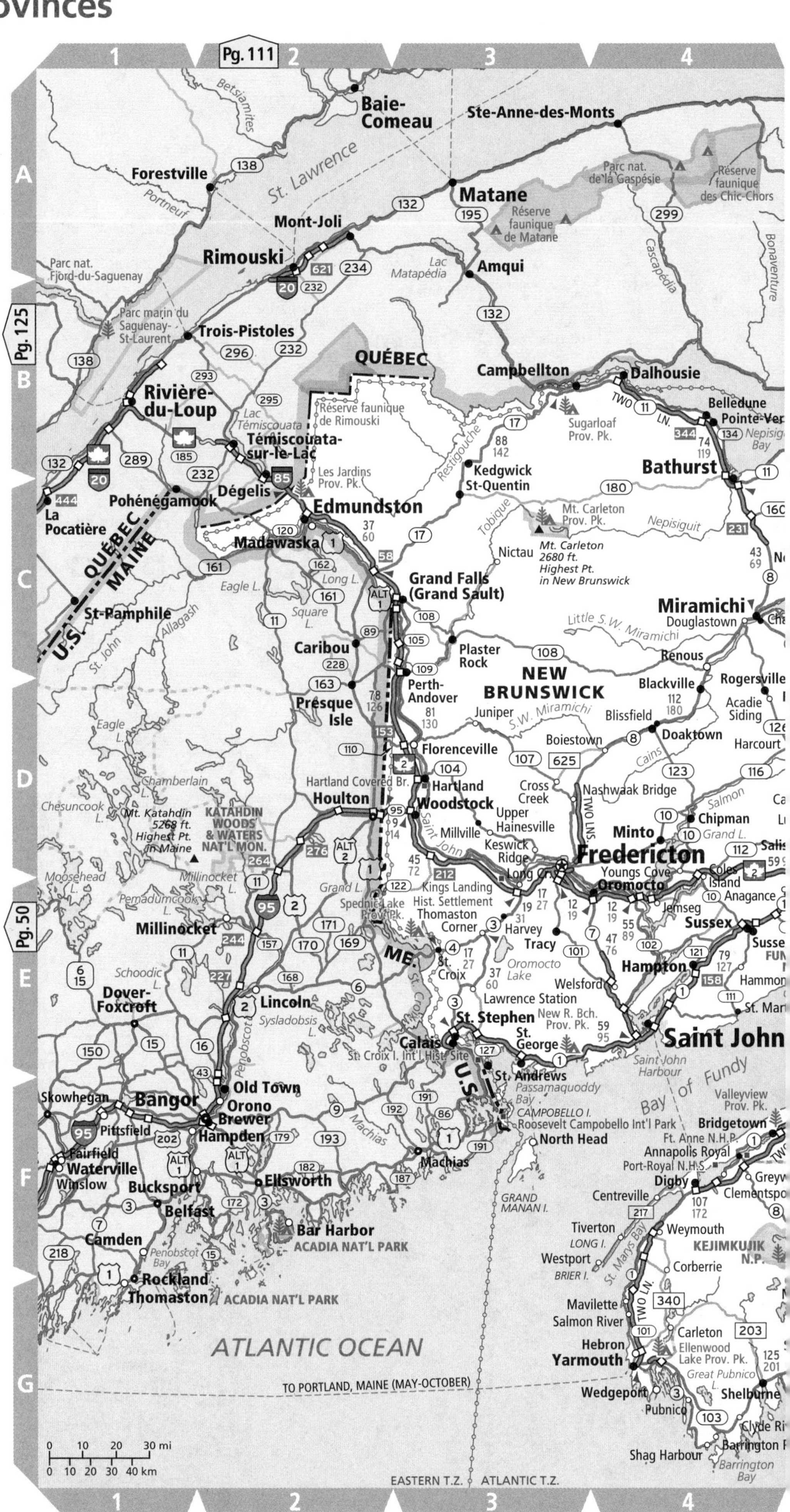

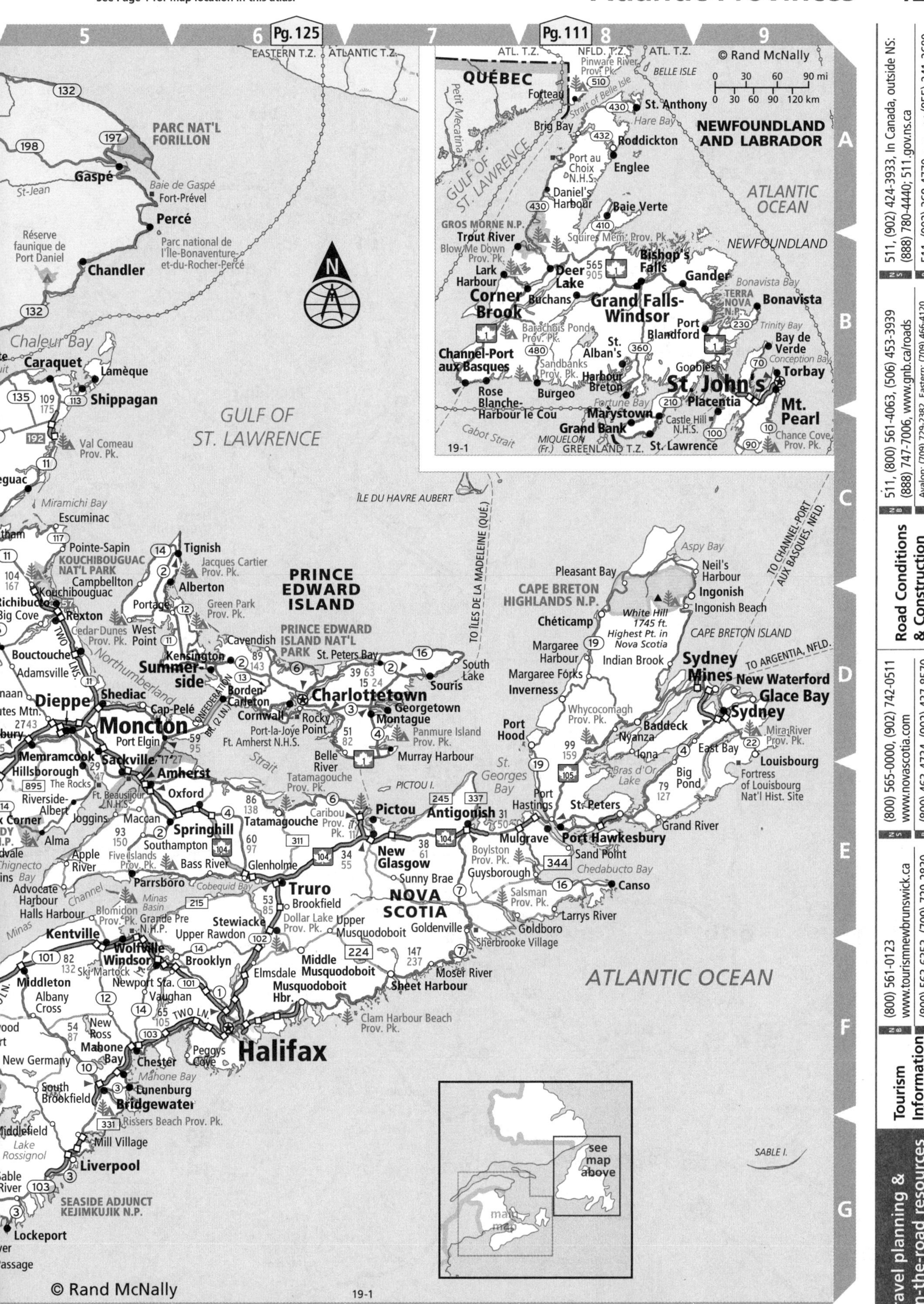

© Rand McNally

19-1

Travel planning & on-the-road resources

Tourism Information

NB (800) 561-0123 www.tourismnewbrunswick.ca

NL (800) 563-6353, (709) 729-2830 www.newfoundlandlabrador.com

NS (800) 565-0000, (902) 742-0511 www.novascotia.com

PEI (800) 463-4734, (902) 437-8570 www.tourismpei.com

Road Conditions & Construction

NB 511, (800) 561-4063, (506) 453-3939 (888) 747-7006, www.gnb.ca/roads

NL Avalon: (709) 729-2382, Eastern: (709) 466-4120 Central: (709) 292-4300, Western: (709) 635-4217 Labrador: (709) 896-7840; www.roads.gov.nl.ca

NS 511, (902) 424-3933, In Canada, outside NS: (888) 780-4440; 511.gov.ns.ca

PEI 511, (902) 368-4770, In Canada: (855) 241-2680 www.gov.pe.ca/roadconditions

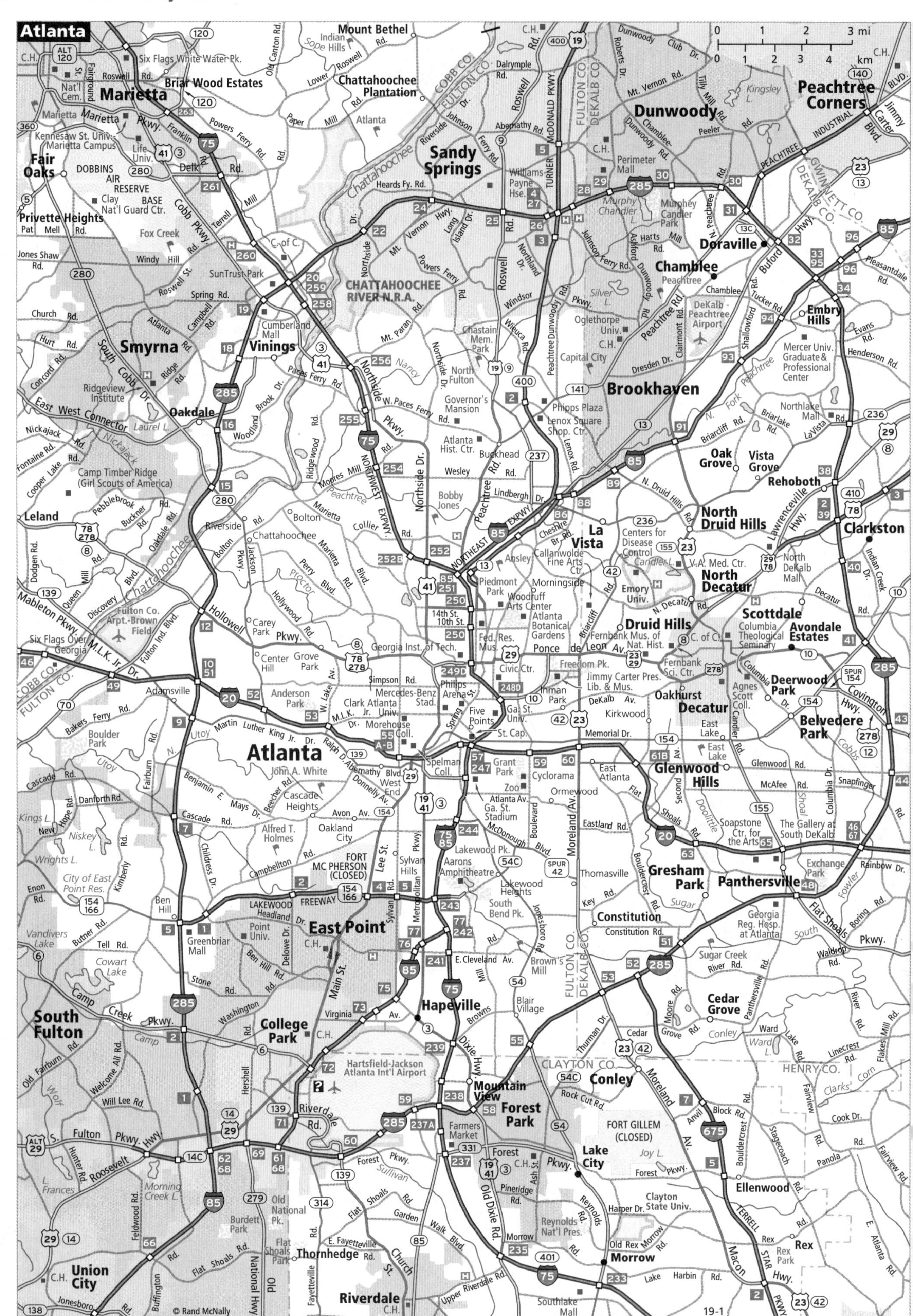
Atlanta
Marietta
Dunwoody
Peachtree Corners
Sandy Springs
Smyrna
Vinings
Fair Oaks
Privette Heights
Oakdale
Leland
Brookhaven
Chamblee
Doraville
Embry Hills
North Druid Hills
Clarkston
La Vista
North Decatur
Druid Hills
Scottdale
Avondale Estates
Decatur
Belvedere Park
Glenwood Hills
Gresham Park
Panthersville
Constitution
East Point
Hapeville
College Park
South Fulton
Mountain View
Forest Park
Conley
Cedar Grove
Lake City
Ellenwood
Morrow
Rex
Union City
Riverdale
Thornhedge
CHATTAHOOCHEE RIVER N.R.A.
DOBBINS AIR RESERVE BASE
Hartsfield-Jackson Atlanta Int'l Airport
FORT MC PHERSON (CLOSED)
FORT GILLEM (CLOSED)
COBB CO.
FULTON CO.
DEKALB CO.
CLAYTON CO.
HENRY CO.
GWINNETT CO.
0 1 2 3 mi
0 1 2 3 4 km
© Rand McNally
19-1

Albuquerque
Los Ranchos de Albuquerque
Albuquerque
Five Points
Armijo
Atrisco
© Rand McNally
Birmingham
Inglenook
Pratt City
Irondale
Mountain Brook
Homewood
Mountain Brook Village
Birmingham
Vestavia Hills
Cahaba Hts.
© Rand McNally
Baltimore
Brooklandville
Lutherville
Stevenson
Chattolanee
Riderwood
Towson
Ruxton
Perry Hall
Baynesville
Carney
Summit Park
Dumbarton
Loch Raven Village
Rodgers Forge
Parkville
Pikesville
Fullerton
Overlea
Villa Nova
Linthigh
Milford
Elmwood
Woodmoor
Lochearn
Rossville
Woodlawn
Rosedale
Catonsville Manor
W. Edmondale
Essex
Catonsville
Eastpoint
Bloomsbury
Dundalk
Arbutus
Halethorpe
Lansdowne
Baltimore Highlands
Baltimore
Relay
Brooklyn Park
Timberview
Elkridge
Arundel Village
Arundel Gardens
Sparrows Point
Harwood Park
Linthicum
Shipley
Hanover
Woodlawn Heights
Rippling Ridge
Garland
Ferndale
Furnace Branch
© Rand McNally

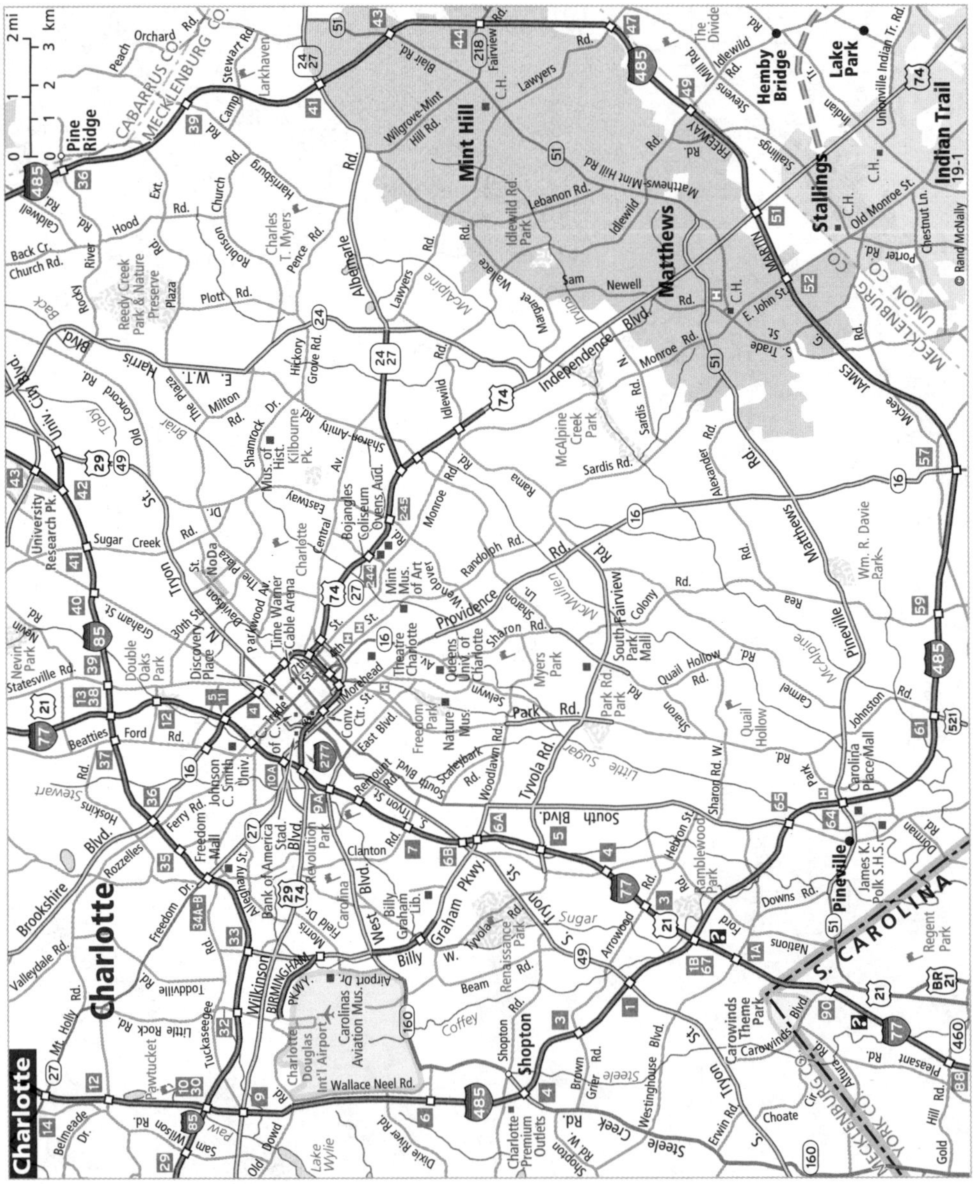
Charlotte
© Rand McNally

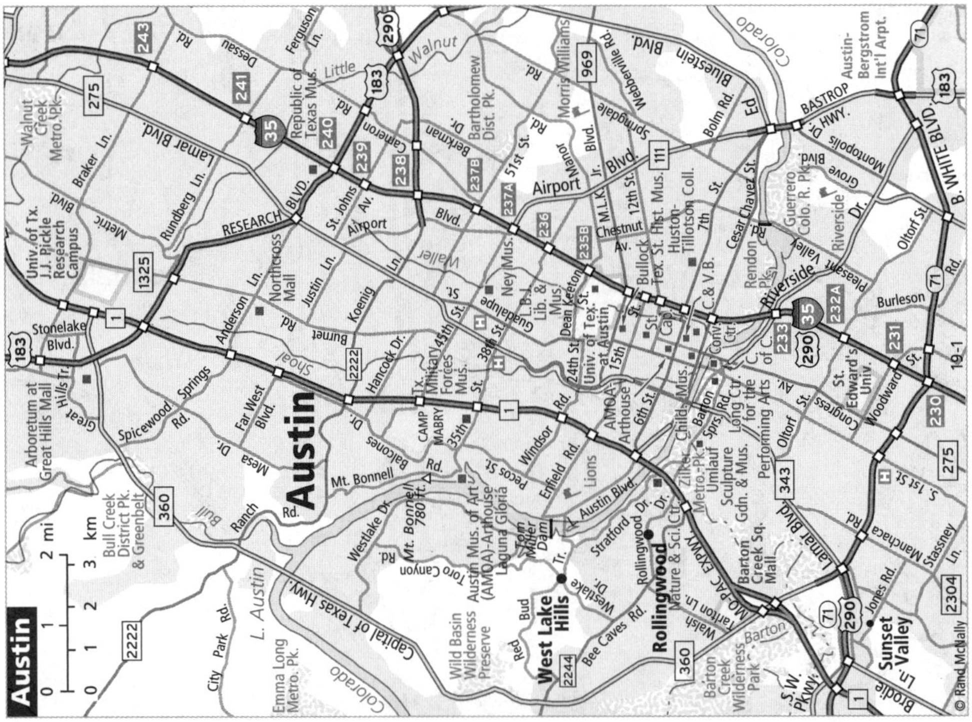
Austin
© Rand McNally

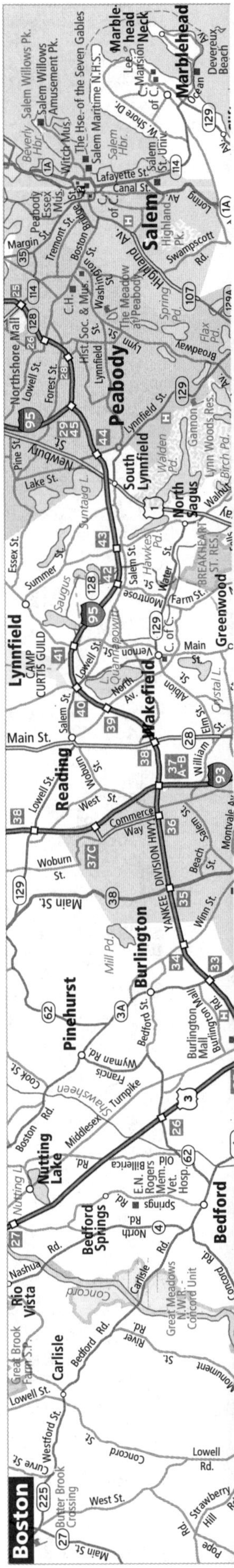
Boston

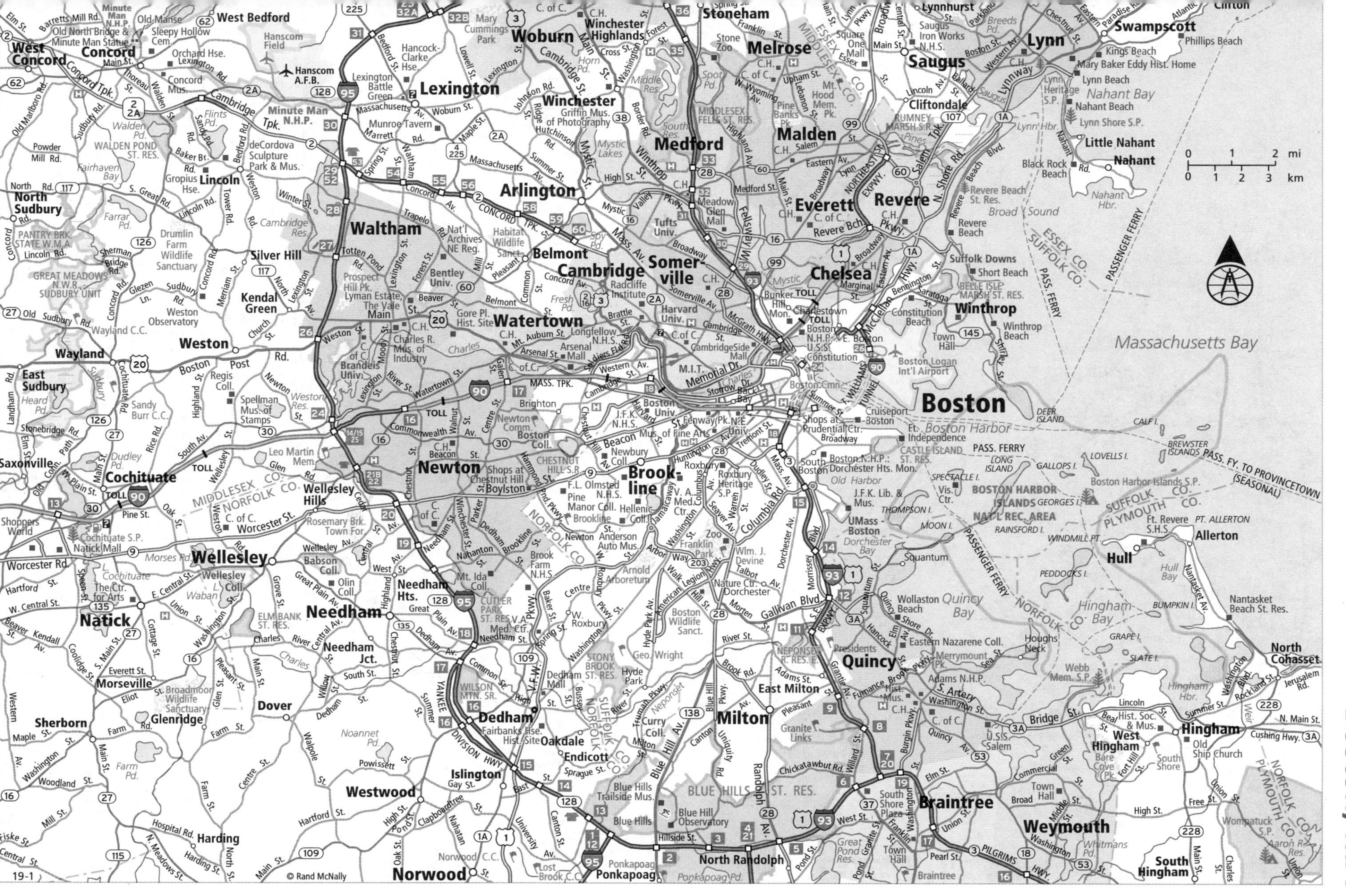
Boston
Massachusetts Bay
Boston Harbor
Quincy Bay
Hingham Bay
Nahant Bay
Broad Sound
Swampscott
Lynn
Nahant
Little Nahant
Saugus
Revere
Winthrop
Chelsea
Everett
Malden
Melrose
Stoneham
Medford
Somerville
Cambridge
Arlington
Belmont
Watertown
Waltham
Newton
Brookline
Winchester
Woburn
Lexington
Lincoln
Concord
West Concord
Weston
Wayland
Wellesley
Needham
Dedham
Milton
Quincy
Braintree
Weymouth
Hingham
Hull
Natick
Cochituate
Dover
Westwood
Norwood
Sherborn
North Randolph
Ponkapoag
Boston Logan Int'l Airport
BOSTON HARBOR ISLANDS NAT'L REC. AREA
BLUE HILLS ST. RES.
PASSENGER FERRY
PASS. FY. TO PROVINCETOWN (SEASONAL)
© Rand McNally

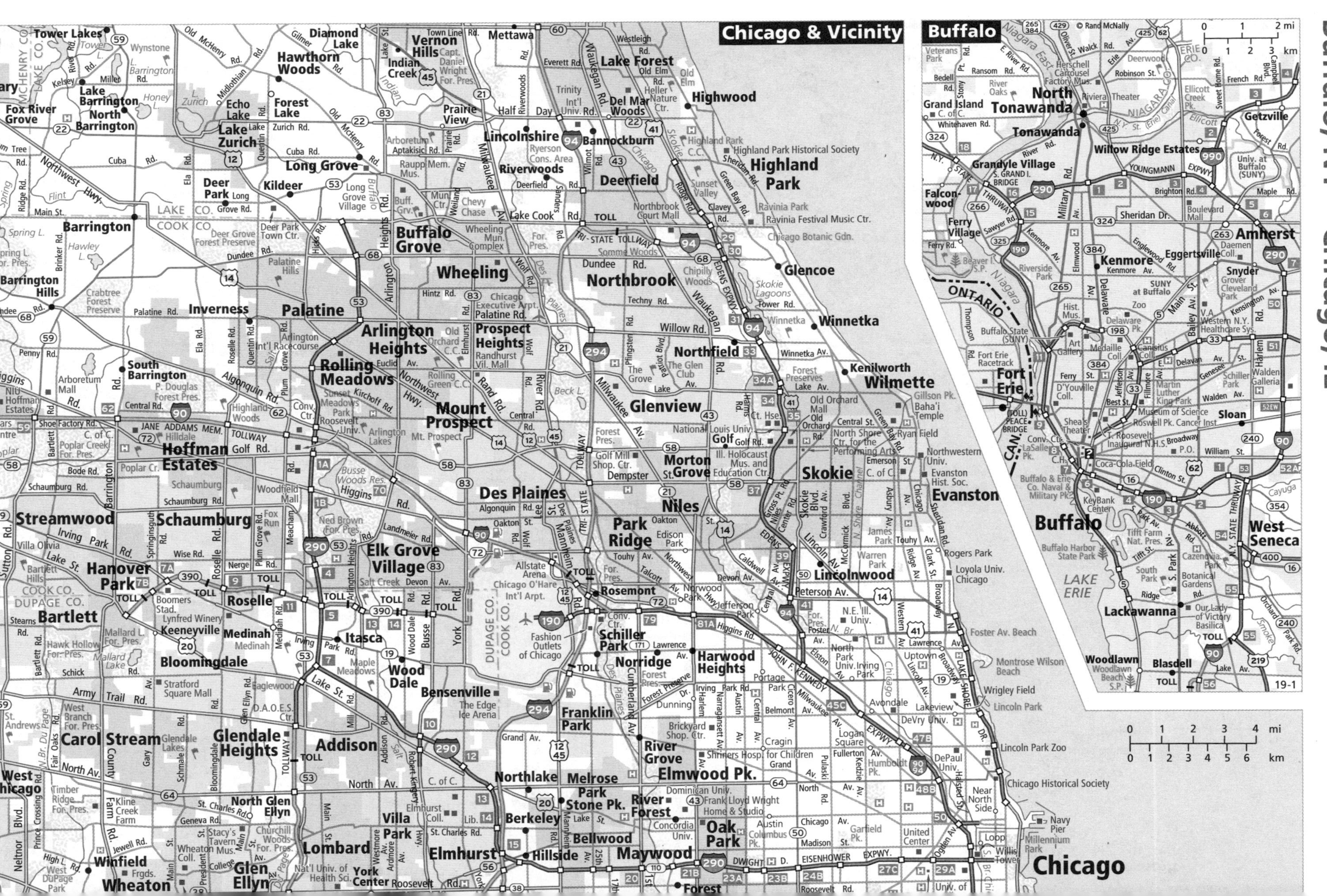
Chicago & Vicinity
Buffalo
© Rand McNally
Chicago
Evanston
Skokie
Wilmette
Winnetka
Glencoe
Highland Park
Highwood
Lake Forest
Deerfield
Northbrook
Glenview
Northfield
Niles
Park Ridge
Des Plaines
Mount Prospect
Arlington Heights
Palatine
Wheeling
Buffalo Grove
Schaumburg
Hoffman Estates
Elk Grove Village
Oak Park
Elmhurst
Lombard
Wheaton
Naperville
Addison
Carol Stream
Glendale Heights
Bloomingdale
Streamwood
Bartlett
Hanover Park
Roselle
Itasca
Wood Dale
Bensenville
Franklin Park
Schiller Park
Norridge
Harwood Heights
Elmwood Pk.
River Grove
Melrose Park
Northlake
Berkeley
Bellwood
Maywood
Hillside
Villa Park
Glen Ellyn
Winfield
West Chicago
Barrington
Lake Zurich
Long Grove
Vernon Hills
Lincolnshire
Mettawa
Cary
North Tonawanda
Tonawanda
Amherst
Kenmore
Fort Erie
Lackawanna
West Seneca
Blasdell
Lake Erie
Ontario
Chicago O'Hare Int'l Arpt.

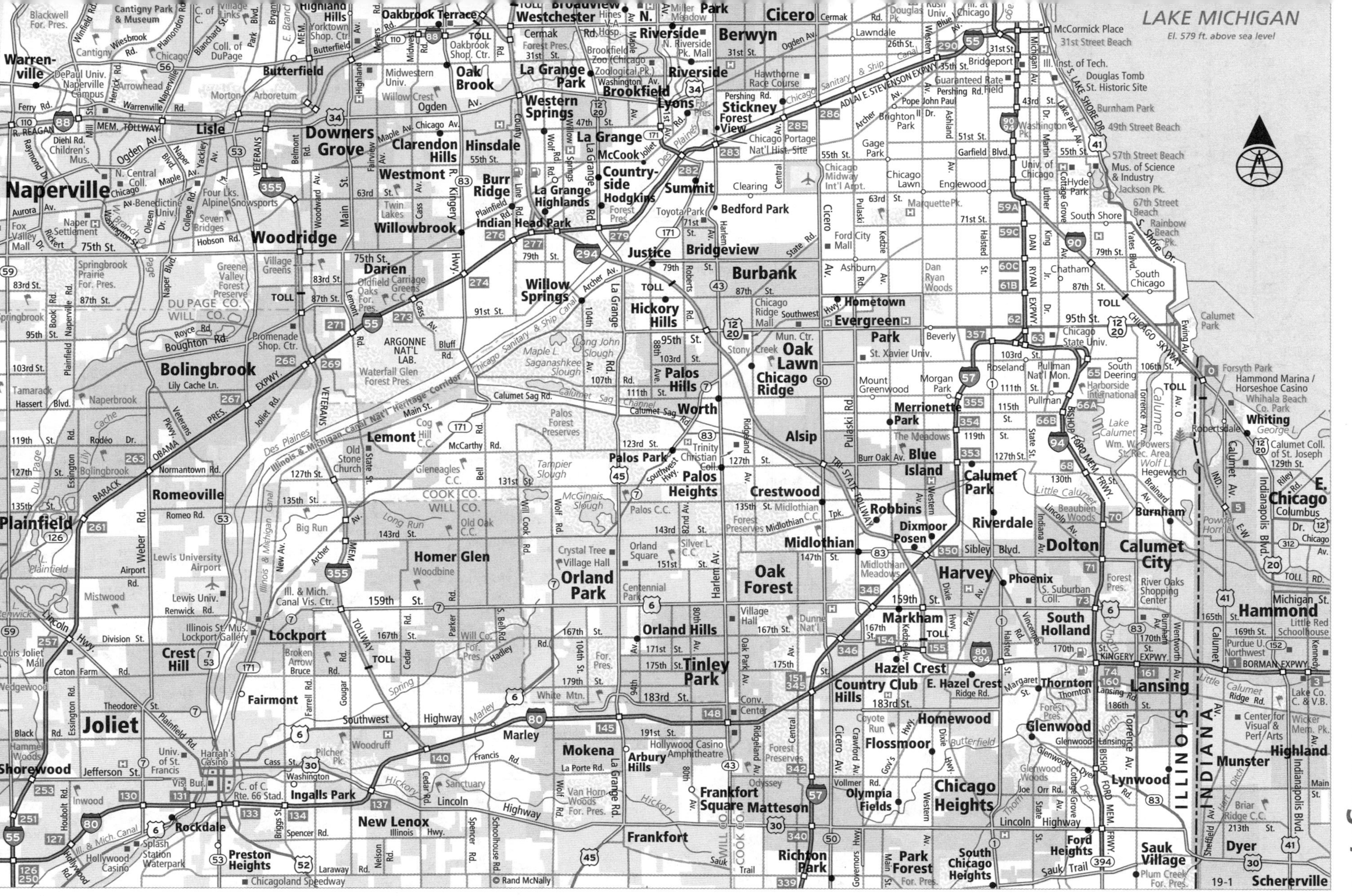
LAKE MICHIGAN
El. 579 ft. above sea level
INDIANA
ILLINOIS
E. Chicago
Whiting
Hammond
Highland
Munster
Dyer
Schererville
Calumet City
Burnham
Lansing
Lynwood
Sauk Village
Dolton
South Holland
Thornton
Glenwood
Ford Heights
Riverdale
Phoenix
Harvey
Calumet Park
Blue Island
Dixmoor
Posen
Robbins
Markham
Hazel Crest
E. Hazel Crest
Homewood
Flossmoor
Chicago Heights
South Chicago Heights
Park Forest
Olympia Fields
Country Club Hills
Richton Park
Matteson
Midlothian
Oak Forest
Tinley Park
Orland Hills
Crestwood
Alsip
Merrionette Park
Evergreen Park
Hometown
Oak Lawn
Chicago Ridge
Burbank
Bridgeview
Bedford Park
Justice
Hickory Hills
Palos Hills
Worth
Palos Heights
Palos Park
Orland Park
Frankfort
Frankfort Square
Mokena
New Lenox
Lockport
Homer Glen
Lemont
Summit
Stickney
Forest View
Cicero
Berwyn
Riverside
Lyons
Brookfield
La Grange
La Grange Park
Western Springs
Countryside
Hodgkins
McCook
Willow Springs
Indian Head Park
Burr Ridge
Hinsdale
Clarendon Hills
Westmont
Willowbrook
Darien
Woodridge
Downers Grove
Oak Brook
Oakbrook Terrace
Westchester
Lisle
Naperville
Warrenville
Bolingbrook
Romeoville
Plainfield
Crest Hill
Joliet
Shorewood
Rockdale
Preston Heights
Fairmont
Ingalls Park
Marley
Arbury Hills
Dan Ryan Expwy
Chicago Skyway
Bishop Ford Mem. Frwy.
Kingery Expwy
Borman Expwy
Tri-State Tollway
Adlai E. Stevenson Expwy
Veterans Mem. Tollway
R. Reagan Mem. Tollway
Chicago Midway Int'l Airport
Argonne Nat'l Lab.
Lewis University Airport
Chicagoland Speedway
COOK CO.
WILL CO.
DU PAGE CO.
19-1
© Rand McNally

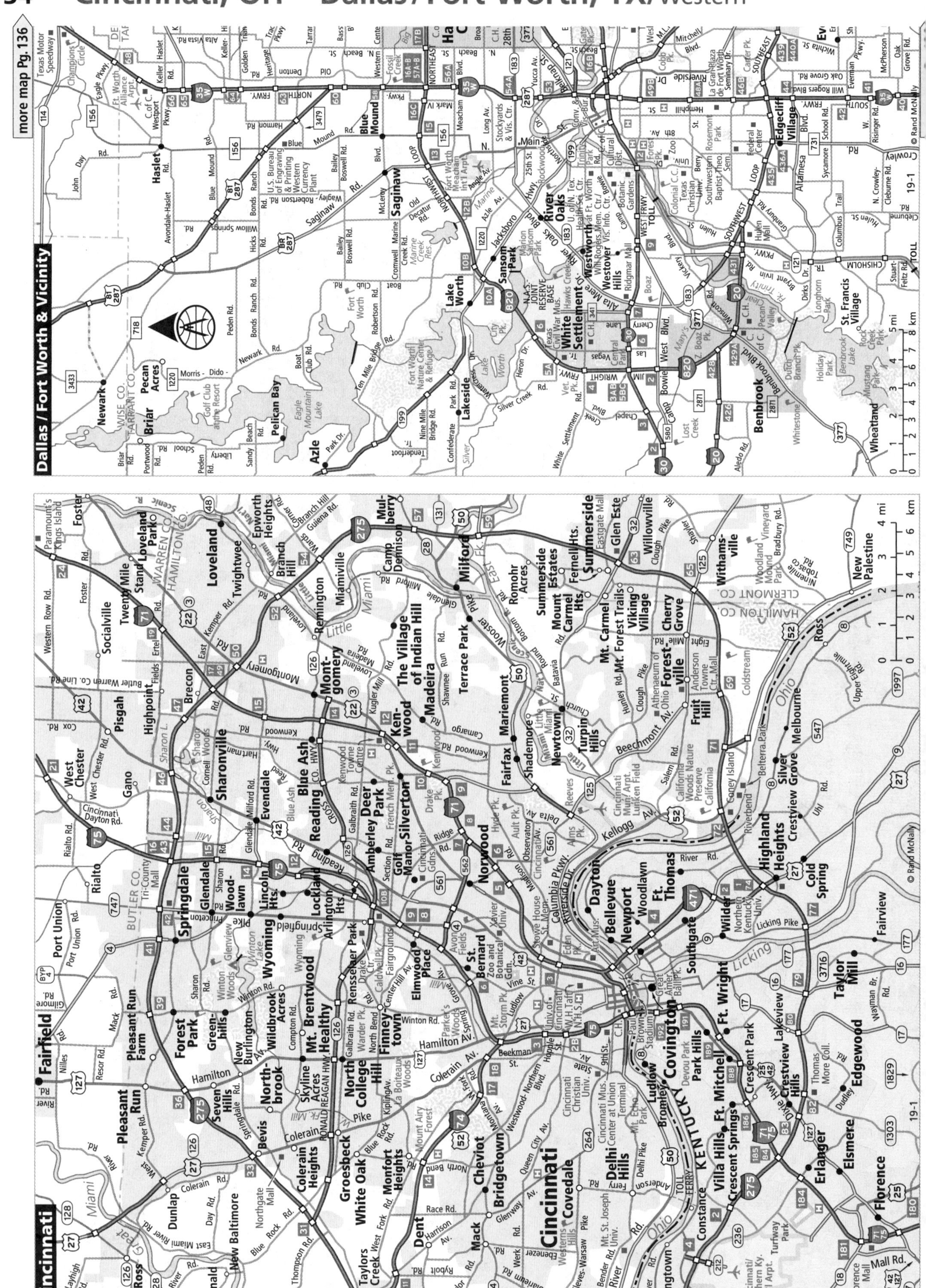
Dallas / Fort Worth & Vicinity
more map Pg. 136
Cincinnati
© Rand McNally

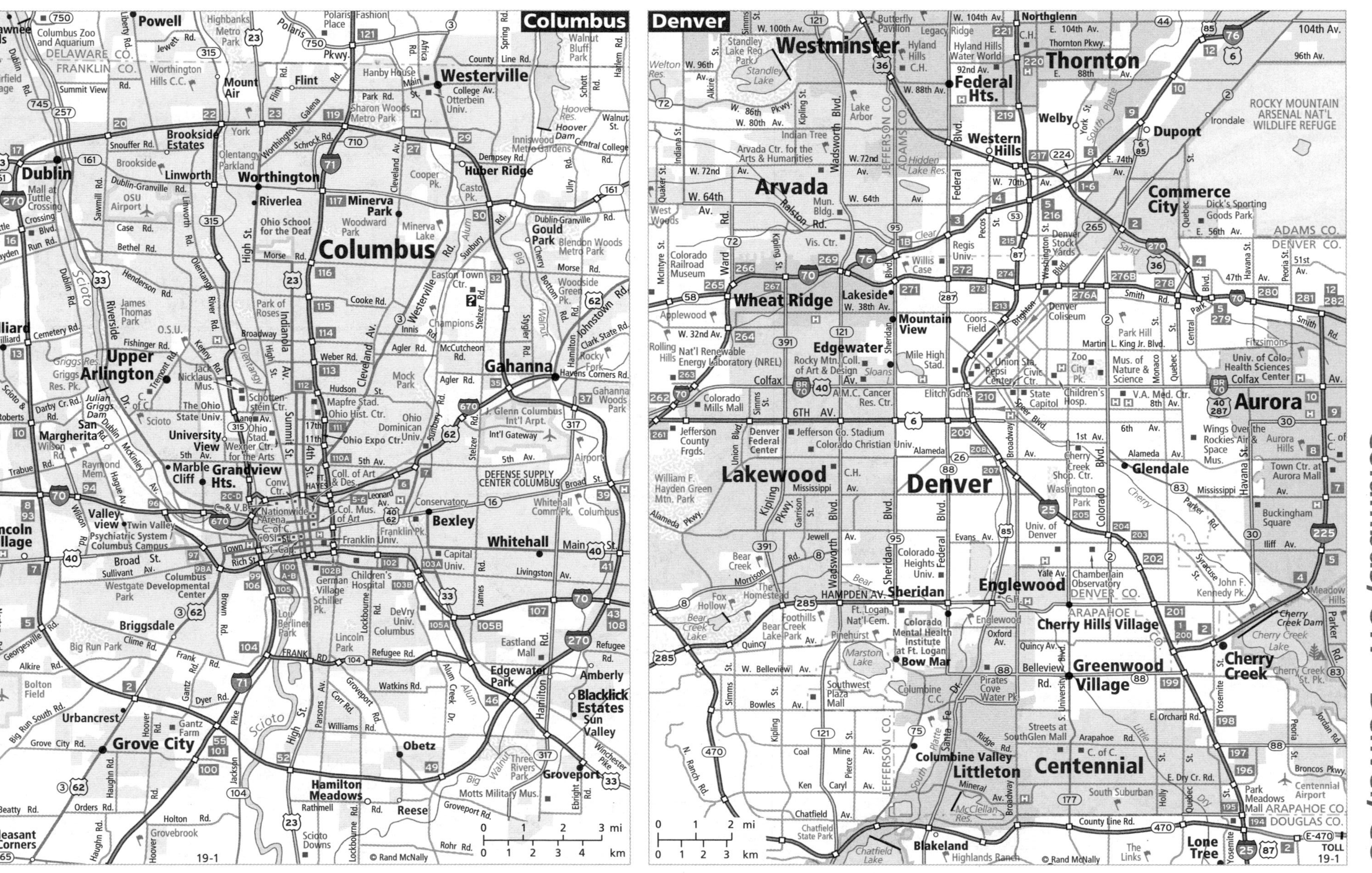
Columbus
Westerville
Columbus
Worthington
Dublin
Upper Arlington
Gahanna
Bexley
Whitehall
Grove City
Hilliard
Obetz
Groveport
Powell
Lincoln Village
Denver
Westminster
Thornton
Federal Hts.
Arvada
Wheat Ridge
Lakewood
Denver
Aurora
Commerce City
Englewood
Littleton
Centennial
Greenwood Village
Cherry Creek
© Rand McNally

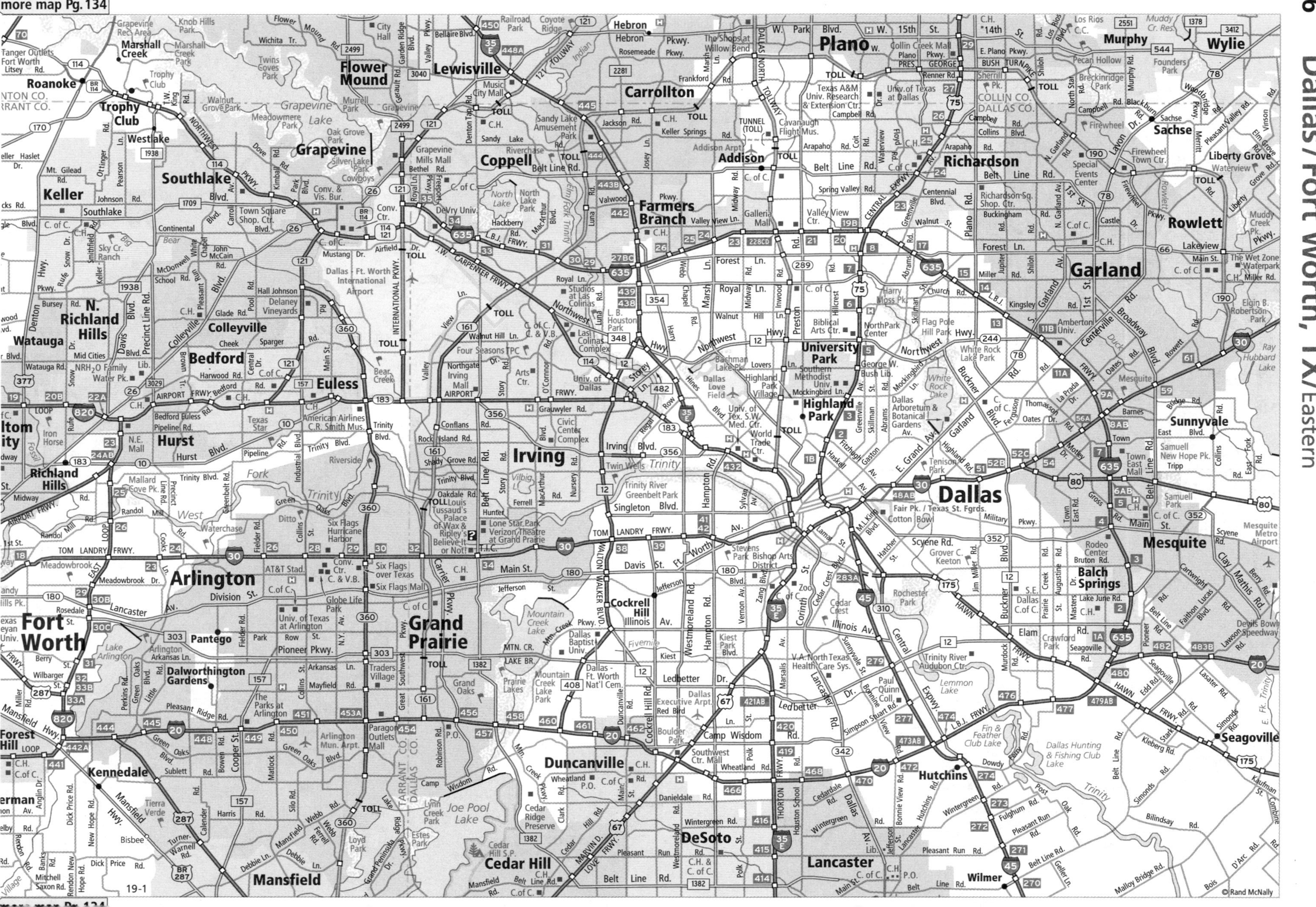
more map Pg. 134
Wylie
Murphy
Sachse
Liberty Grove
Rowlett
Garland
Sunnyvale
Mesquite
Balch Springs
Seagoville
Plano
Richardson
Dallas
Highland Park
University Park
Addison
Carrollton
Farmers Branch
Hutchins
Wilmer
Lancaster
DeSoto
Duncanville
Cedar Hill
Cockrell Hill
Irving
Coppell
Lewisville
Hebron
Flower Mound
Grapevine
Southlake
Colleyville
Euless
Bedford
Hurst
Grand Prairie
Arlington
Pantego
Dalworthington Gardens
Mansfield
Kennedale
Fort Worth
N. Richland Hills
Richland Hills
Keller
Watauga
Trophy Club
Westlake
Roanoke
Marshall Creek
Dallas - Ft. Worth International Airport
Joe Pool Lake
©Rand McNally

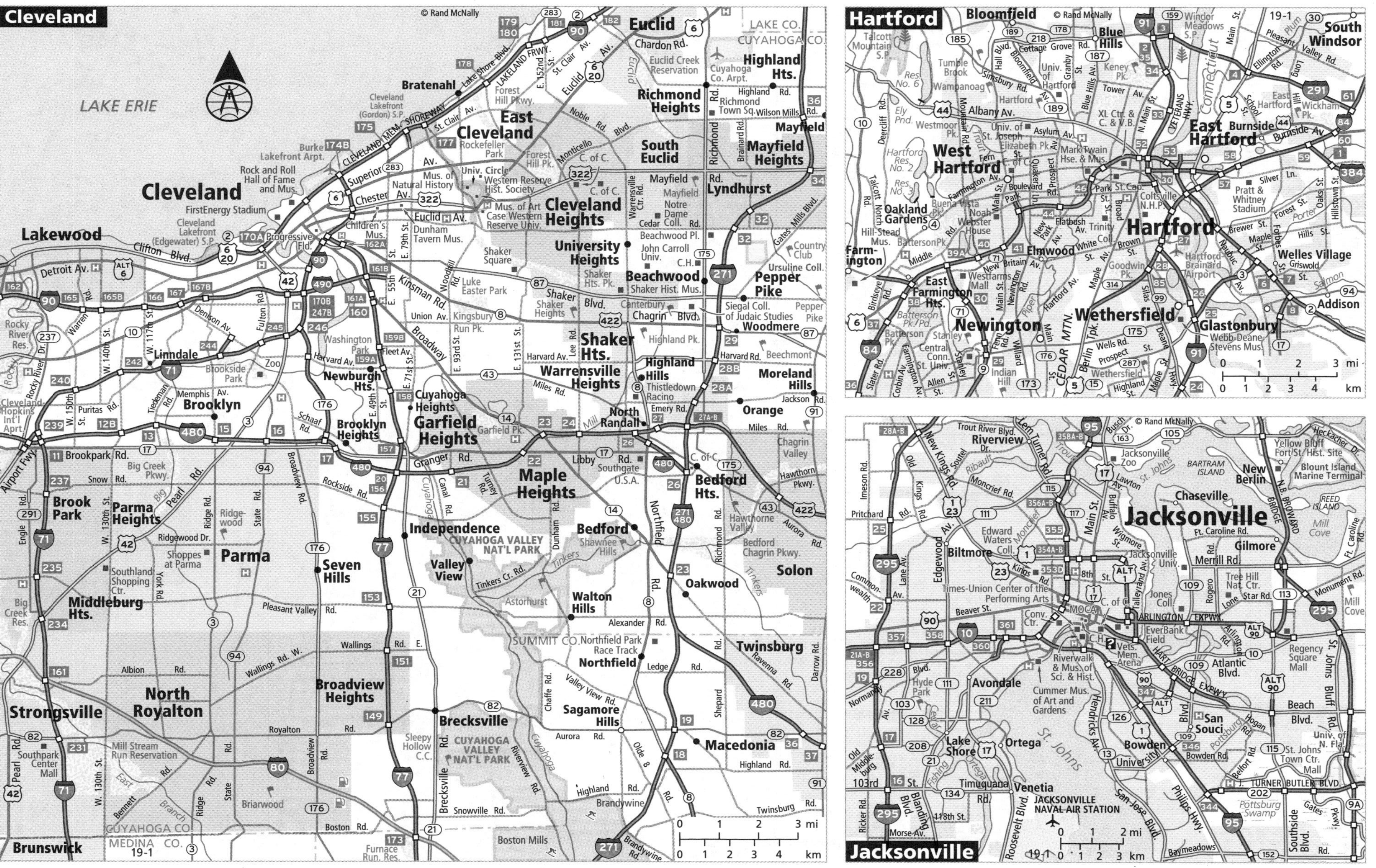
Cleveland
© Rand McNally
LAKE ERIE
Cleveland
Lakewood
Euclid
Bratenahl
East Cleveland
Cleveland Heights
University Heights
Shaker Hts.
Beachwood
Richmond Heights
South Euclid
Lyndhurst
Mayfield Heights
Highland Hts.
Pepper Pike
Moreland Hills
Orange
Woodmere
Warrensville Heights
Highland Hills
North Randall
Maple Heights
Bedford
Bedford Hts.
Garfield Heights
Cuyahoga Heights
Newburgh Hts.
Brooklyn Heights
Brooklyn
Linndale
Parma
Parma Heights
Seven Hills
Independence
Valley View
Walton Hills
Oakwood
Solon
Twinsburg
Macedonia
Northfield
Sagamore Hills
Brecksville
Broadview Heights
North Royalton
Middleburg Hts.
Brook Park
Strongsville
Brunswick
CUYAHOGA VALLEY NAT'L PARK
Hartford
© Rand McNally
Bloomfield
Blue Hills
South Windsor
East Hartford
Hartford
West Hartford
Wethersfield
Newington
Elmwood
Glastonbury
Welles Village
Addison
Burnside
Oakland Gardens
Farmington
East Farmington Hts.
Jacksonville
© Rand McNally
Jacksonville
New Berlin
Gilmore
Chaseville
Riverview
Biltmore
Avondale
Ortega
Venetia
Lake Shore
Bowden
San Souci
JACKSONVILLE NAVAL AIR STATION

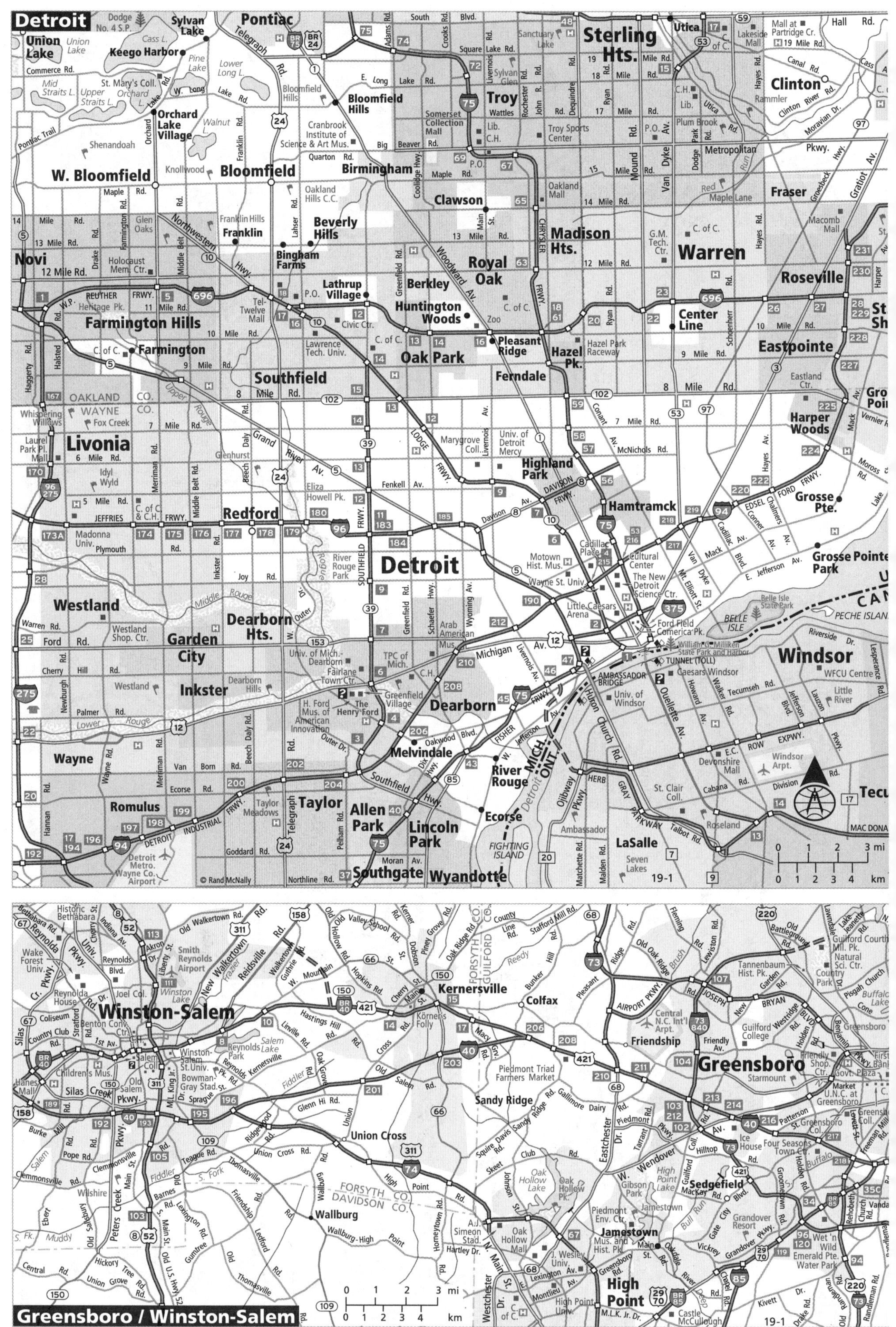

Detroit
Greensboro / Winston-Salem
Pontiac
Bloomfield Hills
Troy
Sterling Hts.
Utica
Clinton
W. Bloomfield
Bloomfield
Birmingham
Clawson
Fraser
Warren
Madison Hts.
Royal Oak
Novi
Farmington Hills
Southfield
Oak Park
Ferndale
Roseville
Eastpointe
Livonia
Redford
Westland
Garden City
Dearborn Hts.
Inkster
Dearborn
Hamtramck
Highland Park
Grosse Pte.
Grosse Pointe Park
Windsor
Wayne
Romulus
Taylor
Allen Park
Lincoln Park
Melvindale
River Rouge
Ecorse
Southgate
Wyandotte
LaSalle
Winston-Salem
Kernersville
Colfax
Greensboro
Friendship
Sandy Ridge
Union Cross
Wallburg
Sedgefield
Jamestown
High Point
© Rand McNally

Indianapolis
Louisville
Indianapolis
Louisville
Speedway
Beech Grove
Lawrence
Jeffersonville
New Albany
Clarksville
Jeffersontown
St. Matthews
Shively
© Rand McNally

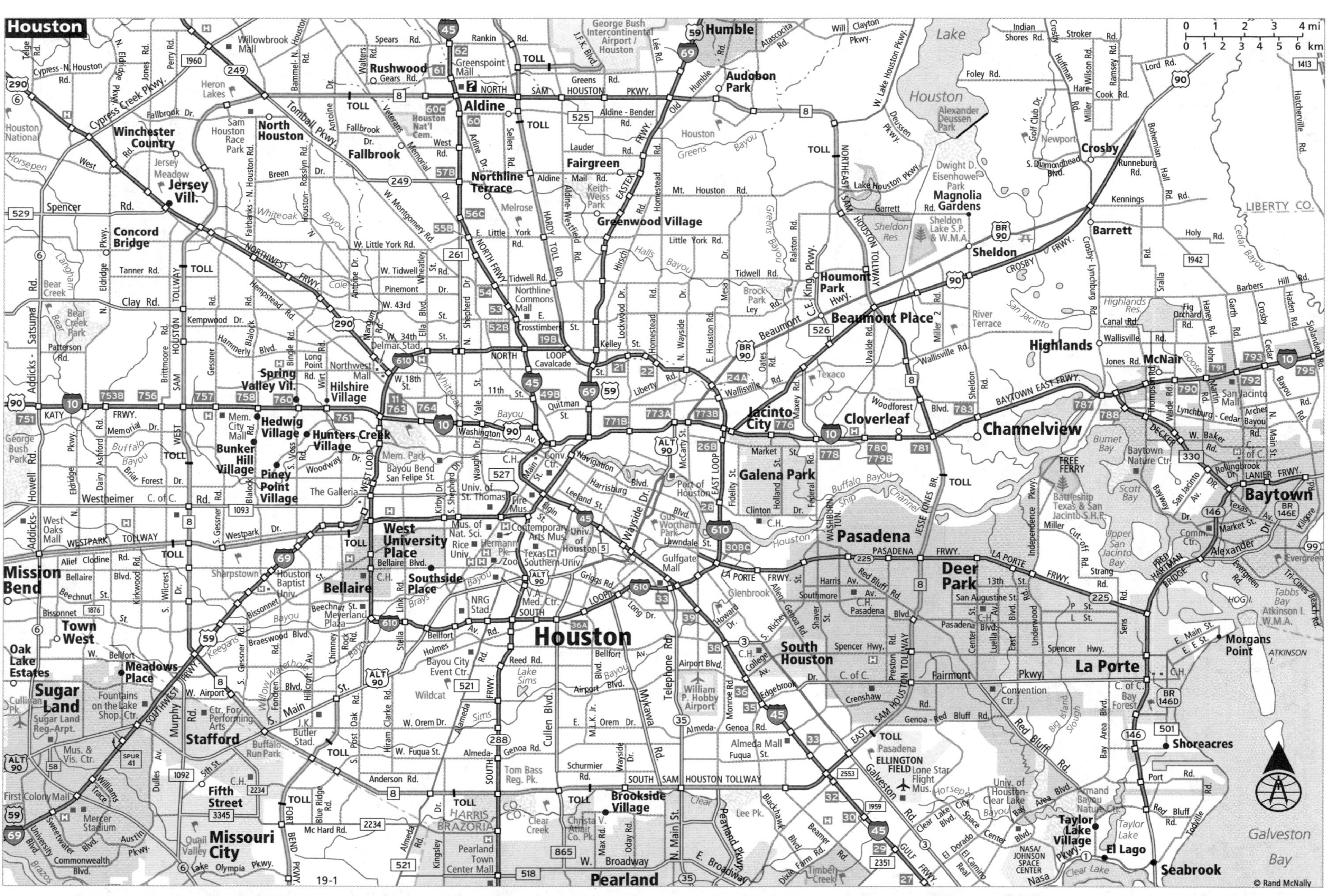
Houston
Humble
Audubon Park
Aldine
Rushwood
Winchester Country
North Houston
Fallbrook
Jersey Vill.
Northline Terrace
Fairgreen
Greenwood Village
Magnolia Gardens
Crosby
Barrett
Sheldon
Concord Bridge
Houmont Park
Beaumont Place
Highlands
McNair
Spring Valley Vil.
Hilshire Village
Hedwig Village
Hunters Creek Village
Bunker Hill Village
Piney Point Village
Jacinto City
Cloverleaf
Channelview
Galena Park
Baytown
Mission Bend
West University Place
Southside Place
Bellaire
Pasadena
Deer Park
Town West
Oak Lake Estates
Meadows Place
Sugar Land
Stafford
South Houston
La Porte
Morgans Point
Shoreacres
Fifth Street
Missouri City
Brookside Village
Pearland
Taylor Lake Village
El Lago
Seabrook
Galveston Bay
Lake Houston
LIBERTY CO.
HARRIS CO.
BRAZORIA CO.
0 1 2 3 4 mi
0 1 2 3 4 5 6 km
© Rand McNally

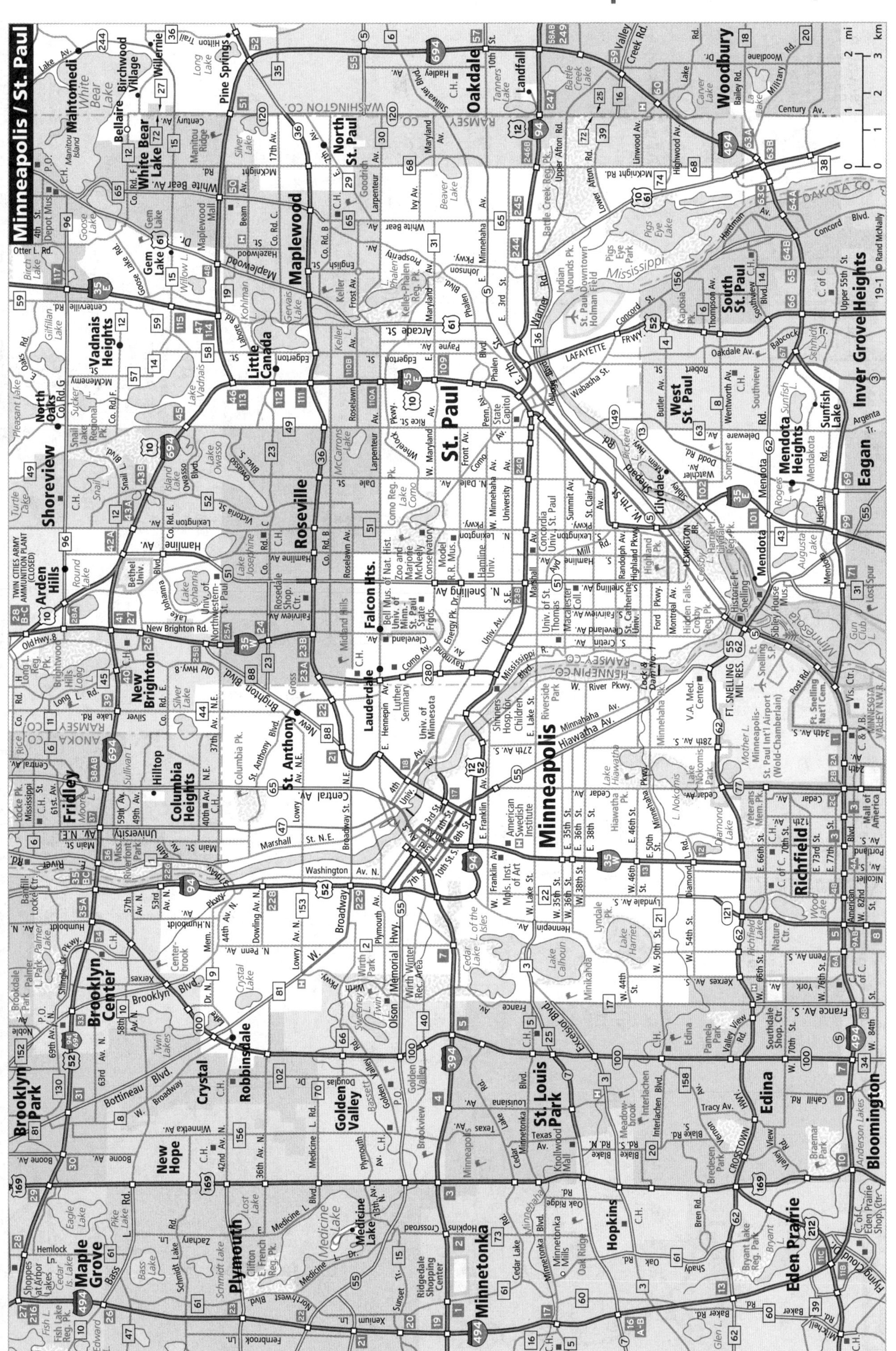
Minneapolis / St. Paul
Mahtomedi
Birchwood Village
Willernie
Pine Springs
White Bear Lake
Gem Lake
Vadnais Heights
North Oaks
Shoreview
Arden Hills
TWIN CITIES ARMY AMMUNITION PLANT (CLOSED)
Little Canada
Maplewood
North St. Paul
Oakdale
Landfall
Woodbury
Roseville
Falcon Hts.
Lauderdale
St. Paul
West St. Paul
South St. Paul
Lilydale
Mendota Heights
Mendota
Sunfish Lake
Inver Grove Heights
Eagan
New Brighton
St. Anthony
Fridley
Hilltop
Columbia Heights
Brooklyn Center
Brooklyn Park
Crystal
Robbinsdale
New Hope
Golden Valley
Minneapolis
St. Louis Park
Edina
Richfield
Bloomington
Hopkins
Minnetonka
Eden Prairie
Plymouth
Medicine Lake
Maple Grove
Minneapolis-St. Paul Int'l Airport (Wold-Chamberlain)
Mississippi
Minnesota
19-1 © Rand McNally

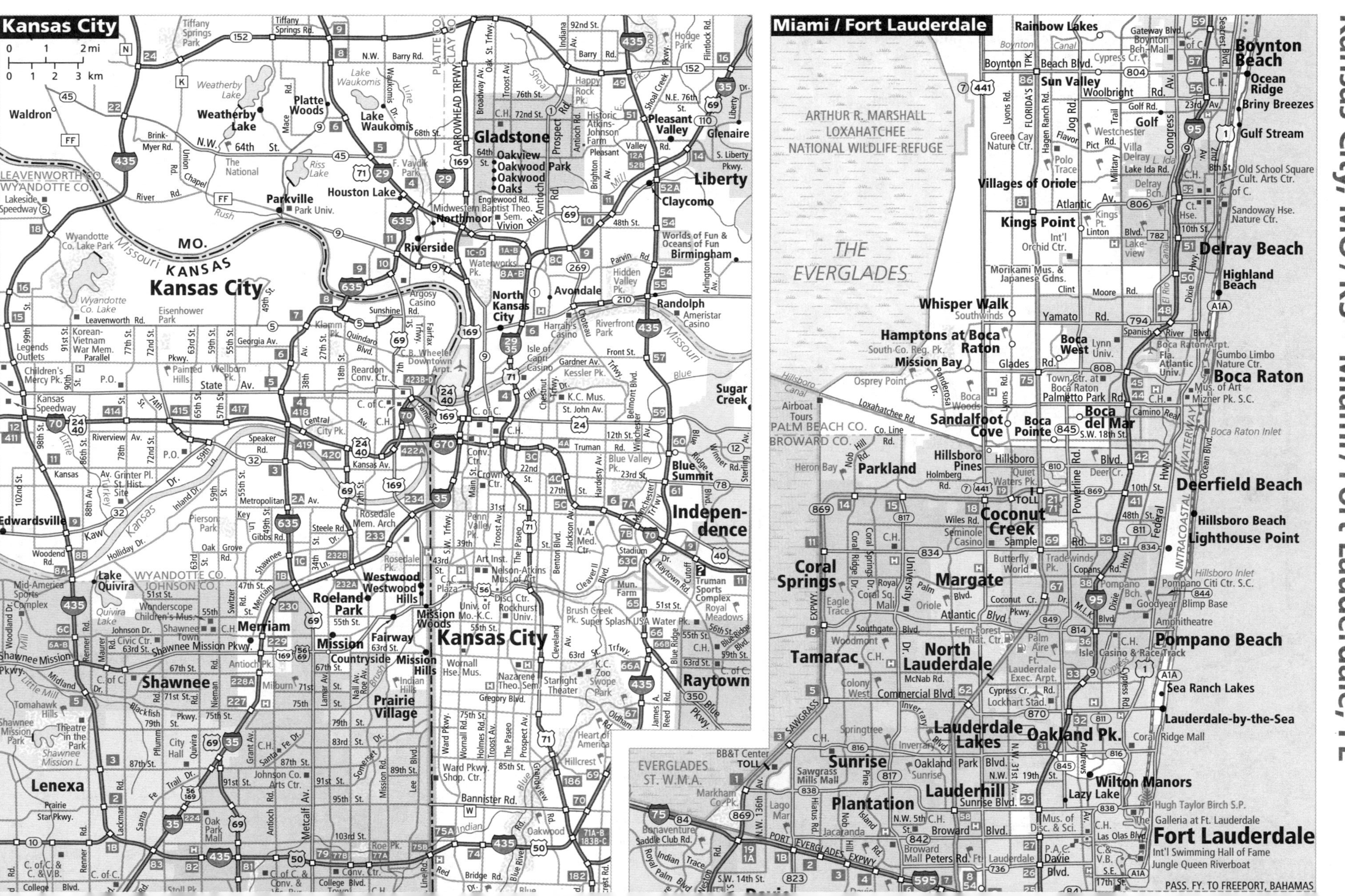

Kansas City
0 1 2 mi
0 1 2 3 km
Miami / Fort Lauderdale
Waldron
Weatherby Lake
Platte Woods
Lake Waukomis
Gladstone
Oakview
Oakwood Park
Oakwood
Oaks
Pleasant Valley
Glenaire
Liberty
Claycomo
Parkville
Houston Lake
Northmoor
Riverside
Birmingham
Avondale
North Kansas City
Randolph
Kansas City
Sugar Creek
Blue Summit
Independence
Edwardsville
Lake Quivira
Roeland Park
Westwood
Westwood Hills
Merriam
Mission
Mission Woods
Fairway
Mission Hills
Kansas City
Raytown
Shawnee
Prairie Village
Lenexa
ARTHUR R. MARSHALL LOXAHATCHEE NATIONAL WILDLIFE REFUGE
THE EVERGLADES
EVERGLADES ST. W.M.A.
Rainbow Lakes
Sun Valley
Golf
Villages of Oriole
Kings Point
Whisper Walk
Hamptons at Boca Raton
Mission Bay
Boca West
Sandalfoot Cove
Boca Pointe
Boca del Mar
Hillsboro Pines
Parkland
Coconut Creek
Coral Springs
Margate
Tamarac
North Lauderdale
Lauderdale Lakes
Oakland Pk.
Sunrise
Lauderhill
Plantation
Wilton Manors
Lazy Lake
Boynton Beach
Ocean Ridge
Briny Breezes
Gulf Stream
Delray Beach
Highland Beach
Boca Raton
Deerfield Beach
Hillsboro Beach
Lighthouse Point
Pompano Beach
Sea Ranch Lakes
Lauderdale-by-the-Sea
Fort Lauderdale
PASS. FY. TO FREEPORT, BAHAMAS

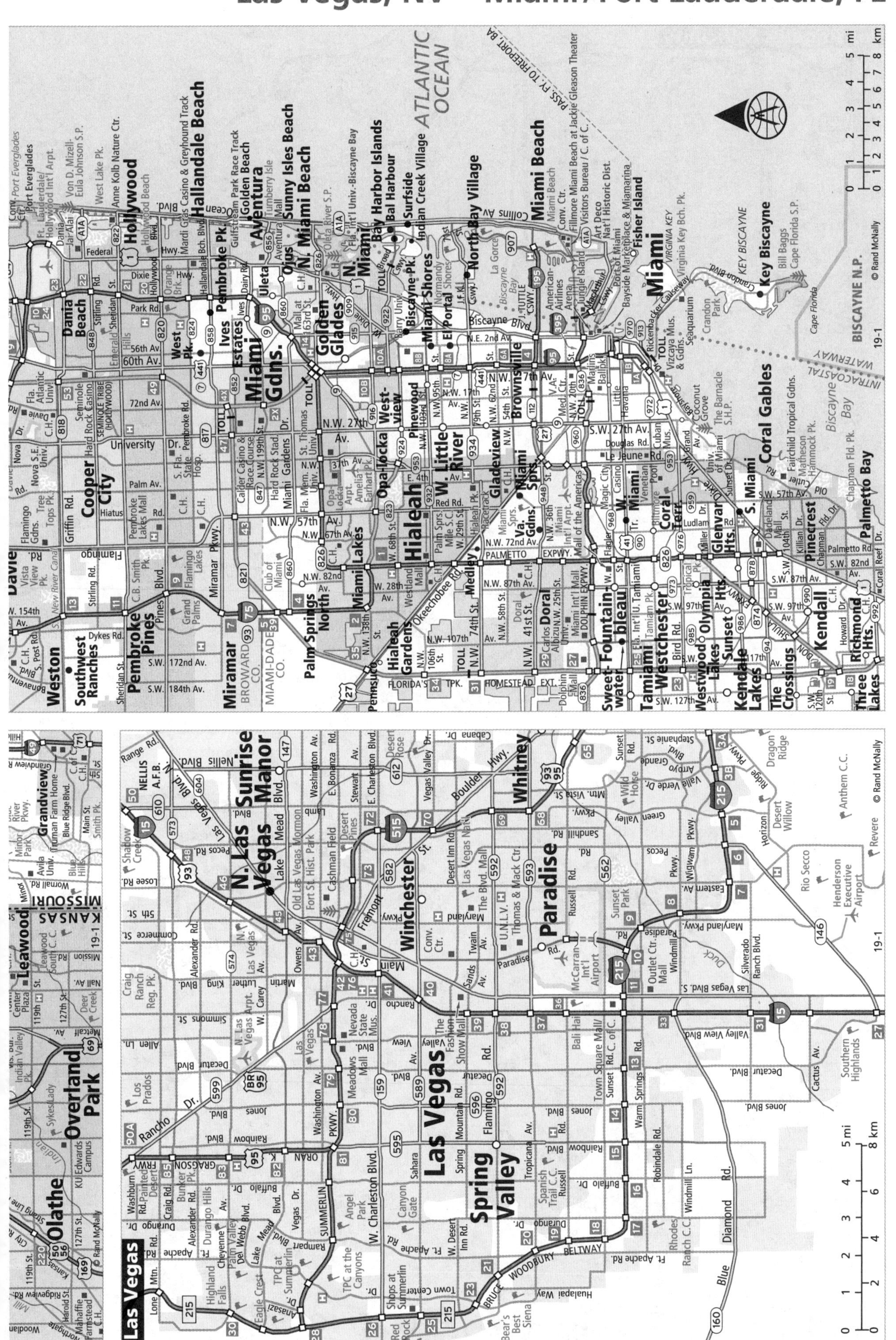
Las Vegas
N. Las Vegas
Sunrise Manor
Winchester
Paradise
Whitney
Spring Valley
Olathe
Overland Park
Leawood
Grandview
KANSAS
MISSOURI
Hollywood
Hallandale Beach
Aventura
Sunny Isles Beach
N. Miami Beach
N. Miami
Miami Gdns.
Hialeah
Miami Beach
Miami
Coral Gables
Key Biscayne
Kendall
Pembroke Pines
Miramar
Weston
ATLANTIC OCEAN
BISCAYNE N.P.
© Rand McNally

Los Angeles & Vicinity
Santa Monica Bay
PACIFIC OCEAN
Los Angeles
Beverly Hills
Santa Monica
Glendale
Burbank
Inglewood
Torrance
Nashville
© Rand McNally

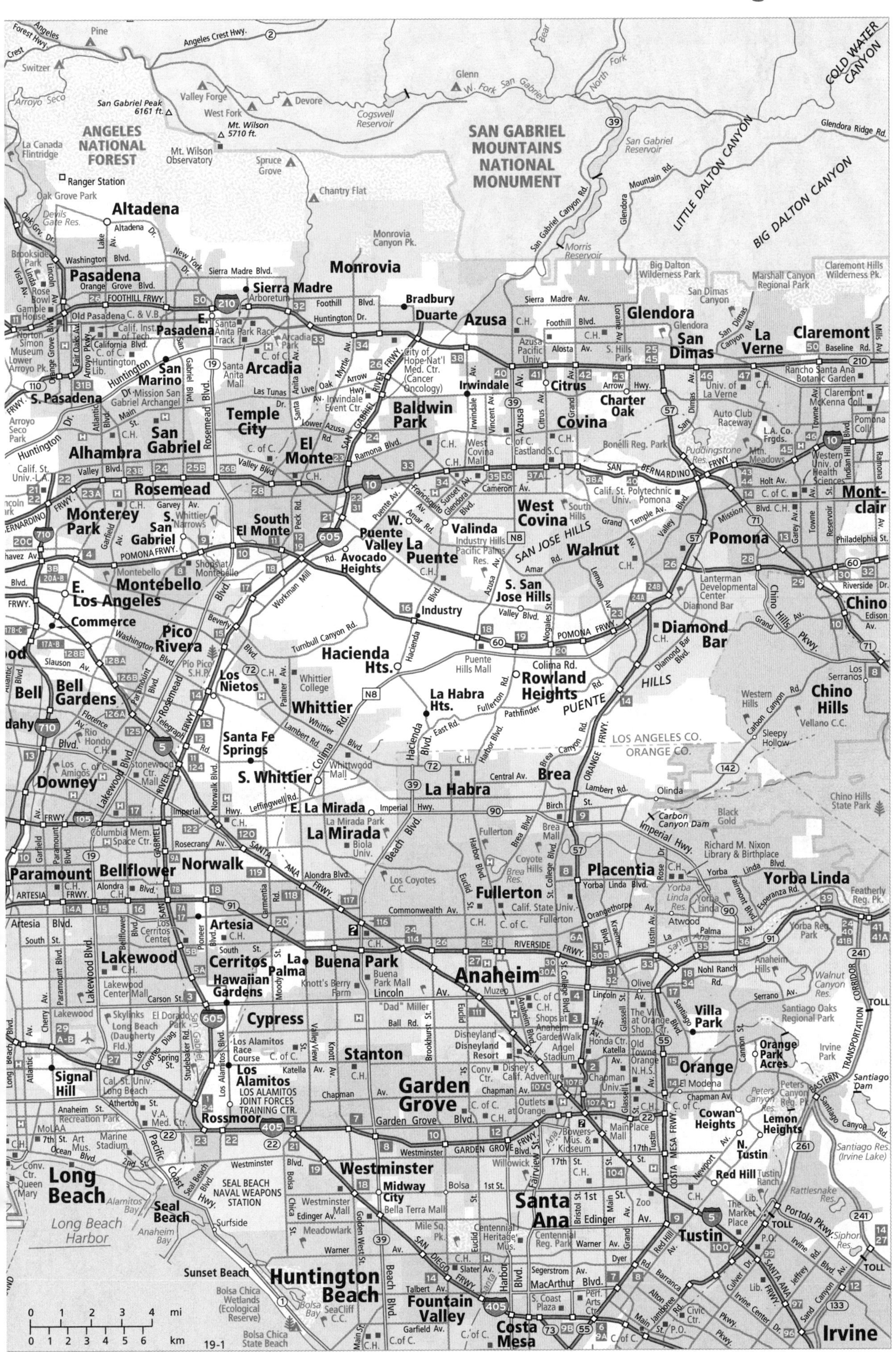
ANGELES NATIONAL FOREST
SAN GABRIEL MOUNTAINS NATIONAL MONUMENT
Altadena
Pasadena
Monrovia
Sierra Madre
Bradbury
Duarte
Azusa
Glendora
San Dimas
La Verne
Claremont
San Marino
Arcadia
Irwindale
Citrus
Charter Oak
S. Pasadena
Temple City
Baldwin Park
Covina
Alhambra
San Gabriel
El Monte
Rosemead
West Covina
Pomona
Mont-clair
Monterey Park
South El Monte
Valinda
Walnut
Puente Valley
La Puente
Avocado Heights
Montebello
E. Los Angeles
S. San Jose Hills
Industry
Chino
Commerce
Pico Rivera
Diamond Bar
Hacienda Hts.
Rowland Heights
Los Nietos
Bell Gardens
Whittier
La Habra Hts.
Chino Hills
Santa Fe Springs
Downey
S. Whittier
La Habra
Brea
E. La Mirada
La Mirada
Norwalk
Paramount
Bellflower
Placentia
Yorba Linda
Fullerton
Artesia
Lakewood
Cerritos
La Palma
Buena Park
Anaheim
Hawaiian Gardens
Cypress
Villa Park
Stanton
Orange
Signal Hill
Los Alamitos
Garden Grove
Rossmoor
Cowan Heights
Lemon Heights
N. Tustin
Long Beach
Seal Beach
Westminster
Midway City
Red Hill
Santa Ana
Tustin
Huntington Beach
Fountain Valley
Costa Mesa
Irvine
LOS ANGELES CO.
ORANGE CO.
Long Beach Harbor
0 1 2 3 4 mi
0 1 2 3 4 5 6 km
19-1

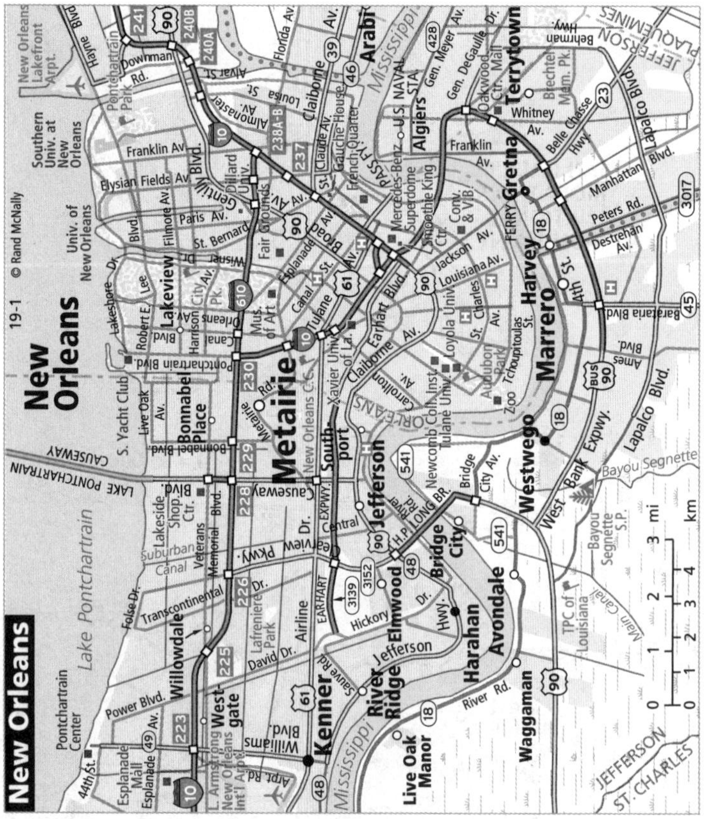
New Orleans
© Rand McNally
New Orleans
Metairie
Kenner
Harahan
Jefferson
Gretna
Marrero
Harvey
Westwego
Avondale
Bridge City
River Ridge
Elmwood
Waggaman
Live Oak Manor
Terrytown
Algiers
Arabi
Lake Pontchartrain
Mississippi
0 1 2 3 mi
0 1 2 3 4 km

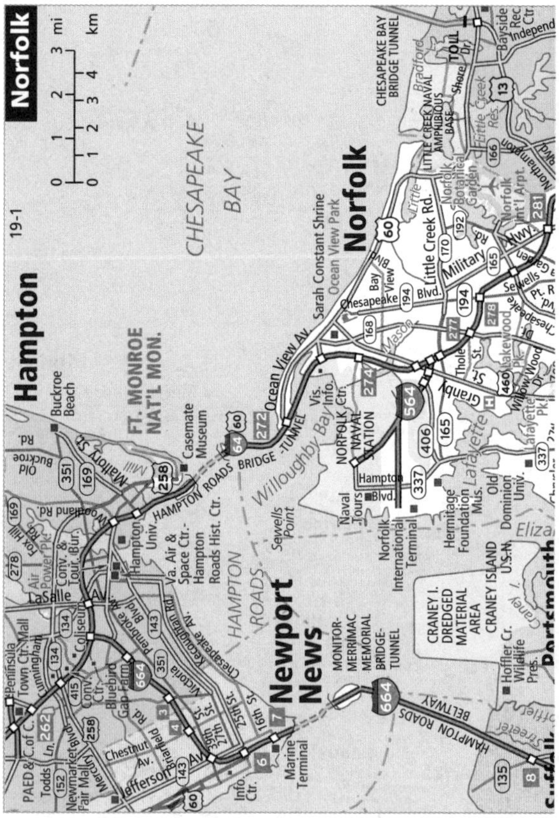
Norfolk
Hampton
Newport News
Norfolk
Chesapeake Bay
Hampton Roads
Ft. Monroe Nat'l Mon.
0 1 2 3 mi
0 1 2 3 4 km

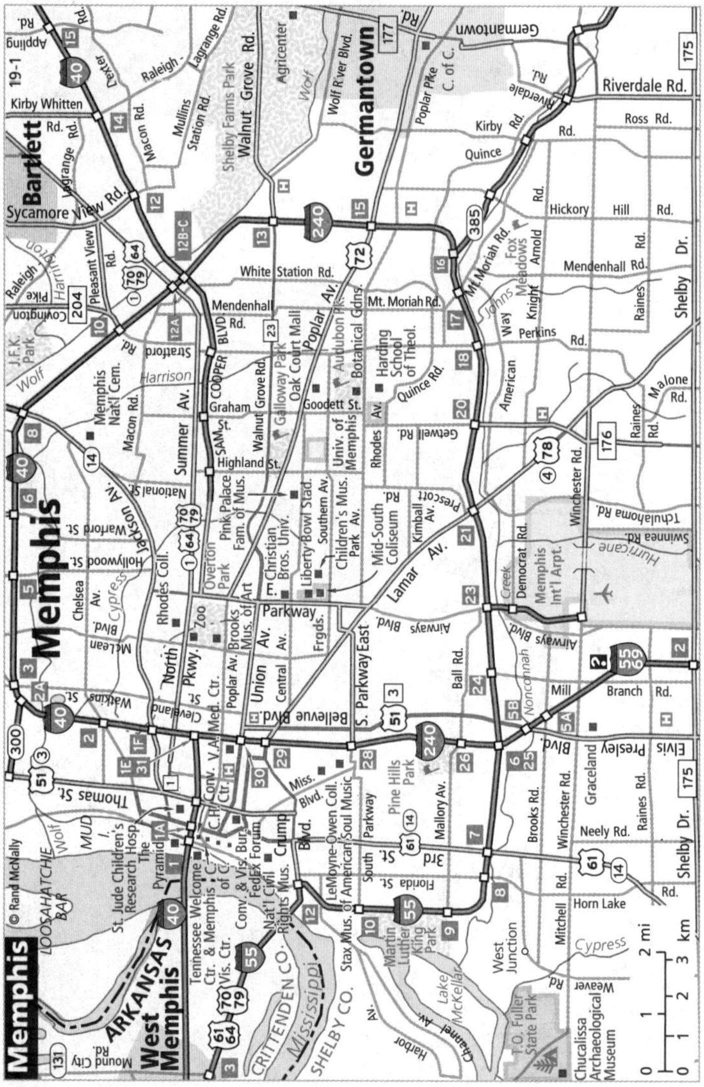
Memphis
© Rand McNally
Memphis
West Memphis
Bartlett
Germantown
Arkansas
Mississippi
Memphis Int'l Arpt.
0 1 2 mi
0 1 2 3 km

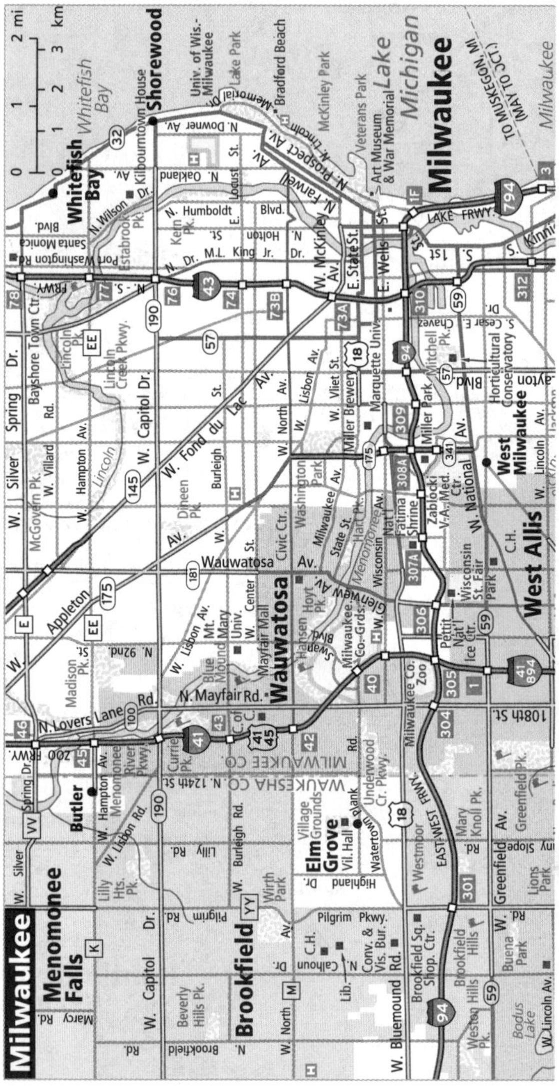
Milwaukee
Milwaukee
Wauwatosa
West Allis
Whitefish Bay
Shorewood
Menomonee Falls
Butler
Brookfield
Elm Grove
Lake Michigan
0 1 2 mi
0 1 2 3 km

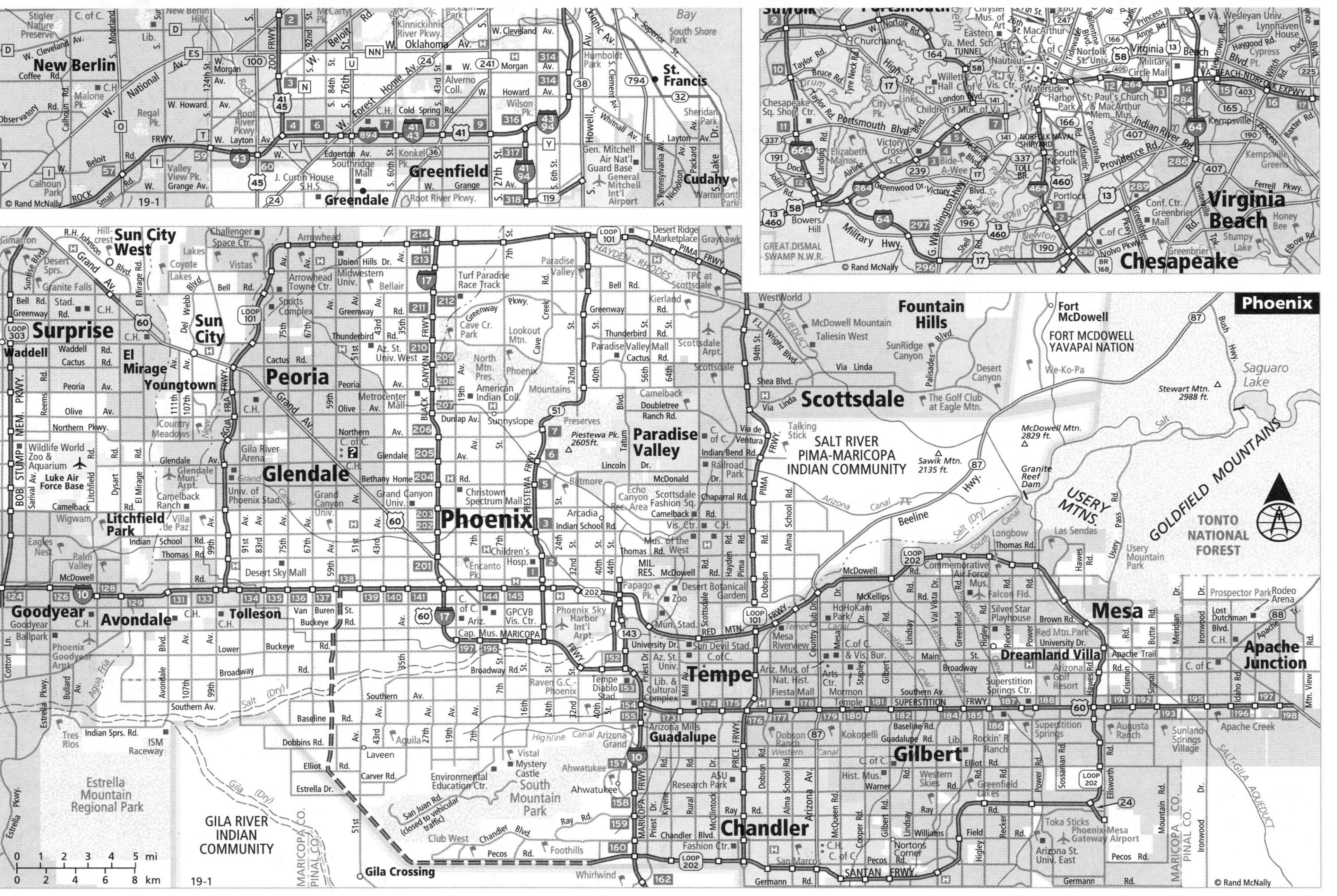
Phoenix
Phoenix
Scottsdale
Tempe
Mesa
Chandler
Gilbert
Glendale
Peoria
Surprise
Goodyear
Avondale
Tolleson
Sun City
Sun City West
El Mirage
Youngtown
Litchfield Park
Paradise Valley
Fountain Hills
Guadalupe
Apache Junction
Dreamland Villa
SALT RIVER PIMA-MARICOPA INDIAN COMMUNITY
FORT MCDOWELL YAVAPAI NATION
GILA RIVER INDIAN COMMUNITY
TONTO NATIONAL FOREST
GOLDFIELD MOUNTAINS
USERY MTNS.
Estrella Mountain Regional Park
South Mountain Park
Gila Crossing
Virginia Beach
Chesapeake
New Berlin
Greenfield
Cudahy
St. Francis
Greendale
© Rand McNally

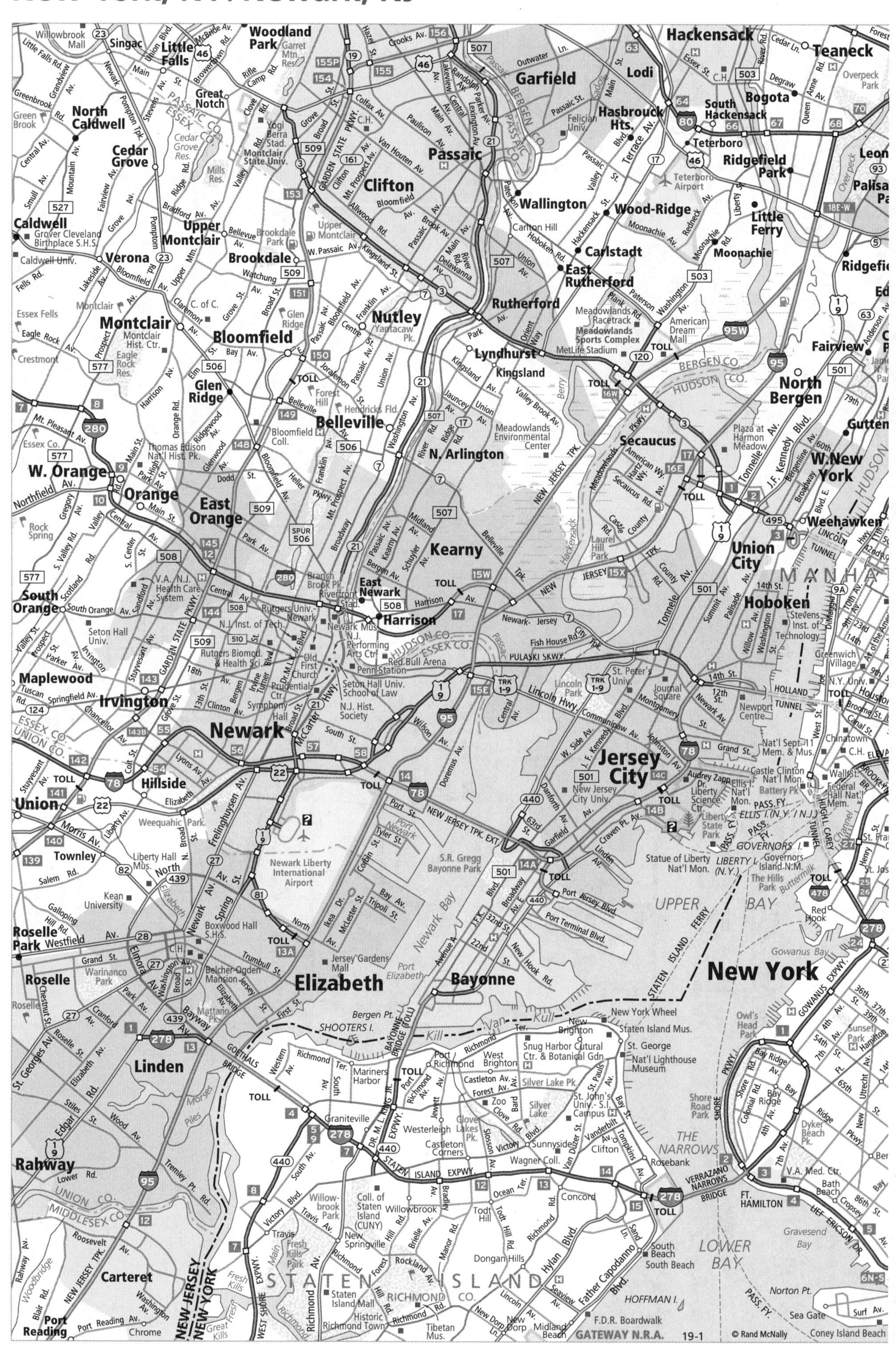
Newark
Jersey City
New York
Elizabeth
Bayonne
Hoboken
Union City
Kearny
Clifton
Passaic
Paterson
Hackensack
Garfield
Montclair
Bloomfield
East Orange
Irvington
Linden
Rahway
Carteret
Staten Island
Newark Liberty International Airport
Statue of Liberty Nat'l Mon.
Upper Bay
Lower Bay
The Narrows
© Rand McNally

New York / Newark & Vicinity
BRONX
QUEENS
BROOKLYN
Englewood
Englewood Cliffs
Fort Lee
Kings Point
Great Neck
Great Neck Plaza
Manorhaven
Sands Point
Saddle Rock
Harbor Hills
Kensington
Great Neck Estates
Russell Gardens
Thomaston
University Gardens
Bellerose
Bellerose Terrace
Valley Stream
Woodmere
Cedarhurst
Lawrence
Inwood
Atlantic Beach
GATEWAY NATIONAL RECREATION AREA
John F. Kennedy International Airport
La Guardia Airport
Jamaica Bay
ATLANTIC OCEAN
RIKERS I.
CITY ISLAND
HART ISLAND
HUNTERS ISLAND
Flushing
Jamaica
Rockaway Beach
Coney Island

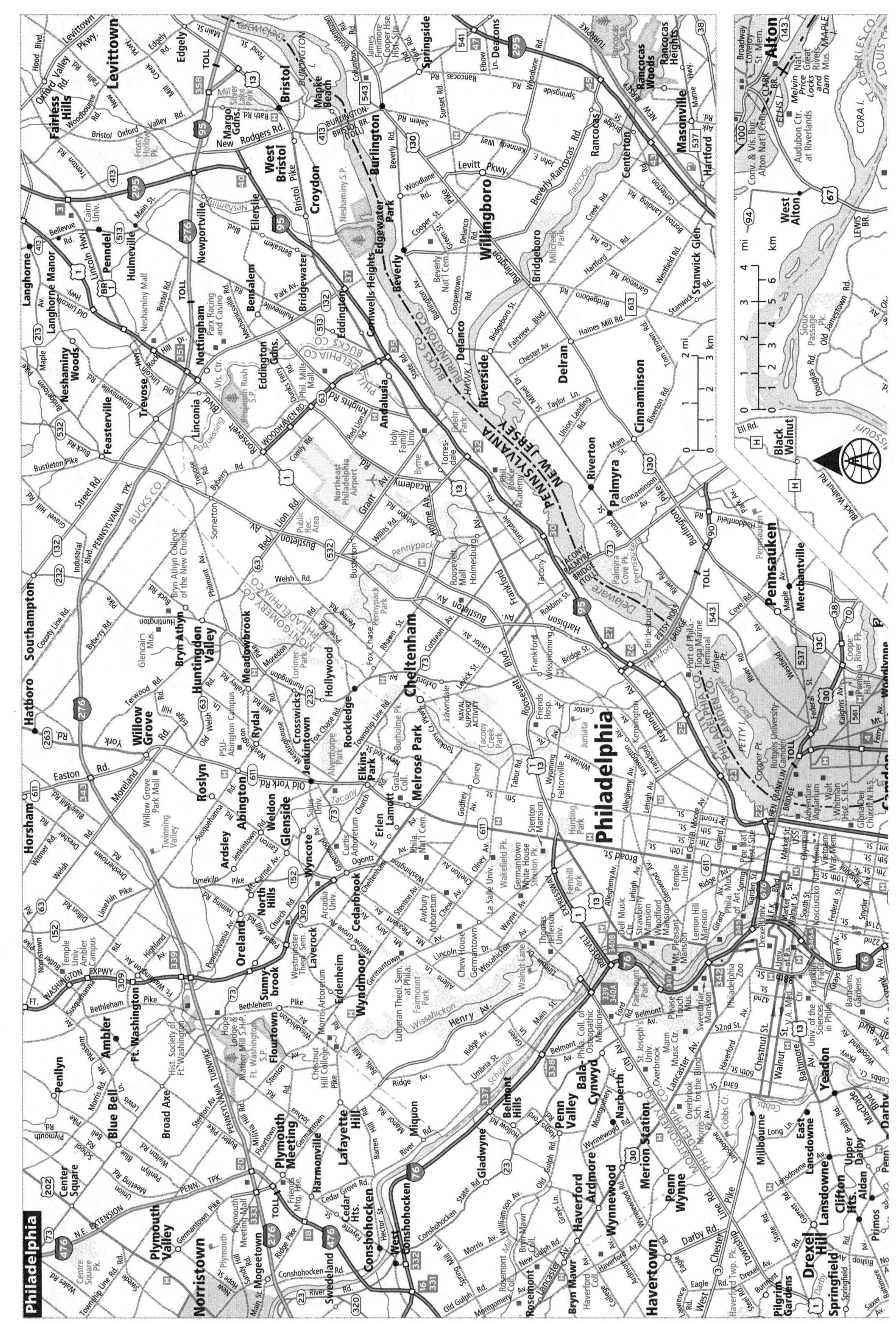
Philadelphia
Levittown
Fairless Hills
Bristol
Burlington
Croydon
Bensalem
Langhorne
Penndel
Newportville
Willingboro
Edgewater Park
Beverly
Delanco
Riverside
Delran
Cinnaminson
Riverton
Palmyra
Pennsauken
Merchantville
Feasterville
Trevose
Southampton
Hatboro
Horsham
Willow Grove
Huntingdon Valley
Bryn Athyn
Cheltenham
Jenkintown
Abington
Glenside
Wyncote
Elkins Park
Melrose Park
Oreland
Flourtown
Ambler
Blue Bell
Plymouth Meeting
Conshohocken
West Conshohocken
Norristown
Gladwyne
Bala-Cynwyd
Narberth
Wynnewood
Ardmore
Haverford
Bryn Mawr
Havertown
Drexel Hill
Yeadon
Lansdowne
Upper Darby
Alton
West Alton
PENNSYLVANIA
NEW JERSEY
Delaware

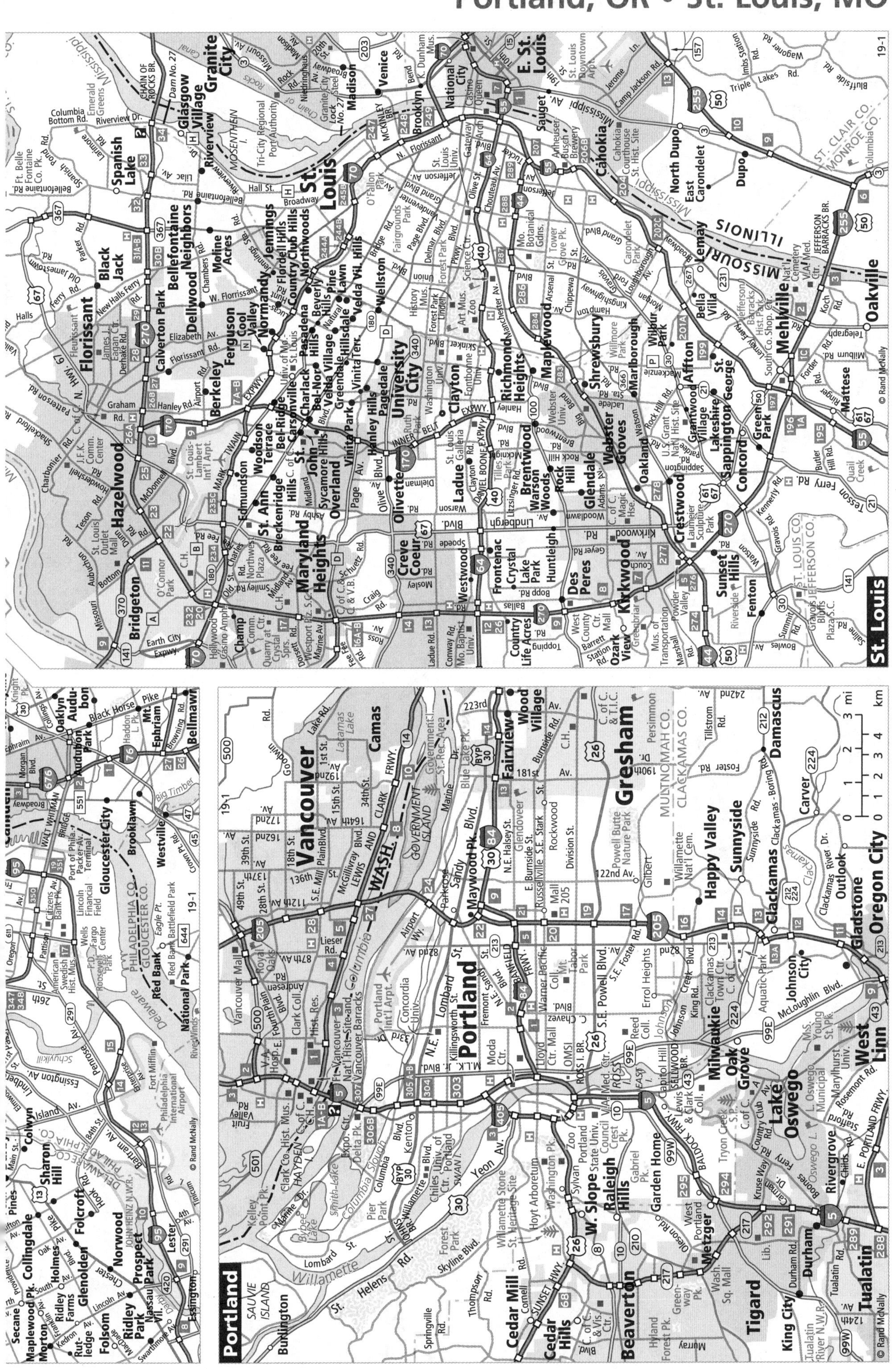
St. Louis
Portland
Vancouver
Gresham
Beaverton
Tigard
Lake Oswego
Oregon City
Milwaukie
Hazelwood
Florissant
Maryland Heights
University City
Clayton
Kirkwood
Webster Groves
Granite City
E. St. Louis
Oakville
Mehlville
© Rand McNally

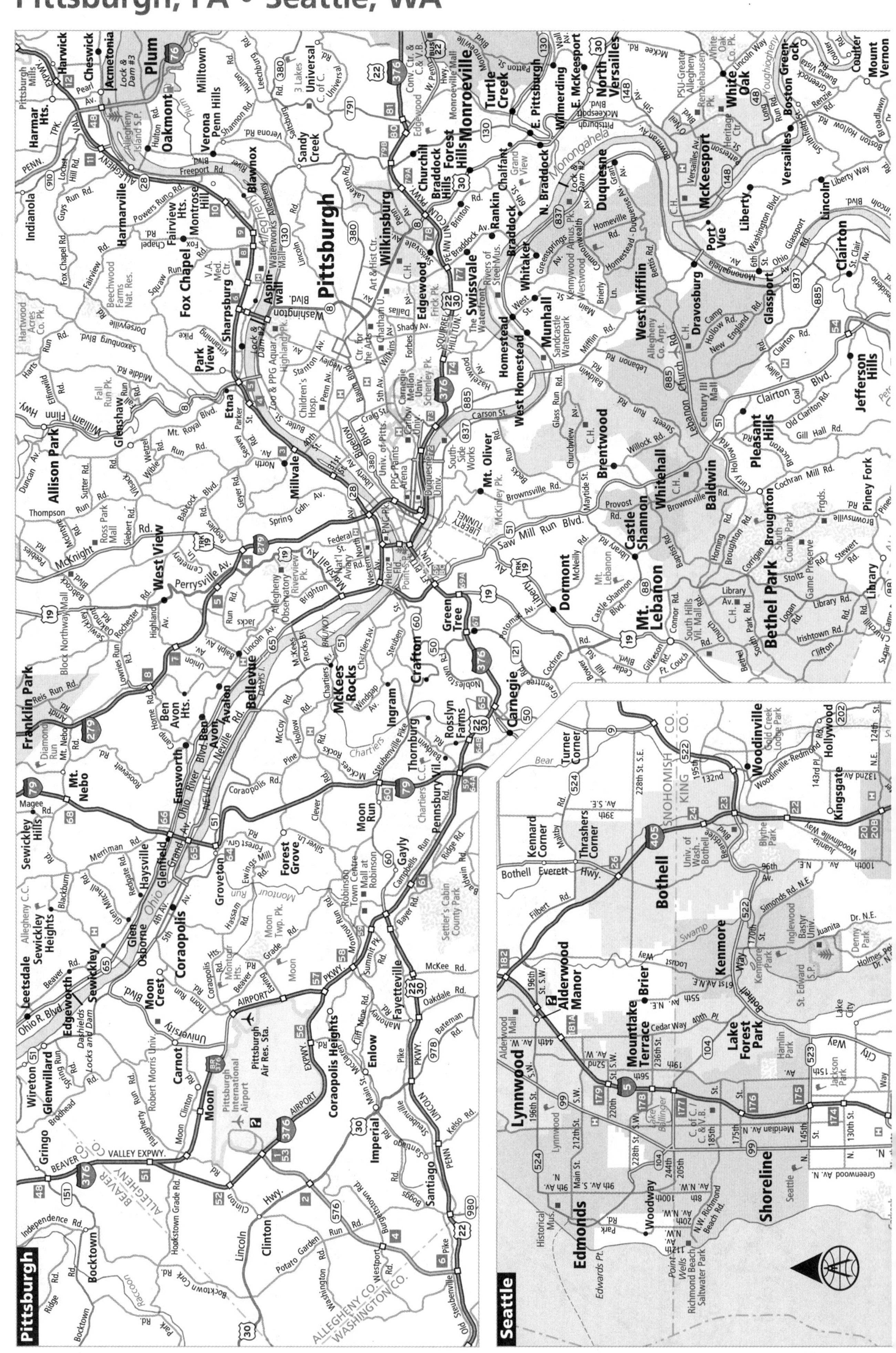

Pittsburgh
Seattle

Orlando
Apopka
Altamonte Springs
Winter Springs
Casselberry
Oviedo
Winter Park
Maitland
Orlando
Pine Hills
Ocoee
Winter Garden
Windermere
Kissimmee
Lake Buena Vista
Lake Apopka
Sanford
Seattle
Bellevue
Kirkland
Redmond
Renton
Mercer Island
Tukwila
SeaTac
Burien
White Center
Kent
Newcastle
Skyway
Lake Washington
Elliott Bay
Puget Sound
Vashon Island
© Rand McNally

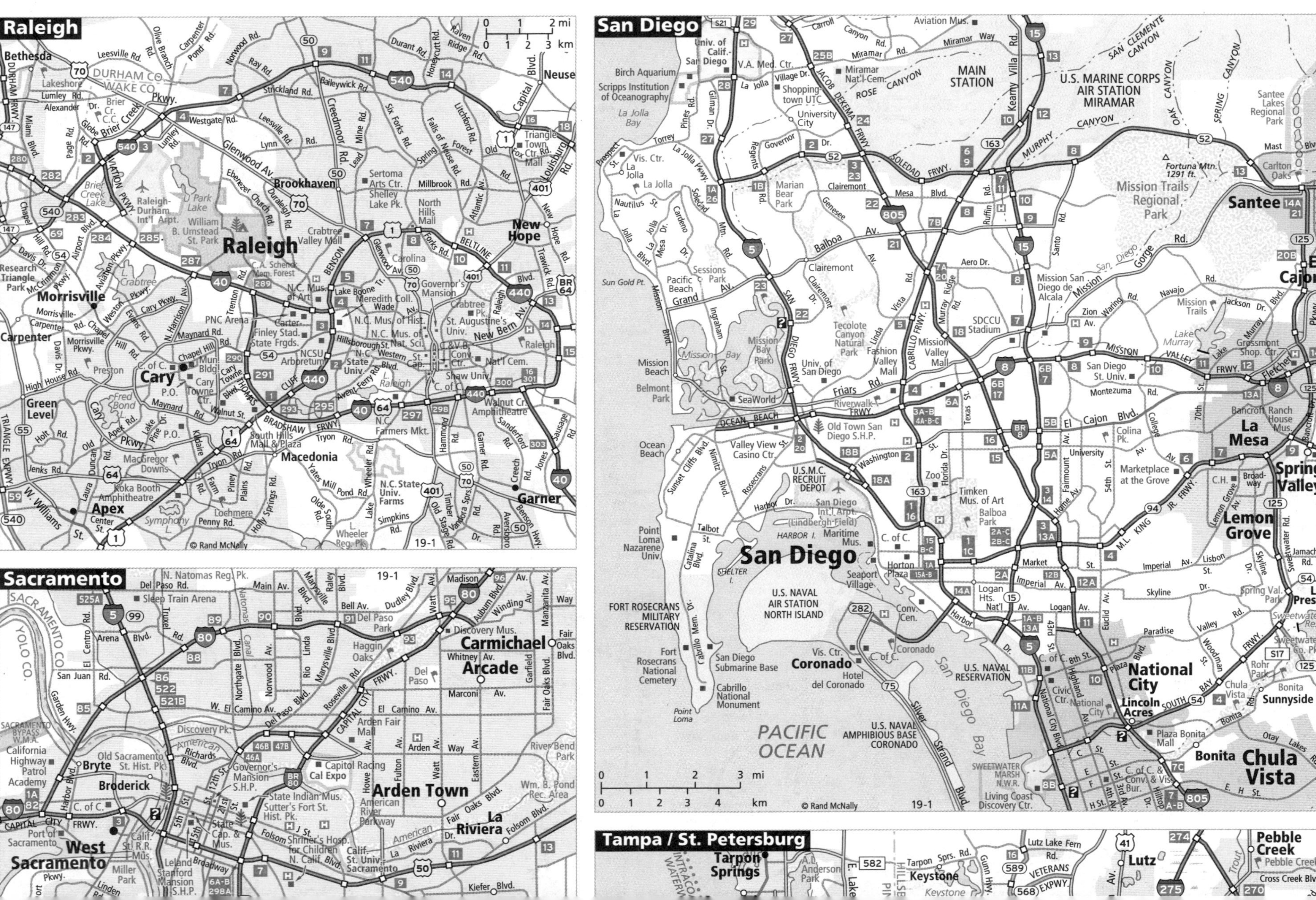
Raleigh
San Diego
Sacramento
Tampa / St. Petersburg
© Rand McNally

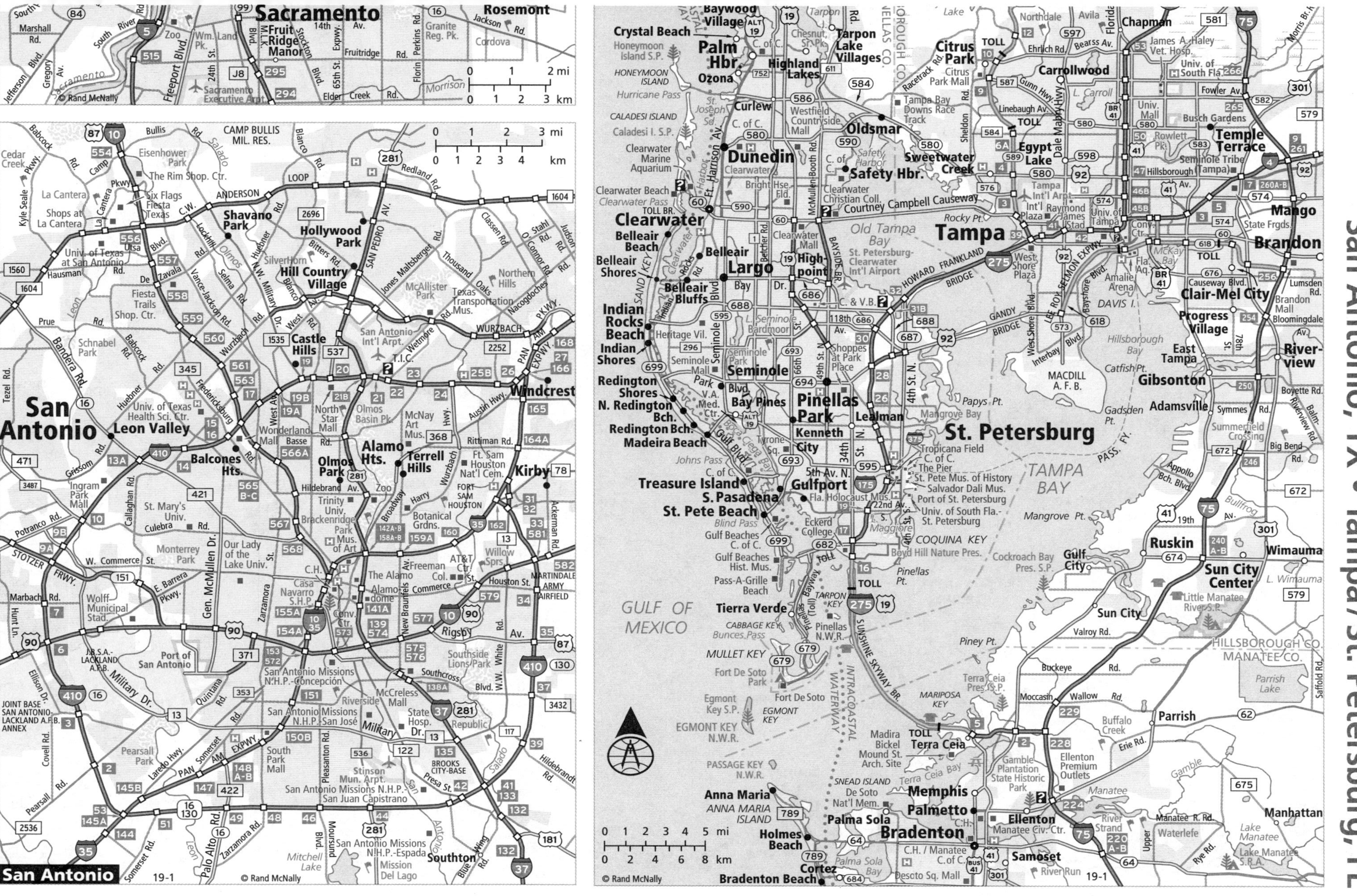

Sacramento
Fruit Ridge Manor
Rosemont
Sacramento Executive Arpt.
© Rand McNally
San Antonio
Leon Valley
Balcones Hts.
Castle Hills
Hollywood Park
Hill Country Village
Shavano Park
Olmos Park
Alamo Hts.
Terrell Hills
Kirby
Windcrest
Southton
San Antonio Int'l Arpt.
CAMP BULLIS MIL. RES.
Univ. of Texas at San Antonio
Univ. of Texas Health Sci. Ctr.
St. Mary's Univ.
Trinity Univ.
The Alamo
Port of San Antonio
JOINT BASE SAN ANTONIO-LACKLAND A.F.B. ANNEX
San Antonio Missions N.H.P.-Concepción
San Antonio Missions N.H.P.-San José
San Antonio Missions N.H.P.-San Juan Capistrano
San Antonio Missions N.H.P.-Espada
San Antonio
19-1
Crystal Beach
Palm Hbr.
Ozona
Tarpon Lake Villages
Highland Lakes
Citrus Park
Carrollwood
Chapman
Temple Terrace
Dunedin
Oldsmar
Safety Hbr.
Sweetwater Creek
Egypt Lake
Clearwater
Belleair Beach
Belleair Shores
Belleair
Belleair Bluffs
Largo
High-point
Tampa
Mango
Brandon
Clair-Mel City
Progress Village
River-view
East Tampa
Gibsonton
Adamsville
Indian Rocks Beach
Indian Shores
Seminole
Pinellas Park
Redington Shores
N. Redington Bch.
Redington Bch.
Madeira Beach
Kenneth City
Lealman
St. Petersburg
Treasure Island
Gulfport
S. Pasadena
St. Pete Beach
MACDILL A.F.B.
TAMPA BAY
Old Tampa Bay
Hillsborough Bay
GULF OF MEXICO
Tierra Verde
Ruskin
Sun City Center
Wimauma
Sun City
Gulf City
SUNSHINE SKYWAY BR.
INTRACOASTAL WATERWAY
HILLSBOROUGH CO.
MANATEE CO.
Parrish
Terra Ceia
Memphis
Palmetto
Ellenton
Bradenton
Samoset
Palma Sola
Anna Maria
Holmes Beach
Cortez
Bradenton Beach
Manhattan
© Rand McNally
19-1

San Francisco Bay Area, CA (San Francisco / Oakland / San Jose)

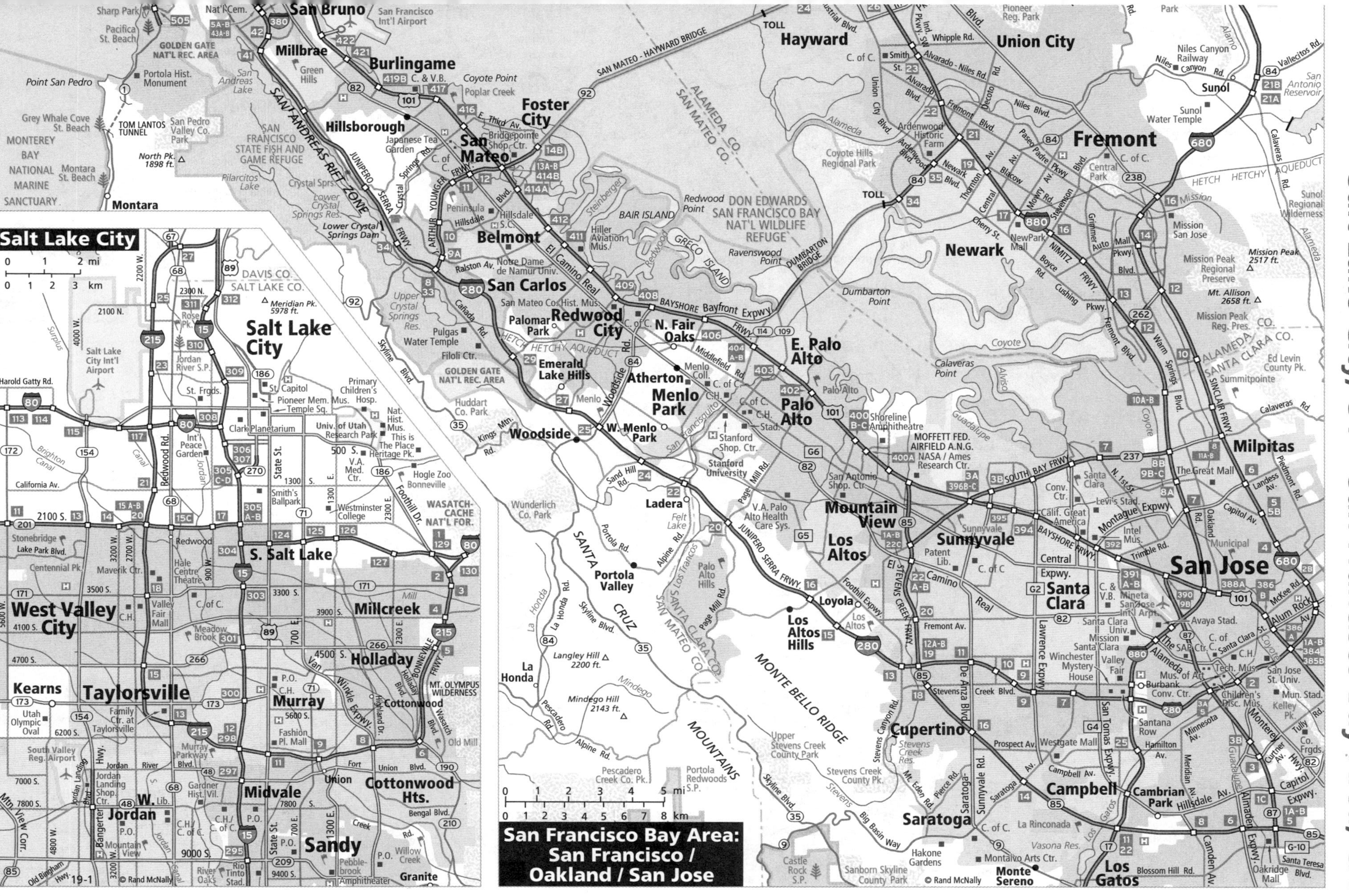
San Francisco Bay Area: San Francisco / Oakland / San Jose
Salt Lake City
0 1 2 3 4 5 mi
0 1 2 3 4 5 6 7 8 km
0 1 2 mi
0 1 2 3 km
© Rand McNally
San Bruno
Millbrae
Burlingame
Hillsborough
Foster City
San Mateo
Belmont
San Carlos
Redwood City
N. Fair Oaks
Emerald Lake Hills
Atherton
Menlo Park
W. Menlo Park
Woodside
E. Palo Alto
Palo Alto
Ladera
Portola Valley
La Honda
Montara
Hayward
Union City
Fremont
Newark
Sunol
Milpitas
San Jose
Santa Clara
Sunnyvale
Mountain View
Los Altos
Los Altos Hills
Loyola
Cupertino
Campbell
Cambrian Park
Saratoga
Monte Sereno
Los Gatos
MONTE BELLO RIDGE
SANTA CRUZ MOUNTAINS
SAN ANDREAS RIFT ZONE
DON EDWARDS SAN FRANCISCO BAY NAT'L WILDLIFE REFUGE
MONTEREY BAY NATIONAL MARINE SANCTUARY
Salt Lake City
S. Salt Lake
Millcreek
Holladay
Murray
Midvale
Sandy
Cottonwood Hts.
Taylorsville
West Valley City
Kearns
W. Jordan
Granite
WASATCH CACHE NAT'L FOR.
MT. OLYMPUS WILDERNESS

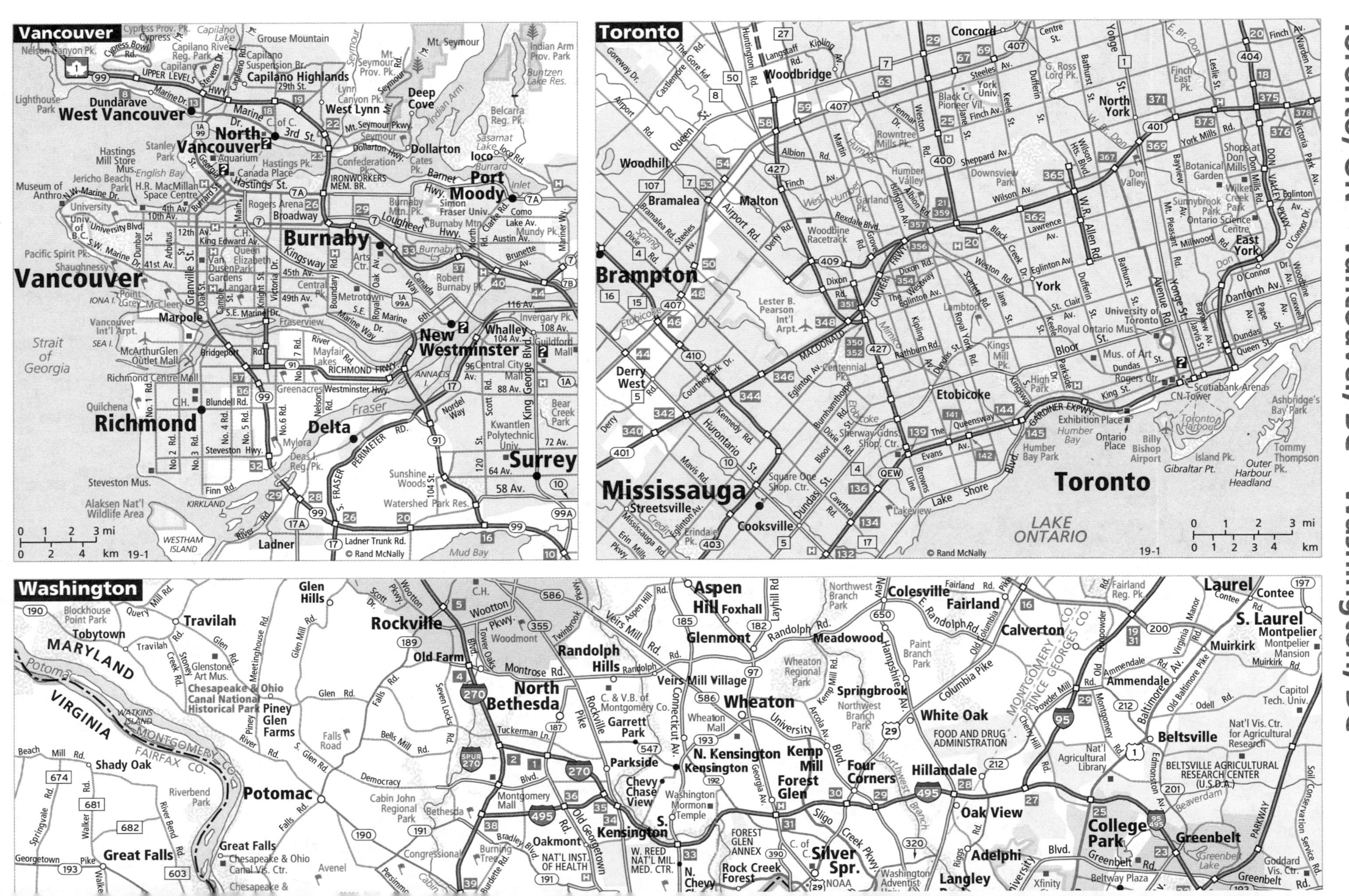
Vancouver
Vancouver
West Vancouver
North Vancouver
Capilano Highlands
Grouse Mountain
Deep Cove
West Lynn
Dollarton
Ioco
Port Moody
Burnaby
New Westminster
Whalley
Marpole
Richmond
Delta
Surrey
Ladner
Strait of Georgia
© Rand McNally
Toronto
Toronto
LAKE ONTARIO
Mississauga
Brampton
Bramalea
Malton
Woodbridge
Woodhill
Concord
North York
East York
York
Etobicoke
Derry West
Streetsville
Cooksville
© Rand McNally
Washington
Rockville
North Bethesda
Randolph Hills
Aspen Hill
Glenmont
Wheaton
Kensington
Silver Spr.
Colesville
Fairland
Calverton
White Oak
Hillandale
Adelphi
Langley
College Park
Greenbelt
Beltsville
Laurel
S. Laurel
Potomac
Great Falls
Travilah
MARYLAND
VIRGINIA

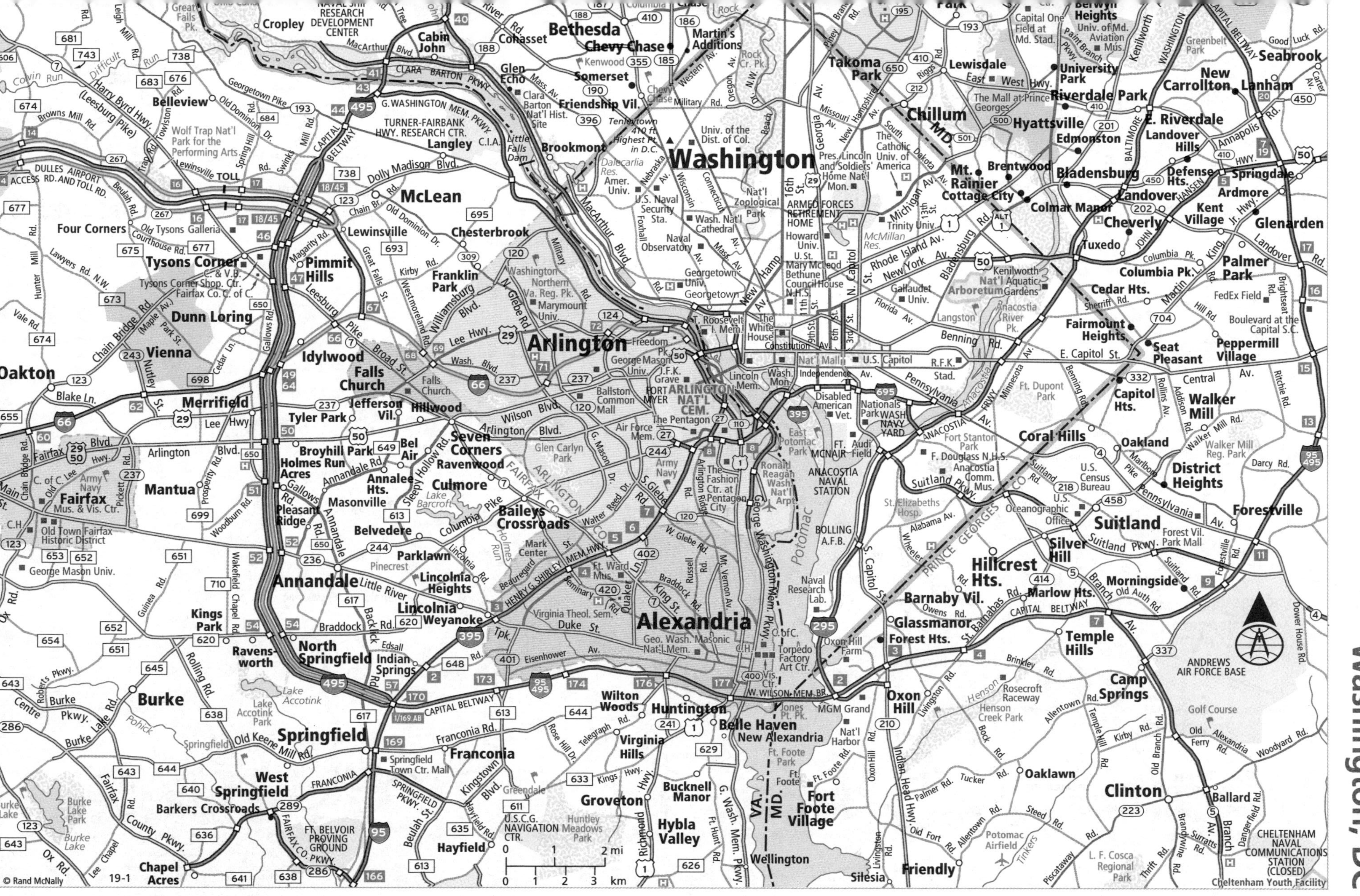
Washington
Arlington
Alexandria
Bethesda
Chevy Chase
McLean
Falls Church
Annandale
Springfield
Fairfax
Vienna
Oakton
Burke
Tysons Corner
Hyattsville
Suitland
Oxon Hill
Clinton
Camp Springs
Temple Hills
Forestville
Seabrook
Lanham
New Carrollton
Riverdale Park
Bladensburg
Takoma Park
Chillum
Silver Hill
Hillcrest Hts.
Fort Foote Village
Huntington
Franconia
Mantua
Merrifield
Dunn Loring
Kings Park
West Springfield
Chapel Acres
Potomac
ANDREWS AIR FORCE BASE
© Rand McNally

Mexico

Population: 112,336,538
Land Area: 758,450 sq. mi.
Capital: Mexico City

Cities and Towns

Acaponeta D-4
Acapulco F-6
Acayucan E-8
Aguascalientes D-5
Arriaga F-8
Atlixco E-7
Autlán de Navarro E-5
Bahía Kino B-3
Bermejillo C-5
Buenaventura B-4
Campeche E-9
Cancún D-10
Champotón E-9
Chetumal E-10
Chihuahua B-4
Chilpancingo F-6
Choix C-4
Cintalapa F-8
Ciudad Camargo C-6
Ciudad del Carmen E-9
Ciudad de México E-6
Ciudad Juárez A-4
Ciudad Madero D-7
Ciudad Mante D-6
Ciudad Obregón B-3
Ciudad Valles D-6
Ciudad Victoria D-6
Coatzacoalcos E-8
Colima E-5
Cozumel D-10
Cuajinicuilapa F-7
Cuauhtémoc B-4
Cuernavaca E-6
Culiacán C-4
Durango D-5
El Fuerte C-4
El Sueco B-4
Ensenada A-2
Escárcega E-9
Fresnillo D-5
Gómez Palacio C-5
Guadalajara E-5
Guamúchil C-4
Guanajuato D-6
Guaymas B-3
Guerrero B-4
Guzmán E-5
Hermosillo B-3
Hidalgo del Parral C-4
Huajuapan de León E-7
Iguala E-6
Irapuato E-6
Jalpa D-5
Jiménez C-5
Juan Aldama C-5
La Paz C-3
La Pesca D-7
León D-6
Linares C-6
Loreto C-3
Los Mochis C-4
Manzanillo E-5
Matamoros C-7
Matehuala D-6
Mazatlán D-4
Mérida D-9
Mexicali A-2
Mexico City E-6
Monclova C-6
Monterrey C-6
Morelia E-6
Navojoa B-3
Nogales A-3
Nueva Rosita B-6
Nuevo Casas Grandes A-4
Nuevo Laredo B-6
Oaxaca F-7
Ojinaga B-5
Orizaba E-7
Pachuca E-6
Parras C-5
Piedras Negras B-6
Pitiquito A-3
Poza Rica E-7
Puebla E-7
Puerto Ángel F-7
Puerto Escondido F-7
Puerto Morelos D-10
Puerto Peñasco A-2
Puerto Vallarta E-5
Punta Prieta B-2
Querétaro E-6
Reynosa C-7
Río Lagartos D-10
Rosario A-2
Sabinas B-6
Sabinas Hidalgo C-6
Sahuaripa B-4
Salamanca E-6
Saltillo C-6
San Blas D-5
San Carlos C-3
San Felipe A-2
San Fernando C-7
San Francisco del Oro C-4
San José del Cabo D-3
San Luis Potosí D-6
Santa Ana A-3
Santa Bárbara C-4
Santa Rosalia B-3
Santo Domingo Tehuantepec F-8
Tamazunchale D-6
Tampico D-7
Tapachula F-8
Taxco E-6
Tepehuanes C-4
Tepic D-5
Tijuana A-1
Tlaxcala E-7
Toluca E-6
Tónichi B-3
Topolobampo C-3
Torreón C-5
Tuxpan D-7
Tuxtla Gutiérrez F-8
Uruapan E-5
Veracruz E-7
Villahermosa E-8
Villagrán C-6
Xalapa E-7
Zacatecas D-5
Zihuatanejo F-6